The
Princeton
Theology
1812–1921

The Princeton Theology 1812–1921

Scripture, Science, and Theological Method
from Archibald Alexander
to Benjamin Breckinridge Warfield

Mark A. Noll, Editor

Baker Book House
Grand Rapids, Michigan 49506

ISBN: 0-8010-6737-5

Library of Congress Catalog Card Number: 83-70836

Printed in the United States of America

The photos on pages 17, 59, 103, 209, and 239
are courtesy of the Presbyterian Historical Society.

To
David Wells
Preceptor and Friend

Contents

Archibald Alexander Hodge *(1823–1886)*

Benjamin Breckinridge Warfield *(1851–1921)*

Acknowledgments

For such a modest work I have incurred a surprisingly large number of debts. Encouragement, bibliographical aid, and many helpful suggestions came from a number of able scholars, none of whom are responsible for my errors of fact or interpretation. They include Randall Balmer, William S. Barker, Nathan Hatch, W. Andrew Hoffecker, George Marsden, David Murchie, Jack Rogers, Gary S. Smith, Jack Stewart, John C. Vander Stelt, and David Wells. I would like to thank especially Roger Nicole and his student Roland Gunn for making available their rich bibliographical work on the Princetonians, and Allan Fisher of Baker Book House for securing in-print copies of Princeton works. John Woodbridge did not contribute directly to this project, but he has regularly forced me to think more carefully about matters Princetonian.

I much appreciated the typing and bibliographical scouring provided by Matthew Floding, Beatrice Horne, Robert Lackie, Molly McCartney, and Kenneth Sawyer. John Stackhouse wrote précis and tracked down out-of-the-way information with great efficiency. Wheaton College administrators Ward Kriegbaum and William Henning were helpful at several stages, not least in loosing the institutional purse strings to cover expenses connected with the project.

Some years ago Maggie Packer introduced me to conservative Presbyterians. For that I am grateful, as well as for the many other good things which, as Maggie Noll, she has given to me. Two of these, Mary and David Noll, could now not care less about Princeton or theology, but in years to come I hope they too will find this book instructive.

Abbreviations

BRPR	*Biblical Repertory and Princeton Review* (includes also *Biblical Repertory and Theological Review*), from 1829 (volume 1).
Essays and Reviews	Charles Hodge, *Essays and Reviews: Selected from the Princeton Review* (New York: Robert Carter & Brothers, 1857).
SSWW	*Selected Shorter Writings: B. B. Warfield*, ed. John E. Meeter, 2 vols. (Phillipsburg, N.J.: Presbyterian and Reformed, 1970, 1973).
ST	Charles Hodge, *Systematic Theology*, 3 vols. (originally published 1872–73; currently published by Wm. B. Eerdmans, Grand Rapids).
WBBW	*The Works of Benjamin B. Warfield*, 10 vols. (originally published 1927–32, currently published by Baker, Grand Rapids):

      I   *Revelation and Inspiration*
      II *Biblical Doctrines*
      III *Christology and Criticism*
      IV *Studies in Tertullian and Augustine*
      V   *Calvin and Calvinism*
      VI *The Westminster Assembly and Its Work*
      VII *Perfectionism Part One*
      VIII *Perfectionism Part Two*
      IX *Studies in Theology*
      X   *Critical Reviews*

Introduction

A N ANTHOLOGY, as historian Peter Gay once put it in introducing a splendid collection of documents on the Enlightenment, "is both an appetizer and an argument."[1] This book too, concerning the theologians of nineteenth-century Princeton Seminary, who with all their hearts distrusted the Enlightenment, is also meant to whet appetites for more and to make a point. The selections from the works of the Princetonians will have to bear the brunt of the advertising. But my argument can be stated immediately: the men of Old Princeton can teach us much about nineteenth-century history and the doing of theology, but only if we resist the temptation to treat them as contemporaries.

In their day, the Princeton theologians exerted a wide influence in American intellectual life, and in our day they have been recognized as important historical figures—for example, by Perry Miller, who once wrote of the "learned and mighty faculty" at Princeton, or by J. David Hoeveler, Jr., who more recently called Charles Hodge "the most brilliant and resolute voice of Princeton Calvinism and the leading spokesman for the Old School [Presbyterians]."[2] Yet for all their acknowledged significance, the Princetonians have been the subject of relatively scant *historical* scrutiny.

To be sure, these theologians remain very much alive for one group of Protestants, those descendants of the fundamentalists who are now called evangelicals. Princeton convictions about Scripture in particular have long been prominent among evangelicals and have recently emerged as a focal point of controversy, hailed by defenders as virtually the last word on the subject, attacked by detractors as shallow and sub-Christian scholasticism. Yet in these ardent polemics only slight attention is paid to the actual situations in which the Princetonians did their work. In the haste to exploit, or to blunt, a Princeton influence in late twentieth-century debate, polemicists forswear careful study of these men as theologians of the nineteenth century and show little interest in dispassionate analysis of their theological methods.

---

1. Peter Gay, *The Enlightenment: A Comprehensive Anthology* (New York: Simon and Schuster, 1973), p. 11.
2. Perry Miller, *The Life of the Mind in America from the Revolution to the Civil War* (New York: Harcourt, Brace and World, 1965), p. 17; J. David Hoeveler, Jr., *James McCosh and the Scottish Intellectual Tradition: From Glasgow to Princeton* (Princeton, N.J.: Princeton University Press, 1981), p. 227.

Nonevangelical theologians and intellectual historians, who might be expected to display greater interest in methodological and historical questions, have a different reason for neglecting Old Princeton. For these moderns, the Princeton theologians have passed into the oblivion assigned to the champions of lost causes. The Princetonians practiced ways of thought and advocated theological positions which have been greatly out of fashion in the twentieth century. As a consequence, historians and theologians who follow these fashions have not been eager to retrieve the Princetonians for disinterested analysis.

Study of the Princeton theology stands, therefore, at an impasse. Concern for a selective list of Princeton convictions flourishes among evangelicals who yet are little interested in the historical contexts of those convictions or in the subtle questions about theological method which so exercised the Princetonians. On the other hand, those nonevangelicals who are best situated to study the history and theological methods of Old Princeton pay them no more than a passing interest.

This is a regrettable state of affairs. It is my hope that this anthology can demonstrate what may be gained by studying the Princeton theologians more historically and more dispassionately. Such study can reveal much about the nineteenth century, and it can be useful—as either model or foil—for those who do Christian theology in the twentieth. Knowledge about Old Princeton is crucial for anyone interested in the theological, intellectual, or ecclesiastical history of nineteenth-century America. The religious viewpoint which these theologians promoted had at least some impact on national character, their beliefs about truth made them full partners in the great American infatuation with Lord Francis Bacon and Sir Isaac Newton, and their dogmatic utterances carried great weight within Presbyterianism while exerting considerable influence beyond.[3] Study of these figures is almost as instructive for theologians as for historians. The Princetonians expressed convictions about theological method forcefully, they took firm stands on the application of Christian belief, and they labored mightily to include both theology and science within a common framework. To this day they continue to be numbered among America's most articulate exponents of Calvinism. Modern theologians who repudiate Princeton views will still be better able to articulate their own for having followed the Princetonians step by step through theirs. Modern theologians who adopt their conclusions will be better able to articulate similar positions in the twentieth century for having taken time to see how they fit into the nineteenth. Finally, it goes almost without saying that for the tiny segment of the reading public that fancies both history and theology, the value of an anthology on the theologians of nineteenth-century Princeton is self-evident.

3. On Princeton ideas and the national character, see Fred J. Hood, *Reformed America: The Middle and Southern States, 1783–1837* (University, Alabama: University of Alabama Press, 1980), pp. 7–87; on Bacon and Newton, see the section on Scottish Common Sense Realism below; on the place of Princeton within Presbyterianism, see Lefferts A. Loetscher, *The Broadening Church: A Study of Theological Issues in the Presbyterian Church Since 1869* (Philadelphia: University of Pennsylvania Press, 1957), pp. 21–25 and *passim;* and George P. Hutchinson, *The History Behind the Reformed Presbyterian Church, Evangelical Synod* (Cherry Hill, N.J.: Mack Publishing, 1974), pp. 175–183 and *passim.*

The Princeton Theologians

Although many individuals contributed to the theology of Old Princeton, this anthology offers selections from only the four men who held the principal chair of theology from the founding of the Seminary in 1812 to the tumultuous decade of the 1920s when the institution was reorganized. These four—Archibald Alexander, Charles Hodge, Archibald Alexander Hodge, and Benjamin Breckinridge Warfield— shared to a remarkable degree a common conception of the theological task, took their bearings from a common view of Scripture, possessed common beliefs about the nature of truth, and reasoned in common ways toward their Calvinistic conclusions. To their day and to our own, their work constituted *the* Princeton Theology.

Archibald Alexander (1772–1851) constructed the framework which shaped the theology at the seminary for over a century.[4] The grand motifs of the Princeton Theology are discussed in greater detail below—devotion to the Bible, concern for religious experience, sensitivity to the American experience, and full employment of Presbyterian confessions, seventeenth-century Reformed systematicians, and the Scottish philosophy of Common Sense. But all of them came to the seminary with its first professor. Alexander had had a full career before he arrived in Princeton in 1812 as the first, and for a time the only, professor at the seminary newly established by the General Assembly of the Presbyterian church. He was born to Scotch-Irish parents in Virginia, educated privately by the Rev. William Graham (a student of Princeton College's John Witherspoon), and ordained as a minister in 1790. After four years of private study and evangelistic itineration, he became the pastor of two Presbyterian churches in Charlotte County, Virginia. He added responsibility as president of Hampden-Sydney College in 1797 before moving a decade later to the Third Presbyterian Church of Philadelphia, whence he was called to Princeton. During the seminary's first year, Alexander gave instruction in all the subjects. With the arrival of Samuel Miller in 1813, he concentrated on the teaching of didactic and polemic theology which he continued until 1840 when, in consideration of his advancing years, his chair was designated the professorship of pastoral and polemic theology. He published widely on theology, history, apologetics, moral philosophy, and religious experience, but his works are not so technical or so weighty as those of his successors. Even his protégé Charles Hodge, for example, did not find it necessary to cite Alexander's writings in his *Systematic Theology,* a work marked otherwise by full interaction with authorities. Yet Alexander was the most winsome of the major Princeton professors. Testimonies concerning the moving power of his preaching, the effectiveness of his spiritual counsel, the relaxed demeanor of his family circle, and the relative latitude of his ecclesiastical views mark him as a forceful and engaging personality of nearly heroic proportions.

Charles Hodge (1797–1878) arrived from his native Philadelphia to study at Princeton College in the summer of 1812, shortly before Alexander entered onto his

---

4. Biographical studies of the four theologians in the anthology are listed in the Bibliography.

duties at the seminary. Hodge attended Alexander's inaugural and soon became his pupil, friend, and colleague. In later life Hodge would speak of Alexander as the one who filled the gap in his life left by the early death of his own father. It was Hodge who fleshed out the framework that Alexander had established by building a full-scale systematic theology on it and by attacking those who did not share its convictions. Hodge graduated from the college in 1815 and from the seminary in 1819. He was then ordained, supplied pulpits, and instructed seminary students in the biblical languages until he was named Professor of Oriental and Biblical Literature in 1822. Hodge made a lengthy tour of German theological institutions from 1826 to 1828, during which time he gained a new appreciation for the benefits of rigorous intellectual effort and a new concern about the dangers of "rationalism," "mysticism," and "ritualism." In 1840 he became Professor of Exegetical and Didactic Theology, to which at Alexander's death in 1852 was added the professorship of polemic theology. Long before this, however, Hodge had become an active literary warrior in the pages of the *Biblical Repertory and Princeton Review,* attacking, among others, the New Haven Theology, Charles Finney's revivalistic New Measures, and Germany's faddish Neologisms. He could be slashing in these polemics, as in his attack on the Mercersburg Theology of John W. Nevin and Philip Schaff, but more generally they displayed the even-handed gravity which led Lutheran theologian C. P. Krauth to say after Hodge's death, that "next to having Hodge on one's side is the pleasure of having him as an antagonist."[5] By 1852 Hodge had also established himself as a writer of popular theology, an observer of American politics, and an active commentator on church affairs both theoretical (how Presbyterians measured up to scriptural ideals) and practical (how Presbyterians were handling major issues of the day). His massive *Systematic Theology* appeared in 1872–1873. Along with several of his other works, it remains in print, and has been at least until very recently assigned as a text in conservative Presbyterian seminaries. His works are forcefully Calvinistic, eminently clear, determinedly logical, and yet infused with a great deal of spiritual ardor. He was a hard-working and earnest individual—indispensable prerequisites, it seems, for employment at Princeton Seminary in the nineteenth century. He was the most complex of the Princetonians, he possessed the most capacious mind (which perhaps explains some of the tensions in his thought), and he has been the least understood by modern observers.

Hodge's son, Archibald Alexander (1823–1886), did not overawe observers like his namesake or impress them like his father, but he had the greatest capacity for precise and concise expression among the major Princetonians. He graduated from Princeton College in 1841 and from the seminary in 1847, served three years as a missionary to India until forced to return by ill health, labored fourteen years as a pastor, twelve years as a professor of systematic theology at Allegheny Seminary, and then was called in 1877 to be his father's associate in didactic and polemic theology, the chair he filled for only seven years from Charles Hodge's death in 1878

5. A. A. Hodge, *The Life of Charles Hodge* (New York: Arno and New York Times, 1969 [1881]), p. 616.

to his own decease at the age of 63. A. A. Hodge published several popular summations of Christian doctrine and a few more technical studies, including an important essay on the inspiration of Scripture, which he wrote with B. B. Warfield in 1881. For the last six years of his life he served as co-editor with the more liberal Charles Briggs of *The Presbyterian Review,* a journal specifically designed to hold together the progressive and conservative wings of American Presbyterianism. Some twentieth-century students have expressed the opinion that A. A. Hodge stated theological propositions better than his father. This was undoubtedly true in some instances, but A. A. Hodge did not—perhaps because of the relative brevity of his career as a teaching theologian—exert the same influence over the Princeton tradition as the others who held his chair.

A. A. Hodge's successor, Benjamin Breckinridge Warfield (1851–1921), maintained Old Princeton views in the trying generation before World War I when many of even the most general convictions of his tradition were being discarded in other parts of the American church. Warfield was born into a wealthy Virginia family and was privately educated before entering Princeton College in 1868. His arrival at the college coincided with the beginning of the tenure of President James McCosh, the last great exponent of Scottish Common Sense Realism in America. Throughout his adolescent years Warfield devoted himself to scientific pursuits—as budding mathematician, geologist, and naturalist—but in 1872 to the surprise of his acquaintances he announced that he planned to enter the ministry. In 1873 he began studies at Princeton Theological Seminary where he sat for a time under the instruction of Charles Hodge.[6] He later memorialized Hodge as a great teacher of Scripture with, however, little interest in exegetical technicalities. On graduation from seminary in 1876 Warfield married, traveled in Europe, served as assistant pastor in Baltimore, and then in 1878 began to teach New Testament Literature and Language at A. A. Hodge's old seminary in Allegheny, Pennsylvania. He succeeded the younger Hodge as Professor of Didactic and Polemic Theology at Princeton in 1887. Unlike his predecessors, Warfield was not an active churchman except in the intellectual sphere. His own reserved personality and the necessity for many years to care for an invalid wife contributed to what his own brother called "a certain intellectual austerity, a loftiness and aloofness."[7] He wrote an incredible number of articles, reviews, and monographs for both popular and scholarly forums (perhaps half of them collected in ten substantial volumes after his death), yet he did not produce a magnum opus on the order of Hodge's *Systematic Theology* or pathbreaking works like those of Alexander. His scholarship was precise, careful, wide-ranging, penetrating, and especially well-grounded in scientific literature. With these scholarly resources, he labored might and main to restrain the rising tide of liberalism, especially as it affected the Old Princeton doctrine of Scripture. Warfield read more widely, possessed more skill in languages, and displayed

6. Warfield, "Dr. Hodge as a Teacher of Exegesis," in *ibid.,* pp. 588–591.
7. Ethelbert D. Warfield, "Biographical Sketch of Benjamin Breckinridge Warfield," WBBW, I: viii.

sharper dialectical powers than any of his three notable predecessors. Yet perhaps because of the nature of his times—with the rise of the university, the increasing specialization and fragmentation of knowledge—his thought seems less comprehensive, less the work of a churchman in society than a theologian in the academy. His death brought to an end the great years of the Princeton theology. No less an observer than J. Gresham Machen described the passing of Warfield as the passing of his theological tradition: "It seemed to me," Machen wrote in a letter describing Warfield's funeral, February 19, 1921, "that the old Princeton—a great institution it was—died when Dr. Warfield was carried out."[8]

Justifiable as it may be to limit attention to these four theologians, a truly complete anthology would include selections from many others who made substantial contributions to the Princeton tradition. Some of these were very important individuals in their own right. Samuel Miller (1769–1850), second professor of the seminary who taught ecclesiastical history and church polity, defended "high Presbyterianism" against all alternatives, and made a strenuous defense of the Old School in the clash that led to Presbyterian division in 1837.[9] James Waddel Alexander (1804–1859), eldest son of Archibald Alexander, polymath, prolific author, pastor of Presbyterian churches in rural Virginia, Trenton, New Jersey, and New York City, professor at Princeton College and Seminary, evangelist, social reformer, and general whirlwind of activity, contributed more material to the *Biblical Repertory and Princeton Review* than anyone else except Charles Hodge.[10] Joseph Addison Alexander (1809–1860), third son of the founder, mastered at least twenty languages and taught several of them in professorships at Princeton College and Seminary, authored commentaries on Isaiah, Psalms, and several New Testament books, and struggled to incorporate elements of both biblical criticism and romantic sensibility into his thoroughly Calvinistic convictions.[11] The last of the major defenders of this tradition was J. Gresham Machen (1881–1937), student of Warfield and teacher of New Testament at the seminary from 1906 to 1929 who was eventually stymied in his effort to maintain the old theology at Princeton and who then founded other institutions in the effort to carry on that tradition.[12]

Beyond these men, an entire corps of able and diligent scholars also made their

8. Quoted in Ned B. Stonehouse, *J. Gresham Machen: A Biographical Memoir* (Grand Rapids: Eerdmans, 1954), p. 310.

9. See Samuel Miller, Jr., *The Life of Samuel Miller* (Philadelphia: Claxton, Remsen & Haffelfinger, 1869); and Belden C. Lane, "Democracy and the Ruling Eldership: Samuel Miller's Response to Tensions Between Clerical Power and Lay Authority in Early Nineteenth-Century America" (Th.D. dissertation, Princeton Theological Seminary, 1976).

10. See "James Waddel Alexander," BRPR, *Index Volume* (1870–71), I: 67–82; and John Hall, ed., *Forty Years' Familiar Letters of James W. Alexander* (New York, 1860).

11. See "Joseph Addison Alexander," BRPR, *Index Volume* (1870–71), I: 82–91; Henry C. Alexander, *The Life of Joseph Addison Alexander* (New York: Charles Scribners, 1870); James H. Moorhead, "Joseph Addison Alexander: Common Sense, Romanticism and Biblical Criticism at Princeton," *Journal of Presbyterian History*, 53 (Spring 1975), 51–65.

12. See Stonehouse, *J. Gresham Machen;* and C. Allyn Russell, "J. Gresham Machen: Scholarly Fundamentalist," in *Voices of American Fundamentalism* (Philadelphia: Westminster, 1976).

Samuel Miller

James Waddel Alexander

Joseph Addison Alexander

J. Gresham Machen

contribution to the Princeton Theology, whether in the pages of the *Biblical Repertory* and succeeding journals, through volumes published under their own names, or by editorial and administrative labors on behalf of the cause. For the most part, the biographies of these leaders lie hidden away in dusty periodicals or forgotten pamphlets, but at least some of their names deserve mention here: Ashbel Green (1762–1848), founding president of the seminary board; Albert Baldwin Dod (1805–1845), a minister and mathematics professor at Princeton College; Lyman Atwater (1813–1883), moral philosopher and Old School polemicist who taught at both the college and seminary; Samuel Tyler (1809–1877), a Maryland lawyer who contributed energetic expositions of Bacon's philosophy to the *Review;* William Henry Green (1825–1900), long-time professor of Old Testament at the seminary; and Francis Landey Patton (1843–1932), Woodrow Wilson's predecessor as president of Princeton University and from 1902 to 1913 the president of Princeton Seminary.[13]

In addition, several theological institutions and a goodly number of individual theologians have carried on the Old Princeton traditions in one form or another to this very day. They include Westminster Seminary in Philadelphia, founded by Machen and other professors from Princeton in 1929, Covenant Seminary (St. Louis), Reformed Seminary (Jackson, Mississippi), Faith Seminary (Philadelphia), and individuals like Roger Nicole of Gordon-Conwell Theological Seminary and John Gerstner, retired professor of church history from Pittsburgh Theological Seminary.

The Institutions of the Princeton Theology

The Princeton theology sprang from the minds of its exponents, but it flowed outward from Princeton through institutions which vastly transcended those individuals. First among these was the seminary itself. Princeton was the second major American theological seminary, founded only four years after the beginning of the Trinitarian Congregationalist school at Andover, Massachusetts.[14] Although other seminaries soon arose within the Presbyterian church, Princeton remained the largest and most influential center of training for the Presbyterian ministry. In 1844, Robert Baird (Princeton Seminary class of 1822) reported in his pioneering survey of *Religion in the United States of America* that there were six Presbyterian seminaries, including Princeton, associated with the Old School, and six more with the

13. See *The Life of Ashbel Green,* ed. Joseph H. Jones (New York: Robert Carter & Bros., 1849); "Albert Baldwin Dod," BRPR, *Index Volume* (1870–71), I: 151–155; Harris Elwood Starr, "Lyman Hotchkiss Atwater," *Dictionary of American Biography* (New York: Charles Scribner's Sons, 1928), I: 416–417; John J. Dolan, "Samuel Tyler," *Dictionary of American Biography* (New York: Charles Scribner's Sons, 1936), XIX: 97–98; John D. Davis, "William Henry Green," *The Presbyterian and Reformed Review,* 43 (July 1900), 377–396; and on Patton, Stonehouse, *J. Gresham Machen,* pp. 64–66, 512.

14. Mark A. Noll, "The Founding of Princeton Seminary," *Westminster Theological Journal,* 42 (Fall 1979), 72–110; (Fall 1979), 72–110; and Lefferts A. Loetscher, *Facing the Enlightenment and Pietism: Archibald Alexander and the Founding of Princeton Theological Seminary* (Westport, Conn.: Greenwood, 1983), pp. 109–138.

New School. Princeton's 110 students and four faculty made it the largest of the Presbyterian institutions. Only Union of New York (New School) with 90 students and four faculty even approached Princeton's size among the Presbyterians, and only Andover with 153 students was larger among all denominations. At that same time the "theological department" at Yale enrolled 72 students, the General Theological Seminary of the Episcopal Church in New York had 74, and the "theological department" at Harvard numbered only 27.[15] By the time of its centennial in 1912, Princeton had the distinction of having enrolled over 1000 more students than any other seminary in the United States. And by 1933, the seminary's biographical catalogue listed a total of 6,386 students in the classes from 1815 (when Alexander's first students graduated) through 1920 (the last year of Warfield's active professorship).[16]

The following figures summarize the total number of students who received their primary training in theology from the four professors anthologized in this volume.[17]

Alexander	1815–1840	1,114
C. Hodge	1841–1878	2,082
A. A. Hodge	1879–1886	440
Warfield	1887–1920	2,750

Many of the students who attended Princeton Seminary, moreover, played unusually important roles in the history of the church, and in broader spheres of American life. In the seminary's first decade, as an example, 254 students attended the classes taught by Alexander and Samuel Miller. Those of this group who later made their mark included the Presbyterian theologians Charles Hodge, John Breckinridge, and James Waddel Alexander; the minister-authors William B. Sprague, Albert Barnes, and Robert Baird; fifteen college presidents, among them John Maclean (Princeton) and Theodore Dwight Wolsey (Yale); and several influential leaders of other denominations like Lutheran Samuel Schmucker and Episcopal bishop John Johns.[18] An enthusiastic speaker at the seminary's centennial

15. Robert Baird, *Religion in the United States of America* (New York: Arno and New York Times, 1969 [1844]), pp. 368–370.

16. Through 1908, Andover had enrolled 3,538 students; through 1912, the Southern Baptist Seminary in Louisville counted approximately 4,500; through 1910, Princeton's total stood at 5,742. "Theological Seminaries," *The New Schaff-Herzog Encyclopedia of Religious Knowledge* (1908–1912), XI: 350, 374. For a complete listing of students, see *Biographical Catalogue of the Princeton Theological Seminary, 1815–1932*, comp. Edward Howell Roberts (Princeton: Trustees of the Seminary, 1933). These figures include all students who attended the various seminaries, not just those who graduated.

17. The division between Alexander and Charles Hodge (1840) is when Hodge took over the bulk of the theological instruction. The figure of 3,000 students which is often cited in reports of Hodge's labors at Princeton include those who studied under him as professor of oriental and biblical literature.

18. *Biographical Catalogue 1815–1932*, pp. 1–24.

rejoiced in the fact that, "besides theological and college teachers, Princeton has contributed to the Presbyterian Church fifty-six moderators of General Assemblies, and five bishops to the Protestant Episcopal Church." The same speaker went on to note that "she has not, as yet, produced a Pope, but has trained three stated clerks of the General Assembly."[19] Other notables who attended the Seminary during its first century included the German Reformed theologian, John Williamson Nevin (class of 1826); Henry James, Sr. (1839), father of psychologist William James and novelist Henry James; missionary statesmen Sheldon Jackson (1858) and Robert Speer (1893); the "many-sided litterateur" Henry van Dyke (1877); and the Episcopalian translator of Sören Kierkegaard, Walter Lowrie (1893).[20] Some of these students, like Nevin, Henry James, van Dyke, and Walter Lowrie, eventually repudiated the Old Princeton theology. Many more, however, would have echoed the sentiments of E. Y. Mullins, president of the Southern Baptist Seminary in Louisville, who had learned his theology from James P. Boyce (class of 1852): "As Mt. Blanc enriches the valleys so Princeton Seminary has stood like Mt. Blanc among the seminaries of this country. In a thousand ways, you have not known, she has sent down her largess of blessing into the valleys, and we rejoice in what she has done. And the reason Mt. Blanc can thus bless the valleys is because she lifts her head to the very skies where, from the inexhaustible heavens themselves, she draws her supply, and so Princeton has drawn her supplies from the eternal sources."[21]

Princeton College was also, in effect, an institution of the Princeton Theology for much of the nineteenth century, even though the college and seminary in Princeton had never been formally connected.[22] In the years immediately preceding the founding of the seminary, negotiators from the General Assembly and the college's board of trustees had contemplated incorporating a seminary into the college as a theological department—the model later followed by Yale and Harvard. But these fell through, and Princeton Seminary came into existence under the direct authority of the General Assembly, while the college remained in the hands of a self-perpetuating board of trustees.[23] Separate as they were officially, however, the two institutions were joined in spirit for most of the nineteenth century through inter-

19. William Hallock Johnson, "Princeton in Theological Education and Religious Thought," in *The Centennial Celebration of the Theological Seminary of the Presbyterian Church in the United States of America at Princeton, New Jersey* (Princeton: At the Seminary, 1912), p. 441.

20. For excellent capsule biographies of Samuel Schmucker, Nevin, Jackson, van Dyke, Lowrie, as well as of Alexander, Charles Hodge, and other prominent graduates of the seminary, see *Sons of the Prophets: Leaders in Protestantism from Princeton Seminary*, ed. Hugh T. Kerr (Princeton: Princeton University Press, 1963).

21. Edgar Young Mullins, "From the Seminaries of Other Churches," *Centennial of Princeton Seminary*, p. 557.

22. The official names of these institutions were The Theological Seminary of the Presbyterian Church in the United States of America at Princeton, New Jersey; and The College of New Jersey (until changed in 1896 to Princeton University). On the college-seminary connection, see Thomas Jefferson Wertenbaker, *Princeton 1746–1896* (Princeton: Princeton University Press, 1946), pp. 118–183, 215–390; and Hoeveler, *James McCosh*, pp. 222–349.

23. Noll, "Founding of Princeton Seminary," pp. 76–85.

locking boards, shared concerns, and their common location. Nearly one-third of the seminary's founding board of 1812 were trustees of the college, and the first president of that board, Ashbel Green, also served as president of the college from 1812 to 1822. Many years later, the first officially designated president of Princeton Seminary, Francis L. Patton, assumed that position in 1902, after serving for 14 years as president of the college. Seminary faculty, including Archibald and James Waddel Alexander, Charles and A. A. Hodge, and William Henry Green, served as prominent members of the college's board throughout the century.[24] It was in fact Charles Hodge, speaking as senior trustee, who officially welcomed James McCosh in 1868 as new president of the college, and reminded him, "We desire that the spirit of true religion should be dominant in this College, that a pure gospel should live here."[25] Throughout the century, a number of professors, like the younger Alexanders and Lyman Atwater, taught alternately at the two institutions. And a number of the college faculty (principally James Carnahan, John McLean, Albert Dod, the Alexanders, and Atwater) were mainstays on the *Princeton Review.* The intimate connection between college and seminary began to dissolve in the last third of the nineteenth century with the growing specialization and secularization of academic life, symbolized in the reorganization of the college as Princeton University in 1896. The parting of ways continued during the presidency of Woodrow Wilson (1902–1910), who attempted to broaden the perspective of the university beyond the parameters of the Princeton Theology.[26] Even so, Wilson's successor, John Grier Hibben (seminary class of 1886 and an ordained Presbyterian minister), could state publicly at the seminary centennial with reference to the shared heritage of the two schools: "we, who are here representing the present Princeton University, pledge you that we will endeavor, so far as lies within us, to preserve the faith and hope of our fathers and to remain true to the gospel which they professed."[27]

Historians of Princeton University regularly look on the influence of the seminary as restrictive.[28] With justice, they note that the doctrinal precision of the seminary held the college back from an earlier adoption of that free inquiry which has characterized the country's great universities for the last 120 years. Still, the college itself benefited greatly from the presence of the seminary, especially over the seminary's first sixty years when it was by far the livelier institution in general scholarship as well as in theology. It is also true that the college, in a subtle way, has had a great influence on the seminary. The philosophy of Scottish Common Sense Realism which played such an important role at the seminary came from the

24. *Biographical Catalogue 1815–1932,* pp. vii–xix; *General Catalogue of Princeton University 1746–1906,* (Princeton: By the University, 1908), pp. 12–47.

25. Hoeveler, *James McCosh,* p. 230.

26. John M. Mulder, *Woodrow Wilson: The Years of Preparation* (Princeton: Princeton University Press, 1978), pp. 158–186.

27. John Grier Hibben, *Centennial of Princeton Seminary,* p. 559.

28. Hoeveler, *James McCosh,* pp. 222–224; Wertenbaker, *Princeton 1746–1896,* pp. 149–151; and "The College of New Jersey and the Presbyterians," *Journal of the Presbyterian Historical Society,* 36 (December 1958), 215–216.

college's two great Scottish presidents, John Witherspoon (president 1768–1794) and James McCosh (1868–1888). Through their philosophical influence the college may have done as much to shape the Princeton Theology as the Princeton Theology did to influence the college.

Apart from the students who had first-hand contact with the proponents of the Princeton Theology, most others in the nineteenth century received their insights from the tradition through the printed page. As influential as the individual volumes penned by the Princetonians were—the systematic and popular theologies of the Hodges being most important—the impact of their learned quarterlies was even greater. The reviews emanating from Princeton contained the discursive expositions of Princeton positions, the carefully articulated attacks on rival theological positions, the thoughtful reflections on matters of church and state, and the general guidelines for reacting to culture that shaped the thinking of many Presbyterians and influenced the reflections even of those who came under attack. Chief among these periodicals was Charles Hodge's *Biblical Repertory and Princeton Review*, which was read with enthusiasm in Old School manses and seminaries throughout the country, with both delight and some exasperation in other Reformed communities, and with mingled amazement and wrath at N. W. Taylor's Yale, Edwards Amasa Park's Andover, John Williamson Nevin's Mercersburg, and Charles Finney's Oberlin.[29] Throughout the last twenty-five years of his life, Hodge's contemporaries paid repeated tribute to the influence of his journal—"beyond all question the greatest purely theological Review that has ever been published in the English tongue" (*British Quarterly Review*, 1871); "I think Dr. Hodge the ablest reviewer in the world" (Irenaeus Prime, *New York Observer*, 1872); "the most powerful organ in the land" (editor, *Autobiography of Lyman Beecher*).[30]

Hodge began the journal in 1825 as the *Biblical Repertory* in order to present translations of European biblical scholarship, but he reorganized it in 1829 as the *Biblical Repertory and Theological Review* in order to give more room to constructive theology from "the association of gentlemen"—that is, the professors of the seminary, and some of the faculty of the college—who took responsibility for it. Hodge was always the driving force behind this journal, which in 1837 changed its name once again, this time to the *Biblical Repertory and Princeton Review*. Many years later at the end of the Civil War, Hodge published a moving piece defending the journal's stance toward the war, in which he called editorial supervision of the publication "a ball-and-chain" that he had carried "for forty years, with scarcely any other compensation than the high privilege and honour of making it an organ for upholding sound Presbyterianism, the cause of the country, and the honour of our common Redeemer."[31] In spite of the effort it cost Hodge, the *Review* was an ideal medium for getting out the Princeton view.

29. See the fulsome and informative "Retrospect of the History of the Princeton Review," by Charles Hodge, BRPR, *Index Volume* (1870–71), I: 1–39.

30. A. A. Hodge, *Life of Charles Hodge*, pp. 257, 259–260.

31. Charles Hodge, "The *Princeton Review* on the State of the Country and of the Church," BRPR, 37 (October 1865), 657.

Articles in the journal were usually responses to published treatises, sermons, or even articles in other periodicals. These reviews dealt expansively with the works in question, but then often broadened into full-scale treatments—sometimes complementary, sometimes in rebuttal—to the presentation of the work under review. The format ideally suited the Princetonians' image of themselves as theological guardians responsible not so much for expounding a theology as defending traditional Calvinism. In the course of their rebuttals, the Princeton men in fact said new things, but always in the effort to conserve. For Charles Hodge's work in particular, the *Review* provided a fuller, more comprehensive picture of the actual contours of his thought than the compressed treatments in the *Systematic Theology* or the amplified discourses in his popular books.

The disorientation within American Presbyterianism in the last third of the century was reflected in the rapidly shifting world of journal publication. Princeton theologians continued in the tradition of the senior Hodge by using the journals as the most advantageous forum for their views, first in the continuation of Charles Hodge's old journal, renamed the *Presbyterian Quarterly and Princeton Review* after Hodge relinquished the editorship in 1872. Then they turned to the *Presbyterian Review* edited by A. A. Hodge and the considerably more liberal Charles Briggs, then to the *Presbyterian and Reformed Review* which Warfield edited with other conservative Reformed leaders from around the country, and finally to the *Princeton Theological Review*, dominated by Warfield and under the exclusive direction of the seminary faculty.

The contributions of A. A. Hodge and Warfield were found in these and several other journals which, if they did not have quite the power of the old *Biblical Repertory and Princeton Review*, still were forceful organs of the Princeton Theology. In addition, the growing practice of presenting self-standing essays on individual topics gave especially Warfield the opportunity to present synthetic monographs on debated topics rather than arguments limited by the coverage of a work under review. Table 1 attempts to sort out the details for the journals associated with the Princeton Theology.

The final institution of the Princeton Theology was the Presbyterian church itself, even though the seminary never enjoyed the full confidence of that entire body. At its inception some Presbyterian leaders wished to see seminary education dispersed in the presbyteries or located further south and west. In the debates over theology, polity, and church organization that led to the Presbyterian division of 1837, Princeton was staunchly Old School. Against the New School Presbyterians, Princeton sided with those who distrusted the theological and practical influence of New England Congregationalism, worried about the effects on Presbyterianism of the voluntary societies which had become so important for Christian activity in the country, and feared lest the revival style favored by the New School would obliterate traditional Calvinism and regular Presbyterian order together.[32] It goes without saying that Princeton attracted few New School scholars

---

32. The nonpareil study of the New School is George M. Marsden, *The Evangelical Mind and the New School Presbyterian Experience* (New Haven: Yale University Press, 1970); on Princeton's opposition, pp. 69, 73–74, and *passim*.

Table 1

Editor	Title	Years
(1) C. Hodge	Biblical Repertory	1825–1828
C. Hodge[33]	Biblical Repertory and Theological Review	1829–1836
	Biblical Repertory and Princeton Review	1837–1871
	(continued as)	
Lyman Atwater & H. B. Smith	Presbyterian Quarterly and Princeton Review	1872–1877
	(continued without the oversight of Princeton Seminary faculty)	
	The Princeton Review	1878–1885
	The New Princeton Review	1886–1889
(2) A. A. Hodge & Charles Briggs	The Presbyterian Review	1880–1889
(3) B. B. Warfield[34]	The Presbyterian and Reformed Review	1890–1902
(4) Warfield & Seminary Faculty	The Princeton Theological Review	1903–1929

in the years of division from 1837 until the breach was healed among Northern Presbyterians in 1869, in spite of Hodge's reservations. A. A. Hodge and Warfield aligned the seminary with the conservative forces in the great theological battles that roiled the Presbyterian waters in the forty years before World War I. Still, the seminary's influence was strong in the denomination. Beginning from 1835 and with but one exception through 1867, Charles Hodge made an annual report and critique on the activities of the General Assembly, usually held in May. Whether or not they liked the report, Presbyterian leaders could not afford to ignore it. It often became the source of further polemics and indeed attained such prominence that one of Hodge's associates on the *Review* once claimed, "there is no inducement to prepare a good article for the July number, because every one turns at once to that on the General Assembly which absorbs all interest."[35]

Princeton's influence in the denomination rested mostly on the power of its ideas. The school did become a center for missionary training.[36] Alexander and A. A. Hodge retained associations in the denomination from their pastoral careers. And all of the Princetonians were in wide demand as interim preachers. Yet their influence was primarily intellectual. The students they taught and the ideas they propounded were not the sole shaping influences on Presbyterians in the nineteenth and early twentieth centuries, but they were among the most powerful.

33. From 1829–1855, with an "Association of Gentlemen," and from 1868–1871 with Lyman Atwater.

34. Warfield's co-editors in 1890 were Wm. G. T. Shedd, Wm. H. Jeffers, Edward D. Morris, S. M. Woodbridge, Talbot W. Chambers, Ransom B. Welch, John DeWitt, William Alexander, and William Caven.

35. BRPR, *Index Volume* (1870–71), II: 206.

36. See the speech by Robert Speer on Princeton's missionary emphasis in *Centennial of Princeton Seminary*, pp. 418–436.

Themes of the Princeton Theology

Writers of theological history regularly leave the impression that the conviction of Old Princeton may be summarized without difficulty. A historian of New England Calvinism wrote scathingly in 1907, for example, about the simplistic thought of Charles Hodge. "In fact, Dr. Hodge showed no ability, and but little desire to understand the New England men. He so constantly misinterpreted them that he soon lost all influence in opposing their speculations among thinking men. . . . He may be safely left by the historian of a progressive school of theology to the natural consequences of his own remark that during the many years of his predominance at Princeton that institution had never brought forward a single original thought."[37] A more even-handed historian has written that "the so-called 'Princeton Theology' seemed to offer an almost mathematical demonstration of an unchanged and unchangeable religious outlook."[38] The best brief accounts of the Princeton Theology, both provided by Sydney Ahlstrom, concede that it was made up of several distinct elements, especially "an almost absolutely rigidified Biblicalism," "a reliance on the Common Sense Realists of Scotland," and the Reformed confessions.[39] But even Ahlstrom implies that the rich complexity which characterized John W. Nevin's Mercersburg Theology or Horace Bushnell's Romantic Christianity was largely absent from Princeton.

In reality, however, the Princeton theology was not a simple matter at all. While it self-consciously taught traditional Calvinism, it did so without smoothing out the various strands of Reformed faith which may not have been so consistent with each other as Princetonians thought. While their theology was rooted in Scripture and the Trinitarian orthodoxy of the early church, it also participated fully in modern philosophical movements—often without fully considering if the religious and secular sources were compatible. While in some respects they remained untouched by the ebb and flow of American life, in others they shared fully in the American experience, with all the vicissitudes which characterized that experience in the nineteenth and early twentieth centuries. It takes only a little unpacking to realize that several guiding themes came together to make the Princeton Theology. No modern historian, however, has adequately explained the complex interrelationships among those themes, nor will this brief introduction accomplish that task. Yet it is possible to present those aspects of their thought which an adequate explanation will one day have to comprehend.

Scripture

The first of these was a conviction that the message of the Bible defined the Christian faith. From Alexander's first call for a seminary (Selection 1) to Warfield's

---

37. Frank Hugh Foster, *A Genetic History of the New England Theology* (Chicago: University of Chicago Press, 1907), p. 432.

38. Loetscher, *The Broadening Church*, p. 21.

39. Sydney E. Ahlstrom, "Theology in America: A Historical Survey," in *The Shaping of American Religion*, ed. James Ward Smith and A. Leland Jamison (Princeton: Princeton University Press, 1961), p. 263; see also Ahlstrom, *Theology in America: The Major Protestant Voices from Puritanism to Neo-Orthodoxy* (Indianapolis: Bobbs-Merrill, 1967), pp. 45–48, 251–292.

last words on the subject as his successor in the chair of theology (Selection 25), the Princetonians propounded and defended a high view of the inspiration and authority of Scripture. Alexander set forth Scripture as the foundation of Christian truth and the norm for Christian life in several contexts: the Bible would stiffen the spine of the church (Selections 1, 4), it would lay bare the inadequacies of Roman Catholic views of authority,[40] and it would provide the boundaries for legitimate science (Selection 5). Charles Hodge maintained Alexander's beliefs, but also sharply contrasted a faith emerging from Scripture with faith arising from what he called "rationalism" (e.g., Higher Criticism of Scripture), or "mysticism" (e.g., Schleiermacher). Hodge also began the process of refining Alexander's concept of biblical authority (Selection 10) which his son and Warfield carried further in their collaborative efforts. These two restated in more precise terms the Princeton doctrine of Scripture in their 1881 article (Selection 19) which was occasioned by a growing sense of alarm over the inroads of Higher Criticism in American Christianity and especially within Presbyterianism. In a series of carefully crafted essays Warfield brought the tradition to its culmination by defining exactly what it meant for Scripture to be inerrant (Selection 23), to be both a divine and human book (Selection 24), and to be the uniquely inspired norm of all divine revelation (Selection 25). Unlike some of their successors in defense of the inerrancy of Scripture, Warfield and the Hodges wrote on this subject with care, precision, learning, careful qualifications, and notable absence of pietistic anti-intellectualism. Princeton's fidelity to the plenary inspiration of the Bible was constant throughout the careers of its first four theologians, even as each successive generation provided increasingly refined statements of the position.

Yet having noted a general Princetonian adherence to Scriptural authority is really only the first step in examining this subject. Why, for instance, accept the Bible as ultimate authority? Alexander and Warfield tended to answer by demonstrating—through an appeal to history, logic, and evidentialist demonstration—that the Scriptures were entirely true (Selections 3, 4, 29). Charles Hodge could write this way also (ST, I:53), but he also argued frequently that an inherent power existed in the Bible (sometimes he called it specifically the work of the Holy Spirit) which compelled belief in its truthfulness.[41] Interestingly, Warfield could

---

40. Alexander wrote his books on Scripture with Roman Catholic conceptions of authority constantly in view. For his specific arguments against Rome, see *The Canon of the Old and New Testaments Ascertained; or, The Bible Complete Without the Apocrypha and Unwritten Traditions* (Edinburgh: Johnstone and Hunter, 1855 [1826]), pp. 33–41, 241–274; he summarized these arguments in *Evidence of the Authenticity, Inspiration, and Canonical Authority of the Holy Scriptures* (expanded edition, Philadelphia: Presbyterian Board of Publication, 1836), pp. 258–265, 303–308.

41. For Hodge's appeal to the Spirit as the authenticator of Scripture, see "The Latest Form of Infidelity," BRPR, 12 (January 1840), 34–35; reprinted in Hodge, *Essays and Reviews* (New York: Robert Carter & Bros., 1857), pp. 90–91. For a general statement of the "internal evidence" of Scripture's divine character, see *The Way of Life* (Philadelphia: American Sunday School Union, 1841), sections 1 and 2 (Selection 9); and "Thornwell on the Apocrypha," BRPR, 17 (April 1845), 271–276; reprinted as "Ground of Faith in the Scriptures," *Essays and Reviews*, pp. 188–193.

sometimes mount a similar argument.[42] The Princetonians also faced the question, to what extent belief in the total truthfulness of Scripture was tantamount to Christian belief itself? Sometimes they seemed to identify the two, sometimes to make a conceptual distinction.[43] Another question was this: what does belief in the inerrancy of Scripture entail for attitudes toward theories of biological evolution? Charles Hodge had extreme difficulties in seeing how belief in the Bible could be squared with any form of evolution; A. A. Hodge could countenance the possibility of considerable evolution if such evolution was not defined naturalistically; and Warfield eventually allowed for a thorough-going theistic evolution which, however, he also carefully distinguished from a naturalistic materialism (Selections 12, 20, 27).

On other questions about the Bible, the Princeton theologians spoke with one voice, but without indicating why their view of Scripture compelled them to speak as they did. Why, for example, read the Bible consistent with confessional Calvinism? Again, why constantly prefer the truth of the Bible as proposition over the truth of the Bible as story or its truth as the molder of piety?[44] In answering these questions, the modern theologian will be driven back into the intricacies of the Princetonians' own thinking to decide whether they were right or wrong. The modern historian, on the other hand, may look outward to the Princetonians' culture and draw the conclusion that they were not mere theologians of the Bible, but actually Reformed theologians of the Bible intimately involved with the cross-currents of nineteenth-century intellectual life.

Reformed Confessionalism

The Princeton theologians stood self-consciously in the Reformed tradition. Warfield in 1904 put with greatest succinctness what they all believed: "Calvinism is just religion in its purity. We have only, therefore, to conceive of religion in its purity, and that is Calvinism."[45] One of the things that makes study of Old Princeton so easy is its consistent advocacy of *the* Reformed faith; one of the things that makes it so difficult is their persistent unwillingness to perceive diversity within Reformed Protestantism. For the Princetonians, Calvin, the great lights of Puritanism, the

---

42. Warfield, "The Inspiration of the Bible," WBBW, I: 53.

43. For the identity, see Charles Hodge, "Inspiration," BRPR, 29 (October 1857), 693: "Christianity always has had a creed. A man who believes certain doctrines is a Christian. If his faith is mere assent, he is a speculative Christian; if it is cordial and appreciating, he is a true Christian." For a statement concerning the subjectivity of faith, see C. Hodge, "What is Christianity?" BRPR, 32 (January 1860), 119: "Christianity objectively considered, is the testimony of God concerning his Son, it is the whole revelation of truth contained in the Scriptures, concerning the redemption of man through Jesus Christ our Lord. Subjectively considered, it is the life of Christ in the soul...."

44. For a discussion of the different ways that American Protestants have read the Bible—whether doctrinally, pietistically, morally, or culturally—see Richard J. Mouw, "The Bible in Twentieth-Century Protestantism: A Preliminary Taxonomy," in *The Bible in America: Essays in Cultural History*, ed. Nathan O. Hatch and Mark A. Noll (New York: Oxford University Press, 1982), pp. 139–162, with pp. 143–144 particularly on the doctrinal emphases of Old Princeton.

45. Warfield, "What is Calvinism?" SSWW, I: 389.

Westminster standards, and the influential dogmaticians of seventeenth-century Europe all spoke with united voice in setting out the Reformed tradition. The Princeton theologians, in their turn, propounded this faith in theological manuals, sermons, commentaries, dogmatic tomes, and polemical writings.[46]

Their Calvinism shared the major emphases of the Reformed tradition: God had created mankind good. In the Fall human beings incurred the wrath of God and brought guilt on themselves. Adam's morally crippling sin was imputed to all humans, who properly deserved the condemnation which their sinfulness entailed. Sinners, because turned from God by their rebellious wills, would not honor God until drawn by his own sovereign mercy. God's love—expressed most clearly in a Covenant of Redemption between Father and Son and a Covenant of Grace between God and his people—brought salvation to the elect. Redeemed sinners must continue to struggle with the lingering effects of the Fall, but could also join in actively working for the Kingdom of God. This was the substantial theology which the Princetonians lived to promote. It remains, through the consistent republication of their works, the aspect of their thought which receives most respected attention today within Reformed circles of conservative Protestantism.

Critical discussion of Princeton's Reformed confessionalism revolves around the modern commonplace that the Reformed tradition was actually a diffuse family of theologies, rather than a repeated expression of the same thing.[47] The Princetonians, however, drew upon different aspects of the Reformed heritage as if it constituted a unified whole. In his *Systematic Theology*, for example, Hodge regularly interweaves testimony from Calvin, the Second Helvetic Confession of 1566, the English Westminster Confession and Catechism of the mid-seventeenth century, and the works of late seventeenth-century polemicist Francis Turretin to support his own Reformed conclusions.

The Princetonians' use of the Reformed dogmaticians of the seventeenth century has been an especially sensitive issue. When Alexander arrived at Princeton to begin instruction, he cast about for a theological text. As his biographer describes it, "Finding no work in English which entirely met his demands, he placed in the hands of his pupils the Institutions of Francis Turretin. It was ponderous, scholastic and in a dead language [Latin], but he believed in the process of grappling with difficulties; he had felt the influence of this athletic sinewy reason on his own mind, and had observed that those who mastered his arguments were apt to be strong and logical divines."[48] Turretin's *Institutio theologiae elencticae* (1679–1685)

46. Examples of each type of work are cited in the bibliography.

47. See, as examples, Jack Bartlett Rogers, *Scripture in the Westminster Confession: A Problem of Historical Interpretation for American Presbyterianism* (Grand Rapids: Eerdmans, 1967); Brian G. Armstrong, *Calvinism and the Amyraut Heresy: Protestant Scholasticism and Humanism in Seventeenth-Century France* (Madison: University of Wisconsin Press, 1969); R. T. Kendall, *Calvin and English Calvinism to 1649* (Oxford: Oxford University Press); and Dewey D. Wallace, Jr., *Puritans and Predestination: Grace in English Protestant Thought, 1525–1695* (Chapel Hill: University of North Carolina Press, 1982).

48. James W. Alexander, *The Life of Archibald Alexander* (Philadelphia: Presbyterian Board of Publication, 1855), p. 331.

remained the theology text at the seminary until replaced by Hodge's *Systematic Theology* in the early 1870s. Francis Turretin (1623–1687) was, in the words of John W. Beardslee III, "a stalwart but in many ways moderate representative of Geneva orthodoxy during what was virtually its last generation—of the orthodoxy based on Calvin's Catechism and the Second Helvetic Confession [1566], plus the Canons of Dort (1619) . . . with a growing rigidity concerning Biblical inspiration, election, reprobation, and unmediated grace expressed in the *Helvetic Consensus Formula* of 1675."[49] Turretin's defense of Calvinism appeared, that is, after more than a century of heated discussion concerning what it meant to be truly Reformed. It responded to Arminius on free will, Amyraut on the nature of the atonement, the Lutherans on the sacraments, and Roman Catholics and rationalists on the authority of Scripture. It is Turretin's precise defense of Reformed positions on these matters—with his intense concern to defend the faith against all detractors—that has earned him the reputation of a "scholastic." Some modern critics see his influence as the dominant note in the Princeton Theology.

There is much to support this contention. Charles Hodge praised Turretin and his generation highly (Selection 7). James Waddel Alexander argued in 1848 that Turretin's "adherence to the received doctrine of the Reformed church is so uniform and strict, that there is no writer who has higher claims as an authority as to what that doctrine was."[50] In 1845 an anonymous note in the BRPR admitted that Turretin's *Institutes* bore "the tincture of scholasticism," but nonetheless recommended him as "the best systematic theological writer with whom we are acquainted" and the work as "remarkably adapted to the present state of theology in this country."[51] And A. A. Hodge seems to have modeled his own *Outlines of Theology* on the question and answer method promoted by Turretin.[52]

Still, it is possible to rate Turretin too highly as a theological guide for the Princetonians. Alexander, who introduced Turretin at Princeton, nonetheless retained other theological mentors.[53] Throughout his life he made much of the advice of his teacher, William Graham, to tackle theological problems by hard thought without written commentary; and many of his works, especially those relating to religious experience, and even some of those on the Bible, reveal little influence from Turretin. Charles Hodge, admittedly, drew heavily on Turretin in the construction of his *Systematic Theology*—for the discussions of the Trinity, the nature of moral responsibility, the covenant, the work of Christ, the power of the

---

49. John W. Beardslee III, *Reformed Dogmatics* (Grand Rapids: Baker, 1977, 1965), p. 14. The recent appearance in English of Francis Turretin, *The Doctrine of Scripture: Locus 2 of Institutio Theologiae Elencticae*, ed. and trans. by John W. Beardslee III (Grand Rapids: Baker, 1981), makes it clear that Turretin's view of the Bible may not have been as mechanistic or as rationalistic as has often been assumed.

50. James Waddel Alexander, "Turretin," BRPR, 20 (July 1848), 461.

51. BRPR, 17 (January 1845), 190.

52. On Turretin's method, see Alexander, "Turretin," p. 462; Charles Hodge, "Historical Sermon," in A. A. Hodge, *Life of Charles Hodge*, p. 553; and illustrated in Beardslee, *Reformed Dogmatics*, pp. 337–459.

53. J. W. Alexander, *Life of Archibald Alexander*, p. 109.

Holy Spirit, and the *ordo salutis*. Turretin also supplied Hodge with several of his arguments against Catholic doctrine. Yet the systematics employs Augustine, Calvin, and the Westminster standards even more widely for a still wider range of topics.[54] A. A. Hodge probably drew on Turretin more obviously and directly than any of the Princeton theologians, especially in his *Outlines of Theology*. But Warfield, who as a seminarian studied Hodge's systematics instead of Turretin, hardly refers to the Genevan at all. That Turretin was a major influence at Old Princeton is clear. That he was dominant in the sense of determining the scope and sweep of their theology is not.

One of the major reasons why it is difficult to sort out the relative influence of the various Reformed influences on the Princeton theologians was their approach to theology itself. The tendency, which continued through Machen, was to regard theological truth in static categories which were not influenced by historical development.[55] Thus, arguments of Calvin against his opponents in 1559, of the Westminster Divines against theirs in 1646, and of Turretin against his in 1679 could be treated simply in kind, as if they were articulated parts of a general framework. This approach to theological assertions had much to do with the Princetonians' conviction that the Bible provided a truthful revelation. It also involved Princeton commitments in philosophy and science. It was a point of view, heavily dependent on the Scottish Philosophy of Common Sense, which itself gave shape to their biblicalism and Reformed confessionalism.

Scottish Common Sense Philosophy

Recent scholarship has shown the broad and deep influence which the Scottish Philosophy of Common Sense enjoyed in the United States from the Revolution into the Gilded Age.[56] The theologians at Princeton were among the American intellectuals who most consistently used the language and the categories of this philosophy even when, as later observers would contend, its tenets seemed to contradict Princeton commitments to Scripture and Reformed tradition.

Scottish Common Sense Realism was a philosophy designed expressly to save the benefits of England's "moderate" Scientific Revolution for good theology, public

54. For an overview of the use of these authorities, see "Index" to Charles Hodge, *Systematic Theology* (Grand Rapids: Eerdmans, n.d.), I, preliminary pp. 1–79.

55. George Marsden explains how this intellectual approach had developed by the early twentieth century in "J. Gresham Machen: History and Truth," *Westminster Theological Journal*, 42 (Fall 1979), 157–175.

56. Outstanding examples of this scholarship include Sydney E. Ahlstrom, "The Scottish Philosophy and American Theology," *Church History*, 24 (1955), 257–272; Douglas Sloan, *The Scottish Enlightenment and the American College Ideal* (New York: Teachers College Press, 1971); D. H. Meyer, *The Instructed Conscience: The Shaping of the American National Ethic* (Philadelphia: University of Pennsylvania Press, 1972); Theodore Dwight Bozeman, *Protestants in an Age of Science: The Baconian Ideal and Antebellum American Religious Thought* (Chapel Hill: University of North Carolina Press, 1977), pp. 3–31; and E. Brooks Holifield, *The Gentlemen Theologians: American Theology in Southern Culture 1795–1860* (Durham, N.C.: Duke University Press, 1978), pp. 110–126.

order, and rational well-being.[57] It was a point of view, developed by learned professors in Glasgow and Edinburgh like Thomas Reid (1710–1796), which attempted to refute the skepticism of David Hume, the idealism of Bishop George Berkeley, and the revolutionary social theories of the radical French Enlightenment. This approach laid great stress on the "common sense" of humankind. It argued that normal people, using responsibly the information provided by their senses, actually grasped thereby the real world. Furthermore, an exercise of the "moral sense," a faculty analogous in all important ways to physical senses, gave humans immediate knowledge about the nature of their own minds. And because all humans, humanity in *common*, were able to grasp the truth of the world in this way—in fact, could not live unless they took for granted that truth was available in this way—this *common sense* could provide the basis for a full-scale philosophy as well. Scottish Common Sense philosophers thus modified and defended the great traditions of modern English thought. They affirmed Francis Bacon's insistence that truth arises from empirical and inductive means. They confirmed John Locke's trust in sense information while eliminating his confusing discussion of ideas. And they hitched their star to the great Sir Isaac Newton by insisting that the highest form of knowledge arises from our empirical study of the outside world and (going beyond Newton) the empirical study of our own minds. The Scottish philosophers regarded truth as a static entity, open equally to all people wherever they lived, in the present or past. They placed a high premium on scientific investigation. They were deeply committed to an empirical method that made much of gathering relevant facts into logical wholes. They abhorred "speculation" and "metaphysics" as unconscionable flights from the basic realities of the physical world and the human mind. And at least some of them assumed that this approach could be used to convince all rational souls of the truth of Christianity, the necessity of traditional social order, and the capability of scientific methods to reveal whatever may be learned about the world.

Considered strictly in terms of philosophical history, this Scottish thought was the chrysalis from which the Princeton Theology emerged. It was brought to America from Scotland in its fullest form by the Rev. John Witherspoon, who became president of Princeton College in 1768 where he taught the teachers of the Princeton Theology. Alexander's sole instructor was William Graham (Princeton College 1773) a single-minded, even naive, philosophical realist who passed Witherspoon's ideas concerning truth, science, and intellectual method to his pupil.[58] Charles Hodge's pastor as a youth and his professor as an adolescent was Ashbel Green (Princeton College 1783), who was just as faithful as Graham in communicating the philosophical perspective of their mentor. In the very year in which Hodge

57. S. A. Grave, *The Scottish Philosophy of Common Sense* (Oxford: Clarendon Press, 1960), is an excellent summary of the school. Henry May, *The Enlightenment in America* (New York: Oxford University Press, 1976), especially pp. 307–362, is superb on the way in which Scottish thought infused what he calls the "didactic" Enlightenment.

58. Wesley Frank Craven, "William Graham," in *Princetonians 1769–1775: A Biographical Dictionary*, ed. Richard A. Harrison (Princeton: Princeton University Press, 1980), pp. 289–294.

entered Princeton College (1812) Green became president of that institution and, as one of his first official actions, restored Witherspoon's text in *Moral Philosophy* to the position it had held when he was an undergraduate—as the culminating and integrating study of the undergraduate curriculum.[59] A. A. Hodge learned Scottish Realism from his father. And Warfield learned it from Scotland's James McCosh, the last great defender of the Scottish Philosophy who became president of Princeton College in 1868 as Warfield was beginning his undergraduate career.[60]

The influence of the Scottish Philosophy is as apparent in the Princetonians' works as in a recital of their educational lineage. Alexander's lecture on the nature of truth, probably the first instruction ever given at Princeton Seminary, is a nearly pure example of the Scottish approach (Selection 3). Charles Hodge began his *Systematic Theology* with a discussion of theological method that was indebted to this same perspective to almost the same degree (Selection 8). And this point of view appears with equal clarity in A. A. Hodge and Warfield.[61] It was commitment to Scottish Common Sense Realism, for example, which more than anything kept Warfield from understanding why his Dutch Reformed contemporaries, Abraham Kuyper and Herman Bavinck, paid so little attention to an empirical apologetics based on Christian evidences (Selection 29). But these theologians, whom Warfield otherwise honored highly, had long since repudiated the reliance on naturalistic "evidences" which Scottish Realism encouraged.

Twentieth-century critics of the Princeton Theology make much of the importance of Scottish Common Sense for their thought. Even those who think more highly of their general contribution often raise questions about their devotion to this philosophy and wonder, as Perry Miller had wondered about the Puritans, if the Princetonians did not introduce "the wooden horse of rationalism into the Trojan citadel of theology."[62] Critics of Scottish Common Sense Philosophy regularly condemn its advocates for being naive, for—that is—failing to recognize how thoroughly all human perceptions, even those of Scripture, are colored by local cultural circumstances. Modern Reformed thinkers who are not Common Sense Realists are among those who insist that it is not only naive, but anti-biblical to begin a chain of reasoning with the assumption that the search for truth involves no moral preconditions in the seeker and no predetermined assumptions about what the

59. See the two critical editions of Witherspoon's *Moral Philosophy*, the first edited by V. L. Collins (Princeton: Princeton University Press, 1912), the second by Jack Scott (Newark, Del: University of Delaware Press, 1982).

60. Before McCosh arrived in America, the Princeton theologians had already expressed their approval of his theological and philosophical efforts; see BRPR, 23 (October 1851), 598–624; *ibid.*, 32 (October 1860), 650–657; *ibid.*, 38 (July 1866), 416–424.

61. On Warfield's adherence to the principles of Scottish Realism, see John H. Gerstner, "Warfield's Case for Biblical Inerrancy," in *God's Inerrant Word*, ed. John Warwick Montgomery (Minneapolis: Bethany Fellowship, 1974), pp. 120–122; and John C. Vander Stelt, *Philosophy and Scripture: A Study in Old Princeton and Westminster Theology* (Marlton, N.J.: Mack, 1978), pp. 182–184.

62. Perry Miller, "The Marrow of Puritan Divinity," in *Errand into the Wilderness* (Cambridge: Harvard University Press, 1956), p. 70.

inquiry will reveal.[63] Some who revile Scottish Realism are moral and epistemological relativists; others believe firmly in the reality of objective truth, but do not believe it is reached by the supposedly value-free inquiries of a putatively neutral science. Both sorts of critics have had a field day with the Princeton theologians.

It is possible, however, to conclude too rapidly that the Princetonians were simply theologians of Scottish Common Sense. Influenced by this perspective as they were, they still retained the fidelity to Scripture and Reformed traditions which kept them from being entirely at the mercy of their philosophy. Indeed, critical work on these theologians can only begin after noting the place of the Scottish philosophy in their thought. For it contains many elements that fit poorly into a scheme dominated by the mechanical categories of Common Sense. Among these elements is the Princeton stress on religious experience.

Religious Experience

For theologians with the reputation of scholastics and rationalists, the Princetonians expended surprisingly great effort in defending the value of religious experience. Professor Andrew Hoffecker has recently published a full book, based on an even fuller dissertation, to argue that the Princeton theologians supported and practiced an active Christian piety.[64] Professor Hoffecker's most difficult task is to convince others to take him seriously; his easiest job is to document the Princetonians' concern for religious experience. The Alexander who could approach theology as a rationalistic Scottish Realist could also write a full book on religious experience in which he quoted with favor the testimony of a man who long read the Scriptures to no avail until "the Lord shined into my mind by them."[65] The Charles Hodge who laid such great store by "facts" and "scientific method" (Selections 8, 17) could also argue for the priority of inner convictions over external argument in the reception of religious truth (Selection 6). The same Hodge who in 1850 so powerfully chastised Edwards A. Park for promoting a theology of the feelings (Selection 9) could in 1872 argue in his systematics for the propriety of a religion of "the heart" (Selection 8).[66] And as David Kelsey has pointed out, even Warfield, the most painstakingly logical of all the Princeton theologians, often described his acceptance of Scripture as much as a result of the luminescent,

63. For popular statements of this point of view from Calvinist theologians, see Nicholas Wolterstorff, "Is Reason Enough?" *Reformed Journal*, April 1981, pp. 20–24; and Alvin Plantinga, "On Reformed Epistemology," *ibid.*, January 1982, pp. 13–17.

64. W. Andrew Hoffecker, *Piety and the Princeton Theologians* (Phillipsburg, N.J., and Grand Rapids: Presbyterian and Reformed, and Baker, 1981); "The Relation Between the Objective and Subjective Aspects in Christian Religious Experience: A Study in the Systematic and Devotional Writings of Archibald Alexander, Charles Hodge, and Benjamin B. Warfield" (Ph.D. dissertation, Brown University, 1970).

65. Archibald Alexander, *Thoughts on Religious Experience* (3rd ed., Philadelphia: Presbyterian Board of Publication, 1844), p. 128.

66. Hoffecker, *Piety and the Princeton Theologians*, pp. 55–94, provides an especially cogent discussion of these two sides of Hodge's theology.

internal power of the written word as from conclusions arising out of a careful skein of reasoning.[67]

These testimonies to Princeton convictions about religious experience do not remove their constant insistence that Christian faith and proper theology must first be propositional. They do, however, show that one-dimensional or simplistic explanations of these theologians are bound to fail. The most important reason for this is that the Princetonians, as much as they sometimes appeared to deny it, were in fact children of their time, participating in the grand intellectual movements of their day. And so to complete a catalogue of the theme of the Princeton theology it is necessary to observe these men as people of their age, especially of the intellectual culture of nineteenth-century America.

Nineteenth-Century Culture

Ahistorical treatments of the Princetonians rush to the conclusion that their ideas may be extracted from the contexts of their own times as timeless guides to the right or egregious examples of error. To return the Princetonians to their own time, however, makes it possible to relate them to their contemporaries and to the shifting intellectual and social worlds of the nineteenth century. This approach represents in the end the only legitimate way to extract value from these thinkers for our own day, for without seeing their theology as it interacted with the conditions of their day, it is impossible for it to interact fruitfully with the conditions of our own. Even simple chronological conjunctions show us that the Princetonians were children of their age who responded to issues that also troubled others in the Western world. Thus, to note that Alexander published his *Thoughts on Religious Experience* (3 eds., 1841–1844) in the same decade that Sören Kierkegaard wrote *The Sickness Unto Death* (1848) suggests that Princeton shared a widespread concern to maintain authentic spirituality in the midst of enthusiasm, nascent rationalism, and creeping modernization. Or to see Hodge's *Systematic Theology*, a massive exposition of theology based on a Calvinistic conception of biblical authority, as belonging to the same era as the First Vatican Council (1870), the great Catholic effort to shore up ecclesiastical authority, is to realize that Princeton too was addressing the issue of religious certainty when most of the West was also rethinking that matter.

A historical examination of the Princetonians also makes it possible to see more clearly where they spoke distinctly and where their voices merely mingled with those of their contemporaries. Such an investigation reveals at the outset that many of the supposed distinctives of the Princeton Theology were simply the common intellectual affirmations of the day. Thus, the Princetonians were devotees of Scottish Common Sense, in large part, because so many American theologians in the nineteenth century were. Early in the century Congregationalist conservatives like Timothy Dwight were almost as diligent as Witherspoon in putting the

---

67. See note 42, and the illuminating discussion of this tendency of Warfield in David H. Kelsey, *The Uses of Scripture in Recent Theology* (Philadelphia: Fortress, 1975), pp. 17–24.

Scottish philosophy to work for the faith. Over the next generation, Congregational moderates like N. W. Taylor or more consistent Calvinists like Edwards A. Park, Unitarians like Andrews Norton, revivalists like Charles Finney, not to speak of the mass of the Presbyterians, whether Old School or New, shared the same philosophical perspective.[68] Yet most of these individuals were opponents of Princeton. At least for much of the nineteenth century, the Princetonians' Scottish Realism shows us more how they sailed along with the American intellectual mainstream rather than against it.

Once again, Princeton was confident about the authority of the Bible because for most of the century almost all evangelical Protestants were. To be sure, developments in the last third of the century constrained A. A. Hodge and Warfield to refine a widely shared view of biblical authority until it bore distinctive Princeton features. Yet before that time, Princeton affirmations concerning the complete authority of Scripture were not distinctive, but in fact only part of a great theological chorus sung by representatives of many denominations.[69]

In a similar manner, Princetonians were drunk on Newton's science, because the whole of American intellectual culture was. The American nineteenth century was densely populated with social scientists, philosophers, and savants in general striving, in Charles Beard's wonderful phrase, to turn "the Newtonian trick,"[70] by ordering the disparate phenomena of a discipline into objective, rational, mechanistic "law." Historians of theology shake their head at the naiveté of Charles Hodge proclaiming early in his systematics that "the Bible is to the theologian what nature is to the man of science" (Selection 8). They are undoubtedly correct in tush-tushing this approach. Yet there was nothing distinctly Princetonian about these words. The honored founder of the American Historical Association, Herbert Baxter Adams, who shared little of Hodge's orthodoxy, would say the same sort of thing about his discipline thirteen years after Hodge's contention: "the historical [seminar] is to the study of history, what the laboratory is to the study of the natural sciences."[71] And similar statements came from practitioners of all disciplines and from all points of the ideological compass.[72]

68. Foster, *The New England Theology*, pp. 246–247, 472–473, and *passim*; Conrad Wright, *The Beginnings of Unitarianism in America* (Boston: Starr King Press, 1955), pp. 135–160; Daniel Walker Howe, *The Unitarian Conscience: Harvard Moral Philosophy, 1805–1861* (Cambridge: Harvard University Press, 1970), pp. 27–44, 69–92; and the sources listed in note 56.

69. See Randall H. Balmer, "The Old Princeton Doctrine of Inspiration in the Context of Nineteenth-Century Theology: A Reappraisal" (M.A. thesis, Trinity Evangelical Divinity School, 1981); and John D. Woodbridge, "Biblical Authority: Towards an Evaluation of the Rogers and McKim Proposal," *Trinity Journal*, 1 new ser. (Fall 1980), 205–208.

70. Charles Beard, "Written History as an Act of Faith," *American Historical Review*, 39 (1934), 223.

71. Herbert Baxter Adams, "On Methods of Teaching History," in *Methods of Teaching History*, ed. G. Stanley Hall (Boston: Ginn, Heath, 1885), p. 176, as quoted by Henry Warner Bowden, *Church History in the Age of Science: Historiographical Patterns in the United States 1876–1918* (Chapel Hill: University of North Carolina Press, 1971), p. 24.

72. For samples, see the essays in Alexandra Oleson and Sanborn C. Brown, eds., *The Pursuit*

For most of the nineteenth century, then, the Princeton theologians merely shared widespread cultural values by believing in a high view of the Bible, expressing their thought in the categories of Scottish Common Sense, and swarming for the comprehensiveness of Newton. What was distinctly Princetonian was how these common cultural legacies were interwoven into more truly distinct convictions (like Princeton's traditional Calvinism), how then that whole cloth became the mantle which defined the Princeton institutions, and how finally the Princeton institutions, themselves a conserving force because of the nature of their development, were able to perpetuate the tradition beyond the time when many other American theologians abandoned both nineteenth-century cultural certainties and the particulars of Princeton's own theology. Regarded historically, the Princeton Theology was the unified sum of three different histories. (1) It is a story of how a group of theologians so effectively joined biblical, Calvinistic confessionalism and nineteenth-century intellectual fashions that they were criticized by contemporaries for being unreasonably Reformed and by succeeding generations for being hopelessly Victorian.[73] (2) It is also a story of how in the nineteenth century a series of powerful institutions arose to embody that theology. (3) It is finally a story of the fate of that set of ideas and those institutions as both convictions and structures passed through the American intellectual revolution that took place in the last third of the nineteenth century.[74]

The selections in the anthology demonstrate amply that first history, but the second and third require some explanation. The great institutions of Princeton shared a common character during the nineteenth century. They were all, more or less, reactionary. The seminary itself was founded in 1812 in response to a feeling that America was undergoing a cultural crisis of unprecedented magnitude. Its founders proposed to remedy defects in the preparation of clergymen, to roll back the tides of secularization in American public life, and to provide a learned defense of Christianity generally and the Bible specifically (Selections 1, 2).[75] The *Biblical Repertory* was founded in 1825 to report on biblical trends from overseas, but was

---

of Knowledge in the Early American Republic: American Scientific and Learned Societies from Colonial Times to the Civil War (Baltimore: Johns Hopkins University Press, 1976); and Alexandra Oleson and John Voss, eds., *The Organization of Knowledge in Modern America, 1860–1920* (Baltimore: Johns Hopkins University Press, 1979).

73. A competent study of the Princeton Theology which criticizes Hodge's turn to Victorian norms is John Oliver Nelson, "The Rise of the Princeton Theology" (Ph.D. dissertation, Yale University, 1935).

74. On that intellectual revolution, see Richard Hofstadter, "The Revolution in Higher Education," in *Paths of American Thought*, eds. Arthur M. Schlesinger, Jr., and Morton White (Boston: Houghton Mifflin, 1963), pp. 269–290; and Laurence R. Veysey, *The Emergence of the American University* (Chicago: University of Chicago Press, 1965). For reflections on the fate of Christian ideas in that revolution, see George M. Marsden, "The Collapse of American Evangelical Academia," in *Faith and Rationality*, ed. Nicholas Wolterstorff (Notre Dame, Ind.: University of Notre Dame, 1983); and Mark A. Noll, "Christian Thinking and the Rise of the American University," *Christian Scholar's Review*, 9 (1979), 3–16.

75. Noll, "The Founding of Princeton Seminary," pp. 85–96.

transformed in 1829, after Hodge returned from Europe, into a watchdog guarding confessional Calvinism from depredations at home and abroad (Selection 13). The Princetonians were also active Old School Presbyterians who from 1837 to 1868 railed against innovations of the "progressive" New School in polity, theology, and attitudes toward the world. Their convictions pushed them to the conservative side of the intradenominational dispute in 1837, but once secured in that position, their conservatism became institutionalized as part of the Princeton tradition.[76] Princeton College, likewise, for as long as it stood shoulder to shoulder with the seminary, was a conserving force. At least through the administration of McCosh, the college reinforced the seminary's determination to guard, protect, and preserve traditional conceptions of philosophical truth, social order, and Christian faith.[77] Charles Hodge's *Systematic Theology*, an institution between covers, not only summed up a lifetime of biblical reflection, but also bequeathed in permanent form conceptions of theology and apprehensions of error that had been shaped in the 1810s and 1820s. The lengthy tenures of the Princeton professors were themselves conservative phenomena, not to speak of the filiopietistic debts which accumulated as the chair passed from father to spiritual son, to actual son, to spiritual son once more. Given the nature of these institutions—all of them harkening back, all of them devoted to preservation, all of them tenacious in guarding a tradition—it is little wonder that Princeton was conservative. It is little wonder that ways of talking about truth, science, the natural world, and mental processes that by 1812 had become traditional for Alexander and Charles Hodge were held so dearly by the successors whom they trained. It is also little wonder that the combination of conservative ideas and conservative institutions survived long after other forms of Christian faith had bowed to modernistic winds.

This singular confluence of ideas and institutions may rightly be described as *the* Princeton Theology. It was the ideas that gave the theology its direction; it was the institutions that made it influential in America. At least some of the Princeton ideas continue to live among evangelicals and to influence instruction in conservative Reformed seminaries. Princeton Seminary itself, though largely disassociated from the principal thrusts of its nineteenth-century theology, continues as a major religious institution. Yet no longer do the powerful ideas speak through the institutions their proponents had created. No longer do great institutions, which compel respect by their very existence, live to promote those ideas. In this sense, which is a historical judgment, the Princeton Theology is no more.

But even the passing of the Princeton Theology cannot be understood apart from a consideration of its historical setting. Soon after the seminary's founding under the leadership of Hodge and Alexander, the Princeton Theology established itself as an important voice in America. Although it stood by its Calvinism while the rest of America swarmed for democracy, it nonetheless spoke the language of the

---

76. Marsden, *Evangelical Mind and the New School Presbyterian Experience*, pp. 73–74, 215–217.

77. Wertenbaker, *Princeton 1746–1896*, pp. 118–183.

American intellectual marketplace so effectively that the marketplace could not but pay attention. From late in Hodge's career to the death of Warfield, the Princeton theology continued to be an important voice in America, but for a different reason. Although it maintained both the intellectual values of the early nineteenth century, while the rest of intellectual America was abandoning them, and its Calvinism, which had not set well even earlier in the century, it nonetheless informed such self-evidently significant institutions that the intellectual world had to give heed. The Fundamentalist-Modernist controversy brought an end to that era and to the Princeton Theology itself.[78] Developments within Presbyterianism turned the seminary over to individuals who did not feel that the Princeton Theology could continue as a viable theological option in the modern world.[79] Even more importantly, Fundamentalist-Modernist disjunctions undercut the synthesis that had created the institutions of the Old Princeton. Fundamentalists believed in the Bible, Modernists in reason, but the Princeton theologians had believed in both. Fundamentalists believed in Newtonian science, Modernists in Darwin, but A. A. Hodge and Warfield had adjusted Calvinism to biological evolution just as Charles Hodge had adopted it to modern geology. Fundamentalists were creedalists who would separate if need be, Modernists breathed toleration and battled to monopolize the intellectual marketplace, but the Princeton Theologians had combined confessionalism with a dominant place in American intellectual life. Fundamentalists stressed piety, Modernists stressed intellect, but the Princeton Theologians had embodied both. In sum, as American Protestants entered the 1930s and Fundamentalists and Modernists went their separate ways, the institutions of the Princeton Theology had ceased to exist and its convictions had been scattered to the winds.

Internal Development

To examine the place of the Princeton Theology within changing American culture raises the question of development within the theology itself. Charles Hodge twice asserted on ceremonial occasions that no new idea had arisen at the seminary. In 1870 he reviewed the course of the *Princeton Review* with these words: "Whether it be a ground of reproach or of approbation, it is believed to be true, that an original idea in theology is not to be found on the pages of the *Biblical Repertory and Princeton Review* from the beginning until now. The phrase 'Princeton Theology,' therefore, is without distinctive meaning."[80] At the semicentennial observance of his election as professor in 1872, Hodge repeated the assertion: "I am not afraid to say that a new idea never originated in this Seminary."[81] Forty years

78. The definitive works on the era are William R. Hutchinson, *The Modernist Impulse in American Protestantism* (Cambridge: Harvard University Press, 1976); and George M. Marsden, *Fundamentalism and American Culture: The Shaping of Twentieth-Century Evangelicalism 1870–1925* (New York: Oxford University Press, 1980).

79. John W. Hart, "Princeton Theological Seminary: The Reorganization of 1929," *Journal of Presbyterian History*, 58 (Summer 1980), 124–140; and Stonehouse, *J. Gresham Machen*, pp. 409–445.

80. Charles Hodge, BRPR, *Index Volume* (1870–71), I: 11.

81. Quoted in A. A. Hodge, *Life of Charles Hodge*, p. 521.

later, seminary president Francis Landey Patton expanded on the claim: Princeton "had no oddities of manner, no shibboleths, no pet phrases, no theological labels, no trademark. She simply taught the old Calvinistic theology without modification: and she made obstinate resistance to the modifications proposed elsewhere, as being in their logical results subversive of the Reformed faith. There has been a New Haven Theology and an Andover Theology; but there never was a distinctly Princeton Theology. Princeton's boast, if she have reason to boast at all, is her unswerving fidelity to the theology of the Reformation."[82]

These claims were not idle self-delusion. The Princeton Theology did preserve vast amounts of classical Reformed thought. The *Princeton Review* became an awesome weapon in American theological debate, in part, because its opponents knew that Hodge and his colleagues had a clear-cut doctrinal standard which they never hesitated to apply to the deviations of others or to expound for the events of the moment. On questions concerning the nature of humanity, the effects of sin, the necessity for redemption, the reliability of Scripture, the person and work of Christ, or the superiority of Presbyterianism, the Princeton Theology stood largely where Calvin, the Westminster divines, and Turretin had stood.

Yet it is also true that as a nineteenth-century expression—employing the tools of Scottish Common Sense, breathing the spirit of Newton, and adjusting to the challenges of the times—the Princeton Theology was not simply a restatement of sixteenth- or even seventeenth-century Calvinism. It was, rather, a restatement in terms that could communicate to Victorian America.[83] And that made a great difference indeed. The theologians at Princeton believed that among the highest forms of truth were those which most carefully imitated Newtonian law. They tended to talk about the Bible as a compendium of data that could be treated scientifically. They had great confidence that the existence of God and the reliability of revelation could be demonstrated by natural reason to all and sundry. And these constituted modifications, even innovations, in the history of Calvinism. Yet again, to make such an assertion is not necessarily to render a value judgment; it is merely to say that in translating Calvinism into the language of nineteenth-century American culture, some things may have been lost and some gained. If a modern evaluator must render a negative judgment on those innovations, the judgment must fall as much upon that culture as a whole as on the Princetonians by themselves.

A less vital, but still intriguing question concerns development within the Princeton Theology itself. Here the conclusion of Lefferts Loetscher accurately reflects the general picture: "In Dr. Alexander is to be found, in germ, the entire Princeton

---

82. Francis Landey Patton, "Princeton Seminary and the Faith," *Centennial of Princeton Seminary,* pp. 349–350.

83. For books suggesting the contours of Victorian intellectual life, see Perry Miller, *The Life of the Mind in America;* Daniel Walker Howe, ed., *Victorian America* (Philadelphia: University of Pennsylvania Press, 1976); Rush Welter, *The Mind of America 1820–1860* (New York: Columbia University Press, 1975); and David S. Reynolds, *Faith in Fiction: The Emergence of Religious Literature in America* (Cambridge: Harvard University Press, 1981).

Theology."[84] And yet innovation, especially as the Princetonians adapted to the changes of the nineteenth century, marked the internal life of their theology as well. Certainly the Princeton Theology was always Calvinistic (though less self-consciously in Alexander than in his successors), certainly it never wavered in fidelity to Scripture as a repository of divine truth (though Alexander and Warfield seemed more confident in demonstrating this than did Charles Hodge), certainly it retained a great confidence in the capacities of evidence, reason, and logic (though not without adding a stress on religious experience), and certainly it always held that proper science and biblical faith were compatible (though attitudes to specific issues varied). As new challenges arose, however, subtle shifts occurred within these general convictions. Alexander was mostly concerned about threats to the faith from Catholics, deists, and enthusiasts, and so stressed proofs for Protestant biblical authority and tests for valid spirituality. Charles Hodge feared human autonomy in its popular and scholarly forms, and so stressed the sole sufficiency of Scripture and the grounding of vital piety on propositional foundations. A. A. Hodge and Warfield faced higher criticism and internalized forms of conservative piety (i.e., the varieties of "perfectionism"), and so refined the Princeton position on Scripture and intensified exposition of traditional Calvinism. On very specific issues changes did take place in the tradition, as for example the attitudes toward evolution that have been noted. Still, even on the general question of which evolution was apart, all of the theologians always took the stance which Hodge stated in the *Systematic Theology:* "As the Bible is of God, it is certain that there can be no conflict between the teachings of the Scripture and the facts of science" (Selection 11).

To be sure, each generation of Princeton theologians was more skilled, better equipped with the technical tools of theology, than its predecessor. Alexander's knowledge of contemporary theological developments in Europe, for example, could not hold a candle to Warfield's. But this was again a matter of changing times rather than of changing substance. The only real question in regard to the internal developments of the theology is again a question of history. Granting that each successive generation propounded the Princeton Theology with greater technical clarity, do we necessarily have the same theology when we have identical statements, but in different situations? This question pertains especially to Warfield, for he was the only representative of the theology who lived in a world where the intellectual assumptions of the early nineteenth century had been replaced by other givens about truth, revelation, and religious knowledge. Such considerations, however, move beyond a strict account of development within the theology. On that head it may be said that if the Princeton Theology was neither as pure a reaffirmation of classical Calvinism nor as internally self-consistent as its advocates or opponents thought, it still retained a remarkable consistency over the course of its remarkable life.

84. Loetscher, *Broadening Church,* p. 23.

The Princetonians and Modern Controversy

The selections in this anthology demonstrate amply how involved the Princeton theologians were in controversy during their own lives. But long after the liberal to moderate theologians of the twentieth century had consigned the Princeton Theology to oblivion, it remained a focus of controversy among conservative Protestants. Its contentions continued to exercise the larger world of Reformed thought that links American Calvinists to the Reformed of Great Britain and the Netherlands. In recent years the Princeton doctrine of an inerrant Scripture has also become a matter of controversy in the broader world of American evangelicalism. Both spheres of controversy—involving debated points on Scripture, apologetics, and the capacity of rational demonstration—deserve brief attention.

It was apparent even in Warfield's lifetime that his picture of the Reformed faith differed in important particulars from that held by Abraham Kuyper (1837–1920) and Herman Bavinck (1854–1921), leaders of the Dutch neo-Calvinist revival at the end of the nineteenth century (Selection 29). Warfield held that history, reason, and objective science could demonstrate the validity of Scripture as divine revelation. Individuals convinced by such demonstration could then rely on Scripture to construct theology. Kuyper and Bavinck, to the contrary, placed very little store by Warfield's kind of evidentialist apologetics. They felt rather that individuals, including their rational capacities, needed to be redeemed before they could reason properly from the Bible. The concept of "antithesis," which played a large role in the Dutch Calvinist response to the Enlightenment, led the Hollanders to feel that rational argument could function properly only as part of allegiance to Christianity, rather than as an anticipation of that allegiance.[85]

Another voice in Warfield's own day made a related criticism, this time, however, in comparing the Princeton view of Scripture to that of the reformers. In what may still be the most trenchant constructive criticism ever published on the Princeton Theology, Scottish church historian Thomas M. Lindsay discussed in 1895, "The Doctrine of Scripture: The Reformers and the Princeton School." Lindsay, who wrote throughout with great appreciation for the Princetonians, yet called them to task for substituting a "purely intellectual apprehension of Scripture," a "formal" conception of biblical authority, for the reformers' "religious idea of the infallibility and authority of Scripture." Against Princeton's concept of "inerrancy," which he felt "to be trivial in the extreme," Lindsay contended that the reformers had properly emphasized scriptural "infallibility," or "the power which compels me to know that God is through this Scripture speaking to me now as He spoke not merely *by*

---

85. For Kuyper's own method, see his *Principles of Sacred Theology,* trans. J. Hendrik De Vries (Grand Rapids: Baker, 1980 [1898]), for example, pp. 89–92 on the effects of sin on the "scientific" enterprise, or pp. 248–256, on the "dependent" nature of theology which exists solely "upon the pleasure of God" (p. 251). Warfield supplied a laudatory introduction to this translation which did not, however, reflect the objections he expressed a few years later (see Selection 29). See also Louis Berkhof, "Introduction to Systematic Theology (Grand Rapids: Baker, 1979 [1932]), pp. 42, 49–50, for specific objections to Princeton method from a Dutch-American in Kuyper's tradition.

the prophets and holy men of old, but *to* them and in them, and giving me through them in word and picture the message of His salvation."[86]

Other Reformed thinkers have continued to make the same sort of criticism of the Princeton Theology since the time of Lindsay and Kuyper. It appears in the works of Cornelius Van Til, who developed Dutch convictions about the noetic effects of the Fall into a complete "presuppositional" theology.[87] It arises in the work of those trained more directly by the successors of Bavinck and Kuyper at the Free University of Amsterdam.[88] Such critics, to one degree or another, acknowledge the continuing value of the Princeton Theology, especially its biblical Calvinism and warm piety. But they demur at the Princeton convictions concerning the natural apologetical powers of even Christians, powers which Alexander took for granted in his opening lecture in 1812 (Selection 3) and which Warfield continued to assert into the twentieth century.[89]

The other strand of criticism is more sweeping. It is based on the conviction that both historical evidence and theological reasoning show not just weaknesses, but fatal flaws in the Princeton Theology, or at least its doctrine of Scripture. Ernest Sandeen sketched the basic framework of this criticism in path-breaking publications in the 1960s and early 1970s.[90] Sandeen argued that the Princeton doctrine of Scripture, especially as presented in the 1881 essay by A. A. Hodge and Warfield, was a startling innovation. Sandeen focused especially on the idea of scriptural "inerrancy in the original autographs" which he felt removed the Bible from serious historical scrutiny and insulated it from meaningful criticism. More recently Jack Rogers and Donald McKim have argued in *The Authority and Interpretation of*

86. Thomas M. Lindsay, "The Doctrine of Scripture: The Reformers and the Princeton School," in *The Expositor*, ed. W. Robertson Nicoll, Fifth ser., vol. I (London: Hodder & Stoughton, 1895), pp. 281, 285, 287, 288.

87. For Van Til's criticism of Warfield's apologetical method, and preference for Kuyper's, see Cornelius Van Til, *The Defense of the Faith* (2nd ed., Philadelphia: Presbyterian and Reformed, 1955), pp. 260–266; and the exchange between Van Til and Jack Rogers, in *Jerusalem and Athens: Critical Discussion on the Philosophy and Apologetics of Cornelius Van Til*, ed. E. R. Geehan (Nutley, N.J.: Presbyterian and Reformed, 1971): Rogers, "Van Til and Warfield on Scripture in the Westminster Confession," pp. 154–165, with a "Response by C. Van Til," pp. 165–171.

88. For example, Vander Stelt, *Philosophy and Scripture;* and Ralph J. Danhof, *Charles Hodge as a Dogmatician* (Goes, Netherlands: Oosterbaan and Le Cointre, ca. 1930), especially pp. 171–213.

89. Other modern critics of the Princetonian approach to theology include T. F. Torrance, who feels that Warfield succumbed to a kind of rationalism, Review of Warfield's *Inspiration and Authority of the Bible, Scottish Journal of Theology*, 7 (1954), 104–108; and Daniel P. Fuller, who feels that Warfield did not take historical evidence quite seriously enough, "Benjamin B. Warfield's View of Faith and History: A Critique in the Light of the New Testament," *Bulletin of the Evangelical Theological Society*, 11 (Spring 1968), 75–83. For defenses specifically of Warfield's views on theology and Scripture, see Gerstner, "Warfield's Case for Biblical Inerrancy," and Roger Nicole, "The Inspiration of Scripture: B. B. Warfield and Dr. Dewey M. Beegle," *Gordon Review*, 8 (Winter 1964–65), 93–109.

90. Ernest R. Sandeen, "The Princeton Theology: One Source of Biblical Literalism in American Protestantism," *Church History*, 31 (September 1962), 307–321; and *The Roots of Fundamentalism: British and American Millenarianism 1800–1930* (Chicago: University of Chicago Press, 1970), pp. 103–131.

Scripture that the Princeton doctrine of the Bible was a scholastic, Aristotelian, and rationalistic conception which gravely distorted "the central Christian tradition" on Scripture.[91] Augustine and the Reformers who exemplify that central tradition regarded Scripture as a source of divine truth transcending quibbling concerns about propositional detail.

The Princeton Theology has not lacked defenders in response to this criticism. Against Sandeen, Randall Balmer has argued convincingly that the view of Scripture expressed by A. A. Hodge and Warfield in 1881 was essentially that of the entire Princeton tradition and of much American theology generally to that time.[92] Against Rogers and McKim, John Woodbridge has contended that the entire history of the church reflects a broad, if sometimes amorphous, commitment to the inerrancy of Scripture in its original autographs.[93] Others who have taken Rogers and McKim's volume to task agree with Woodbridge on the weaknesses of their historical reconstruction, but suggest that the book's fundamental problem is its own inadequate conception of how best to express a doctrine of Scripture.[94] In this modern controversy over the Princeton conception of the Bible, Sandeen, Rogers, and McKim have successfully made the point that a conception of Scripture which was thoroughly at home in the intellectual world of the nineteenth century may not answer every legitimate question in the second half of the twentieth. Their critics, on the other hand, have succeeded in showing that the Princetonians were not the historical innovators that a superficial glance might indicate. They suggest further that there is a danger in throwing the baby out with the bath if the substance as well as the form of the Princeton doctrine of Scripture is jettisoned.

Recent debate over the Princeton Theology can be regarded as a commentary on the present state of evangelical intellectual life, which has moved beyond the anti-historical character of Fundamentalism, but which is still not sure of its footing in the contemporary world of ideas. As evidence of this uncertainty, the major statements in the current debate over Princeton and inerrancy have been marked by either creative theology and sloppy history or superb history and wooden theology.[95] Evangelicals still await a treatment of Old Princeton that is as sophisticated and as refined as the work of the Princetonians was itself.

91. Jack B. Rogers and Donald K. McKim, *The Authority and Interpretation of the Bible: An Historical Approach* (San Francisco: Harper & Row, 1979).

92. Balmer, "The Old Princeton Doctrine of Inspiration"; and "The Princetonians and Scripture: A Reconsideration," *Westminster Theological Journal,* 44 (1982), 352–365.

93. Woodbridge, "Biblical Authority," pp. 165–236.

94. The most perceptive reviewers make this common point from their own different theological perspectives: see the reviews by J. I. Packer, *Crux,* 16 (March 1980), 31–32; William S. Barker, *Presbyterion: Covenant Seminary Review,* 6 (Fall 1980), 96–107; David F. Wells, *Westminster Theological Journal,* 43 (Fall 1980), 152–155; Gerald T. Sheppard, *Theology Today,* 38 (October 1981), 330–337; and John H. Leith, *Interpretation,* 35 (January 1981), 75–78.

95. For brief but carefully nuanced statements on the controversy, see George M. Marsden, "Everyone One's Own Interpreter? The Bible, Science, and Authority in Mid-Nineteenth-Century America," in *The Bible in America,* pp. 97–98n26–28; and Grant Wacker, "The Demise of Biblical Civilization," *ibid.,* p. 135n13. An interesting proposal for a more sensitive treatment of the historical

Such an evaluation of other contemporary attempts to take the measure of the Princeton Theology lays me under obligation to express my own evaluation of the school. As a Calvinist and an evangelical I find myself edified and encouraged by the vast bulk of the Princeton writings. I am especially struck with Charles Hodge as one who combined in unusual measure personal piety, biblical profundity, and theological balance. The Princetonians as a group still communicate exactly, or very nearly so, what needs to be communicated to a man-centered world about the realities of God's sovereignty. They are filled with insight on the debilities of fallen human nature, the illuminating truthfulness of Scripture, the unity of all truth under God, and the errors of subjective mysticism, presumptuous rationalism, and scientistic naturalism. Yet as one who favors the Calvinism of Jonathan Edwards, which bears striking formal resemblances to that of Abraham Kuyper, I find the Princeton Theology weak on the relationship of natural and revealed theology, confused on the proper place of affective knowledge, and overly sanguine about the powers of rational apologetics. In addition, I do not feel that they adequately acknowledged the seriousness of Kant's challenge to static conceptions of knowledge or Kierkegaard's contentions about the subjectivity of Christian faith. They were no doubt correct to pounce on the efforts of E. A. Park to chart a theology of the feelings (Selection 17), or to lambaste the Mercersburg Theology for incautious acceptance of mystical elements from Schleiermacher and Hegel (Selection 14), or to score Bushnell for emptying language of propositional content (Selection 16). But they overstated their case. In their own devotional works, and occasionally in their more systematic efforts, the Princetonians paid due heed to the way in which character, emotion, and historical conditioning can be as important to Christianity as logic, reason, and objective demonstrations. Yet they continued to write their formal theology as if Christianity were basically applied doctrine, basically a set of propositions on which life is built. Their uneasiness about efforts to incorporate subjectivity, historical conditioning, and personal knowledge into Christian theology did in fact preserve much that was in dire jeopardy. But it also prevented the faith they loved so dearly from achieving the full effects that its Author—who was at once the Way, the Truth, and the Life—intended. It is only speculation, but it may also be that Princeton's vehement attacks on those who were trying to incorporate an element of subjectivity into orthodoxy may have contributed to the rapid demise of orthodoxy itself in the last third of the nineteenth century when subjectivity was torn from Christian moorings and transformed into a great weapon attacking traditional Protestantism in America.[96]

The effect of this Princeton imbalance remains with evangelicals to this day. The

---

problem has been made by Ian Rennie, "Mixed Metaphors, Misunderstood Models, and Puzzling Paradigms: A Contemporary Effort to Correct Some Current Misunderstandings Regarding the Authority and Interpretation of the Bible. An Historical Response," paper presented at the conference, "Interpreting an Authoritative Scripture," Institute for Christian Studies, Toronto, June 1981.

96. This idea is suggested by David F. Wells in an unpublished paper, "The Atonement in American Theology 1820–1840."

Princeton doctrine of Scripture, because of its proper insistence on the objectivity of divine truth, contributed a vital element to the fundamentalist reaction to modernism.[97] Yet because the Princetonians had themselves made this doctrine a more or less mechanical principium independent of the rest of their theology, it was readily detached from their own substantive convictions about living faith. And thus we have the irony, for which their own theological methods were partly responsible, of modern fundamentalists and conservative evangelicals relying on the Princeton doctrine of Scripture as a cardinal mainstay, while at the same time blithely disregarding the positive convictions of the Princetonians themselves. The case of Warfield is instructive here. As an inerrantist, Warfield retains a place of high honor among conservative evangelicals. He was also a Calvinist who believed in predestination and the definite atonement, and he was a vehement critic of all forms of what he called "perfectionism," whether Pentecostal, "higher life," Keswick, or "victorious living."[98] In less central concerns, he was a postmillennialist who regarded premillennialism as a doctrinal aberration; and he was a theistic evolutionist.[99] But these substantive convictions of Warfield are little known among evangelicals today, in large part because he himself sanctioned a theological method which provided for an independent, humanly-rooted verification of Scriptural infallibility. This allowed others to adopt his doctrine of Scripture without necessarily paying attention to what he felt those Scriptures actually taught. For my part, I would like to see more evangelical concern for the Princetonians' substantive theology and their general confidence in Scriptural authority, where they most transcended the limitations of their age, and less for their theological method and approach to apologetics, where they were most time-bound.

The Anthology

John Updike has commented that "anthology making, like sculpting in marble, is in large measure an act of taking away."[100] Such taking away is a particularly painful process for the Princeton theologians because of their prolific output. Charles Hodge himself was responsible for over 5,000 pages, as tightly packed in print as in reasoning, of the *Princeton Review* during the more than forty years in which he edited that journal. He probably published as much again elsewhere, including his 2,000-page systematics, several biblical commentaries, a small shelf of

97. Sandeen, *Roots of Fundamentalism,* pp. 103–131; Marsden, *Fundamentalism and American Culture,* pp. 109–118; George W. Dollar, *A History of Fundamentalism in America* (Greenville, S.C.: Bob Jones University Press, 1973), pp. 173–177.

98. This point is made nicely by Roger Nicole in his review of Rogers and McKim, *Christian Scholar's Review,* 10 (1980), 161–165; see especially Warfield's own *Calvin and Calvinism, Perfectionism Part One, Perfectionism Part Two,* and *Studies in Theology* (WBBW, V, VII, VIII, IX).

99. Warfield, "The Gospel and the Second Coming," SSWW, I: 348–355; on evolution, see Selection 27.

100. John Updike, Review of *The New Oxford Book of Christian Verse, New York Times Book Review,* April 11, 1982, p. 18.

sermons, ecclesiastical treatises, and devotional works. While Alexander, A. A. Hodge, and other Princeton leaders published somewhat less, Warfield was nearly as prolific. The Princetonians themselves would almost certainly have had doubts about a selection of their works limited, as this anthology is, to statements on theological method, Scripture, and science, and to their differences with other theologians. They would perhaps have objected most strenuously to giving more attention to formal questions about the Bible, truth, and theology than to their expositions of Scripture, their applications of Christian teaching, and the positive constructions of the Calvinistic perspective they cherished so dearly.

There are, however, good reasons why a twentieth-century anthology may be excused for concentrating on these topics. In the first place, the Princetonians' positive theology and their biblical expositions were rooted in convictions about Scripture and truth. Because they wrote in the nineteenth century, such convictions ultimately involved questions about the domain of science. In addition, much of their constructive theology is still in print,[101] while many of their crucial statements on theological method, as well as their most sharply expressed differences with other theologians, lie buried in forgotten tomes. A number of modern studies have explicated the place of the Princetonians in nineteenth-century Presbyterian history, and a wealth of detailed scholarship is available on their theology as such.[102] Some good works have explored the intellectual framework which undergirded the Princetonians' positive theology and their ecclesiastical convictions, but this is still the area which requires most careful attention.[103]

For the historically minded, this focus on the Bible, science, and theological method offers information on how the Princetonians fit into an intellectual era bracketed by Thomas Jefferson on one end and William James on the other. In particular, the selection from their polemical works displays how Old Princeton was situated vis-à-vis other schools of theology, whether the moderate Calvinism of the New England Theology, the romantic theologies of Mercersburg or of Bushnell, the revivalism of Finney, or—later in the century—the varieties of Liberalism and Fundamentalism. By presenting Princeton reflections on "natural philosophy," geology, Darwin, and evolution—from Alexander early in the nineteenth century to Warfield early in the twentieth—we also have a miniature case study on the progressive accommodation of theology and science within this prominent tradition. Almost all of the excerpts also shed at least some light on how conservative Calvinists dealt with the two great intellectual reorientations of the era: the democratization of the American mind in the early national period and the manifest secularization at the turn of the twentieth century.

For the theologically minded, the anthology's selections of Princeton views on Scripture should stimulate ongoing efforts to determine the nature of the Bible's

101. See bibliography for in-print works.
102. See especially the checklist of dissertations in the bibliography.
103. The best interpretations of the Princeton theologians in the intellectual contexts of their times are found in Bozeman, *Protestants in an Age of Science*, and Marsden, *Fundamentalism and American Culture*.

message and its role in the church. The anthology's selections concerning science should advance reflection on the specific question of relating scientific conclusions and biblical statements and the more general question of living in a world where forms of knowledge appear increasingly disjointed. Its selections on theological method illustrate how one community of scholarly believers tried to bridge the gap between ultimate realities and the contingencies of intellectual life. Some who read this anthology will find themselves agreeing with both the methods and conclusions of the Princetonians, others will agree with conclusions and not methods, or methods and not conclusions, while still others will reject both. All, however, should be moved to more careful theological endeavors for having followed the Princetonians through theirs.

The anthology, unfortunately, does not include selections illustrating the Princetonians' attitudes toward social and political dimensions of American life. This is regrettable inasmuch as an examination of how these theologians moved (or failed to move) from theological conviction to social response is a logical extension of the examination of those convictions. Space limitations, and the desire to offer rounded treatment on Scripture, science, and theological method made this deletion necessary.[104]

Selections in the anthology are arranged chronologically and topically. The book begins with excerpts from two documents illustrating the concerns which lay behind the founding of Princeton Seminary. The four theologians appear in historical sequence, and the selections follow the same order: (1) considerations of theological method, (2) explanations concerning Scripture, (3) reflections on science, and for Charles Hodge and Warfield, (4) polemical responses to other theologians. Within each category works are presented chronologically.

The Princeton theologians were as prolix as they were profound, so abridgment has been necessary for nearly every selection. References to sources make it possible for interested readers to secure the complete works from which the abridgments come. In each selection I have attempted to present the kernel of a Princeton argument, or response, and have, therefore, regularly omitted lengthy quotations from secondary authorities, footnotes, compendious biblical citations, and material found elsewhere in the anthology. In order to keep footnoting to a minimum in the text, capsule identifications of all the names mentioned are included as part of the index of names. The bibliography suggests paths for further study.

104. It is, however, encouraging to see significant studies appearing on this theme—for example, Hood, *Reformed America;* William S. Barker, "The Social Views of Charles Hodge (1797-1878): A Study in 19th-Century Calvinism and Conservatism," *Presbyterian: Covenant Seminary Review,* 1 (Spring 1975), 1-22; David N. Murchie, "Morality and Social Ethics in the Thought of Charles Hodge" (Ph.D. dissertation, Drew University, 1980); two works by Gary S. Smith, "Calvinism and Culture in America, 1870-1915" (Ph.D. dissertation, Johns Hopkins University, 1981), and "The Spirit of Capitalism Revisited: Calvinists in the Industrial Revolution," *Journal of Presbyterian History,* 59 (Winter 1981), 481-497; and Ronald W. Hogeland, "Charles Hodge, the Association of Gentlemen and Ornamental Womanhood: A Study of Male Conventional Wisdom, 1825-1855," *Journal of Presbyterian History,* 53 (Fall 1975), 239-255.

The documents themselves have been edited very lightly. They are presented verbatim, except where the punctuation of the original distorts the sense for modern readers. The major alteration here is that, especially for material from the first half of the nineteenth century, commas that are confusing by more recent standards are omitted. Obvious typographical errors have been corrected silently. Notes to the documents are the editor's except where indicated.

The process of selecting which writings to include, and which parts of those works, must by its nature be precarious. Guided by the general themes of the anthology, I have tried to present as representative material as possible. I have not intentionally skewed the selections. The anthology attempts to present the Princeton theologians at their best and at their worst, but even more, at their most characteristic.

The Founding of
Princeton Theological Seminary

1

Archibald Alexander's General Assembly Sermon

1808

In the year 1808 two events concentrated Presbyterian attention on the need for specialized training of ministers. The first was the founding of Andover Seminary in Massachusetts by Trinitarian Congregationalists smarting over the appointment of a Unitarian as Hollis Professor of Divinity at Harvard. The steps taken at Andover offered a model for what Presbyterians could do to meet the urgent demand for ministers and to check the nation's growing secularization. The second event was a powerful sermon at the Presbyterians' General Assembly in May by the retiring moderator, Archibald Alexander. In retrospect, it is clear that this sermon initiated the public push for seminary education among the Presbyterians.

Concern for specialized training of ministers had existed for some time before 1808 among the Presbyterians. New Jersey's Jacob Green had called for special schools for aspiring pastors as early as 1775, but to no avail.[1] A generation later Green's son, Ashbel, pastor of Philadelphia's Second Presbyterian Church, began corresponding with Samuel Miller, one of the ministers of New York City's United Presbyterian Church, about the same idea.[2] Ashbel Green carried plans further than his father when he submitted a moving overture to the General Assembly in 1805 pleading for the denomination to "give us ministers" for the needs of frontier and settled regions alike.[3] The next year's General Assembly passed a resolution urging better preparation of more ministers, and it heard from the president of Princeton College, Samuel Stanhope Smith, who spoke up for his own institution's ability to train the needed pastors.[4] Yet nothing concrete had been done when Alexander rose to speak in May, 1808. He chose as his text I Corinthians 14:12 ("seek that ye may excel to the edifying of the church").

1. See Mark A. Noll, "Jacob Green's Proposal for Seminaries," *Journal of Presbyterian History* 58 (Fall 1980): 210-23.

2. For brief biographical identifications of all the people mentioned in introductions or selections, see the index of names.

3. Miller to Green, March 12, 1805, and related correspondence, Samuel Miller, Jr., *Life of Samuel Miller*, 1:192; *Minutes of the General Assembly of the Presbyterian Church in the United States . . . from . . . 1789 to . . . 1820* (Philadelphia: Presbyterian Board of Publication, 1847), p. 341.

4. *Minutes of the General Assembly,* pp. 362-63, 366.

Although he could not have known it at the time, themes of his sermon would become the principles of his own activities at the denomination's seminary at Princeton. The message painted a convincing picture of the dangers of the times—error and infidelity, "rational Christianity" and "enthusiasm." And it pointed to what would be the bedrock of the future Princeton Theology, the foundational authority of Scripture as the sole source for Christian teaching. The excerpt below is from pp. 10-12 and 24-26 of Archibald Alexander, *A Sermon Delivered at the Opening of the General Assembly of the Presbyterian Church in the United States. May 1808* (Philadelphia: Hopkins and Earle, 1808).

CHRIST HIMSELF IS the truth. He has not only revealed the truth, but all the rays of this divine light are concentrated in him. From his face the divine glory beams forth with its brightest lustre. The wisdom, power, justice, purity, love, and faithfulness of God are here clearly exhibited. In *his* actions and sufferings, the spirituality and extent of the law of God, and the nature and just deserts of sin are set forth in a stronger light than any works could represent them. So completely does the character of Jesus Christ as Mediator involve all important truth, that no dangerous error can be conceived which does not affect our views of his personal dignity or mediatorial work. This, therefore, is said to be "eternal life," or all that is necessary to obtain "eternal life," to "know the only true God and *Jesus Christ* whom he hath sent." To "preach Jesus Christ and him crucified" includes the whole range of doctrines taught by the apostle Paul. The aspect of every dispensation, of every institution, of every leading fact and principal prediction in the whole system of revelation is turned toward the incarnate Son of God. In him is contained that mystery of godliness, which through eternity will be developing, for the instruction and entertainment of saints and angels.

In proportion as the doctrines which relate to Christ the Redeemer are understood, received, and reduced to practice, does the edifice of the church stand firmly on its basis; and in proportion as these are extended and propagated, the glorious building is enlarged. The prophets and apostles who speak of the Messiah may, on that account, be called the foundation; but "Jesus Christ himself is the chief cornerstone, in whom all the building fitly framed together, groweth into a holy temple in the Lord."

Both in ancient and modern times, the assaults of the enemies of the church have been directed against this cornerstone; and although the *gates of hell* have failed of success in their attempts to shake this *rock* on which the church is built, yet as the malice of Satan is incapable of being extinguished or mitigated, we may expect renewed attacks, until the time of his confinement shall arrive. In our own times, infidelity has come in like a flood, and threatened to inundate the church with a horrible species of philosophical atheism. The torrent swelled high and raged with fearful impetuosity; but its violence has now abated, and the danger from this *source* appears to be in a good measure over. But the watchmen on the walls of Zion ought not to lie supinely down, or nod upon their posts, but should endeavour to observe the motions of the enemy so successfully, that they may be able to give seasonable warning of the kind of assault which may next be expected.

From the signs of the times, I apprehend the danger to evangelical truth which will now arise will be from two opposite points: From what is called *rational Christianity*, and *enthusiasm.*

Most of those speculative men, who were lately inclined to deism, will now fill the ranks of Socinianism, or Unitarianism, as they choose to denominate their religion. The errors of idolized reason are very dangerous, because they have for their abettors the learned and powerful of this world, and the influence of their example is very extensive.

These opinions, however, are not likely to spread very widely amongst the common people, as they divest religion of all its awful and interesting attributes; so that the more sincerely and fully any person becomes a convert to this system, the more indifferent he will become to all religion. But no religion will engage the attention of people generally, unless it be calculated to interest their feelings. It appears to me, therefore, that enthusiasm is likely to spread more extensive mischief among the unlearned than any species of free-thinking. The passions excited by enthusiasm, it is true, are too violent to be lasting; but the evil produced is, nevertheless, often permanent. Enthusiasm and superstition have commonly been represented as the two extremes in religion; but to me it appears that they are near akin, and succeed each other as cause and effect. The wild ebullitions of enthusiasm, when they subside, leave their subjects under the fatal influence of some absurd opinions which become the creed of a new sect; and almost invariably such superstitious customs are adopted as are effectual to shield them from every approach of truth. So that these errors are often perpetuated for many generations, and at last die only with the extinction of the people who held them.

It is curious to observe how nearly extremes sometimes approach each other in their ultimate effects. No two things appear more opposite in their origin and operation, than Unitarianism and enthusiasm—the one proceeding from the pride of reason, the other from the exuberance of the imagination—the one renouncing all pretensions to divine assistance, the other professing to be guided by inspiration at every step: yet in this they agree, that they equally tend to discredit and set aside the authority of the scriptures of truth. The rationalist will not receive many of the doctrines of revelation because they do not accord with his preconceived notions, which he calls the dictates of reason. The enthusiast will not submit to the authority of scripture because he imagines that he is under the direction of a superior guide. The one makes his own reason the judge of what he will receive as true from the volume of revelation; the other determines every thing, whether it relate to opinion or practice, by the suggestions of his fancied inspiration.

On the errors which arise from both these quarters, we should keep a watchful eye; and against them we should make a firm and faithful stand. On the one hand, we must unequivocally deny to *reason* the high office of deciding at her bar what doctrines of scripture are to be received and what not; and on the other, we must insist that all opinions, pretensions, experiences, and practices must be judged by the standard of the Word of God.

"To the law and to the testimony" let us make our appeal against every species of error; "if they speak not according to these, it is because there is no light in them."

I WILL NOW make a few remarks on the subject of purity as it respects the discipline of the church. The first thing here which deserves our attention is the introduction of suitable men into the ministry. If you would have a well-disciplined army, you must begin by appointing good officers. There is no subject which more deserves the attention of our church when met in general assembly than this. The deficiency of preachers is great. Our vacancies are numerous, and often continue for years unsupplied, by which means they are broken up or destroyed. Our seminaries of learning, although increasing in literature and numbers, furnish us with few preachers. This state of affairs calls loudly for your attention. Some measures have already been adopted by the recommendation of the general assembly to remedy this evil; but although they promise considerable success, yet they are inadequate to the object. In my opinion, we shall not have a regular and sufficient supply of well-qualified ministers of the gospel, until every presbytery, or at least every synod, shall have under its direction a seminary established for the single purpose of educating youth for the ministry, in which the course of education from its commencement shall be directed to this object: for it is much to be doubted, whether the system of education pursued in our colleges and universities is the best calculated to prepare a young man for the work of the ministry. The great extension of the physical sciences, and the taste and fashion of the age, have given such a shape and direction to the academical course, that, I confess, it appears to me to be little adapted to introduce a youth to the study of the sacred scriptures.

The consequence of the deficiency of well-qualified preachers has been that some have been disposed to venture upon the dangerous expedient of introducing men who were destitute of the literary qualifications required by our directory. And here permit me to suggest, whether the rule, which prescribes the kind and degree of learning which presbyteries shall require of candidates, is not susceptible of amendment. As it now stands, it is rather a standard to which we wish to be conformed, than a rule with which we strictly comply. I believe it is a fact that no presbytery in our body has been able, uniformly, to obey the letter of this law; and this frequency of violation in all, has led some to dispense with it altogether. I think, therefore, if from the circumstances of our churches, there be a necessity for deviating from this rule in any degree, it would be better to recommend to the presbyteries such an alteration as would authorize this proceeding.

The end of all our labours, however, should be to promote holiness in the great body of the church. The necessity of purity of heart and life, in order to salvation, is indispensable. "Blessed are the pure in heart, for they shall see God." "Follow peace with all men and holiness, without which no man shall see the Lord." But on this subject it would be improper for me to enlarge at present.

2

Plan of the Theological Seminary
1811

After Alexander's sermon in 1808, Ashbel Green took the lead in the maneuvers which eventually led to the founding of Princeton Seminary.[1] Green's presbytery of Philadelphia overtured the 1809 General Assembly to establish "a theological school." That body appointed a committee to canvass the various presbyteries concerning their wishes in the matter. Some Presbyterian leaders, as indeed Alexander (Selection 1), expressed the desire for many such schools established in many parts of the country. But Green and Samuel Miller felt that this proposal would spread the energies and resources of the denomination too thin. Instead, they lobbied over the winter of 1809-10 and at the 1810 General Assembly for a centralized seminary. When Miller was named in 1810 to chair the committee reporting on the situation, his committee turned in a strong recommendation for the establishment of a single seminary. The 1810 Assembly also commissioned Green to draw up a constitution for the school. The plan which resulted, as modified only slightly by the 1811 Assembly, became the founding document for the seminary. The 1812 General Assembly authorized its beginning and located it at Princeton.

The plan left full authority over the seminary in the hands of the General Assembly, which was to appoint a board for the actual supervision of the institution. This board was to supervise a faculty which, in its turn, was to be sworn defenders of the Westminster Confession and Catechisms. Students were to follow a three-year course of study, similar to the one that had been established at Andover, but provisions were also made for those who could not remain for the entire course. As the following selections from the plan also make clear, the institution was to specialize in positive knowledge of Scripture and a learned defense of the faith. Ministers who had been trained at the seminary would be better equipped to promote missions, ecclesiastical harmony, and social order. They would also be able to defend Scripture and to refute assaults on the faith like those involved in the "deistical controversy." The selections are from *The Plan of a Theological Seminary adopted by the General Assembly of the Presbyterian Church in the United States of America, in their session of May last, A.D. 1811; Together with the measures taken by them to carry the plan into effect* (Philadelphia: Aitken, 1811), pp. 4-6 and 12-13.

1. For a full recital of the details involved in negotiations at the General Assemblies and with the trustees of Princeton College concerning a seminary, see Noll, "The Founding of Princeton Seminary," pp. 76-85.

[Purposes]

It is to form men for the Gospel ministry, who shall truly believe, and cordially love, and therefore endeavour to propagate and defend, in its genuineness, simplicity, and fulness, that system of religious belief and practice which is set forth in the Confession of Faith, Catechisms, and Plan of Government and Discipline of the Presbyterian Church; and thus to perpetuate and extend the influence of true evangelical piety, and Gospel order.

It is to provide for the church an adequate supply and succession of able and faithful ministers of the New Testament; workmen that *need not to be ashamed,* being qualified *rightly to divide the word of truth.*

It is to unite, in those who shall sustain the ministerial office, religion and literature; that piety of the heart which is the fruit only of the renewing and sanctifying grace of God, with solid learning: believing that religion without learning, or learning without religion, in the ministers of the Gospel, must ultimately prove injurious to the Church.

It is to afford more advantages than have hitherto been usually possessed by the ministers of religion in our country, to cultivate both piety and literature in their preparatory course; piety, by placing it in circumstances favourable to its growth, and by cherishing and regulating its ardour; literature, by affording favourable opportunities for its attainment, and by making its possession indispensable.

It is to provide for the Church, men who shall be able to defend her faith against infidels, and her doctrines against heretics.

It is to furnish our congregations with enlightened, humble, zealous, laborious pastors, who shall truly watch for the good of souls, and consider it as their highest honour and happiness to win them to the Saviour, and to build up their several charges in holiness and peace.

It is to promote harmony and unity of sentiment among the ministers of our Church, by educating a large body of them under the same teachers, and in the same course of study.

It is to lay the foundation of early and lasting friendships, productive of confidence and mutual assistance in after life among the ministers of religion; which experience shows to be conducive not only to personal happiness, but to the perfecting of inquiries, researches, and publications advantageous to religion.

It is to preserve the unity of our Church, by educating her ministers in an enlightened attachment, not only to the same doctrines, but to the same plan of government.

It is to bring to the service of the Church genius and talent, when united with piety, however poor or obscure may be their possessor, by furnishing, as far as possible, the means of education and support, without expense to the student.

It is to found a nursery for missionaries to the heathen, and to such as are destitute of the stated preaching of the gospel; in which youth may receive that appropriate training which may lay a foundation for their ultimately becoming eminently qualified for missionary work.

It is, finally, to endeavour to raise up a succession of men, at once *qualified for* and thoroughly *devoted to* the work of the Gospel ministry; who, with various endowments, suiting them to different stations in the Church of Christ, may all possess a portion of the spirit of the primitive propagators of the Gospel; prepared to make every sacrifice, to endure every hardship, and to render every service which the promotion of pure and undefiled religion may require.

Article IV: Of Study and Attainments

As the particular course of study pursued in any Institution will, and perhaps ought to be modified in a considerable degree, by the views and habits of the teachers; and ought, moreover, to be varied, altered, or extended, as experience may suggest improvements; it is judged proper to specify, not so precisely the course of study, as the attainments which must be made. Therefore,

Section 1

Every student, at the close of his course, must have made the following attainments, viz., he must be well skilled in the original languages of the Holy Scriptures. He must be able to explain the principal difficulties which arise in the perusal of the Scriptures, either from erroneous translations, apparent inconsistencies, real obscurities, or objections arising from history, reason, or argument. He must be versed in Jewish and Christian antiquities, which serve to explain and illustrate Scripture. He must have an acquaintance with ancient geography, and with oriental customs, which throw light on the sacred records.—Thus he will have laid the foundation for becoming a sound biblical critic.

He must have read and digested the principal arguments and writings relative to what has been called the deistical controversy.—Thus he will be qualified to become a defender of the Christian faith.

He must be able to support the doctrines of the Confession of Faith and Catechisms, by a ready, pertinent, and abundant quotation of Scripture texts for that purpose. He must have studied, carefully and correctly, Natural, Didactic, Polemic, and Casuistic Theology. He must have a considerable acquaintance with General History and Chronology, and a particular acquaintance with the history of the Christian Church.—Thus he will be preparing to become an able and sound divine and casuist.

He must have read a considerable number of the best practical writers on the subject of religion. He must have learned to compose with correctness and readiness in his own language, and to deliver what he has composed to others in a natural and acceptable manner. He must be well acquainted with the several parts, and the proper structure of popular lectures and sermons. He must have composed at least two lectures and four popular sermons, that shall have been approved by the professors. He must have carefully studied the duties of the pastoral care.—Thus he will be prepared to become a useful preacher, and a faithful pastor.

He must have studied attentively the form of Church Government authorized by the Scriptures, and the administration of it as it has taken place in Protestant Churches.—Thus he will be qualified to exercise discipline, and to take part in the government of the Church in all its judicatories.

Archibald Alexander
1772–1851

3

Nature and Evidence of Truth
1812

In May 1812 the General Assembly elected Archibald Alexander as the first professor of its new seminary. Alexander was inaugurated in August and began instruction with three students. By the time of the seminary's first annual report to the General Assembly, six more students had arrived and another five would begin their studies before the start of the second full year.[1] Alexander taught this handful of students in all the theological subjects, but he gave early attention to philosophical matters as well. A manuscript has been preserved at Princeton of Alexander's first lecture on philosophical subjects, the substance of which is presented below.

Alexander's discussion, "Nature and Evidence of Truth," stands squarely in the tradition of Scottish Common Sense Realism. His great intellectual nemesis, as it had been for the Common Sense philosophers, was David Hume. His defense against Hume, similarly, involved an assertion of self-evident truths, the reliability of physical senses, moral senses, and human testimony, and the givenness of cause-and-effect relationships. Although Alexander never mentioned Hume by name, he spent most of the lecture refuting Hume's assertions— that cause and effect can never be more than a mental construct and that testimony concerning the miraculous can never adequately ground religious belief.[2]

Alexander's various preceptors had rung the changes on Hume's assertions, and Alexander repeats their arguments for the sake of his students. In this he employed the strategy of his own teacher, William Graham, who "carried on his investigations," according to Alexander, "not so much by books, as by a patient and repeated analysis of the various processes of thought as these arose in his own mind, and by reducing the phenomena thus observed to a regular system."[3] Graham had also given his pupil a manuscript copy of John Witherspoon's *Lectures on Moral Philosophy* as part of Alexander's training for the ministry.[4] And before Alexander began lecturing at Princeton, he also read the

---

1. A copy of the first annual report from 1813 is found in *Centennial of Princeton Seminary,* pp. 9-16. For a list of the first year's students, see *Biographical Catalogue 1815-1932,* pp. 1-2.

2. For a good, brief summary, see D. G. C. MacNabb, "David Hume," *The Encyclopedia of Philosophy* (New York: Macmillan, 1967) 4: 74-90.

3. J. W. Alexander, *Life of Archibald Alexander* (Philadelphia: Presbyterian Board of Publication, 1855), p. 18. See also p. 106 for discussion of Graham's methods.

4. Ibid., p. 108.

great Scottish philosophers (Thomas Reid, James Beattie, and Dugald Stewart) whose ideas Witherspoon had popularized.

Alexander's convictions about truth were those which Graham, Witherspoon, and the Scots had also expressed:[5] "The constitution of our nature," as Alexander phrases it, makes it necessary to accept the basic reliability of sense information, reasoning, and human testimony. "Intuitions" about our own character and about human nature are valid sources of knowledge, if carefully distinguished from flights of "imagination." Information derived from the common-sense experience of humanity is self-evidently true. Alexander had only scorn for the "Metaphysical sophister" who could doubt these fundamental certainties. And for him, such basic truths constituted not only a solid philosophy, but also a means to demonstrate the existence of God and the reliability of God's own testimony (i.e., Scripture). It is not entirely clear where Alexander derives each aspect of his thought in the lecture, but his overwhelming debt to the Scottish tradition is beyond question. (See the appendix for Alexander's own list of sources for the lecture.)

Also beyond question is the debt of the entire Princeton Theology to the kind of philosophy expounded in this lecture. It was not just a matter of treating theology as a science, which meant something less specific for Alexander in 1812 than for Hodge in 1872 (Selection 8). The Princetonians also remained convinced that intuition or common sense provided certain unquestionable starting points from which good arguments could rise to rebut skepticism, defend the existence of God, and support the truthfulness of Scripture. This conviction plays less of a role for Hodge (e.g., Selection 6) than it did for Warfield (e.g., Selection 29), but it still was a constant in the development of the theology. Many other convictions also gave shape to the Princeton Theology, but it never moved far beyond the philosophical assertions which Alexander delivered in the seminary's first term.

The manuscript of this lecture, in Alexander's own hand, is found in the Speer Library, Princeton Theological Seminary, and is here used by permission of the Seminary. Alexander titled it, "Theological Lectures, Nature and Evidence of Truth, October 1812." In this transcription, contractions have been expanded and punctuation brought into conformity with modern usage. Capitalization and italicization remain as in the original.

T HE DISCOVERY OF truth is the object of every science. To become acquainted with those truths which relate to the being, character, and works of God, and the relations subsisting between him and his creatures, is the object of Theological Science.

That man is capable of real knowledge to a certain degree all must admit; for if we should even suppose that it could be proved that all human knowledge is

---

5. Grave, *The Scottish Philosophy of Common Sense,* provides an excellent summary of these principles.

uncertain, this very supposition destroys itself, by taking it for granted that the uncertainty of our knowledge may be *proved*, i.e., certainly known. No man can consistently assert that he is a universal skeptic; for if he doubts of all things he must of course doubt about the reality of this act, and therefore must be uncertain whether he doubts or not.

The fact is that we are so constituted that we are under the necessity of believing many propositions. By no reasoning, or voluntary effort, can a man cease to believe *that he exists, that he perceives, that he feels pleasure and pain,* that *other beings exist,* etc. Many things are so obvious, and so necessarily engage the attention of all rational beings, that we cannot conceive any period of their active existence in which they do not assent to them. But there are other propositions which when presented to the mind, we believe as firmly and necessarily as these; yet they are not so constantly obtruded on our attention; and persons possessing some rationality may live for a considerable time without having distinctly thought of them. Of this class are the axioms on which the science of Mathematics is founded, concerning which it is impossible for anyone to doubt who is capable of comprehending the meaning of the terms by which they are expressed; and yet many persons may have lived a long time in the world without having had their attention directed to them. There is also in the minds of all men an implicit belief in many things which it does not appear have ever been distinctly and explicitly comprehended. For instance, all men act upon the principle that every effect must have a cause; that the *energy* and *quantity* of the cause may be inferred from the nature of the effect, as far as it is known; that similar causes will produce similar effects; that we are the same persons today that we were yesterday, or twenty years ago; that the concurring testimony of all men with whom they have had opportunity of conversing, or of any considerable number of disinterested persons, is worthy of credit.[6] All men, and even children advanced beyond infancy, invariably act upon these principles, and prove by their conduct that by the constitution of their nature they are led to believe these things in every particular case which occurs, without having even considered the proposition in the general, or abstracted from the particular instances. And indeed all our knowledge is originally particular. The forming of these particulars into general propositions is an operation of the mind which is to be ranked among the latest in the unfolding of its powers. Now these propositions which from the constitution of our nature we are under the necessity of believing, as soon as they are presented to the mind, we call by the name self-evident truths.

As a great part, however, of our knowledge does not consist in self-evident propositions but is the result of reasoning, or attained by some intermediate process; and as it is of great importance in receiving opinions to examine into the grounds and reasons on which they rest, some inquirers after truth have considered it necessary to extend their caution so far as to refuse to assent even to

6. Alexander is here addressing specifically assertions that Hume had made against traditional proofs for God and for Christianity. See Hume, *A Treatise of Human Nature* (1739, 1740) on cause and effect, and *Enquiry Concerning Human Understanding* (1748), section X, "On Miracles."

self-evident truths, until by reasoning or some other legitimate means they could be fairly established. They have therefore laid it down as the proper method of commencing our search after truth *to doubt of everything* until we could establish something by proof. This is the method of investigation proposed by *DesCartes* and his followers. Agreeably to this plan, this celebrated philosopher began with attempting to prove his own existence and reasoned thus, *Cogito ergo sum.* But it is obvious to remark that he violated his own principle in the very first step. It was as necessary to prove that we think or that we exist. Indeed, the conclusion is necessarily implied in the premises; for evidently there can be no thought without existence. And such absurdity will ever be the consequence of attempting to establish by reasoning those self-evident truths on which all reasonings are founded. Without some such principles which needed no proof reasoning would be impossible, as is evident by the above example.[7]

There can be no reasoning without premises, and these premises in the commencement of our investigation must be self-evident truths. For what is reasoning, but a comparison of ideas already known, and thereby inferring others which were before unknown? But it may be said that a rational being ought to be able to give a reason for every thing which he believes; but according to this view of the subject, he assents to the most important truths without any reason. To this I answer, that the best reason which anyone can have for believing any proposition is that it is so evident to his intellectual faculty that he cannot disbelieve it. If he is as certain as he

7. Some time later, Alexander added to this manuscript a lengthy note on Descartes which, as an illustration of his convictions about the relationship between physical senses and mental processes, deserves to be cited:

"The first object of this philosopher was to free himself from all the prejudices of education; in the prosecution of this object he called every thing into question of which it was possible to doubt.

"He went back to the first and clearest principle of human knowledge, the consciousness of thought; taking this for granted, he immediately and justly inferred his existence as included in this truth. Thus far there seems to be nothing amiss in his process; but having observed that in many cases we are liable to be deceived in regard to the objects of sense he concluded that no reliance could be placed on the information of our senses until it was demonstrated that they were true inlets of knowledge. There was his first and greatest mistake. For assuming nothing as true but the existence of mind and its exercises, he undertook in the next place to prove the being of a God without any assistance from the visible creation.

"He found that he could form the idea of an infinitely perfect being; such an idea he inferred must have an infinite being for its author, therefore there was a God, or an infinitely perfect being. Then he proceeded to prove the existence of the world thus: our senses are given to us by an infinitely perfect being, but an infinitely perfect being will not deceive his dependent creatures, therefore the information received by our senses is true. Now it was upon his principles as necessary to prove that consciousness could not deceive us, or that the senses could not. And if he could not trust his senses until he had proved that they were not deceptions, how could he consistently acquiesce in the deductions of reasoning, until he should demonstrate that this faculty was incapable of deceiving us?

"It is true, that we make many mistakes in regard to the objects of our senses; but we are liable to mistakes in reasoning also, and to a greater extent. The truth is that all our faculties give us true information when exercised within their peculiar sphere, but whenever we attempt to go beyond this narrow circle we are apt to err."

can be already of the truth of a proposition, why should he wish for further light? Of what advantage would proof be if it could be had? Again, if it should be established by a process or reasoning, that logical process, if correct, must depend upon some principle, or principles which have been taken for granted, and surely the conclusion can never be more certain than the premises. The greatest possible assurance which we can have of any truth is that the constitution of our nature obliges us to assent to it. If it be asked whether it is not possible that our constitution might be so formed as to lead us into error, the answer would be that the case would admit of no remedy. We would have as much reason, if we should entertain a suspicion of this sort, to suspect the correctness of our reasoning faculty, as of that faculty by means of which we intuitively perceive fundamental truths; and indeed from what has been already said, it does appear that the conclusions from reasoning cannot in the nature of things possess more certainty than those first principles on which all reasonings are founded.

To prove that our faculties are not so constituted as to misguide us, some have had recourse to the *goodness* and *truth of God,* our creator, but this argument is unnecessary. We are as certain of these intuitive truths as we can be. No supposition of the possibility of deception shakes in the least my belief that I exist, and that the world exists; and if it did, this argument or any other would be unavailing; because, if I supposed that my faculties were deceptious, I should have as much reason to doubt of their correctness in forming such an argument, as in any other case. Besides, we must be sure that we exist, and that the world exists, before we can be certain that there is a God, for it is from these *data* that we prove his existence.[8] But it may be asked, are we not actually imposed upon in many cases in things which appear self-evident, until reason is consulted, by the light of which illusion is banished? For instance, it is laid down as a first principle that we must implicitly rely on the information of our senses; and yet how often do they impose upon us? What appears more evident to us than that the sun and stars are constantly moving round us, and that the moon is much larger than any of the Heavenly bodies except the sun; but by the assistance of reason and Philosophy we correct these mistakes. In answer, it may be observed that although our senses give us certain information of the real existence of external objects, yet they cannot give us correct ideas of the nature, size, shape, and motions of the objects by which we are surrounded. And if we form opinions on these subjects merely from the impressions on the senses, we shall fall into many mistakes. For instance, when we judge of the distance of an object by the eye, we apply that organ to a use for which it is by no means adapted. We can, it is true, in many cases judge pretty correctly of the distance of an object by looking at it, but this is the effect of experience. The

8. Alexander here affirms the necessity of apologetics, as he does later in the lecture when showing why God's existence is not a self-evident truth and why arguments are proper "to prove that what is alleged to come from [God] is really his word." This defense of apologetics appears again in Alexander's inaugural sermon (Selection 4) when he argues for the Scriptures as God's word. It is the same note which Hodge strikes in his discussion of the proofs for God's existence (ST, I: 202–240) and Warfield in expressing his differences with Bavinck and Kuyper (Selection 29).

knowledge of distance is undoubtedly acquired originally by the sense of feeling, and when we have ascertained the distance of an object, observing that at this distance it exhibits a certain appearance, we gradually learn, when a similar appearance is exhibited, to refer it to the same distance. But without experience, we should not have the least idea of the relative distances of visible objects, as has been proved by fact; and when we undertake to judge of the distance or size of objects entirely beyond the sphere of our experience, we must of necessity fall into gross mistakes. Similar observations might be made respecting the error into which people fall respecting the motions of the Heavenly bodies. For we cannot judge of absolute motion of bodies by the sense of seeing.

The senses give certain and correct information in all cases where they are exercised on their proper objects and within their proper sphere; and the mistakes into which we are led in relation to objects of sense are commonly *judgements* and *inferences* which we rashly draw in consequence of certain sensations. And when these erroneous judgements are corrected, it is not properly by the light of reason; for by reasoning alone the errors of sense can never be corrected, but it is by the senses exercised in more *favourable* circumstances.

But if all men must necessarily assent to these intuitive truths, how does it happen that they have been denied by some Philosophers? If a man could be found who did not believe in these things, he would be a natural fool or madman, and would be esteemed so by all men. It would be a degree of folly and madness, too, never witnessed on earth. For the greatest idiot or most raving madman does still retain the belief of some self-evident truths and act upon them. And as to those few philosophers who in their books have pretended to call in question the existence of a material world, they have, nevertheless, in common life acted upon the same principles with other men. They have as cautiously avoided running into the fire, or striking their heads against a post, as common people. And *conduct* is the best evidence of the nature and strength of our belief.

But it may be inquired whether vulgar errors may not be mistaken for self-evident truths, as many embrace them with unwavering confidence. Undoubtedly it may be so; and there is great need to guard against falling into this error. These truths which are the first principles of all our knowledge are evident to all who contemplate them. All men in all ages and countries have agreed in them, and no man can disbelieve them if he would. . . .

The exact number of self-evident truths cannot be ascertained. With respect to many, we can say with certainty that they belong to this class; but there are many others concerning which it may be doubted whether they are known by the faculty of *common sense*, or by a short and obvious process of reasoning. Some have considered the existence of Deity as belonging to the class of self-evident truths; but however clear and convincing the argument may be by which truth may be established, yet it ought to be considered rather as a conclusion of reason or subject of revelation than as an intuitive proposition.

It has been objected to this doctrine of *first principles of knowledge* that it is merely a revival of the old exploded doctrine of *Innate* Ideas. To which I answer that very possibly some who talked of innate ideas meant no more than that as soon as the mind was exercised, there were some truths which it could not but *assent* to, without any other light than that which is contained in the proposition itself. But considering innate ideas in the light in which they are set by Mr. Locke in his refutation of that doctrine, as being certain impressions or notions which exist in the mind previous to and independent of sensation and reflexion, there is nothing in common between that opinion and the one which we have now proposed.[9] Which is that to a mind furnished with the common ideas received by sensation and reflexion there are some truths or propositions which immediately on being proposed are perceived to be true without any process of reasoning in the case. Indeed, this doctrine is necessarily implied in the receiving ideas by sensation and reflexion; for if we were not so constituted as to believe implicitly in the reality of what we perceive by the senses and are conscious of in ourselves, we should remain forever as incapable of acquiring knowledge as a brute. It cannot be said that we learn these truths by experience; for without such a constitution there could be no such thing as learning by experience. Perceiving the sun in the firmament a thousand times, without any belief in his existence, would never bring us any nigher to the knowledge of that Luminary.

It is reasonable to suppose that to a perfect intelligence all truths are intuitive. The necessity of reasoning to discover truth is an argument of the weakness of the human mind. The omniscient God beholds every truth evidently without the intervention of any process of reasoning.

The ability in man therefore to perceive some truths intuitively is one of the greatest perfections of his intellect; and we may conclude that beings of a higher grade in the intellectual scale perceive many more things intuitively than we do; and that if our minds should be enlarged in another state of existence, one effect will be that many things which are in the present state only to be discovered by a tedious process will there be self-evident.

Indeed, when we attend to the nature of that operation of the mind called reasoning, it appears that the truth which forms the conclusion is viewed at last in the same manner by the mind as self-evident truths; and the use of this process is merely to bring it fairly before the mind. It may be laid down as a maxim therefore that the ultimate evidence on which we receive any truth is contained *in itself*.

The truths which may be considered self-evident are of several distinct kinds:

1. The existence of the objects of sense and consciousness.
2. Necessary truths, such as Mathematical axioms.
3. Philosophical principles, such as "Every effect must be produced by some cause," etc.
4. Moral truths, as for instance, that there is an essential difference between moral good and evil; that benevolence is better than malevolence, etc.[10]

9. John Locke, *Essay Concerning Human Understanding* (1690), Book I, "Of Innate Ideas."
10. Alexander regularly presented expanded lectures on the nature and extent of these moral

5. Facts, reported to us by a sufficient number of competent witnesses, past or present, as that such men as Caesar and Pompey did once exist; that there was a beautiful building formerly in Jerusalem called the Temple, etc.

6. Truths founded on uniform experience as that the sun will rise tomorrow; that fire will burn the next hour as well as the present.

7. Memory.

With regard to all these, if a man should be asked why he believes, he can give no other reason than that his mind is so constituted that he cannot do otherwise than assent to these things. And if he attempt to dive deeper into the reasons of his assent he will only perplex his own mind.

1. I believe, for instance, that I am now thinking on a particular subject because *I am conscious of it,* but other reasons for my belief of this proposition I can assign none, and I need none; for what effect can reasons and arguments produce on the mind but to confirm its belief in some propositions; but my assent to this is as strong as it can be. I make an effort to believe the contrary—I find it to be impossible. I try to doubt whether I am now thinking—the effort is absurd. All men possess this certainty of the reality of the exercises of their own minds. *Assent* is essential to consciousness. Certainty is inseparable from it. But no reason can be assigned for it but that we are constrained by the nature of our intellect thus to think and believe.

2. Again, *I see and feel* the pen with which I am writing. I have no more doubt of its existence than of my own. I cannot doubt of it. If some Metaphysical sophister should attempt to prove to me by a long proof of reasoning that I was mistaken—that there was no such thing as matter and that the sun which I supposed to exist was nothing more than an idea in my own mind, I might be utterly unable to answer his arguments, or detect their sophistry; but as long as I feel the pen with my fingers, and see it with my eyes, my conviction of its existence remains unaltered. Call it an *idea,* or by what name you please, this cannot shake the certain confidence which I have of its existence. I am so constituted that I find it utterly impossible to doubt of the reality of what I perceive by my senses. This certainly does not invoke any opinion respecting the nature and philosophical properties of matter. It relates only to its existence and capacity of affecting our senses in a particular way.

3. In the third place. I remember that more than a year ago I saw the sun eclipsed. I believe with invincible firmness in the fact which my memory has preserved. When it took place it was believed on the evidence of sense, but ever since on the authority of memory. And I find that my assent is as unwavering on this ground as the former, though the impression of the object is less vivid on the mind; but if I am asked why I credit memory, and how I can be sure that it will not deceive me, I have nothing to reply but that I am under a necessity of believing

truths. The lectures were published after his death in *Outlines of Moral Science,* ed. James W. Alexander (New York: Charles Scribner, 1852).

what I remember, as well as what I perceive or am conscious of; but here I must stop. And if I could give a reason it might as well be asked how do you know but your reason deceives you.

It may be inquired here whether we implicitly credit every thing which we remember and whether memory does not often deceive us. In answer to the first question, it is evident that to remember a thing necessarily implies a belief of its existence in every instance, for we cannot conceive of a greater absurdity than to disbelieve or doubt of what we distinctly remember; and with respect to the second inquiry, I would say that memory never does deceive us. It is true we are often doubtful about certain things which have been deposited in the memory; we are uncertain whether they existed or not, and are often mistaken in what we supposed we remembered. But the fact is we only doubt whether we do actually remember an event. And when we are mistaken in our recollection it is by confounding memory with imagination. Many things remain so obviously in the mind that we know not how they came there; and certain impressions may be made on the imagination which lead us to think that they are the suggestions of memory. But experience will satisfy every one that when we distinctly remember anything or suppose we do, we never hesitate; and when we do actually remember anything we are never deceived by memory.

4. The next class of self-evident truths may be called *Philosophical principles,* because on these *data* all the sciences are founded. These, however, may be divided into *necessary, moral,* and *analogical.*

Of the first class are the mathematical axioms, such as that "A whole is greater than a part"—"All the parts are equal to the whole," etc. And such first principles as these, "That every effect must have an adequate cause." "Like causes will produce similar effects," etc.

Of moral self-evident truths we may give as an instance, "that there is a difference betwixt moral good and evil"; "that justice, kindness, etc., are better than cruelty and injustice"; "that conscience ought to be obeyed," etc.

Of the third class are these, "that the qualities which have been uniformly found in certain beings will continue to qualify them, as for instance that fire will continue to burn, food to nourish, etc. That the sun will rise and set tomorrow and the day following." These last mentioned truths, it is true, are founded on experience. We must have observed, or others for us, what the nature of things is for a long time before we can conclude that the same will continue. But if we ask ourselves why we believe that the qualities of things and regular course of nature will continue, it must be resolved into a law of our nature. So it is with respect to the other first principles under this kind, we believe them because we cannot do otherwise.

5. But most of the knowledge which man acquires he receives upon testimony. Our belief in testimony is not the effect of experience, as some have asserted, but is a consequence of the peculiar constitution of our nature. If it were the former it would be very weak in children and increase with our years and experience; but the reverse is the fact. Children believe every thing which is told them, and only begin to doubt of the truth of any testimony after they have had experience of the

falsehood of some things which have been told them. Though we are naturally inclined to credit all testimony, yet it would be absurd to suppose that we were under a necessity of doing this; for often men contradict one another in what they assert, and our own experience contradicts many things which we may have heard. But still testimony may be so general or so circumstanced as to produce as full and necessary an assent of the mind as truths of any kind.

It is only by the information of others that I know there is such a place as London or Paris, and yet I have no more doubt that there are such towns than I have that there is such a place as Philadelphia which I have been accustomed to see every day. I try to suppose that I may be mistaken in this belief, but the effort is ineffectual. I cannot doubt of what so many have testified to be true. One man or a few men might deceive me, but the testimony of thousands who never saw each other to the same thing must be true. My belief in the existence of certain persons whom I have never seen is of the same invincible kind. It would be perfectly unavailing for any one to suggest that men were so false and deceitful that there was no dependence to be put in their testimony and that therefore our belief that there was such a man as Bonaparte, or Lord Wellington, might be without foundation. We are sure in such cases that we are not deceived, and cannot be deceived. And we find on trial that it would be as easy to disbelieve the existence of our next neighbor whom we see every day as of many persons whom we have never seen. This certainty of many truths resting on testimony alone is not confined to such as have existed as facts in our time. We are equally certain of many things which took place before we were born. Some hundreds of years have elapsed since the time of Luther and Calvin, and yet I believe as firmly that there were such men as I do in any other truth. So that it is not necessary that the testimony which commands my assent should be that [of] persons now alive, or delivered *viva voce*. Written records which received the uncontradicted assent of all capable of judging at the time when they were formed, and which have come down to us sanctioned by the belief of all intermediate generations, are commonly sufficient to produce an unwavering assent, and this especially is the case when we observe that the present state and circumstances of the world correspond with what we read in such records; or when some visible and permanent monuments commemorative of the truths and facts recorded are still in existence. To give an example. We read in the oldest history extant that the earth was once inundated with a flood. This history has been firmly believed by the people among whom it was published ever since. A tradition of the same event has been handed down through successive generations in almost every country.

In confirmation of this fact we find traces of the deluge in every part of the world, such as marine substances on the highest mountains, and in such quantities that nothing but an event like this could have brought them thither; and to silence the cavils of vain theorists we find the bones and relics of sea and land animals promiscuously mingled together in many parts of the earth, which can never be reconciled with the theories of unbelievers, that the sea and land have by degree changed places, etc., which have been invented without the shadow of historical proof, and indeed, in contradiction to all tradition as well as all history.

When I consider the testimony by which the fact of a general Deluge is established and the present appearance of the earth, I am constrained to believe that such an event did at some former period take place.

As we naturally are disposed to credit the testimony of our fellow creatures, much more will we be under a necessity of believing the testimony of God, if he should deign to speak to us in such a way that we should be certain that it was indeed he who was speaking, whether mediately or immediately. We need no arguments to prove that God will speak the truth. This we [take] as a self-evident truth. The only use of argument in the relation to the testimony of God is to prove that what is alleged to come from him is really his word. The Israelites who stood at the foot of Mt. Sinai and saw the symbols of his majesty and glory and heard his awful voice stood in no need of reasoning or argument to convince them that what was spoken was true.

6. Finally. It has been intimated that many truths capable of being known are not self-evident; but must be discovered by the process of the mind called *reasoning*. It is, for instance, *evident* to every mind that things equal to the same are equal to one another; but it is not evident until proved by a chain of reasoning that the square on the side of a right-angled triangle is equal to both the squares of the sides including the right angle, yet when the reasoning by which this is demonstrated is understood, it is believed as firmly as the axiom stated above. By means of this faculty which may be exercised on subjects of every class, the boundaries of knowledge have been greatly enlarged, and may be still further extended without limit. . . .[11]

11. See the Appendix for the sources which Alexander used in preparing the lecture.

4

Inaugural Address
1812

The inauguration of Archibald Alexander as America's first Presbyterian professor of theology took place on August 12, 1812. The day's activities included a sermon by Samuel Miller on a "faithful ministry" from II Timothy 2:2, Alexander's address, and a charge to the professor and three entering students by Miller's colleague from New York City, Phillip Millerdoler. The young Charles Hodge witnessed the activites "lying at length on the gallery rail" in Princeton's Presbyterian church, and was enthralled.[1]

Alexander's sermon, on John 5:39, "Search the Scriptures," was a memorable performance. It was filled with forthright declamation, sprinkled with scholarly erudition, and—at the end—quickened with pious fervor. More importantly, the sermon's approach to the Bible presented briefly what the whole history of the Princeton Theology labored to accomplish extensively—in Alexander's own phrase, "First, to ascertain that the Scriptures contain the truths of GOD: and, secondly, to ascertain what those truths are." Accordingly, the first two-thirds of the sermon set out proofs for the integrity and authority of Scripture. Alexander cited prophecy and miracles, the reforming power of the gospel and the beneficial social effects of Christianity, and many other arguments to demonstrate the trustworthiness of Scripture. He silenced Roman Catholics, Deists, and "enthusiasts" of various kinds. After a brief excursus describing how to study and interpret Scripture, he pointed to the role of the Holy Spirit in illuminating and confirming the truths of the Bible. The sermon closed with a fervent evocation of the positive teachings of Scripture, including its testimony to divine creation, human sinfulness, supernatural redemption, and God's law.

The address deserves careful attention not only as the inauguration of Alexander but also the inauguration of the Princeton Theology. The blend of reasoning and piety, evidentialism and fideism, defense and proclamation which would characterize the school emerged full-blown. While not as self-consciously Calvinistic as Charles Hodge (e.g., Selection 15), as careful in its evidence as A. A. Hodge (e.g., Selection 19), or as sensitive to nuances of biblical phraseology as Warfield (e.g., Selection 25), Alexander nonetheless was marking out the path which they would one day follow. The sermon appears below as it was published in 1812 by J. Seymour of New York City: *The Sermon, Delivered at the Inauguration of the Rev. Archibald Alexander, D. D., as Professor of Didactic and Polemic*

---

1. John Oliver Nelson, "Charles Hodge: Nestor of Orthodoxy," in *The Lives of Eighteen from Princeton,* ed. Willard Thorp (Princeton: Princeton University Press, 1946), p. 194.

Theology, in the Theological Seminary of the Presbyterian Church, in the United States of America. To Which are Added, the Professor's Inaugural Address and the Charge to the Professor and Students, pp. 57–104. The only deletions are three brief catalogues of scholarly authorities and Alexander's more lengthy recommendations for studying the Septuagint and Chaldean and Syriac translations of the Bible. Punctuation and capitalization have been brought into conformity with modern usage.

HIGHLY RESPECTED AND venerable Directors of the Theological School; and other learned and respectable Auditors, convened on the present solemn occasion!

The institution and commencement of a Theological Seminary, under the patronage and direction of the General Assembly of our church, ought to be a subject of mutual congratulation to all its members. But it cannot be concealed that the same causes which have operated to render such an institution urgently necessary have also opposed serious obstacles in the way of carrying it into effect. The deficiency among us of that kind and extent of learning requisite to confer dignity and respect, as well as usefulness, on the professor's chair, is too obvious to require remark. But every important institution must have its infancy and growth before it can arrive at maturity; and however long we might have deferred this undertaking, the same difficulties would probably have met us at its commencement, which we are now obliged to encounter. The sentiments and emotions by which my own mind is agitated, in consequence of the new and important station in which I find myself placed by the choice of my brethren, and especially, the deep sense which I entertain of my insufficiency for the work, I shall not attempt to express. If the design be of GOD, he will prosper the undertaking, notwithstanding the weakness of the instruments employed in carrying it on; and will crown our feeble efforts with success. On HIM therefore may our hope and confidence be firmly fixed; and may "his will be done on earth as in heaven!"

I have selected, as the subject of the discourse now required of me, the words of our LORD, recorded in the 5th Chap. and 39th ver. of the Gospel according to John: Ἐρευνᾶτε τὰς γραφὰς *Search the Scriptures.*

The verb here used signifies to search with diligence and attention. Its literal meaning appears to be, to pursue any one, by tracing his footsteps. Thus it is employed by *Homer* to express the lion's pursuit of the man who had robbed him of his whelps, by his footsteps; and the dog's pursuit of his game, by his track. The precise meaning of the word, therefore, both in its literal and figurative application, is expressed by the English word, *investigate.* It may be read, either in the indicative, or in the imperative mood. Doctor *Campbell,* in his new translation of the Gospels, prefers the former, and renders the passage, *"Ye do search the Scriptures";* but *Wetstein* and *Parkhurst* consider it to be in the imperative, agreeably to our version: and certainly this rendering gives more point and force to the sentence, *"search the Scriptures, for in them ye think ye have life, but they are they which testify of me."*

Although the word, γραφὰς, *Scriptures,* is of such general import as to include writings of any kind; yet there can be no doubt but what the Scriptures of the Old Testament were here intended. This phrase is used in the New Testament, as we use the word *Bible,* which, though literally signifying any book, yet is now appropriated to designate the volume of inspiration.

The history of the origin of alphabetical writing is involved in considerable obscurity. The first notice which we find of the existence of such an art, is contained in the command given to *Moses,* in the seventeenth [chapter] of Exodus, *to write* a certain transaction *in a book:* and soon afterwards, we read that the law was written by the finger of JEHOVAH, on the two tables of testimony. To me, it appears very probable, therefore, that it was about this time a subject of revelation to *Moses.* As a precise pattern of the tabernacle was shown to him in the mount, and as certain persons were inspired with wisdom to fit them for the execution of that work, why may we not suppose that this wonderful art, so necessary for recording the revelations received from God, for the use of posterity, was also made known to *Moses?* One thing is certain; that all the alphabets of the western portion of the globe, and probably those of the eastern also, have had a common origin: and we have no authentic account of the invention of an alphabet by any people; so that whenever this art of writing may have had its origin, I am persuaded it was no invention of man, but a revelation from GOD.

With respect to the antiquity of these writings, I know of none which can bear any competition with the Pentateuch. Some, indeed, have supposed, that some part of the Vedas of the Brahmins, was written before the books of *Moses;* but there is no historical evidence on which we can depend in support of this opinion. And we are too well acquainted with the fraudulent pretensions of the Hindoos to antiquity, to place any confidence in their assertions. The ultimate opinion of that incomparable scholar, Sir *William Jones,* on this subject, was that the writings of *Moses* were the oldest of any in the world: and a more competent and impartial judge could not easily be found.

As the words of the text are indefinite, they should be considered as imposing an obligation on all sorts of persons, according to their ability and opportunity, to search the Scriptures. We cannot help therefore being struck with the impiety, as well as absurdity, of the practice of the Papists, in withholding the Scriptures from the people.

Will it be said, that when they misinterpret and pervert them, they should be taken away? But such was the conduct of the persons here addressed by Christ. They were so blinded by prejudice that they could not perceive in the Scriptures that person who was the principal subject of them. But does the divine Saviour forbid them the use of the Scriptures, on this account? No; he enjoins it on them, *to search them.* To study them with more care, and with minds more free from prejudice.

Though the duty of searching the Scriptures is common to all Christians, yet there are some on whom it is more peculiarly incumbent. Teachers of religion, and candidates for the sacred office, are bound by an obligation of uncommon force to attend to this duty. In particular relation to such I propose to consider the subject in the sequel of this discourse. But before I proceed further, I would observe that although the words of our Lord in the text refer to the Old Testament, (for at the time of their being spoken there were no other Scriptures extant) yet the reason of the command will apply with full force to other inspired writings as soon as they are promulgated. We shall therefore consider the Scriptures of the New Testament, as well as the Old, embraced within the scope of our Saviour's command.

It will be important to bear in mind that there are two distinct things comprehended in the object of this investigation. First, to ascertain that the Scriptures contain the truths of GOD: and, secondly, to ascertain what these truths are.

Let us now suppose the two volumes containing the Old and New Testaments, the one in the original Hebrew, the other in the Greek, to be put into the hands of the theological student, accompanied with the command of Christ, *search the Scriptures*. Investigate these volumes with diligence. What should be the first step in this investigation? Ought he not to be well satisfied of the identity of these books, with those which formerly existed? Here is a Hebrew volume; but does it contain the same writings to which our Saviour referred? And does this Greek volume comprehend the very books which were received as inspired in the Apostolic age? In this inquiry, the biblical student may obtain complete satisfaction. With respect to the canon of the Old Testament, one fact will be sufficient to remove all doubt. These books have been in the possession of both Jews and Christians ever since the commencement of the gospel dispensation; and they now agree in acknowledging the same books to be canonical; which, considering the inveterate opposition subsisting between them, is a convincing evidence that the canon of the Old Testament has undergone no change since the introduction of Christianity. And that it had undergone none before that period may be proved from this circumstance, that although our Lord often upbraids the Jews with having *perverted* the Scriptures, he never insinuates that they had *altered* or *corrupted* them.

In confirmation of what has been said respecting the canon of the Old Testament, we might adduce the testimony of *Josephus,* and of the Christian Fathers; who not only agree with one another in their catalogue of the books of the Old Testament, but with the canonical list which we now hold. The books called *Apocrypha,* were never received into the canon by the Jews, nor by the earlier Christian Fathers and councils, and have therefore no just claim to be considered as belonging to the Old Testament.

With regard to the New Testament, the evidence is equally convincing. The Christian Church was, in a short time, so widely extended, and embraced so many different languages and nations, that a universal agreement, in this whole body, through all the successive periods of the church, in acknowledging the same books to be canonical, must satisfy every impartial mind that our New Testament is the very same which was received and held sacred by the primitive church. To strengthen this conclusion, it may be added, that at a very early period, these books were translated into many different languages; several of which early translations, either in whole or in part, have come down to our times: and some of them have been preserved among Christians unknown to their brethren of other countries, for many centuries.

In addition to this, it may be observed that accurate lists of the books of the New Testament were made by early ecclesiastical writers, and also by general councils, which are still extant, and agree with our catalogue of canonical books. It deserves to be mentioned also that the churches in every part of the world held copies of these Scriptures, which they preserved with the utmost vigilance; and quotations were made from them, by all the fathers; so that a large portion of the New Testament might be collected from the works of the early ecclesiastical writers. Besides there are still extant manuscript copies of the whole, or a part of the New Testament, from twelve to fifteen hundred years old, which contain the same books that are comprehended in our printed volumes.

What has now been asserted, respecting the universal consent with which the books of the New Testament were received by the ancient church, in all its parts, must be admitted, with the exception of those few books, which have been termed, *Antilegomena,* because their divine authority was denied or disputed by some. Impartiality requires us also to state that these books are not found in some of the oldest versions, as the Syriac, for instance; and therefore it must be admitted that the evidence for their canonical authority is not so complete, as of the rest which were ever undisputed. At the same time, it ought to be observed that the chief reason of doubting was because these books, for a while, were not so generally known to the churches: but as soon as they were accurately examined, and their evidence weighed, opposition to them ceased; and at no late period they obtained an undisturbed place in the sacred canon.

The theological student, having obtained satisfaction respecting the perfection of the canon of Scripture, the next step in his investigation should relate to the *integrity* of the sacred text. For it is possible that the canon might be complete, and yet the text might be so corrupted and mutilated as to leave it uncertain what the original of these books might have been. It is of importance, therefore, to be able to prove that the Scriptures have suffered no material injury, from the fraud of designing men, or from the carelessness of transcribers. In the former part of the last century this was a subject of warm altercation in the church. For whilst some maintained that the sacred text had not received the slightest injury from the ravages of time, others boldly asserted that it was greatly corrupted. The agitation of this question led to a more extensive and accurate examination and collation of manuscript *codices* than had been before made, and gave rise to that species of Biblical criticism, which has, within the last half-century, assumed so conspicuous a place in Theological science. Distant countries were visited, the dark cells of cloisters and monasteries explored, and all important libraries ransacked in search of copies of the Scriptures. Learned men, with unparalleled diligence, employed their whole lives in the collation of manuscripts, and in noting every, even the smallest variation, in their *readings*. Their indefatigable labour and invincible perseverance in prosecuting this work are truly astonishing. It has indeed, much the appearance of laborious trifling; but upon the whole, though not always so designed, has proved serviceable to the cause of truth. For though the serious mind is at first astonished and confounded, upon being informed of the multitude of various readings, . . . yet it is relieved, when on careful examination it appears that not more than one of a hundred of these, makes the slightest variation in the sense, and that the whole of them do not materially affect one important fact or doctrine. It is true, a few important texts, in our received copies, have by this critical process, been rendered suspicious; but this has been more than compensated by the certainty which has been stamped on the great body of Scripture, by having been subjected to this severe scrutiny. For the *text* of our Bibles having passed this ordeal, may henceforth bid defiance to suspicion of its *integrity*. And with respect to the disputed texts referred to above, one thing should ever be kept in mind; that, granting that the evidence from the present view of ancient manuscripts, is against their genuineness, yet this may not be decisive. The learned *Cave* lays it down as a rule to direct us in judging of the comparative excellence of the editions of the Fathers. "That the older the editions are, by so much the more faithful are they."[2] And assigns this reason for the rule, that the first editions were made from the best manuscripts, which were commonly lost or destroyed, when the edition was completed. And I see not why the same reason will not equally apply to the early editions of the Scriptures. In fact, there is historical evidence that the manuscripts used by cardinal *Ximenes* in his Polyglott, have been destroyed, and they appear, from several circumstances, to have been both numerous and ancient: and I am persuaded also, notwithstanding what *Wetstein* and *Michaelis* have said to the contrary, that some of those used by *Stephanus* in his editions of the New Testament, have also been lost. We cannot tell, therefore, what the evidence for these texts might have been to these learned editors. Certainly very strong or they would not have inserted them.

The next step in this investigation would be to ascertain that these books are genuine; or were written by the persons whose names they bear; but as this appears to me to be substantially answered by what has been already said and by what will be added under the next article, I will not now make it a subject of particular discussion; but will proceed to inquire into the *authenticity* and *inspiration* of the Scriptures. I join these two things together because, although a book may be authentic without being inspired; yet if the Bible be authentic, it must have been given by inspiration, for the writers profess that they were inspired.

The truth of this point may be established by several species of evidence quite distinct from each other.

It may, in the first place, be demonstrated by proving the truth of the facts

---

2. Alexander's note: *"Historia Literaria Proleg.* Sec. v.R.1." The Anglican patristic scholar, William Cave (1637–1713), published his *Scriptorum ecclesiasticorum historia literaria* in 1688; it was a history of editions of the Bible to the fourteenth century.

recorded in the scriptures. These facts, many of them being obviously of a miraculous nature, if admitted to have existed, will indubitably prove that those persons by whom they were performed must have been sent and assisted of God: for, as the Jewish ruler rightly reasoned, "no man could do these things unless God were with him." Now the truth of these miracles may be established by testimony like other ancient facts; and also by the history of them being so interwoven with other authentic history, that we cannot separate them: and especially, by that chain of events, depending on them, and reaching down to our own time which has no other assignable origin but the existence of these miracles. For, to believe in the events which the history of the church presents to us, and yet deny the miracles of the gospel, would be as absurd as believing that a chain which hung suspended before our eyes had nothing to support it because that support was out of sight. As to the witnesses of these facts, they are such, and deliver their testimony under such circumstances, and in such a manner, as to *demand* our assent. The impossibility of successfully impugning this testimony obliged the most insidious enemy of Christianity[3] to resort to the principle, "that no testimony is sufficient to confirm a miracle": but the absurdity of this position has been fully demonstrated by *Campbell, Vince,* and others, and it has also been shown by an ingenious writer that the gospel was true, even upon this author's own principles, because its falsehood would involve a greater miracle than any recorded in it.

The next species of evidence in support of the proposition under consideration is derived from prophecy. If the Scriptures contain predictions of events which no human sagacity could have foreseen; if they have foretold events the most improbable which have occurred in exact conformity with the prediction; and if they have described a person combining in his character and life, traits and events apparently incompatible and inconsistent; and yet a person has appeared answering literally to this description, then certainly the writers of these predictions were inspired. But such is the fact. "This sure word of prophecy" is, indeed, like "a light that shineth in a dark place"; but it is also like the light of the dawn which "shineth more and more unto the perfect day." Other evidence may lose something of its force by the lapse of time, but this grows brighter and stronger with every revolving year; for the scope of prophecy comprehends all ages; and new events are continually occurring which had been long foretold by the oracles of GOD. The third species of evidence for the authenticity and inspiration of the Scriptures arises out of their contents. The extraordinary and superlatively excellent nature of the Christian religion proves that it could not have been the production of impostors, nor of unassisted fishermen; nor indeed, of any description of uninspired men. Its doctrines exhibit that very information which is necessary to satisfy the anxious inquiries of man, conscious of his guilt and desirous of salvation. Its precepts are so sublimely excellent, so marked with sanctity and benevolence; and at the same time so perfectly adapted to human nature and human circumstances that the brightest wit can detect no flaw, nor suggest any improvement. "The heavens declare the glory of

---

3. Alexander is referring to Hume and the works cited under Selection 3, n. 6 above.

God"; and so does the holy page of Scripture. It bears the stamp of divinity in its face; and breathes a spirit which could originate no where else but in heaven. Another evidence, but connected with the last, is the blessed tendency and holy efficacy of the gospel to reform the hearts and lives of men, and to produce peace and joy in the mind and conscience; which effects never could result from any false religion.

The success of the gospel, in its commencement, is also an important consideration. When we contemplate the resistance which was to be overcome, both external, from religious and civil establishments, and internal, from the inveterate prejudices and vices of men; and then take into view the means by which all these obstacles were surmounted, we cannot refuse to admit that the power of the Almighty accompanied them.

The beneficial effects of Christianity on those nations which have received it is a striking fact, and furnishes a strong argument in favour of the authenticity and inspiration of the Scriptures. Under their benign influence, war has become less sanguinary and ferocious; justice has been more equally distributed: the poor have been more generally instructed, and their wants supplied; asylums have been provided for the unfortunate and distressed; the female character has been appreciated and exalted to its proper standard in society; the matrimonial bond has been held more sacred; and polygamy, the bane of domestic happiness, discountenanced. In short, the whole fabric of society has been meliorated; and real civilization promoted by Christianity wherever it has been received: and the above mentioned effects have borne an exact proportion to the purity in which this holy religion was preserved, and the degree of conformity to its precepts which has existed among any people.

The next question which should engage the attention of the Theological student, is, for what purpose were the Scriptures given? In answer to this, all are ready to agree, that they were intended to be a guide to man in matters of religion; *a rule of faith and practice.* But here several important questions occur. Are the Scriptures the *only* rule? Are they a *sufficient* rule? Are they an *authoritative* rule? and, Were they only designed to guide us in matters of religion?

Our first controversy is with the Romanists, who maintain that *tradition* is also a rule of faith; and that the Scriptures without tradition are neither a sufficient nor intelligible rule. But this opinion takes away all that fixedness and certainty which a written revelation was intended and calculated to give to religion. Wherein consists the advantage of having a part of the will of GOD committed to writing, if the interpretation of this depends on the uncertain and varying light of oral tradition? We might as well have nothing but tradition, as be under the necessity of resorting to this uncertain guide to lead us to the true meaning of the written word. But had it been intended to make this the channel of communicating the divine will to posterity, some method would have been divised to preserve the stream of tradition pure. No such method has been made known. On the contrary, the Scriptures predict a general and awful apostasy in the church. It could not be otherwise but that during this period tradition would become a corrupt channel of information.

This apostasy has taken place; and the stream of tradition has, in fact, become so muddy, and so swelled with foreign accessions from every quarter, that Christianity, viewed through this medium, exhibits the appearance of a deformed and monstrous mass of superstition. But, if we should admit the principle that the constant tradition of the church should be our guide, where shall we go to look for it? To the Greek, to the Latin, or to the Syriac church? To the 4th, 9th, or 14th century? For there is no uniformity; not even in *the infallible Catholic Church*. Every one in the least acquainted with ecclesiastical history must know that not only has the practice varied at different times, in very important matters; but also the Bulls of Popes, and Decrees and Canons of Councils, have often been in perfect collision with one another: and, what is worst of all, have often been in direct hostility with the word of GOD. For the same thing has happened to tradition in the Christian, as formerly in the Jewish church. *"It hath made the word of God of none effect, teaching for doctrines the commandments of men."*

But whilst we reject tradition as a rule of truth, we do not deny the utility of having recourse to the early practice of the church, for the illustration of Scripture where there is any doubt respecting apostolic practice or institution.

There are two other opinions by which the sufficiency and authority of the Scriptures as a rule of faith and practice are invalidated. These, though held by persons erring on opposite extremes, agree in derogating from the respect due to the Scriptures.

The first is the opinion of those who will not believe any thing, though contained in Scripture, which does not correspond with their own reason. If, for instance, a thousand passages of Scripture could be adduced, explicitly teaching the doctrine *of the Trinity, of original sin, of efficacious grace, of vicarious sufferings,* or *eternal punishments,* they would not admit them, because they have determined all these to be contrary to reason; and therefore the Scriptures *must be* so interpreted as to exclude all such doctrines; and the texts which support them must be tortured by the critical art, or perverted by the wiles of sophistry, until they are silent, or speak a different language. Now, the only mystery in the religion of these sons of reason is that they should want a revelation at all. Certainly it would be more consistent to reject Christianity wholly, than whilst professing to receive it in the general, to deny almost all the particular doctrines of which the general system is composed. For my own part, I cannot consider Socinianism in any other light than Deism masked.[4] At any rate, they are *nearly related.* If *that* has a little stronger faith, *this* has the advantage on the score of consistency.

The other opinion referred to is that of fanatics in general, who, whilst they confess that the Scriptures are divinely inspired, imagine that *they* are possessed of the same inspiration. And some, in our own times, have proceeded so far as to boast of revelations by which the Scriptures are entirely superseded as a rule of

4. Socinianism, after Faustus Socinus (1539–1604), included the belief that Christ was not divine. Deism is the name given to the loose collection of seventeenth- and eighteenth-century cosmologies that depended on God for creation and for the establishment of natural laws, but for little else.

faith and practice. Now, the difference between these persons and the holy men of God who wrote the Scriptures consists in two things. First, the inspired writers could give some external evidence, by miracle or prophecy, to prove their pretensions; but enthusiasts can furnish no such evidence: and secondly, the productions of the prophets and apostles were worthy of God, and bore his impress; but the discourses of these men, except what they repeat from Scripture, are wholly unworthy of their boasted origin, and more resemble the dreams of the sick, or the ravings of the insane, than the "words of truth and soberness."

But, on the other hand, there have been some who believed that the Scriptures not only furnish a rule to guide us in our religion, but a complete system of *philosophy;* that the true theory of the universe is revealed in the first chapters of Genesis; and that there is an intimate connexion betwixt the natural and spiritual world. The one containing a sort of emblematical representation of the other; so that even the high mystery of the Trinity is supposed to be exhibited by the material fluid, which pervades the universe, in its different conditions, of fire, light, and air. *John Hutchinson,* Esq. of *England,* took the lead in propagating this system, and has been followed by some men of great name and great worth. . . . But, although, we acknowledge, that there is something in this theory which is calculated to prepossess the pious mind in its favour; yet it is too deeply enveloped in clouds and darkness to admit of its becoming generally prevalent. And if what these learned men suppose had been the object of revelation, no doubt some more certain clue would have been given to assist us to ascertain the mind of the Spirit, than the obscure, though learned, criticisms of *Hutchinson.*

The next question which occurs in the course of this investigation is very important. How should the Scriptures be interpreted in order that we may arrive at their *true* and *full* meaning? The obvious answer would be, by attending to the grammatical and literal sense of the words employed, to the force and significance of the figures and allusions used, and to the idiom of the languages in which they are written. But here we are met by a very important and embarrassing question. Is the literal meaning of Scripture always, or generally, the principal and ultimate sense; or, are we to suppose that under this there is a recondite, spiritual meaning contained? Most of the Fathers considered the Scriptures to contain a double sense; the one literal, the other mystical or allegorical; and they regarded the first very little except in relation to the second. The Romanists maintain an opinion very similar; but the mystical sense they divide into several parts. And among Protestants there are many who discover a strong predilection for this mode of interpretation.

But this principle, admitted without limitation or qualification, has a direct tendency to overthrow all certainty in divine revelation. For, as there is no certain key to this mystical or spiritual meaning, every man makes it out according to the liveliness of his own imagination: and weak men by their fanciful expositions greatly degrade the dignity and mar the beauty of revealed truth.

The followers of Baron *Swedenborg,* not contented with two, maintain that the

Scriptures contain three senses, the *celestial, spiritual,* and *natural,* which are connected by *correspondences.* This doctrine of correspondences, is, according to them, the only key to open the true meaning of Scripture; which was, for many ages, lost, but recently was made known to this extraordinary nobleman. Notwithstanding the extravagance of this system, it has charms for some persons, and these not of the illiterate vulgar. It is a sort of refined mysticism, which corresponds with the peculiar turn of some minds that are fond of novelty and disdain to walk in the old beaten track. Reasoning or argument with those who profess to hold familiar intercourse with angels would, I presume, be superfluous. We shall leave them therefore to enjoy their visions of a *terrestrial* heaven, without interruption, whilst we proceed to observe that among the orthodox themselves there is no small difference of opinion respecting the *extent* which may be given to the meaning of Scripture. The celebrated *Cocceius* laid it down as a rule *that Scripture should be considered as signifying all that it could be made to signify.* The whole of the Old Testament, in his opinion, was either typical or prophetical of Messiah and his kingdom. Here, as in a glass, he supposed the future destinies of the church might be viewed. The learned *Grotius* verged to the very opposite extreme in his ideas of the interpretation of Scripture. This gave rise to a saying which became proverbial, respecting these two great men; and which is highly creditable to the piety of the former; *"Grotium nusquam in sacris literis invenire Christum, Cocceium ubique."* "That *Grotius* could find Christ no where in the Bible, *Cocceius* every where."

This rule of *Cocceius,* however, is liable to great abuse; and as *Limborch* justly observes, "is calculated to make of the Scriptures a mere Lesbian rule, or nose of wax, which may be bent into any shape; and seems to be no other than the old allegorical method of interpretation, introduced under a new name."

But, on the other hand, it is certain that many of the *persons, occurrences,* and *ceremonies* of the Old Testament are typical; and some things are thus interpreted in the New Testament which we never should have conjectured to possess any meaning beyond the literal, unless we had been otherwise taught by inspiration. Besides, all judicious commentators are forced to admit that many of the prophecies have a primary and secondary reference, even the most important of those which relate to Messiah are of this description. Those who insist that one meaning and no more belongs to every text are greatly at a loss how to reconcile with their opinion the quotations made from the Old Testament in the New, where they are expressly said to be fulfilled, though certainly, many of them, not in their primary and literal sense. Under the guidance of sound sense and just criticism, we should pursue a middle course between these two extremes. But although we cannot admit the rule of *Cocceius* in all its latitude, nor go the whole way with his followers; yet it is but justice to acknowledge that some of them deserve to be ranked with the first expositors and theologians who have appeared in the church. . . .

Upon the whole, our conclusion respecting this matter is that every particular passage of Scripture should be interpreted according to the peculiar circumstances of the case: the literal should be considered as the true and only meaning, unless some remoter sense be indicated by some peculiar aptitude, correspondence, or fitness, in the words and ideas of the text; or unless it be referred to something else in the Scriptures themselves. Good sense and the analogy of faith are the guides which we should follow in interpreting the Bible.

We come now to consider the *helps* which the Biblical student needs to enable him to search the Scriptures with success. The volumes which we have already supposed to be put into his hands are not written in our vernacular tongue. We have, it is true, an excellent translation of the Scriptures; but this was not made by inspiration, and cannot therefore possess the same authority and infallibility, with the originals. We admit the lawfulness and utility of translations for the use of the people; but nothing can be more evident than that the expounder of Scripture should be well acquainted with the very "words by which the Holy Ghost teacheth" us the will of GOD. The knowledge of the Hebrew and Greek languages, therefore, is a necessary prerequisite to the successful study of the Scriptures. I think I may venture to assert that this single acquisition will be of more importance to the Theological student than all the commentaries which have ever been written. By this means he will be able to see with his own eyes; and will be qualified to judge for himself.

Every person who has had experience will acknowledge that even in reading the plainest texts, there is a satisfaction and advantage to be derived from the original, which cannot easily be explained. It becomes therefore a duty incumbent on all who are candidates for the sacred office, or invested with it, to endeavour to become acquainted with the *original Scriptures.*

But in all writings, and especially such as contain historical facts, there are frequent allusions to the existing customs of the country, and to the prevailing opinions of the people, where the book was written. The same is found to be the case with the Scriptures. Many passages would be quite unintelligible without some acquaintance with Jewish antiquities. The customs and manners of that people should, therefore, be studied with particular attention.

And as scriptural history frequently refers to the condition, character, and transactions of contemporaneous nations, it is of importance to be well acquainted with their history, as delivered to us by profane authors. There is, however, a more important reason why the Biblical student should be well versed in history, ancient and modern; and that is, because *there* he must look for the accomplishment of many important prophecies. Even the fulfilment of the remarkable prediction of Christ respecting the destruction of *Jerusalem* is not recorded in Scripture, but must be sought in the *Jewish* and *Roman* historians.

Chronology and geography are also requisite helps to enable us to understand many parts of Scripture. These have been called the eyes of history; and they are not more so of civil, than sacred history.

Even modern travels have been turned, by some learned men, to a very important account in explaining the Scriptures. For oriental customs and modes of living have not been subject to the same capricious changes which have prevailed in the western nations. And therefore, by observing carefully what oriental customs are, at this day, a very probable opinion may be formed of what they were two thousand years ago. This observation holds good, particularly, in relation to such Eastern nations as have never been conquered, nor incorporated with any other people; as the Arabs, for instance.

Indeed, to speak the truth, there is scarcely any science or branch of knowledge which may not be made subservient to Theology. Natural history, chemistry, and geology have sometimes been of important service in assisting the Biblical student to solve difficulties contained in Scripture; or in enabling him to repel the assaults of adversaries which were made under cover of these sciences. A general acquaintance with the whole circle of science is of more consequence to the Theologian than at first sight appears. Not to mention the intimate connexion which subsists between all the parts of truth, in consequence of which important light may often be collected from the remotest quarters; it may be observed that the state of learning in the world requires the advocate of the Bible to attend to many things which may not in themselves be absolutely necessary. He must maintain his standing as a man of learning. He must be able to converse on the various topics of learning with other literary men; otherwise the due respect will not be paid to him; and his sacred office may suffer contempt, in consequence of his appearing to be ignorant of what it is expected all learned men should be acquainted with.[5]

But next to the knowledge of the original languages, an acquaintance with early translations is most important. The Septuagint, the Chaldaic paraphrase, the Syriac, and the Vulgate, deserve to be particularly mentioned. . . .

The Vulgate is commonly supposed to have been made by *Jerome,* and to have succeeded to older Latin versions. It was, for many ages, the only medium through which the revelation contained in holy Scripture was viewed in the western part of the church. The Romanists, considering that this version could be made to favour their pretensions and corruptions, more than the original, bent all their force to the support of its authority; whilst at the same time, they let slip no opportunity of disparaging the Hebrew text. At length they proceeded so far as to decree, in the Council of Trent, "that it should be reckoned as *the authentic standard by which all disputations, preachings, and expositions, should be judged; and that no person should dare to reject its authority on any pretext whatever."* The more liberal Catholics themselves, are ashamed of the unblushing effrontery of this decree; and what slender foundation there was for so high a claim may be conjectured from this circumstance, that a learned man of their own communion declares that he had himself noted *eighty thousand* errors in this version.[6] But, nevertheless, it may be useful in many ways to the Biblical student, and being written in Latin, is accessible to every scholar. And here I will take occasion to remark, the great importance of a familiar acquaintance with the Latin language, to the Theologian. Although no part of Scripture is written in that language, yet it is almost essentially

5. Samuel Miller shared the same concern for clerical status in his arguments for a seminary; see Miller, *Sermon at the Inauguration,* pp. 9, 43; *Minutes of the General Assembly,* pp. 457–58.
6. Alexander's note: "Isidore Clarius."

necessary to pass through this vestibule in order to arrive at the knowledge of any other ancient language; most valuable grammars and dictionaries being written in Latin: and almost all Theological works, not designed for the immediate use of the people, were composed in this language, prior to the middle of the last century, a very small portion of which have been translated into English. The course of Theological study would indeed be very much circumscribed, if we were destitute of this key to unlock its rich treasures. It would lead me into a discussion too long, to consider what assistance may be derived from the writings of the Fathers; what from the Schoolmen; what from the Reformers; and what from more modern commentators and critics, in the interpretation of the Scriptures. The time allotted for this discourse would be entirely insufficient to do justice to this subject. I shall therefore leave it untouched, and proceed to mention,

A HELP which, though put in the last place in this discourse, is of more real importance than all the rest; and that is *the illumination and assistance of the Holy Spirit.* Illumination differs from inspiration in this respect; that whereas by the latter we are made acquainted with truths before unrevealed, or unknown, by the former we are enabled to discern the beauty and real nature of the truths contained in a revelation already made. It is obvious that in the study of divine truth much depends on the temper and condition of the student's mind. A proud and self-sufficient person, however endowed with acuteness of intellect, and furnished with stores of literature, is continually prone to fall into pernicious error; whilst the humble man occupies a station from which truth may be viewed to advantage. Prejudice, proceeding from education or passion, blinds the mind and warps the judgment; but the sincere and ardent love of truth disposes us to view the whole evidence, and impartially to weigh the arguments on both sides of any question. As much therefore depends upon preserving our own minds in a proper state, as upon the diligent use of external means of information. The conclusion from these premises is that the student of sacred literature should be possessed of sincere and ardent piety. He should be a man "taught of GOD," conscious of his own insufficiency, but confident of the help of the Almighty. Indeed, when we consider the weakness of the human intellect, and the various prejudices and false impressions to which it is constantly liable, we must be convinced that without divine assistance, there is little hope of arriving at the knowledge of truth, or preserving it when acquired. He, who would understand the Scriptures, therefore, ought not to "lean to his own understanding," but by continual and earnest prayer should look unto the "Father of lights," from whom proceedeth every good and every perfect gift; and who hath promised to give wisdom to those who lack it, and ask for it.

There is no person who needs more to be in the constant exercise of prayer than the Theological student: not only at stated periods, but continually in the midst of his studies, his heart should be raised to heaven for help and direction. A defect here, it is to be feared, is one principal reason why so much time and labour are often employed in theological studies with so little profit to the church. *That* knowledge which puffeth up is acquired; but charity, which edifieth, is neglected.

When the serious mind falls into doubt respecting divine truths, the remedy is not always reasoning and argument, but divine illumination. The mind may be in such a state that it is rather perplexed, than relieved, by mere human reasoning; but at such times a lively impression made by the Spirit of truth banishes all doubt and hesitation; and then the same texts or arguments which were before unavailing to our conviction and satisfaction exhibit the truth in a light as clear as demonstration. This may appear to some to savour of enthusiasm. Be it so. It is, however, an enthusiasm essential to the very nature of our holy religion, without which it would be a mere dry system of speculation, of ethics and ceremonies. But this *divine illumination* is its *life*, its *soul*, its *essence*. It is true, this influence is not peculiar to the Theologian. Every sincere Christian, in his measure, partakes of this "anointing," by which he is taught to know all things; but the teacher of religion needs a double portion of this spirit. How often does the minister of the Gospel labour and toil with all his might without producing any thing of importance, for edification! But if he receive the aid of the Spirit, his text is opened and illustrated without any painful exertion of his own. He is conscious, indeed, that he is a mere recipient. The train of thought which occupies his mind appears to originate in some occult cause which he cannot trace. And happy would it be for preachers, happy for their hearers, if there were more dependence on divine assistance, not only in the composition, but in the delivery of sermons! When God shall appear in his glory, to build up Jerusalem, he will raise up, I have no doubt, a race of preachers, who shall partake of this heavenly gift in a much higher degree than has heretofore been common. He will bring forward to the sacred office men possessing *boldness*, founded on their reliance upon divine assistance; *clearness*, proceeding from divine illumination; and that *unction* which flows from the sweet and lively experience of the truth delivered, in the heart of the preacher. The solicitous, and often unsuccessful, effort to rise to some artificial standard of oratory, shall then yield to nobler motives; and the preacher, like *Paul*, shall be willing to make a sacrifice of his own reputation for learning, and refinement, at the foot of the cross: and to count all things but loss for the excellency of the knowledge of Jesus Christ his LORD. Gospel simplicity and sincerity shall then be preferred by the Man of God to all the soaring flights of eloquence, and to all the splendid trappings and tinsel of human science. May it please the Lord of the vineyard speedily to send forth many such labourers into his harvest; *for the harvest is great, and the labourers are few!*

I will now bring this discourse to a conclusion, by offering some motives to excite the Theological student to diligence in the perusal of the sacred Scriptures.

A book has a claim upon our time and study, on account of the authority by which it comes recommended, the excellency of the matter comprehended in it, and the interest which we have involved in the knowledge of its contents. On all these accounts the Bible has the highest possible claim on our attention. It comes to us, as we have proved, authenticated as the word of God; stamped as it were with the signature of heaven; and recommended to our diligent perusal by the Lord Jesus Christ. The matter which it contains is, like its origin, divine: *truth*, pure, glorious and all important truth, constitutes the subject of this Book. The saying ascribed to Mr. Locke when he took leave of a beloved relation, shortly before his end, was worthy of that profound genius; "Study," said he, "the Sacred Scriptures; they have God for their author, truth without mixture of error for their matter, and eternal life for their end."[7] If we should take the lowest view of the subject, and form our opinion of the Scriptures by the same rules by which we judge of human compositions, they will be found to transcend the highest efforts of human genius, as far as the heavens are above the earth. Hear on this subject the decision of a scholar, in whom learning and taste in their highest perfection were combined; "I have regularly and attentively read these holy Scriptures, and am of opinion that this volume, independently of its divine origin, contains more sublimity and beauty, purer morality, and finer strains of poetry and eloquence, than can be collected from all other books, in whatever age or language they may have been composed."[8] But the excellency of the Scriptures cannot be appreciated by the rules of human criticism. As well might we think of judging of the proportions of the celestial arch, or the location of the stars in the vast expanse, by the rules of architecture. The word of God, like his works, is on a plan too vast, too sublime, too profound, to be measured by the feeble intellect of man.

Fully to explain how worthy the Scriptures are of our attention, on account of the matter comprehended in them, would require us to exhibit all the truths which they contain; but as this cannot be done in one, or a few discourses, I will now content myself with mentioning a few leading points, on which the Scriptures furnish us with information of the most important kind.

In the first place, then, it is here, and here alone, that we can learn the true character of God. The indistinct outline which may be traced in the works of creation is here filled up. The knowledge of God which could be derived from a view of his works would not be sufficient for man, even in a state of innocence; and much less so when he is fallen into sin. None have ever been able to form just conceptions of the Deity from the light of nature alone. A revelation was absolutely necessary to teach man what God is; and the Bible contains all the information which we need on this subject. Here the divine glory is revealed. The moral attributes of Deity, especially, are represented in the clearest, strongest light. Truths respecting the divine nature are here revealed, concerning which reason and philosophy could never have formed a conjecture. The glorious and mysterious doctrine of a Trinity in unity is taught from the beginning to the end of the Bible; a doctrine offensive to the pride of man, but one which will afford subject for profound contemplation through eternity. From the Scriptures we learn not only that God is holy, just, merciful, and faithful; but we behold these attributes harmonizing in a work which, according to all the views that finite wisdom could have taken of it, must have placed them in a state of complete variance; that is, in the justification and salvation of a sinner. In the redemption of Christ these divine perfections not

---

7. Alexander included no citation for this quotation.

8. Alexander's note: "Found written in his own hand, on a blank leaf of Sir *William Jones's* Bible, after his death." William Jones (1726–1800) was an Anglican editor, founder of the theological quarterly *British Critic*, and prolific author on theological topics.

only appear harmonious; *"mercy and truth having met together, and righteousness and peace having kissed each other";* but in the cross are exhibited with a lustre and glory which, according to our conceptions, could not have been given to them in any other circumstances. If we would know *the only true God,* then we must "search the Scriptures."

In the next place, we obtain from the Bible a satisfactory account of the origin of evil, natural and moral. Not, indeed, an explanation of the reason why it was permitted; but such an account of its introduction as is perfectly consistent with the honour and purity of the divine government. We here learn that God created man "in a state of innocency, with freedom and power to will and do that which was well pleasing to himself, but yet mutable, so that he might fall from it."[9] This liberty was abused by man: sin therefore owes its origin to the creature, who is wholly chargeable with its blame; although it did not take place without the knowledge, nor contrary to the purpose, of the infinite God. The first man being the root of all his posterity, and being appointed to act for them as well as for himself, they are involved with him in all the consequences of his fall; for *"they sinned in him and fell with him in his first transgression."* All the streams of sin and misery in the world flow from this original fountain. And so deep and dreadful is this fall of man that he is utterly unable to recover himself from the guilt and depravity into which he is by nature sunk.

The last mentioned article of information would be only calculated to plunge us into the depths of misery and despair, were it not, that the Scriptures teach us the consoling doctrine of *redemption.* Indeed, the whole Bible may be considered as a history of Redemption. Here we can trace the wondrous plan up to its origin, in the eternal counsels of peace. Here we read of the early development of this plan, after the fall, in paradise. The incarnation and victory of the glorious Redeemer was clearly intimated in the promise, *"that the seed of the woman should bruise the serpent's head."* To this object, the faith of the pious was directed by every new revelation and institution. Prophets, in long succession, with lips touched with hallowed fire described and predicted *Immanuel.* Although their prophecies are often expressed in dark symbolical language, yet sometimes from the midst of this darkness there are vivid coruscations of light which exhibit the promised Messiah as visibly, as if he had already come. At length the fulness of time arrived, and *"God sent forth his Son made of a woman, made under the law to redeem them that were under the law." "God was now manifest in the flesh."* And he *"who being in the form of God, thought it no robbery to be equal with God, made himself of no reputation, and took upon him the form of a servant, and was made in the likeness of men; and being found in fashion as a man, he humbled himself and became obedient unto death, even the death of the cross; wherefore God also hath highly exalted him, and given him a name which is above every name."* The redemption of the church by the blood of the Son of God is a subject on which angels look with

9. Westminster Confession 9.2.

wonder; and it is a subject, which through eternity will furnish a theme for the songs of the redeemed of the LORD.

But the Scriptures give us information, not only of the work of the Redeemer in procuring for us an "everlasting righteousness"; but also of the work of the Spirit in uniting the redeemed soul to Jesus Christ; in regenerating, sanctifying, supporting, guiding, and comforting it; until it is "made meet for the inheritance of the saints in light."

Another important article of information which we find in the Scriptures of truth is a clear expression of the will of God in relation to the duty of man. There are, it is true, traces of the law of God still remaining on the heart of every man; but these are far from being sufficient to show him the full extent, and the spiritual nature, of the duties required of him. And what might be known from honestly inquiring of our own consciences respecting our duty is often missed through the influence of false principles, instilled into the mind by a defective education, and by customs become universally prevalent, through the corruption of human nature. But we need be no longer at a loss about the law of God. He condescended to publish it, with his own voice, in the hearing of all *Israel;* and to write it with his own finger, on tables of stone. To explain this law, we have many comments from inspired men; but especially we have the lucid exposition of the Lawgiver himself; and, what is more important, we behold it fully illustrated and exemplified in the obedience which HE, in our nature, and for our sakes, rendered to it; so that, if we now wish to know our duty, we have only to contemplate the character of Jesus Christ. If we wish to do it, we have only to walk in his foot-steps.

Finally, the Scriptures contain a distinct and full revelation of futurity, as far as it is necessary for us to know what is to be hereafter. In them, "life and immortality are brought to light." Full assurance is given, by the testimony of one who cannot lie, that "an exceeding great and eternal weight of glory" is reserved for the people of God in another world. In the New Testament we are made familiar with heaven by the frequency with which it is mentioned and described. The existence of a future world is no longer left to be collected by uncertain reasoning and probable conjecture. It is now a matter of testimony. Faith has a firm ground on which to rest; for this truth is linked with every fact and doctrine of the Gospel; is seen in every promise and threatening under the new dispensation. But the Scriptures reveal not only a heaven of glory, but a hell of horror; a dark and "bottomless pit," *"where the worm dieth not, and where the fire is not quenched," and where "there is weeping, and wailing, and gnashing of teeth."* They give us the certain assurance, also, of a day being appointed in which God will judge the world in righteousness by that man whom he hath ordained; and in which they that are in their graves shall rise, some to everlasting life and glory, and others to everlasting shame and contempt.

From this brief survey of what the Scriptures teach us, we must be convinced of the great importance of being well acquainted with them. Our own salvation is involved in the right knowledge of this book; and if we are teachers of others, how important is it that we "as good stewards of the mysteries of GOD" be "able rightly to divide the word of truth, giving to every one his portion in due season." We should, therefore, "meditate on these things, and give ourselves wholly to them, that our profiting may appear unto all." We must "take heed unto ourselves, and to our doctrine, and continue in them; for by so doing we shall both save ourselves and them that hear us."

But we shall not only find the Scriptures to be a source of profitable instruction; a rich mine of truth which has never yet been fully explored; but also a source of pure and permanent delight.

As the natural light is pleasant to the eyes, so is truth to the understanding, unless some moral disease render its approach unacceptable. "They whose deeds are evil, love darkness rather than light"; but the regenerate soul "rejoices in the truth." Food to the hungry is not more pleasant, nor cold water more refreshing to the thirsty, than evangelical truth to the pious mind. It is, indeed, the bread of life which cometh down from heaven; the hidden manna, with which the spiritual Israel are fed, whilst they sojourn in this wilderness. The person who has been taught of God prefers the truths of his word to all earthly treasures, and to all the sweets of nature. "More are they to be desired, than gold, yea, than much fine gold: sweeter also than honey and the honey comb." "The law of thy mouth is better unto me than thousands of gold and silver." "Thy statutes have been my song in the house of my pilgrimage." How delightful must it be to sit as a disciple at the feet of Jesus, and with a child-like docility imbibe precious instruction from his word and Spirit! When we fall under the power of some overwhelming temptation, or when dark clouds of adversity thicken around us, in the truths and promises of our GOD, we find our only refuge. In the sanctuary, when the oracles of God are delivered, doubt and unbelief, sorrow and despair, are driven away. Here divine beauty beams with mild effulgence on the soul, and the troubled spirit is charmed to rest. *"One day in thy courts is better than a thousand." "One thing have I desired of the Lord, that will I seek after, that I may dwell in the house of the Lord, all the days of my life, to behold the beauty of the Lord."*

When Jesus joins himself to his disconsolate disciples, how soon is their sorrow turned into joy! And whilst he "opens their understandings to understand the Scriptures," "how do their hearts burn within them!" That which above all things makes the Scriptures precious, and the study of them delightful, is that there we can find *Jesus Christ.* We have no need to say, "who shall ascend into heaven, that is, to bring Christ down from above; or who shall descend into the deep, that is, to bring up Christ again from the dead?" For, "the word is nigh *us,* even in *our* mouth, and in *our* heart; that is, the word of faith which we preach." "Christ and him crucified," is the centre of the Christian's religion, the foundation of his faith and hope, and the perennial spring of all his pleasures and his joys. When at any time it pleases God to shine upon his word, whilst the believer reads its sacred contents, what a divine glory illuminates the holy page! What attractive beauty draws forth the best affections of his heart! What wonders do his opened eyes behold in the cross! He seems to be translated into a new world, and is ready to exclaim, "I have heard of thee by the hearing of the ear; but now mine eye seeth thee." "Old things are passed away, and behold, all things are become new." O! could the pious reader of the Scriptures constantly retain these spiritual views and these holy impressions, heaven would be begun. This wilderness would "bud and blossom as the rose," and paradise be renewed on earth. But "this is not our rest, it is polluted"; that *re-maineth for the people of God;* even *"an inheritance incorruptible, undefiled, and that fadeth not away, reserved in the heavens for us, who are kept by the power of God through faith unto salvation, ready to be revealed in the last time."*

But whilst we are on our pilgrimage to this promised land, the Scriptures will be "a light to our feet and a lamp to our paths." They will answer the same purpose to us which the pillar of cloud and of fire did to the Israelites. They will guide us in the right way through all our journey. Let us, then, be persuaded diligently "to search the Scriptures."

I beg leave to conclude this discourse in the words of the pious *Weller*, the friend and disciple of *Luther:* "I admonish you again and again, that you read the sacred Scriptures in a far different manner from that in which you read any other book: that you approach them with the highest reverence, and most intense application of your mind; not as the words of a man, nor an angel, but as the words of the Divine Majesty, the least of which should have more weight with us, than the writings of the wisest and most learned men in the world."[10]

10. Alexander's note: "Consilium De Studio Theologiae." Hieronymus Weller von Molsdorf (1499–1572) was a colleague of Luther from 1527 to 1535 and a staunch advocate of Luther's views.

5

The Bible and the Natural World
1829

The stake of the Princeton theologians in science was great. In the first place they regularly conceived of theology as a science (as in the first words of Selection 3), and this gave them a great concern to understand the nature, domain, and prospects of scientific inquiry. In the second, they were evidentialists who thought that study of the natural world would necessarily demonstrate the existence of God and the validity of divine revelation. It was, therefore, a matter of grave concern when the name of science and the reputation of scientists were ranged against their orthodox convictions. To such threats they reacted not only by defending the integrity of orthodoxy, but also by defining the proper domain for the scientific enterprise. They themselves struggled hard to be "scientific" in both the medieval sense of the word (systematic inquiry generally) and the modern (systematic study of nature particularly). Alexander's essay which appears below is an early example of those efforts.

It begins with natural law arguments—cosmological and teleological, as well as proofs from Design—to demonstrate the necessity of a Creator. It then goes on to show how Scripture tells the same, and more. "Common sense," especially, shows that alternative theories—whether atheism, pantheism, or something in between—do not work. Nearly half the essay, however, treats arguments concerning the unity of the human race. This was an absolutely central concern for the Princeton theologians. The unity of humanity was vital because the Bible taught it. But the unity of the race was also vital because it was on the basis of *common* sense—the collective perceptions of all humanity—that the Princetonians rested their arguments for God and for Scripture. To suggest that the human race was not a single, unified species thus undercut not only a longstanding interpretation of early Genesis, but also the very premise of a common-sense apologetics. Alexander's arguments for the unity of humanity follow in general those presented by Witherspoon's successor as president of Princeton College, Samuel Stanhope Smith (1751-1819), who made them in a well-received volume published first in 1787 and then expanded in 1810, *An Essay on the Causes of the Variety of Complexion and Figure in the Human Species.*[1] They are arguments to which both Charles Hodge and Warfield returned as they too contended against the idea of multiple origins for humankind (e.g., Hodge, "The Unity of Mankind," BRPR, 31 [January 1859], 103ff.; Warfield, Selection 26).

1. Smith's expanded work has been published in a modern edition, with careful notes, by Winthrop D. Jordan (Cambridge: Harvard University Press, 1965).

It is fitting that this essay, which stakes out the proper domain of scientific inquiry, should have appeared in the first issue of the reorganized BRPR, 1 (January 1829), 101-120, a journal which itself existed to define and defend the boundaries of orthodoxy. The essay's full title was "The Bible, A Key to the Phenomena of the Natural World." It is presented here in its entirety.

T HE STUPENDOUS FABRIC of the universe, part of which we see, and part of which we ourselves are, cannot but become an object of earnest contemplation to the inquisitive mind. The great majority of men, it is true, pass through life without reflection. Their intellectual powers are so little cultivated, and they are so much occupied with objects of sense, and in making provision for their immediate and pressing wants, that they never attempt to raise their minds to the contemplation of the wonderful works by which they are surrounded: but accustomed from infancy to behold these objects, they excite no surprise, and seldom call forth a single reflection. There have always been, however, among nations enjoying any degree of civilization, men of minds more cultivated than the rest, and more disposed to investigate the causes of those phenomena, which they continually beheld. These sages, when they looked upon the heavens and the earth, upon themselves and other organized and living beings, have been led to inquire, whence all these things? Have they always existed? or have they been produced? To those who have been conversant with the truth all their lives, it may seem that it would have been an easy thing for any rational mind to ascend, at once, from the creature to the invisible Creator: but we cannot readily conceive of the perplexity and darkness which surround the intellect of men whom no ray of divine revelation has visited. The reasonings of such men are also impeded and perverted by prejudices and erroneous opinions imbibed from their forefathers; and, not unfrequently, pride and other evil passions influence speculative men to adopt extravagant opinions, for the sake of their paradoxical character, or because they are naturally grateful to the feelings of depraved nature. It is, therefore, not an unaccountable fact that men, unenlightened by divine revelation, should have fallen into so many egregious errors respecting the origin of the world and its inhabitants.

A considerable number of those called philosophers entertained the opinion that the universe always existed as we now behold it. They observed that from age to age the heavenly bodies move on in their orbits, undisturbed and unchanged; and that on earth the same changes of day and night, of winter and summer, of seed time and harvest, succeed each other in regular order: and no other power being manifest to the senses but that which operates through all nature, they concluded, that the universe existed without any cause of itself; and that it ever had existed, and ever would exist as it now appears.

Some, however, observing in all things, as they imagined, a tendency to dissolution, and perceiving in our globe evidences of a former destruction, adopted the opinion that the universe contained in itself the principles of its own dissolution and regeneration; —that, after running through a period of unknown and inconceivable duration, it falls into a chaotic state, in which catastrophe all organized bodies are destroyed and return to their simplest elements; but, from this chaos, by degrees, springs up a new order of things or a renewal of that which before existed; and thus, while they conceived the universe to be eternal, they imagined that it is in a state of perpetual change by a kind of circular progression which has neither beginning nor end.

Others of those called philosophers, who seem to have paid a more minute attention to the curious structure of organized bodies, were of opinion that they must, by some means, have been formed or produced; but, not being able to rise to the conception of a Creator—or what is more probable, not liking to retain the idea of God in their minds—they invented the hypothesis of the eternal existence of the elements of the universe, which they supposed to consist of atoms or indivisible bodies of all manner of shapes, and in perpetual motion among each other. These atoms, possessing various affinities, came together in every conceivable form of organized bodies, until, by degrees, and in a long process of time, the universe assumed its present aspect, and vegetables and animals of every species were produced by the fortuitous concourse of atoms.

Such a hypothesis might seem too absurd to be seriously entertained by any rational mind, and yet we find among its abettors men of high and cultivated intellect among the ancients. It has, however, met with less favour among modern atheists than the fore-mentioned theories; although, in point of absurdity, all systems of atheism may be said to stand on a perfect level; for no folly can be conceived greater than that which says, "there is no God."

The idea of the necessity of a cause, wherever we observe what we must consider an effect, is so deeply engrained in human nature that most men have professed themselves dissatisfied with any system which assigned no cause, or no better cause than chance or necessity for the existence of all things. Many have been led, therefore, to adopt the opinion that the universe was God, believing that whatever distinctness and variety there may seem to be in the world, there existed but one substance or being of which the heavens and the earth, vegetables and animals are only so many parts, or rather manifestations. This theory differs from the first mentioned in this important respect, that it recognizes a great first cause, which is God; but the difference, as to any useful end, is more in appearance than in reality; for, according to this hypothesis, there is still nothing in existence besides the universe itself. There is no free, sovereign, independent being whom we should worship or obey; or in whom we can confide for help or safety. In fact, it differs from blank atheism in nothing, except that it gives the name of God to the universe of creatures: and thus we come to the horrible conclusion that we and all other things are parts of God.

Although this hypothesis had its advocates among the ancients, yet Benedict Spinoza has the credit of reducing it to a regular system which he exhibited in the imposing form of mathematical demonstration. As this atheistical theory was published in an enlightened age, and in a Christian country, it might have been expected that it would attract but few admirers: and, indeed, the number of avowed disciples of Spinozism has been small; yet the same system, new-modelled but not improved, has become a favourite with a large number of philosophers of the present day on the continent of Europe, and especially in Germany, under the appropriate name of Pantheism. And so great is the infatuation of some calling themselves Christians, that they have thought that this disguised atheism might be reconciled with Christianity.

A system less absurd than any of the former was that the world has an all-pervading, active, and intelligent soul, which moved and directed all the operations of nature, as the human soul moves and governs the body.

Near akin to this was the opinion that the planets and stars were all animated bodies, possessed of the power of moving themselves, and of intelligence sufficient to guide and regulate their own motions.

Many students of the physical sciences in our times seem to have adopted a theory similar to that which gives a soul to the world. They ascribe all effects to *nature* and to the laws of nature. In all the remarkable contrivances and evidences of design which abound in the animal and vegetable worlds, they see nothing but the plastic power of nature. The idea of a God, distinct from the world, and from whom nature derives all its powers, seems to have no place in their philosophy.

But sometimes the doctrine of *the soul of the world*, has been combined with that of one supreme God, as in the sublime but mystical theory of Plato.

From what has been said, it is evident that the human intellect is prone to wander from the truth; and that reason is liable to be perverted, even in matters of the highest importance; and in which the light of evidence seems to us to shine most clearly.

A just and impartial consideration of the universe, cannot fail to lead the sincere seeker of truth to the opinion, that there must exist a great first cause, powerful and intelligent, who has made the world for some particular end. As sound reason would constrain us, if we should find a curiously contrived machine, evidently formed for a useful purpose, to ascribe it to an intelligent artificer, how can we refuse to ascribe the structure of the universe, in which the evidences of design are more numerous and more striking, infinitely, than in any of the works of men, to a wise and powerful architect?[2] If a watch or steam-engine could not be formed by the accidental aggregation of particles, brought together by the winds or waves, how can we suppose that such a structure as a completely organized animal body could be formed by a fortuitous concourse of atoms? There is in a small part of the

---

2. Alexander here reasons very similarly to William Paley, who began his famous *Natural Theology* (1802) by speaking of the valid inference we could make of a purposeful designer if, on crossing an empty heath, we discovered a watch. Elsewhere, however, Alexander speaks disparagingly of Paley: "No man . . . has done more to corrupt the true theory of morals than Dr. Paley"; "The Elements of Moral Science," BRPR 8 (July 1835): 377–401. Alexander was particularly offended by the utilitarian thrust of Paley's *Moral and Political Philosophy* (1785). On the use and dismissal of Paley in America, see D. H. Meyer, *The Instructed Conscience: The Shaping of the American National Ethic* (Philadelphia: University of Pennsylvania Press, 1972), pp. 7–9, 22.

human body, more profound wisdom in designing the texture and organization of the parts for the attainment of a particular end, than in all the curious mechanism of man's contrivance. And if we should even suppose (absurd as it is) that such an organized system could come into existence without design, how could we account for the wonderful adaptation of other things, existing in an entirely separate state, to the necessities and conveniences of the animal body? Without light the eye would be useless, but when we examine the mechanism of this organ, and observe that it is constructed upon the most perfect principles of optics, can we for a moment hesitate to believe that the eye was formed by a designing agent to receive, refract, and concentrate the rays of light for the purposes of vision? The same adaption is remarkable between the air and the organ of hearing; and between the air and the lungs; the same is also true in regard to the stomach and the food which it so eagerly craves. In these, and a thousand other things, the evidences of design are as strong as they possibly can be. If we can resist these, no other proofs would answer any purpose in removing our incredulity.

Reason, then, clearly indicates that this universe is not God, but is the work of God, and that he must be a being of transcendent perfection. But having arrived at this conclusion, who would not wish to have his faith confirmed by some clear manifestation of this august Being? If he exists and formed our bodies, and gave us our rational powers, surely he can find out ways by which he can make himself known to us. He cannot, indeed, render himself visible to our bodily eyes because he is a spirit; but he who indued man with the faculty of communicating with his fellows by the use of speech, can speak to us in a language which we can understand. Now this very thing he has done, by divine revelation. By inspiring chosen individuals, and attesting their communications, he has plainly informed us not only that he exists, but that he is the Creator, Preserver, and Governor of the universe; that he is above all, and independent of all; and that all things were produced by his own pleasure, and for his own glory.

That which reason often missed, or mistook, and at best spelled out with hesitation, the voice of revelation declares with decisive authority.

Reason may vaunt herself when the discovery is made, but she owes her clearest light and firmest convictions to the voice of inspiration.

The Bible furnishes the full and satisfactory commentary on the book of nature. With the Bible in our hands, the heavens shine with redoubled lustre. The universe, which to the atheist is full of darkness and confusion, to the Christian is resplendent with light and glory. The first sentence in the Bible contains more to satisfy the inquisitive mind than all the volumes of human speculation. "In the beginning God created the heavens and the earth." Here, in a few words, is comprehended the most sublime of all truths—the production of a universe out of nothing by the word of the Almighty. If God created the heavens and the earth, then he existed before they were brought forth—even from eternity; for he who gives beginning to all other things can have none himself. Before the world was, this august Being existed, independent and happy, in the plenitude of his own infinite perfections. This first word of written revelation teaches us what reason in her boldest flights could never reach, namely, that the universe sprang from nothing—not from nothing as its cause, but from the inconceivable working of almighty power where nothing existed from which it could be made. None of the heathen sages ever believed such a creation possible. They universally received it as an axiom, that *ex nihilo nihil fieri* [nothing comes from nothing]: but here we learn "That the worlds were framed by the word of God, and that the things which are seen, were not made of things which do appear." This stupendous work, of giving being to so great a multitude and variety of creatures, is often celebrated in the sublime strains of sacred poetry and in the commanding eloquence of the inspired prophets. "Thus saith the Lord, that created the heavens and stretched them out, he that spread forth the earth and that which cometh out of it." "Which made heaven and earth, the sea, and all that therein is." "He hath made the earth by his power, he hath established the world by his wisdom, and hath stretched out the heavens by his discretion."

"O Lord God, behold thou hast made the heavens and the earth, by thy great power."

"The Lord which stretcheth forth the heavens, and layeth the foundations of the earth, and formeth the spirit of man within him."

The apostles tread in the footsteps of the prophets, in ascribing the creation of the universe to God alone, "The living God, which made the heavens and the earth, and all things therein."

"God that made the world and all things therein." "For the invisible things of him from the creation of the world, are clearly seen, being understood by the things that are made, even his eternal power and Godhead."

"He that built all things is God."

With such declarations as these coming from the mouth of God himself, how is the mind enlarged and elevated in contemplating the heavens and the earth! How grand, how beautiful, how wise, how harmonious, is the universe, when viewed through the medium of divine revelation. "The heavens declare the glory of God, and the firmament sheweth his handy work: day unto day uttereth speech, and night unto night teacheth knowledge."

"O Lord our Lord, how excellent is thy name in all the earth! who hast set thy glory above the heavens"—"When I consider thy heavens, the work of thy fingers, the moon and the stars which thou hast ordained; what is man that thou art mindful of him? And the son of man that thou visitest him?"

Without the book of revelation, the book of nature would be as a volume sealed; but with this key, we can open its wonderful pages, and receive instruction from every creature of God.

2. But let us descend from the contemplation of the universe, to the consideration of some of its parts. Here is the race of mankind and multitudes of living creatures in the earth, the air, and the water; whence have they proceeded? What can reason and philosophy answer? Had man and the other animals a beginning, or were they from eternity? If the former, from what cause and by what steps did they arrive at their present condition? On no subject has philosophy betrayed her

weakness more than in her speculations respecting the origin of the human race. It would be poorly worth our while to review the absurd theories of ancient and modern philosophers, which more resemble the dreams of the sick than the sober deductions of reason. One will give to the earth I know not what prolific power to produce men and animals; another chooses to place man in his origin on a level with the speechless brutes, from which condition he is supposed to arise by long and assiduous exertion; acquiring for himself the use of articulate and written language, and inventing, from time to time, all the arts which now minister to the comfort of civilized life. But such theories are too absurd for refutation. The idea of the production of animals or vegetables by what was called equivocal generation, that is, without progenitors or organized seeds and roots has long since been exploded. Experiments the most decisive have demonstrated the falsehood of the notions, entertained by the ancients, of the generation of animated beings from mere corruption. The men and animals now on the earth belong to a series reaching back to eternity; or, they were formed and placed on our globe, by an almighty Being. Let us then, for a moment, look at the theory which assigns to man an existence without beginning. While the individuals die, the species is immortal. If such a hypothesis does not do violence to common sense, it would be difficult to say what does. Each individual is dependent, and yet the whole series of individuals, independent. The absurdity and contradiction of such a theory is only concealed by the darkness of eternity. By running back until we are overwhelmed with a subject which our minds cannot grasp, we are apt to lose sight of the unreasonableness of a supposition, which on a limited scale, every one can clearly see. As if one should say, here is a chain suspended consisting of a thousand links, each one depending on the next above it; could such a chain of a thousand links remain suspended without any thing to support it? To such a problem, every child would give the correct answer. The thing is manifestly impossible. Well, suppose the number of links be increased to a hundred million, could the chain support itself any better than when it consisted of a thousand, or even ten links? Certainly not; would be the answer of every person of common sense; and such a person would be apt to say, the more links there are in the chain, the more support does it require, seeing its tendency to fall will be in proportion to its weight. But then, suppose the links so increased that our minds can no longer conceive of the number, will such an increase, however great it may be, render a support less necessary? The answer ought be as decisively as before in the negative. We have seen that the increase of the number, while within the limits of our conception, did not lessen the necessity for a supporting power, and why should such an increase as goes far beyond our power of imagination be supposed to have this effect? The idea of a series of men without beginning and without any Creator to give them being is one of the greatest absurdities which can be conceived.

Besides, when we consider the number of men; when we trace their history; when we reflect upon their small advancement in the arts and sciences; and how recent the most useful inventions are; how can we, unless we renounce our reason, believe that mankind has existed on this globe from eternity? The thing is impossible.

The only reasonable hypothesis, therefore, is that the human race, together with the various species of animals and vegetables, had a beginning and that they were created by a wise and omnipotent Being, by whose care and sustaining power they are still preserved.

But man feels too little satisfied with his own reasonings to rest contented with such conclusions as he can himself deduce. He wishes to see the face, or hear the voice, of his great Creator. He wants an explicit declaration from the mouth of his Father in heaven, assuring him of the truth of his own reasonings; and authorizing him to claim the relation of a creature formed by the power and goodness of God.

Such a desire of divine instruction is neither sinful nor unreasonable in creatures situated as we are. Who would not wish to know his own earthly father? And who would like, on such a subject, to be left to reasonings founded on abstract principles? But how much more interesting is it for us to know our heavenly Father, to whom we owe our very being, with all its faculties and capacities? Now this reasonable desire the great Creator has condescended to gratify. He has, in the revelation which is contained in the Holy Scriptures, informed us not only that he is our Maker, but has given us most particular information of the time and circumstances of man's creation. After the heavens and the earth, and beasts, fishes, and birds, were formed; in short, after all things on earth were created, God, speaking in the glorious council of his own Being, said, "Come, let us make man in our own image, and after our own likeness: and let them have dominion over the fish of the sea, and over the fowl of the air, and over the cattle, and over all the earth."—"So God created man in his own image; in the image of God created he him." "And the Lord God formed man of the dust of the ground, and breathed into his nostrils the breath of life: and man became a living soul." "And the Lord God said, it is not good that the man should be alone, I will make an help-meet for him." "And the Lord God caused a deep sleep to fall upon Adam; and he slept, and he took one of his ribs, and closed up the flesh instead thereof. And the rib which the Lord God had taken from man made he a woman, and brought her unto the man; and Adam said, this is now bone of my bone, and flesh of my flesh: she shall be called woman, because she was taken out of man."

I have, somewhere, met with an account of an infidel, more ingenious than wise, who proposed to put the Mosaic history to the test by examining whether man was deficient of a rib in one of his sides. It would have been as reasonable to have examined whether every male descendant of Adam had the scar of the wound made in the side of the first man. If Adam had remained all his life destitute of the rib which was taken away, why should it be supposed that this defect should be transmitted to his posterity? But he laboured under no such defect, for the opening made was closed up with flesh instead of that which was taken away. The rib was not taken on account of any difficulty to obtain materials, but to show that a man and his wife were one, and that a man should ever cherish his wife as his own flesh. The word here translated *rib*, properly means, *a side:* for aught that appears, the whole side of the man might have been taken to form the woman; but this is a matter of no consequence.

Infidels have been fond of turning this simple and beautiful history of the formation of the first man and the first woman, into ridicule; but if man had a beginning, and was created by the Almighty, what account could be imagined more natural and reasonable than this? Let the scoffer produce his own hypothesis, and subject it to the test of examination—but he has none. He laughs at the Bible history, and at the same time has nothing to answer as a substitute. But to men of sober minds who wish to be acquainted with their own origin, this narrative is most satisfactory and instructive. We know that man must have had a beginning, and consequently a Creator; but reason could not inform us how, or in what circumstances, he commenced his existence: *that*, therefore, which we wish to know, and need to know, is distinctly revealed and plainly recorded in the Bible. Man, instead of being from eternity, is of yesterday; instead of springing like a mushroom from the putrid earth, he came from the forming hand of the great Creator; instead of being at first an ape or orang-utang, he was made in the likeness and after the similitude of God. The Bible, then, explains to us, our own origin and the origin of all creatures. It teaches that man was made out of the clay of the earth but this clay was wrought into shape and wonderfully and fearfully organized by a divine hand.

3. The physical history of man exhibits some very remarkable phenomena, among which none have attracted the attention of the inquisitive so much as the striking variety in the complexion, hair, size, and figure of the species in different countries. Of complexion we find every shade of colour from white to sooty black; and of hair from the silken or flaxen locks of the north of Europe, to the crisped and curled wool of the Guinea-Negro. In the formation and prominence of the nose, lips, and cheeks, there is also a remarkable difference in different nations. These striking and numerous varieties have led some philosophers to adopt the opinion that mankind are not descended from one stock; but that originally there must have been parents corresponding with the several classes of men. It is an obvious objection to this theory that the several complexions of mankind are not distinctly marked, but run into each other by imperceptible shades; so that, if we suppose more species of men than one, we know not where to stop. If every considerable variety must be the foundation of a distinct species, we must adopt the hypothesis that originally God created a multitude of human beings of different complexions.

It is also a fact unfavourable to this hypothesis that there are striking varieties in complexion, hair, &c., among those known to have proceeded from one stock. In the same nation, some whole families or tribes are distinguished by fair hair and a ruddy complexion, while others are equally remarkable for dark complexion and black hair and eyes. These varieties in the same nation are known also to be transmitted from father to son for many generations. But we are unable to account for this variety; and if such a difference may take place when the external circumstances are nearly similar, why may not the greater varieties of the human species be owing to the great difference of climate and other circumstances of the nations of the earth?

Since a more accurate knowledge has been obtained of the numerous tribes inhabiting the islands of the great South Sea, some very interesting facts have been brought to light respecting the origin of these insulated savages. The information collected by Dr. Prichard and published in his *Physical History of Man* goes far to prove that men who have at a remote period sprung from the same stock may so diverge from each other in features, complexion, hair, &c., that they form distinct classes, and seem to be as widely apart from each other as almost any of the differing tribes of men. The identity of the origin of some of these islanders, whose appearance is so dissimilar, is ascertained by the radical sameness of their language; and it is a thing unknown in the history of savages to change their vernacular tongue. It is manifest, therefore, that there are natural causes in operation, whether we understand what they are or not, sufficient to produce all the varieties observed in the human species.

The diversity of features and complexion in the Jews, who have long resided in widely different climates, and who it is known do not intermix with other people, affords a strong confirmation of the same truth.

It is also as remarkable as it is obvious that, for the most part, men of a certain complexion are found in a particular latitude, unless they have been recently removed from their own country. We do not find the black skin and crisped hair in high latitudes; nor the fair complexion and light-coloured hair under the equator. From the first glance, therefore, it would seem that there is some connexion between climate and the complexion. Whether a difference of climate is sufficient of itself to account for these varieties, need not be determined. There may be other causes combined with this, some of which may be unknown to us. Animals carried from the temperate regions, far to the North, become white and their fur becomes much thicker and warmer. The final cause of this change is manifest and indicates the wisdom and goodness of the great Creator, but we know not how to account for it. The fact is certain, but the process of nature by which it is brought about is concealed; at least, it has not yet been discovered. Now, there may be, in the constitution of man a principle which accommodates itself to different climates, for purposes equally important. Indeed it is a well-known fact, that black people can endure a tropical sun much better than white men.

The analogy derived from other animals and vegetables, also, forbids the multiplication of the human species. The changes produced in the different species of animals which can live in climates widely different are as great, and in some much greater, than in the human species. Take, for an example, the canine species. How great the difference between the large mastiff and the diminutive lap-dog. These varieties in animals of the same species extend not only to their size, colour, and shape, but in a very remarkable degree to their instincts.

Seeing then that this is the common law of animal nature, why should we expect that the physical nature of man should be exempt from changes induced by a diversity of climate? And when we observe that the varieties of the human race have a manifest relation to the climate of the respective nations, the conclusion, upon all just principles of natural science, must be that the human species is one.

In all cases, where there is a difference of species, there is a marked difference in the internal structure of the body; but among the different tribes of men, no such diversity has been observed as can be the foundation of a diversity of species. The most exact anatomical dissections have discovered no permanent parts or contrivances in one nation which are not found also in all others. They all have the same bones, the same joints, the same system of nerves, the same number, use, and position of muscles, the same blood-vessels, glands, and digestive organs. Not only is the external appearance of the parts the same, but the interior texture and constituent particles composing the respective parts of the human body are the same in the white man, as in the black, the olive, the red, or the yellow.

It is scarcely necessary to observe that all men have the same external senses, the same bodily appetites, the same instincts, the same susceptibility of forming habits, and the same natural passions and desires. Those things in the constitution of man which have no resemblance in other species of animals are found in all the nations of the earth. The risible faculty and the faculty of weeping, and especially the possession of articulate speech, all serve to prove the identity of the human species. And if, from the body and its functions we ascend to the mind, here we find the same original faculties in all the varieties of the human race. We observe in all not only perception, consciousness, and memory, of which the inferior animals seem to partake, but the power of reasoning; the faculty of imagination; the power of association and abstraction; and what is more decisive still, the moral sense, of which there is no vestige in the brutes; and the faculty of taste; for all men perceive a difference between right and wrong and feel moral obligation; and all men have some sense of beauty and deformity. Moreover, all men are capable of improvement, and those nations which are now the most learned and refined were once among the most barbarous of the human race.

This perfect similarity in mind and body is sufficient to lead all impartial men to the conclusion that the human race are all descended from one pair, and that the varieties are accidental—the effect of a variety of causes, all of which we are unable to explore.

Some philosophers have, however, thought themselves justified in considering men of different species, not so much from the variety in their complexion and external appearance, as from the different degrees of flatness or rotundity in the skulls of different nations. On this ground, the learned Blumenbach has reduced the whole human race to five classes or species. But in the first place, the examination of human skulls has not been sufficiently extensive to furnish correct data for such a classification; and in the next place, if the difference exist, it affords no philosophical reason for supposing an original diversity of species. The causes which have operated other changes may as easily have produced a difference in the mere form of the skull: and those who give credit to the discoveries of the craniologists will find no difficulty in accounting for any varieties which are found in the skulls of men of different tribes.

Some time since, a radical difference of intellect was insisted on, as a criterion to determine a difference of species: but since our acquaintance with the most degraded and stupid of the human race has become more accurate; and especially, since we have witnessed the improvements which these are capable of, and the rapid advancement of some of them in knowledge and civilization, the whole ground of this opinion is taken away.[3]

There is another criterion of the identity of species, which by some naturalists has been considered decisive. It has been found that although animals of different species may be made to propagate a mongrel breed, their offspring are, for the most part, barren, and are seldom known to propagate. But the various classes of men mingle as freely and propagate the species with as much facility as people of the same tribe. Of late, however, some doubt has been expressed respecting the correctness of the fact first stated, on which the whole argument rests. It is alleged that sufficient experiments have not been made on the subject of the natural want of fertility in mules and other hybrids; and that, as far as experience goes, they are found to be fruitful in as many cases as they are barren. Leaving, therefore, the degree of barrenness in such animals in doubt, it is clear that no new species capable of continuing itself by propagation has been formed by the union of animals of different species, and that there exists a natural obstruction which does not exist in the case of men of the different classes.

But why might not a number of pairs of the same species, or exactly similar in parts and powers, have been produced as well as one? To which we answer that although the thing is possible, yet sound philosophy never resorts to such a supposition. Naturalists always go on the principle that more causes of the phenomena of nature than are sufficient are not to be admitted, and where every effect can as well be accounted for by supposing one original pair, as by many, the hypothesis of more than one ought, on general principles, to be rejected.

Having seen that reason itself leads us to believe that all the various nations of men are derived from one stock and form but one species, it cannot but add strong confirmation to our belief that the Sacred Scriptures clearly inform us that when God created man upon the earth, he created them male and female—one man, and one woman—from whom proceeded all the nations of the earth.

The idea which some have entertained that there were men before Adam, is destitute of all shadow of proof. The apostle Paul, in his discourse before the Senate of Areopagus, explicitly declares what reason and revelation unite in teaching to be the truth. "And hath made of one blood all nations of men, for to dwell on all the face of the earth." One word from the inspiration of God goes farther to establish our minds in the belief of the truth than volumes of arguments depending merely on the fallible reason of man.

The Bible teaches us that every man of every tribe and of every colour, whether his skull be flat or prominent, is our brother, and has a claim upon us for all the kindness and beneficence which it is in our power to show him. The same God is the Father of us all; and the same man is our common earthly father; and we are all rapidly tending to the same judgment and to the same eternity.

3. Samuel Stanhope Smith had made much of the development of blacks, when brought into contact with white "civilization" and a northern climate; Smith, *Essay on the Causes of Variety*, ed. Jordan, pp. 57ff.

But if any should, after all, be of opinion that the diversity among men cannot be accounted for by natural causes; yet it does not follow that the Mosaic history is false, or that there are several species of men entirely distinct from each other. At some period of the history of man, for some special reason, the Governor of the universe may have given a distinctive colour to one or more families of the earth. And some believers in the Bible are so fully impressed with this idea that they have undertaken to affirm that we have an intimation of this very thing in the sacred history. While some, however, would refer the black colour of the skin to the mark set upon Cain (which is irreconcilable with the history of the deluge), others with more probability, refer it to the curse upon Canaan, the son of Ham. As his posterity were doomed to be the servants of servants, it is thought that some peculiar mark was set upon them, which, it is presumed, was the dark colour of the skin, and the crisped and wooly hair. And in confirmation of this opinion, they allege that the black people are the descendants of Ham, and that they are the slaves of all the world until this day.

While I am willing to admit that God might, for reasons unknown to us, have miraculously changed the complexion and features of a part of the human race, I must think that the idea that the black colour was inflicted as a disgrace and a curse is a mere prejudice. Why should not the white colour be considered as a mark of God's displeasure? for, no negro from the burning sands of Africa can appear more shocking to the inhabitants of northern regions than the white man does to the people of the interior of that continent.

It seems, moreover, to be a prejudice without foundation that the colour of the whites was that of the first man. Much the larger part of the inhabitants of the earth are of a complexion nearly midway between the two extremes. Is it not, therefore, much more probable that our first parents were red men or of an olive or copper colour? And this opinion derives some support from the name of the first man; for the radical signification of *Adam* is *red*. And if this be assumed as a fact, then it will be much easier to account for the various complexions of men from natural causes, than if we suppose that either white or black was the original complexion.

But from what has been said, it will be seen that no valid argument against the truth of the Bible can be derived from the variety in the human species; whether that variety can be accounted for by natural causes or not.

Charles Hodge
1797–1878

6

Lecture to Theological Students
1829

The Princeton theologians often appear very rationalistic. Alexander, for example, frequently made much of human ability to demonstrate Christian truth (e.g., Selections 3, 4). Warfield labored long to hone his apologetical methods (e.g., Selections 21, 25). And even Charles Hodge devoted considerable attention to proving the faith (e.g., Selection 17; ST, I: 202-40, 633-36 on miracles). Yet the other side of apologetics at Princeton was a forthright advocacy of piety.[1] All of the major Princeton theologians published complete works that appealed directly to living faith as a ground for truth and life (Alexander, *Thoughts on Religious Experience;* C. Hodge, *The Way of Life, Princeton Sermons;* Warfield, *Faith and Life*). Charles Hodge, in particular, argued repeatedly that Christian faith did not rest on the power of Christians logically to demonstrate its truthfulness. In fact, Hodge felt that error in doctrine should be regarded as an effect, not as a cause of impiety. Besides the selections excerpted in this anthology (below and Selection 9), Hodge made similar arguments on many other occasions. In 1840, for instance, he took Congregationalist Andrews Norton to task for speaking as if Christianity rested on the verifiability of miracles. "It is hardly necessary to remark," Hodge responded, "that every Christian knows that such is not the foundation of his faith: he has firmer ground on which to rest the destiny of his soul. He does not believe Grotius or Paley [who propounded arguments defending belief in God]; he believes God himself, speaking in his word. The evidence of the truth is in the truth itself" ("The Latest Form of Infidelity," BRPR 12 [January 1840]: 33; quoted from *Essays and Reviews,* p. 89; see also "Ground of Faith in the Scriptures," BRPR 17 [April 1845]: 271-76, reprinted in *Essays and Reviews,* pp. 188-93; and "Beecher's Great Conflict," BRPR 26 [January 1854]: 138). Were this the only side of Hodge we saw, we would be justified in labeling him a pietist or fideist.

The following excerpt from a lecture to the theological students, made shortly after Hodge returned from his European sojourn (1826-28), reveals how he regarded the relationship between truth and life. A few years later in a similar lecture he would lay greater stress on the necessity for a minister to ground his

---

1. On Hodge's deep strain of piety, especially as it relates to the doing of theology, see W. Andrew Hoffecker, *Piety and the Princeton Theologians* (Phillipsburg, N.J., and Grand Rapids: Presbyterian and Reformed, and Baker, 1981), pp. 44-94. Also helpful on Hodge's early religious life are the journal entries introduced by Charles D. Cashdollar, "The Pursuit of Piety: Charles Hodge's Diary, 1819-1820," *Journal of Presbyterian History* 55 (Fall 1977): 267-84.

life on the truth ("Suggestions to Theological Students," BRPR 5 [January 1833]: 100-113). Fresh from Europe, however, he wanted to show them that truth was grounded in life.[2] Throughout his career, Hodge would be a stickler for propositions. But even at his most mechanistic (e.g., Selection 8) he retained a sense of how much Christian truth depended on Christian faith (cf. last section of Selection 8). For him thought and action, belief and character, came closer together than for any of the other Princetonians.

There is a certain irony here, for Hodge justly deserved his reputation as a diligent defender of orthodox propositions. He regularly lambasted opponents for giving in to "enthusiasm," "mysticism," or other devices by which *they* were trying to take account of subjectivity, inwardness, or states of character (Selections 14-17). Yet this selection, with its reference to "feeling" concerning Christ, Hodge's later description of a theology of the "heart" standing beside one of "the intellect" (ST, I: 16, in Selection 8), and his admission as an old man that "language is an imperfect vehicle of thought; as an expression of emotion it is utterly inadequate"[3]—all push toward the conclusion that he was not so much objecting to Bushnell, Finney, Nevin and Schaff, or E. A. Park for trusting their hearts, but rather reproving them for letting heart move head in the wrong direction. For most of his career, Hodge spoke as if he could best save piety by zealously guarding the truth. But on more than one occasion he sounded more like his opponents who felt they could save the truth by zealously guarding piety.

Hodge began his 1829 address by telling the students how much superior American "civil and religious liberty" was to that of Europe. He next conceded that, while the church was healthier in the United States, European education was vastly superior. He then turned to an analysis of Europe's recent religious history, which led him to this discussion on the relationship of learning and piety. The excerpt is from Charles Hodge, "Lecture, Addressed to the Students of the Theological Seminary," BRPR 1 (January 1829): 90-98.

A THIRD GREAT TRUTH which an observation of the state of European churches is adapted to impress upon the mind is *the intimate connexion between speculative opinion, and moral character.*

There is no sentiment more frequently advanced than that a man's opinions have little to do with his moral character, and yet there is none more fundamentally erroneous. The fact is that opinions on moral and religious subjects depend mainly on the state of the moral and religious feelings. Mere argument can no more produce the intimate persuasion of moral truth than it can of beauty. As it depends on our refinement of taste, what things to us are beautiful, so it depends upon our

2. On Hodge's time in Europe, see A. A. Hodge, *Life of Charles Hodge*, pp. 104-201.
3. Charles Hodge, response at the semicentennial of his teaching at Princeton, 1872, quoted in ibid., p. 519. See ibid., pp. 488-90, for a letter from Hodge to a Scottish correspondent on "the witness of the Spirit" in which Hodge ascribes to the Holy Spirit the Christian's conviction that Scripture is true and that the believer is a child of God.

religious feelings, what doctrines for us are true. A man's real opinions are the expression of his character. They are the forms in which his inward feelings embody themselves and become visible. The secret conviction of this truth is the reason that the ascription of obnoxious opinions is always regarded as an aspersion on character. Why is the denial of God's existence regarded with horror by all classes of men, but because it presupposes a heart dead to all the manifestations of his glory in creation, in our own nature, and in his word? The denial of God's justice is a proof of insensibility to sin; the rejection of Jesus Christ, of blindness to his moral loveliness. It is, therefore, an important truth that no serious religious error can exist without a corresponding perversion or destruction of religious feelings.

To prevent misapprehension, it may be proper to remark that while it is asserted that if a man's feelings be in a proper state, he will embrace and believe the truth as soon as it is presented; it is freely admitted that a man's opinions may be correct, and yet his moral character corrupt. But in this case these opinions are merely nominal; they form no part of the intimate persuasion of his soul, and hence, are no expression of his character.

In support of the point we are considering, we might refer to the different systems of religion throughout the world, and observe their correspondence with the peculiar character of the people who embrace them. The contemplative and effeminate systems of Eastern Asia; the mixture of loftiness and sensuality in the religion of Mohammed; the refinement, licentiousness, and general disregard of principle in the theology of the Greeks; the more rigid features of the religion of the early Romans; or the sanguinary creed of the warlike nations of Northern Europe. Or we might refer to the characteristic traits of the various sects in christendom, and observe how the leading features of each are expressed in their peculiar opinions. Those in whom the imagination predominates, who have liveliness without depth of religious feeling and but little reflection, have a religion of pomp and splendid forms, of fasts and festivals and of easy means of satisfying the conscience. All those in whose systems the sovereignty of God, the helplessness and dependence of man, his depravity and solemn responsibility occupy the leading parts have been distinguished for severity, strictness, separation from the world, depth of feeling and fixedness of purpose: a strong determined character, whose tendency is to make the severer prevail over the milder features of religion. The Arminian system is the natural expression of feelings less strongly marked, of less reverence for God, less humiliating views of man, and in general of less prominence and depth of religious character. Those who have no inward necessity for the doctrines of the gospel, no apprehension of God's holiness, no fear of his justice, no adequate sense of sin, need no atoning Saviour, and no sanctifying Spirit, and thus easily satisfy themselves with the doctrines of natural religion. Another proof of this point is that whenever a change occurs in the religious opinions of a community, it is always preceded by a change in their religious feelings. The natural expression of the feelings of true piety is the doctrines of the Bible. As long as these feelings are retained, these doctrines will be retained; but should they be lost, the doctrines are either held for form's sake or rejected, according to circumstances;

and if the feelings be again called into life, the doctrines return as a matter of course. The proof of this remark must be sought in ecclesiastical history. Its truth can only be observed, however, where there is freedom of opinion; where the mind is left to assume its natural form, and adopt opinions most congenial with its state. When every thing is fixed and immoveable, as in the Catholic church, there will, of course, be little change visible, whatever may actually take place beneath the unvarying surface. But in Protestant countries we see abundant evidence of the correctness of the remark. In Scotland the doctrines of the church are retained only by those who retain the spirit of the framers of their confession. In Geneva the system of Calvin did not survive the spirit of its author. The same may be said of France, and all parts of Germany. In this latter country the truth of our remark is more observable, because more violent changes have there occurred than in any other portion of christendom.

After the struggle against infidelity had been sustained in England, it passed over into France and thence into Germany. Here it achieved its greatest triumph. Christianity had well nigh ceased to be even the nominal religion of the land—men began to talk of the introduction of a new Bible—of the abolition of the clergy—and of the very form of the church. To this remarkable event, this distressing fall of so large and important a part of Protestant christendom, the eyes of all interested in religion have been naturally turned, and a general demand made, what could have been the cause of so general and lamentable a defection. Much has been written on this subject, and a thousand causes assigned, while the most obvious has been the least regarded. The simple fact is, that vital religion had been long declining. There seem to be certain cycles through which almost every church is more or less regularly passing. During one age, there are many revivals of religion, and a general prevalence of evangelical spirit and exertion; to this succeeds a period of revival or of open departure from the faith. In Germany at the period of the reformation, there was a general revival of religion; to this succeeded a period of cold orthodoxy brought about principally by perpetual controversy on unimportant subjects. This long period was but partially interrupted by the revival under Franke and Spener, after which things relapsed into their former course. The preaching of the gospel was so tiresome and controversial that it could produce little effect upon the people. Practical religion was no necessary requisite for admission into the ministry; and the clergy soon became as little distinguished for piety as any other class of men. This being the case, their holding or rejecting the doctrines of the gospel was a mere matter of circumstance. As long as their interest, or standing, depended upon their nominal faith, they retained it; but as soon as fashion and interest was on the side of rejecting it, they rejected it. Under Frederick the Great, infidelity became the fashion; no opprobrium was attached even to the clergy, declaring themselves superior to the opinions and prejudices of darker ages. They had lost their hold on the doctrines of the gospel and stood ready to be carried away by the first blast that blew.

The fact that at this juncture, the philologians, Heyne and Wolf, gave a new spring to historical criticism, and commenced distinguishing on critical grounds the genuine from the spurious parts of the ancient classics, led Semler and his school to follow the same course with regard to the Bible. And as they had no inward necessity for believing, their fancying that they discovered critical grounds for the rejection of this or that book of scripture, or the whole, they renounced their faith in the word of God. New systems of philosophy now making their appearance, moulding religion into a hundred different shapes, completed the effect of turning the already really unbelieving clergy and others into the ranks of open infidelity. It was not until severe national and private afflictions began to turn the minds of all classes of men towards God, and awaken feelings which found no appropriate objects in the barren systems of philosophical religion, that men began to return to the doctrines of the Bible. And just in proportion as this revival of religion has advanced, has been the return to orthodoxy. Thus as irreligion preceded infidelity, the revival of religion has preceded a return to soundness of faith.[4] It is this vital connexion between piety and truth that is the great and solemn lesson taught by the past and present state of the German churches.

This correspondence between opinion and character is strikingly observable in the various religious parties in that section of the church. The leading parties are the Orthodox, the Rationalists and the Pantheists. Wherever you find vital piety, that is, penitence, and devotional spirit, there you find, the doctrines of the fall, of depravity, of regeneration, of atonement, and the Deity of Jesus Christ. I never saw nor heard of a single individual who exhibited a spirit of piety who rejected any one of these doctrines. There are many who have great reverence for Jesus Christ and regard for the scriptures, but having no experience of the power of the gospel, they have no clear views nor firm conviction of its doctrines; they are vacillating on the borders of two classes of opinion, exactly as they are in feeling.

The Rationalists as a body are precisely like common men of the world. In general, orderly in their lives, but without the least semblance of experimental piety. They regard it as mysticism, exaggeration, enthusiasm, or hypocrisy. Some few, from the natural turn of their minds, have something of the poetry and sentimentality of religion but nothing of vital godliness. In Pantheism there is room and expression for a variety of character. Some men of elevated intellects, discourse much of the sublimity and grandeur of the infinite, and bow with a sort of adoration before the living universe. But as this infinite is not a person, is neither moral nor intelligent, this system, while it inflates the imagination, gives no object for the moral feelings: and hence, when men who have much of these feelings fall into its snares, they are in torment until they find deliverance. Others of this class, from the idea that the all-pervading principle is most completely developed in intelligent

---

4. Hodge discusses the revival in Germany in his letters and diary from the time of his European travels, ibid., pp. 148–52 and *passim*. The terms *Orthodox, Rationalist,* and *Pantheist,* which Hodge used in this lecture (next paragraph) were also found in his diary. Hodge considered Friedrich August Gottreu Tholuck, Johann August Wilhelm Neander, and Ernst Wilhelm Hengstenberg to be orthodox (ibid., *passim*). He called theologian F. E. D. Schleiermacher and philosopher G. W. F. Hegel pantheists (ibid., p. 119). Without naming any names, he described the rationalists as deists (ibid., pp. 136–137).

beings, and most of all, in those who have come to a consciousness of their identity with this principle, are filled with the most amazing pride; they are God in the highest state of his existence. These are self-idolaters. Others again, of a different cast, love to feel themselves a part of an illimitable whole, which moves on and must move on, through its vast cycles without their cooperation or responsibility, and look forward with complacency to going out, like a spark in the ocean, unnoticed and unremembered in the infinitude of being.

Now, brethren, if these things be so, if a man's religious opinions are the result and expression of his religious feelings, if heterodoxy be the consequence rather than the cause of the loss of piety, then "keep your hearts with all diligence, for out of them are the issues of life." Remember that it is only in God's light that you can see light. That holiness is essential to correct knowledge of divine things, and the great security from error. And as you see that when men lose the life of religion, they can believe the most monstrous doctrines, and glory in them; and that when the clergy once fall into such errors, generations perish before the slow course of reviving piety brings back the truth; "what manner of men ought you to be in all holy conversation and godliness." Not only then for your own sake, but for the sake of your children, and your children's children, forsake not your God; who is our God, because he was the God of our fathers. The fate of future ages rests with every present generation.

Again, beware of any course of life or study which has a tendency to harden your hearts and deaden the delicate sensibility of the soul to moral truth and beauty. There are two ways in which this may be done, a course of sin, and indulgence in metaphysical speculations on divine things. The reason why such speculations produce this effect is that the views of truth thus taken are not of its moral nature, and of course produce no moral feeling, but the reverse. Let a man, when contemplating the grandeur of alpine scenery, begin to examine the structure of the mountains, and study their geological character; what becomes of his emotions of sublimity? Thus also religious truth, viewed in the general, produces devotion; metaphysically analyzed it destroys it. Where is our reverence and awe of God, while prying into his essence or scrutinizing his attributes? Where are our feelings of penitence, when disputing on the origin of evil? our sense of responsibility when discussing free-will and dependence? That it may be necessary to attend to these subjects, and get as far as possible definite ideas respecting them, no one will deny; but when our habitual views of truth are of this nature, there is an end of all feeling on the subject. There is another remark which may here be made. When a man prefers examining the geological structure of a mountainous region to the contemplation of its grandeur; he only prefers the acquisition of knowledge to the enjoyment of an elevating emotion; but as the objects of his examination are external and have no connexion with the emotions of his mind, his insensibility is no obstacle to his progress. But with regard to moral subjects the case is far different; the feelings destroyed by metaphysical investigation are the very objects to be investigated, for their moral quality is their essence. If this be weakened or destroyed, there is nothing left; and a man in this state is no more qualified to speak on these subjects than the deaf to discourse on music. This is the reason that metaphysicians so often advance doctrines which the whole world knows to be false because they contradict the strongest moral feelings of the soul. Will the mass of pious people ever be brought to believe that God is the author of sin? that man is not free, and consequently not accountable? that sin is not a moral evil, not mere imperfect development? or the still more horrible opinion that God himself is merely the blind instinctive principle which animates and constitutes the universe, of which neither moral nor intellectual qualities can be predicated?[5] Yet metaphysicians teach all these doctrines. Look around you, brethren, and see if these things be not so. As far as my observation extends, it is the uniform tendency of such speculations to deaden the moral sensibility of the soul. Beware then of unhallowed speculations on sacred subjects. Bring all your doctrines to the test of God's word and of holiness. Go with your new opinions to the aged children of God who have spent years in close communion with the Father of lights. Propose to them your novel doctrines, should they shock their feelings, depend upon it, they are false and dangerous. The approbation of an experienced Christian of any purely religious opinion is worth more than that of any merely learned theologian upon earth.

Finally, lean not to your own understanding. If there be any declaration of the Bible confirmed by the history of the church, and especially by the recent history of European churches, it is that "he that leaneth to his own understanding is a fool." When men forsake the word of God, and profess to be wise above that which is written, they inevitably and universally lose themselves in vain speculation. Look at the state of things when every man is following the light of his own reason. Each boasts that he alone has the truth, and yet each is often a miracle of folly to every man but himself. True, such men are often men of great intellect; but can mere intellect perceive moral truth? Can man by wisdom find out God? can he find out the Almighty unto perfection? No man knoweth the Father but the Son and he to whom the Son shall reveal him. Submit yourselves, therefore, to the teaching of him in whom "are all the treasures of wisdom and knowledge." It is only when thus taught that you will be able to teach others also.

One word more—keep as you would your hold on heaven your reverence for Jesus Christ. Reverence for the Redeemer of sinners is the very last feeling which deserts a falling Christian, or a sinking church. When all other evidence and all other arguments for the Bible had lost their force, this solitary feeling has held up the soul from sinking into infidelity and thence into perdition. When this is lost, all is lost. The soul that is insensible to the glory of the Son of God, is "as a tree twice dead and plucked up by the roots."

5. Hodge is here describing Hegel; see ibid., p. 119.

7

The Virtues of Seventeenth-Century Theologians

1844

A review of J. A. W. Neander's *History of the Planting of the Christian Church,* which Hodge published in 1844, offered an opportunity to reflect on theologians of an earlier day. Neander had been one of the professors in Germany who, as a Christian and a scholar, had favorably impressed the young Hodge almost twenty years earlier.[1] Yet Hodge was uneasy with Neander's penchant for "development," a penchant which always bore for him the taint of Schleiermacher. After praising Neander's history as scholarly and as basically Christian, Hodge took it to task for its imprecision. This then allowed him to comment positively on the theology of the Protestant Reformation and negatively on the "pantheism" of modern Germany. It also provided him with an occasion to say yet another good word about the common sense of British and American thinkers. And, finally, it gave him an opportunity to hymn the writers with whom he felt most at home, the dogmaticians of the seventeenth century, including Turretin, whose text was still serving in 1844 as the seminary's basic theological resource as it would for another twenty-eight years. This selection is from Charles Hodge, "Neander's History," BRPR 16 (April 1844): 180–83. Brief biographical sketches of the theologians mentioned in this selection can be found in the index of names.

IN LOOKING BACK upon the ground over which this accomplished, ardent and delightful writer has led us, and in reconsidering the peculiarities of his scheme, both good and evil, we are more and more inclined to trace his singular deviations from the beaten way of orthodox divinity to his grand characteristic opinion that Christianity is a development. If this proposition is understood of subjective Christianity, nothing could be more safe or more important. The Kingdom of God, as light, as leaven, and as fire, will go on until it has reached new subjects, and affected all souls. Divine Truth will be—not more clearly revealed—but more fully comprehended; and the result will be the subjugation of all human minds on earth.

1. On Hodge's contacts with Neander in Berlin, see ibid., pp. 142, 164–165, 170, and 181–182.

But if the meaning is that the objective revelation of truth is a development; that as the gospel was unfolded from the root of Judaism, so a future growth is yet to spring from scriptural Christianity and perpetually bud and bloom into new truths and systems, in comparison with which the New Testament is but a germ—we confess we regard the opinion as fundamentally erroneous. Such an assumption lies equally at the basis of the modern pantheistic theology and the figments of St. Simonianism.[2] And the history of modern opinion in Germany teaches us that there is no safety in any lower ground than that of the Reformers and in the more rigid views of divine inspiration. If, as is maintained, theology is advancing and maturing itself by new discoveries, the progress should bear a closer analogy with the march of other sciences. More positive truth should be brought to light. Dogmatic statements should be more clear and explicit. Definitions and distinctions should be precise and above the danger of mistake. Great principles having been ascertained, the more minute ramifications of truth should be made apparent. But instead of this, the whole tendency of German theology, including that of the work before us, has been a marked retrocession from all fixed points. Dimness and generality have succeeded to precision and unequivocal enunciation. Formulas have been adopted which may be the vehicles as well of error as of truth. And the prospect was never less than at the present moment, of anything like a new creation.

"I cannot agree," says Neander, "with the conviction of those who think that this new creation will be only a repetition of what took place in the sixteenth or seventeenth century, and that the whole dogmatic system, and the entire mode of contemplating divine and human things, must return as it then existed." Neither can we; but at the same time we must protest against those who would sweep away as rubbish the whole of that glorious structure with cries of *Rase it, rase it, even to the foundation thereof.* We have no respect for speculations which refuse all aid from those great spirits whom God raised up. They militate against their own theory of development. Rejecting that theory in its excess, we nevertheless do not believe that every race is to lay a new foundation. The system of the Reformers was not only a great advance upon that which it superseded, but was vastly superior to that which would now displace it. The same service which was rendered to Luther and Calvin by Augustine, may be rendered to Neander and Twesten by Luther and Calvin. Though we would not swear by the names of these masters, we would, if the question were inevitable, prefer the system of any one of them, as a whole, to that of the work under review. We would adopt the *Loci Communes* of Melanchthon or of Peter Martyr in preference to any dogmatic system which modern Germany has produced. Nay, we are so thoroughly convinced that honest, bold and categorical declarations are better than wavering ambiguities and transcendental amphibologies that we would rather let a pupil take his chance of truth between two opposite systems, for instance those of Arminius and Gomar, than to refer him to the misty generalities of the ablest modern syncretist.

2. The followers of Claude Henri de Rouvroy, Count de Saint-Simon (1760–1825), held the socialistic views of their mentor, and with him believed that a religion of humanity could adequately enshrine the benevolent principles of a now outdated Christian faith.

After all the alleged improvements in theological research, we never feel so much disposed to take down one of the old Latin dogmatic writers of the seventeenth century, as immediately on closing a fresh work from Germany. These antiquated writers have a thousand faults, it may be; they are stiff, they are prolix, they are technical, they are intolerant and austere, they are scholastic in their distinctions, but they have one great merit—they always let us know what they mean. Their atmosphere, if wintry and biting, is clear. They boldly march up to difficulties, and beard even those which they fail to conquer. Their dialectic was an armour of proof, which might be used as well on the wrong as on the right side, but it was of the finest temper, and of such weight as to be unwieldy to champions of our day. The frequent perusal of their disquisitions has a value independent of the truths evolved. It promotes patient thought, prompts to exact definition, whets the discriminative acumen, and exercises the intellect in logical strategy. Especially does it beget a repugnance to dreamy contemplation and the use of vague diction for concealment. It is precisely this point in which lies the great difference between the two classes of writers. It is a difference not so much of opinion or system, as of intellectual habitude. The clearness which we applaud, is found not only in Turretin, Rivet, and Chamier, but in Crellius, Grotius and Le Clerc.[3] That objects are made more luminous in the writings of the orthodox, we readily grant; for whatsoever doth make manifest is light. It is this description of writers, and this style of disquisition, which we would unhesitatingly recommend to young theologians. They have one obvious claim upon our preference, that they accord in their chief peculiarities with the characteristic of the American, or what is the same thing, the British mind. It is the school from which proceeded the clear-sighted and unambiguous Bulls, Pearsons, Chillingsworths, Tillottsons, Baxters, Watsons, Edwardses, and Paleys, of a former age. On the other hand, the taste for German writers on dogmatic theology is factitious, alien to the genius of the Anglo-American mind, and productive, wherever it exists, of debilitating and rhapsodical musing.

3. Hodge counted the first three as orthodox allies and considered the last three erroneous or heretical.

8

Introduction to *Systematic Theology*
1872

When Charles Hodge set out in the early 1860s to write a systematic theology, he had over twenty years of teaching experience and mountains of lecture notes to draw on. Yet the theology which emerged was more than a reshaping of those notes, even as it was more than a translation into an American idiom of Princeton's previous textbook, the *Institutes* of Turretin. While the systematics that he delivered to the printers in the early 1870s made use of his earlier work in the classroom and the BRPR, it represented a fresh statement of his convictions. This was particularly true for his considerations of theological method. According to his son, "the preparation of the first part of this vast work, treating on the foundations of Natural Theology, and its relation to materialism and other antitheistic theories, scientific and philosophical and traditional, exacted of him a great amount of special reading and reflection."[1]

In spite of this extra effort, however, the methodological principles that emerge in the *Systematic Theology* are consistent with long-standing traditions of the Princeton Theology. The ST treats theology as a science (see Alexander, Selection 3, first paragraph). It makes much of Common Sense principles concerning physical and moral nature (Alexander, Selection 3). It treats the Bible as the sole authoritative source for revealed theology (Alexander, Selection 5). And it continues to see a connection between bad methods and bad theology (as he had in earlier polemics, Selections 14-17). These continuities notwithstanding, Hodge's discussion of method does show that the Princeton Theology had grown more sophisticated over the years. Hodge does not waver on the primacy of propositions, but he gives much more scope in the theological enterprise to "moral nature," the messages of the "heart," and the work of the Holy Spirit than had Alexander. He does not retreat from the Princeton insistence on the "facts" of Scripture, but he shows more sensitivity than had Alexander to the way in which human perspective may distort an apprehension of facts. He relies almost as heavily on a mechanistic picture of the world, but he does not place the principal emphasis on evidentialist apologetics that Alexander did before him and Warfield would after.

The discussion of theological method which begins Hodge's *Systematic Theology* is, in sum, a microcosm of his entire work. It is clear and filled with logical force. It thus remains a potent guide to the doing of theology for many

---

1. A. A. Hodge, *Life of Charles Hodge,* p. 451, where other details concerning the composition of the ST may also be found.

conservative evangelicals today. But the *Systematic Theology* also displays what J. I. Packer has called "Charles Hodge's ever-simple view of scientific method."[2] Its value for a time like the late twentieth century when science seems to be as much a creative art as a mechanistic system of arrangement can thus be called into question.[3]

Historically considered, Hodge's discussion of method contains the same parallel emphasis on objective revelation and subjective Christian experience that mark him as the most comprehensive of the Princeton theologians. Theologically considered, it raises again the question whether a simple inductive view of science is as necessary to the continuation of Augustinian-Calvinistic theology as Hodge himself so obviously believed it was.

The following selection is from ST, I: 1-19.[4]

On Method*

Theology a Science

In every science there are two factors: facts and ideas; or facts and the mind. Science is more than knowledge. Knowledge is the persuasion of what is true on adequate evidence. But the facts of astronomy, chemistry, or history do not constitute the science of those departments of knowledge. Nor does the mere orderly arrangement of facts amount to science. Historical facts arranged in chronological order are mere annals. The philosophy of history supposes those facts to be understood in their causal relations. In every department the man of science is assumed to understand the laws by which the facts of experience are determined, so that he not only knows the past but can predict the future. The astronomer can foretell the relative position of the heavenly bodies for centuries to come. The chemist can tell with certainty what will be the effect of certain chemical combinations. If, therefore, theology be a science, it must include something more than a mere knowledge of facts. It must embrace an exhibition of the internal relation of those facts, one to another, and each to all. It must be able to show that if one be admitted, others cannot be denied.

The Bible is no more a system of theology, than nature is a system of chemistry or of mechanics. We find in nature the facts which the chemist or the mechanical philosopher has to examine, and from them to ascertain the laws by which they are

2. J. I. Packer, Review of Rogers and McKim, *The Authority and Interpretation of the Bible*, in *Crux*, 16 (March 1980), 31.

3. Representative works that speak of science in these terms include Thomas S. Kuhn, *The Structure of Scientific Revolutions* (2nd ed., Chicago: University of Chicago Press, 1970), which describes scientific "development" as something vastly different than the orderly progress of empirical induction; and Michael Polanyi, *Personal Knowledge* (Chicago: University of Chicago Press, 1958), which treats scientific "progress" as a function of human experience rather than impersonal information. For a sensitive reflection from a generally Calvinistic perspective on modern relationships between science and theology, see Thomas F. Torrance, *Christian Theology and Scientific Culture* (New York: Oxford University Press, 1981).

4. Sydney Ahlstrom's fine anthology, *Theology in America*, also reprints parts of Hodge's methodological considerations from the ST on pp. 251-64.

*Chapter 1, *Systematic Theology*.

determined. So the Bible contains the truths which the theologian has to collect, authenticate, arrange, and exhibit in their internal relation to each other. This constitutes the difference between biblical and systematic theology. The office of the former is to ascertain and state the facts of Scripture. The office of the latter is to take those facts, determine their relation to each other and to other cognate truths, as well as to vindicate them and show their harmony and consistency. This is not an easy task, or one of slight importance.

It may naturally be asked, why not take the truths as God has seen fit to reveal them, and thus save ourselves the trouble of showing their relation and harmony? The answer to this question is, in the first place, that it cannot be done. Such is the constitution of the human mind that it cannot help endeavoring to systematize and reconcile the facts which it admits to be true. In no department of knowledge have men been satisfied with the possession of a mass of undigested facts. And the students of the Bible can as little be expected to be thus satisfied. There is a necessity, therefore, for the construction of systems of theology. Of this the history of the Church affords abundant proof. In all ages and among all denominations such systems have been produced.

Second, A much higher kind of knowledge is thus obtained than by the mere accumulation of isolated facts. It is one thing, for example, to know that oceans, continents, islands, mountains, and rivers exist on the face of the earth; and a much higher thing to know the causes which have determined the distribution of land and water on the surface of our globe; the configuration of the earth; the effects of that configuration on climate, on the races of plants and animals, on commerce, civilization, and the destiny of nations. It is by determining these causes that geography has been raised from a collection of facts to a highly important and elevated science. In like manner, without the knowledge of the laws of attraction and motion, astronomy would be a confused and unintelligible collection of facts. What is true of other sciences is true of theology. We cannot know what God has revealed in his Word unless we understand, at least in some good measure, the relation in which the separate truths therein contained stand to each other. It cost the Church centuries of study and controversy to solve the problem concerning the person of Christ; that is, to adjust and bring into harmonious arrangement all the facts which the Bible teaches on that subject.

Third, We have no choice in this matter. If we would discharge our duty as teachers and defenders of the truth, we must endeavor to bring all the facts of revelation into systematic order and mutual relation. It is only thus that we can satisfactorily exhibit their truth, vindicate them from objections, or bring them to bear in their full force on the minds of men.

Fourth, Such is evidently the will of God. He does not teach men astronomy or chemistry, but He gives them the facts out of which those sciences are constructed. Neither does He teach us systematic theology, but He gives us in the Bible the truths which, properly understood and arranged, constitute the science of theology. As the facts of nature are all related and determined by physical laws, so the facts of the Bible are all related and determined by the nature of God and of his creatures. And as He wills that men should study his works and discover their wonderful organic relation and harmonious combination, so it is his will that we should study his Word, and learn that, like the stars, its truths are not isolated points, but systems, cycles, and epicycles, in unending harmony and grandeur. Besides all this, although the Scriptures do not contain a system of theology as a whole, we have in the Epistles of the New Testament, portions of that system wrought out to our hands. These are our authority and guide.

The Theological Method

Every science has its own method, determined by its peculiar nature. This is a matter of so much importance that it has been erected into a distinct department. Modern literature abounds in works on Methodology, i.e., on the science of method. They are designed to determine the principles which should control scientific investigations. If a man adopts a false method, he is like one who takes a wrong road which will never lead him to his destination. The two great comprehensive methods are the à priori and the à posteriori. The one argues from cause to effect, the other from effect to cause. The former was for ages applied even to the investigation of nature. Men sought to determine what the facts of nature must be from the laws of mind or assumed necessary laws. Even in our own day we have had Rational Cosmogonies, which undertake to construct a theory of the universe from the nature of absolute being and its necessary modes of development. Every one knows how much it cost to establish the method of induction on a firm basis, and to secure a general recognition of its authority. According to this method, we begin with collecting well-established facts and from them infer the general laws which determine their occurrence. From the fact that bodies fall toward the centre of the earth has been inferred the general law of gravitation which we are authorized to apply far beyond the limits of actual experience. This inductive method is founded upon two principles: First, That there are laws of nature (forces) which are the proximate causes of natural phenomena. Secondly, That those laws are uniform; so that we are certain that the same causes, under the same circumstances, will produce the same effects. There may be diversity of opinion as to the nature of these laws. They may be assumed to be forces inherent in matter; or they may be regarded as uniform modes of divine operation; but in any event there must be some cause for the phenomena which we perceive around us, and that cause must be uniform and permanent. On these principles all the inductive sciences are founded; and by them the investigations of natural philosophies are guided.

The same principle applies to metaphysics as to physics; to psychology as well as to natural science. Mind has its laws as well as matter, and those laws, although of a different kind, are as permanent as those of the external world.

The methods which have been applied to the study of theology are too numerous to be separately considered. They may, perhaps, be reduced to three general classes: First, The Speculative; Second, The Mystical; Third, The Inductive. These terms are, indeed, far from being precise. They are used for the want of better to designate the three general methods of theological investigation which have prevailed in the Church.

The Speculative Method

Speculation assumes, in an *à priori* manner, certain principles, and from them undertakes to determine what is and what must be. It decides on all truth, or determines on what is true from the laws of the mind, or from axioms involved in the constitution of the thinking principle within us. To this head must be referred all those systems which are founded on any *à priori* philosophical assumptions. There are three general forms in which this speculative method has been applied to theology.

Deistic and Rationalistic form. The first is that which rejects any other source of knowledge of divine things than what is found in nature and the constitution of the human mind. It assumes certain metaphysical and moral axioms, and from them evolves all the truths which it is willing to admit. To this class belong the Deistical and strictly Rationalistical writers of the past and present generations.

Dogmatic Form. The second is the method adopted by those who admit a supernatural divine revelation, and concede that such a revelation is contained in the Christian Scriptures, but who reduce all the doctrines thus revealed to the forms of some philosophical system. This was done by many of the fathers who endeavored to exalt πίστις into γνῶσις, *i.e.*, the faith of the common people into philosophy for the learned. This was also to a greater or less degree the method of the schoolmen, and finds an illustration even in the "Cur Deus Homo" of Anselm, the father of scholastic theology. . . .[5] This method is still in vogue. Men lay down certain principles, called axioms, or first truths of reason, and from them deduce the doctrines of religion by a course of argument as rigid and remorseless as that of Euclid. This is sometimes done to the entire overthrow of the doctrines of the Bible, and of the most intimate moral convictions not only of Christians but of the mass of mankind. Conscience is not allowed to mutter in the presence of the lordly understanding. It is in the spirit of the same method that the old scholastic doctrine of realism is made the basis of the Scriptural doctrines of original sin and redemption. To this method the somewhat ambiguous term *Dogmatism* has been applied, because it attempts to reconcile the doctrines of Scripture with reason, and to rest their authority on rational evidence. The result of this method has always been to transmute, as far as it succeeded, faith into knowledge, and to attain this end the teachings of the Bible have been indefinitely modified. Men are expected to believe, not on the authority of God, but on that of reason.

Transcendentalists. Thirdly, and preeminently, the modern Transcendentalists are addicted to the speculative method. In the wide sense of the word they are Rationalists, as they admit of no higher source of truth than reason. But as they make reason to be something very different from what it is regarded as being by ordinary Rationalists, the two classes are practically very far apart. The Transcendentalists also differ essentially from the Dogmatists. The latter admit an external,

---

5. "Cur Deus Homo" ("Why God Became a Man," 1097–98) was the great work of Anselm (1033–1109) on the atonement, which described Christ's death as a ransom paid to the devil and also in terms of God's justice and mercy.

supernatural, and authoritative revelation. They acknowledge that truths not discoverable by human reason are thereby made known. But they maintain that those doctrines when known may be shown to be true on the principles of reason. They undertake to give a demonstration independent of Scripture of the doctrines of the Trinity, the Incarnation, redemption, as well as of the immortality of the soul and a future state of retribution. Transcendentalists admit of no authoritative revelation other than that which is found in man and in the historical development of the race. All truth is to be discovered and established by a process of thought. If it be conceded that the Bible contains truth, it is only so far as it coincides with the teachings of philosophy. The same concession is freely made concerning the writings of the heathen sages. The theology of Daub, for example, is nothing more than the philosophy of Schelling. That is, it teaches just what that philosophy teaches concerning God, man, sin, redemption, and the future state. Marheinecke and Strauss find Hegelianism in the Bible, and they therefore admit that so far the Bible teaches truth....

These are the principal forms of the speculative method in its application to theology. These topics will present themselves for fuller consideration in a subsequent chapter.

The Mystical Method

Few words have been used with greater latitude of meaning than *mysticism.* It is here to be taken in a sense antithetical to speculation. Speculation is a process of thought; mysticism is [a] matter of feeling. The one assumes that the thinking faculty is that by which we attain the knowledge of truth. The other, distrusting reason, teaches that the feelings alone are to be relied upon, at least in the sphere of religion. Although this method has been unduly pressed, and systems of theology have been constructed under its guidance which are either entirely independent of the Scriptures or in which the doctrines of the Bible have been modified and perverted, it is not to be denied that great authority is due to our moral nature in matters of religion. It has ever been a great evil in the Church that men have allowed the logical understanding, or what they call their reason, to lead them to conclusions which are not only contrary to Scripture but which do violence to our moral nature. It is conceded that nothing contrary to reason can be true. But it is no less important to remember that nothing contrary to our moral nature can be true. It is also to be admitted that conscience is much less liable to err than reason; and when they come into conflict, real or apparent, our moral nature is the stronger and will assert its authority in spite of all we can do. It is rightfully supreme in the soul, although, with the reason and the will, it is in absolute subjection to God who is infinite reason and infinite moral excellence.

Mysticism as applied to theology. Mysticism, in its application to theology, has assumed two principal forms, the supernatural and the natural. According to the former, God, or the Spirit of God, holds direct communion with the soul; and by the excitement of its religious feelings gives it intuitions of truth and enables it to attain a kind, a degree, and an extent of knowledge unattainable in any other way. This has been the common theory of Christian mystics in ancient and modern times. If by this were meant merely that the Spirit of God by his illuminating influence gives believers a knowledge of the truths objectively revealed in the Scriptures which is peculiar, certain, and saving, it would be admitted by all evangelical Christians. And it is because such Christians do hold to this inward teaching of the Spirit that they are often called mystics by their opponents. This, however, is not what is here meant. The mystical method, in its supernatural form, assumes that God by his immediate intercourse with the soul reveals through the feelings and by means, or in the way of intuitions, divine truth independently of the outward teaching of his Word; and that it is this inward light, and not the Scriptures, which we are to follow.

According to the other, or natural form of the mystical method, it is not God but the natural religious consciousness of men, as excited and influenced by the circumstances of the individual which becomes the source of religious knowledge. The deeper and purer the religious feelings, the clearer the insight into truth. This illumination or spiritual intuition is a matter of degree. But as all men have a religious nature, they all have more or less clearly the apprehension of religious truth. The religious consciousness of men in different ages and nations has been historically developed under diverse influences, and hence we have diverse forms of religion—the Pagan, the Mohammedan, and the Christian. These do not stand related as true and false but as more or less pure. The appearance of Christ, his life, his work, his words, his death, had a wonderful effect on the minds of men. Their religious feelings were more deeply stirred, were more purified and elevated than ever before. Hence the men of this generation, who gave themselves up to his influence, had intuitions of religious truth of a far higher order than mankind had before attained. This influence continues to the present time. All Christians are its subjects. All therefore, in proportion to the purity and elevation of their religious feelings, have intuitions of divine things such as the Apostles and other Christians enjoyed. Perfect holiness would secure perfect knowledge.

Consequences of the mystical method. It follows from this theory: (1) That there are no such things as revelation and inspiration in the established theological meaning of those terms. Revelation is the supernatural objective presentation or communication of truth to the mind by the Spirit of God. But according to this theory there is, and can be, no such communication of truth. The religious feelings are providentially excited, and by reason of that excitement the mind perceives truth more or less clearly, or more or less imperfectly. Inspiration, in the Scriptural sense, is the supernatural guidance of the Spirit which renders its subjects infallible in communicating the truth to others. But according to this theory, no man is infallible as a teacher. Revelation and inspiration are in different degrees common to all men. And there is no reason why they should not be as perfect in some believers now as in the days of the Apostles. (2) The Bible has no infallible authority in matters of doctrine. The doctrinal propositions therein contained are not revelations by the Spirit. They are only the forms under which men of Jewish culture gave expression to their feelings and intuitions. Men of different culture, and under other circumstances, would have used other forms or adopted other doctrinal statements. (3) Christianity, therefore, neither consists in a system of doctrines, nor does it contain any such system. It is a life, an influence, a subjective state; or by whatever term it may be expressed or explained, it is a power within each individual Christian determining his feelings and his views of divine things. (4) Consequently, the duty of a theologian is not to interpret Scripture, but to interpret his own Christian consciousness; to ascertain and exhibit what truths concerning God are implied in his feelings toward God; what truths concerning Christ are involved in his feelings toward Christ; what the feelings teach concerning sin, redemption, eternal life, etc.

This method found its most distinguished and influential advocate in Schleiermacher, whose "Glaubenslehre" [dogmatics] is constructed on this principle.[6] By Twesten—his successor in the chair of Theology in the University of Berlin—it is held in greater subjection to the normal authority of Scripture. By others, again, of the same school, it has been carried out to its utmost extreme. We are at present, however, concerned only with its principle, and neither with the details of its application, nor with its refutation.

The Inductive Method

It is so called because it agrees in everything with the inductive method as applied to the natural sciences.

First, The man of science comes to the study of nature with certain assumptions.[7] (1) He assumes the trustworthiness of his sense perceptions. Unless he can rely upon the well-authenticated testimony of his sense, he is deprived of all means of prosecuting his investigations. The facts of nature reveal themselves to our faculties of sense, and can be known in no other way. (2) He must also assume the trustworthiness of his mental operations. He must take for granted that he can perceive, compare, combine, remember, and infer; and that he can safely rely upon these mental faculties in their legitimate exercise. (3) He must also rely on the certainty of those truths which are not learned from experience, but which are given in the constitution of our nature. That every effect must have a cause; that the same cause under like circumstances will produce like effects; that a cause is not a mere uniform antecedent but that which contains within itself the reason why the effect occurs.

Second, The student of nature having this ground on which to stand and these tools wherewith to work, proceeds to perceive, gather, and combine his facts. These he does not pretend to manufacture, nor presume to modify. He must take them as they are. He is only careful to be sure that they are real, and that he has them all, or

---

6. If there is a villain in the ST, it is F. E. D. Schleiermacher (1768–1834), whom Hodge scores repeatedly for a vast number of errors, e.g., on the nature of "dependence" (I: 21, 65, 173), on the nature of God and divine omniscience (I: 370, 395, 402, II: 138), on the Trinity (I: 481), on sin (II: 138), on Christ (II: 441–442), to mention only the most important.

7. This section and the one which follows on "The Inductive Method as applied to Theology" follow very closely the principles of Scottish Common Sense Realism first expounded by Alexander in 1812 (Selection 3).

at least all that are necessary to justify any inference which he may draw from them or any theory which he may build upon them.

Third, From facts thus ascertained and classified, he deduces the laws by which they are determined. That a heavy body falls to the ground is a familiar fact. Observation shows that it is not an isolated fact; but that all matter tends toward all other matter; that this tendency or attraction is in proportion to the quantity of matter; and its intensity decreases in proportion to the square of the distance of the attracting bodies. As all this is found to be universally and constantly the case within the field of observation, the mind is forced to conclude that there is some reason for it; in other words, that it is a law of nature which may be relied upon beyond the limits of actual observation. As this law has always operated in the past, the man of science is sure that it will operate in the future. It is in this way the vast body of modern science has been built up, and the laws which determine the motions of the heavenly bodies; the chemical changes constantly going on around us; the structure, growth, and propagation of plants and animals, have, to a greater or lesser extent, been ascertained and established. It is to be observed that these laws or general principles are not derived from the mind, and attributed to external objects, but derived or deduced from the objects and impressed upon the mind.

The Inductive Method as Applied to Theology

The Bible is to the theologian what nature is to the man of science. It is his store-house of facts; and his method of ascertaining what the Bible teaches is the same as that which the natural philosopher adopts to ascertain what nature teaches. In the first place, he comes to his task with all the assumptions above mentioned. He must assume the validity of those laws of belief which God has impressed upon our nature. In these laws are included some which have no direct application to the natural sciences. Such, for example, as the essential distinction between right and wrong; that nothing contrary to virtue can be enjoined by God; that it cannot be right to do evil that good may come; that sin deserves punishment, and other similar first truths, which God has implanted in the constitution of all moral beings, and which no objective revelation can possibly contradict. These first principles, however, are not to be arbitrarily assumed. No man has a right to lay down his own opinions, however firmly held, and call them "first truths of reason," and make them the source or test of Christian doctrines. Nothing can rightfully be included under the category of first truths, or laws of belief, which cannot stand the tests of universality and necessity, to which many add self-evidence. But self-evidence is included in universality and necessity, in so far, that nothing which is not self-evident can be universally believed, and what is self-evident forces itself on the mind of every intelligent creature.

In the second place, the duty of the Christian theologian is to ascertain, collect, and combine all the facts which God has revealed concerning himself and our relation to Him. These facts are all in the Bible. This is true, because everything revealed in nature, and in the constitution of man concerning God and our relation to Him, is contained and authenticated in Scripture. It is in this sense that "the

Bible, and the Bible alone, is the religion of Protestants."[8] It may be admitted that the truths which the theologian has to reduce to a science, or, to speak more humbly, which he has to arrange and harmonize, are revealed partly in the external works of God, partly in the constitution of our nature and partly in the religious experience of believers; yet lest we should err in our inferences from the works of God, we have a clearer revelation of all that nature reveals, in his Word; and lest we should misinterpret our own consciousness and the laws of our nature, everything that can be legitimately learned from that source will be found recognized and authenticated in the Scriptures; and lest we should attribute to the teaching of the Spirit the operations of our own natural affections, we find in the Bible the norm and standard of all genuine religious experience. The Scriptures teach not only the truth, but what are the effects of the truth on the heart and conscience when applied with saving power by the Holy Ghost.

In the third place, the theologian must be guided by the same rules in the collection of facts as govern the man of science.

1. This collection must be made with diligence and care. It is not an easy work. There is in every department of investigation great liability to error. Almost all false theories in science and false doctrines in theology are due in a great degree to mistakes as to matters of fact. A distinguished naturalist said he repeated an experiment a thousand times before he felt authorized to announce the result to the scientific world as an established fact.

2. This collection of facts must not only be carefully conducted, but also comprehensive, and if possible, exhaustive. An imperfect induction of facts led men for ages to believe that the sun moved round the earth and that the earth was an extended plain. In theology a partial induction of particulars has led to like serious errors. It is a fact that the Scriptures attribute omniscience to Christ. From this it was inferred that He could not have had a finite intelligence, but that the Logos was clothed in Him with a human body with its animal life. But it is also a Scriptural fact that ignorance and intellectual progress, as well as omniscience, are ascribed to our Lord. Both facts, therefore, must be included in our doctrine of his person. We must admit that He had a human as well as a divine intelligence. It is a fact that everything that can be predicated of a sinless man, is in the Bible, predicated of Christ; and it is also a fact that everything that is predicated of God is predicated of our Lord; hence it has been inferred that there were two Christs—two persons—the one human, the other divine, and that they dwelt together very much as the Spirit dwells in the believer; or, as evil spirits dwelt in demoniacs. But this theory overlooked the numerous facts which prove the individual personality of Christ. It was the same person who said, "I thirst"; who said, "Before Abraham was I am." The Scriptures teach that Christ's death was designed to reveal the love of God and to secure the reformation of men. Hence Socinus denied that his death was an

---

8. The saying is from William Chillingworth (1602–1644), latitudinarian Anglican and briefly convert to Rome whose views Hodge otherwise did not approve; see Ahlstrom, *Theology in America*, p. 290n13.

expiation for sin or satisfaction of justice. The latter fact, however, is as clearly revealed as the former; and therefore both must be taken into account in our statement of the doctrine concerning the design of Christ's death.

Illustrations without end might be given of the necessity of a comprehensive induction of facts to justify our doctrinal conclusions. These facts must not be willfully denied or carelessly overlooked or unfairly appreciated. We must be honest here, as the true student of nature is honest in his induction. Even scientific men are sometimes led to suppress or to pervert facts which militate against their favorite theories; but the temptation to this form of dishonesty is far less in their case than in that of the theologian. The truths of religion are far more important than those of natural science. They come home to the heart and conscience. They may alarm the fears or threaten the hopes of men, so that they are under strong temptations to overlook or pervert them. If, however, we really desire to know what God has revealed we must be conscientiously diligent and faithful in collecting the facts which He has made known, and in giving them their due weight. If a geologist should find in a deposit of early date implements of human workmanship, he is not allowed to say they are natural productions. He must either revise his conclusion as to the age of the deposit, or carry back to an earlier period the existence of man. There is no help for it. Science cannot make facts; it must take them as they are. In like manner, if the Bible asserts that Christ's death was a satisfaction to justice, the theologian is not allowed to merge justice into benevolence in order to suit his theory of the atonement.[9] If the Scriptures teach that men are born in sin, we cannot change the nature of sin and make it a tendency to evil and not really sin in order to get rid of difficulty. If it be a Scriptural fact that the soul exists in a state of conscious activity between death and the resurrection, we must not deny this fact or reduce this conscious activity to zero because our anthropology teaches that the soul has no individuality and no activity without a body. We must take the facts of the Bible as they are, and construct our system so as to embrace them all in their integrity.

In the fourth place, in theology as in natural science, principles are derived from facts, and not impressed upon them. The properties of matter, the laws of motion, of magnetism, of light, etc., are not framed by the mind. They are not laws of thought. They are deductions from facts. The investigator sees, or ascertains by observation, what are the laws which determine material phenomena; he does not invent those laws. His speculations on matters of science, unless sustained by facts, are worthless. It is no less unscientific for the theologian to assume a theory as to the nature of virtue, of sin, of liberty, of moral obligation, and then explain the facts of Scripture in accordance with his theories. His only proper course is to derive his theory of virtue, of sin, of liberty, of obligation, from the facts of the Bible. He should remember that his business is not to set forth his system of truth (that is of no account), but to ascertain and exhibit what is God's system, which is a matter of

9. From this point, and for several paragraphs, Hodge is rehearsing his own polemical history, especially with the Congregationalists of New England.

the greatest moment. If he cannot believe what the facts of the Bible assume to be true, let him say so. Let the sacred writers have their doctrine, while he has his own. To this ground a large class of modern exegetes and theologians, after a long struggle, have actually come. They give what they regard as the doctrines of the Old Testament; then those of the Evangelists; then those of the Apostles; and then their own. This is fair. So long, however, as the binding authority of Scripture is acknowledged, the temptation is very strong to press the facts of the Bible into accordance with our preconceived theories. If a man be persuaded that certainty in acting is inconsistent with liberty of action; that a free agent can always act contrary to any amount of influence (not destructive of his liberty) brought to bear upon him, he will inevitably deny that the Scriptures teach the contrary, and thus be forced to explain away all facts which prove the absolute control of God over the will and volitions of men. If he hold that sinfulness can be predicated only of intelligent, voluntary action in contravention of law, he must deny that men are born in sin, let the Bible teach what it may. If he believes that ability limits obliga-tion, he must believe independently of the Scriptures, or in opposition to them, it matters not which, that men are able to repent, believe, love God perfectly, to live without sin, at any and all times, without the least assistance from the Spirit of God. If he deny that the innocent may justly suffer penal evil for the guilty, he must deny that Christ bore our sins. If he deny that the merit of one man can be the judicial ground of the pardon and salvation of other men, he must reject the Scriptural doctrine of justification. It is plain that complete havoc must be made of the whole system of revealed truth, unless we consent to derive our philosophy from the Bible, instead of explaining the Bible by our philosophy. If the Scriptures teach that sin is hereditary, we must adopt a theory of sin suited to that fact. If they teach that men cannot repent, believe, or do anything spiritually good, without the super-natural aid of the Holy Spirit, we must make our theory of moral obligation accord with that fact. If the Bible teaches that we bear the guilt of Adam's first sin, that Christ bore our guilt, and endured the penalty of the law in our stead, these are facts with which we must make our principles agree. It would be easy to show that in every department of theology—in regard to the nature of God, his relation to the world, the plan of salvation, the person and work of Christ, the nature of sin, the operations of divine grace, men, instead of taking the facts of the Bible, and seeing what principles they imply, what philosophy underlies them, have adopted their philosophy independently of the Bible, to which the facts of the Bible are made to bend. This is utterly unphilosophical. It is the fundamental principle of all sciences, and of theology among the rest, that theory is to be determined by facts, and not facts by theory. As natural science was a chaos until the principle of induction was admitted and faithfully carried out, so theology is a jumble of human speculations, not worth a straw, when men refuse to apply the same principle to the study of the Word of God.

The Scriptures Contain All the Facts of Theology

This is perfectly consistent, on the one hand, with the admission of intuitive truths, both intellectual and moral, due to our constitution as rational and moral beings; and, on the other hand, with the controlling power over our beliefs exercised by the inward teachings of the Spirit, or, in other words, by our religious experience. And that for two reasons: First, All truth must be consistent. God cannot contradict himself. He cannot force us by the constitution of the nature which He has given us to believe one thing, and in his Word command us to believe the opposite. And, second, All the truths taught by the constitution of our nature or by religious experience are recognized and authenticated in the Scriptures. This is a safeguard and a limit. We cannot assume this or that principle to be intuitively true, or this or that conclusion to be demonstrably certain, and make them a standard to which the Bible must conform. What is self-evidently true, must be proved to be so and is always recognized in the Bible as true. Whole systems of theologies are founded upon intuitions, so called, and if every man is at liberty to exalt his own intuitions, as men are accustomed to call their strong convictions, we should have as many theologies in the world as there are thinkers. The same remark is applicable to religious experience. There is no form of conviction more intimate and irresistible than that which arises from the inward teaching of the Spirit. All saving faith rests on his testimony or demonstration (1 Cor. 2:4). Believers have an unction from the Holy One, and they know the truth, and that no lie (or false doctrine) is of the truth. This inward teaching produces a conviction which no sophistries can obscure and no arguments can shake. It is founded on consciousness, and you might as well argue a man out of a belief of his existence, as out of confidence that what he is thus taught of God is true. Two things, however, are to be borne in mind. First, That this inward teaching or demonstration of the Spirit is confined to truths objectively revealed in the Scriptures. It is given, says the Apostle, in order that we may know things gratuitously given, *i.e.*, revealed to us by God in his Word (1 Cor. 2:10–16). It is not, therefore, a revelation of new truths, but an illumination of the mind, so that it apprehends the truth, excellence, and glory of things already revealed. And second, This experience is depicted in the Word of God. The Bible gives us not only the facts concerning God and Christ, ourselves, and our relations to our Maker and Redeemer, but also records the legitimate effects of those truths on the minds of believers. So that we cannot appeal to our own feelings or inward experience, as a ground or guide, unless we can show that it agrees with the experience of holy men as recorded in the Scriptures.

Although the inward teaching of the Spirit, or religious experience, is no substitute for an external revelation, and is no part of the rule of faith, it is, nevertheless, an invaluable guide in determining what the rule of faith teaches. The distinguishing feature of Augustinianism as taught by Augustine himself, and by the purer theologians of the Latin Church throughout the Middle Ages, which was set forth by the Reformers, and especially by Calvin and the Geneva divines, is that the inward teaching of the Spirit is allowed its proper place in determining our theology. The question is not first and mainly, What is true to the understanding, but What is true to the renewed heart? The effort is not to make the assertations of the Bible harmonize with the speculative reason, but to subject our feeble reason to the mind of God as revealed in his Word, and by his Spirit in our inner life. It might be

easy to lead men to the conclusion that they are responsible only for their voluntary acts, if the appeal is made solely to the understanding. But if the appeal be
made to every man's, and especially to every Christian's inward experience, the
opposite conclusion is reached. We are convinced of the sinfulness of states of mind
as well as of voluntary acts, even when those states are not the effect of our own
agency, and are not subject to the power of the will. We are conscious of being sold
under sin; of being its slaves; of being possessed by it as a power or law, immanent,
innate, and beyond our control. Such is the doctrine of the Bible, and such is the
teaching of our religious consciousness when under the influence of the Spirit of
God. The true method in theology requires that the facts of religious experience
should be accepted as facts, and when duly authenticated by Scripture, be allowed
to interpret the doctrinal statements of the Word of God. So legitimate and powerful is this inward teaching of the Spirit that it is no uncommon thing to find men
having two theologies—one of the intellect, and another of the heart. The one may
find expression in creeds and systems of divinity, the other in their prayers and
hymns. It would be safe for a man to resolve to admit into his theology nothing
which is not sustained by the devotional writings of true Christians of every denomination. It would be easy to construct from such writings received and sanctioned
by Romanists, Lutherans, Reformed, and Remonstrants [i.e., Arminians], a system
of Pauline or Augustinian theology such as would satisfy any intelligent and devout
Calvinist in the world.

The true method of theology is, therefore, the inductive, which assumes that the
Bible contains all the facts or truths which form the contents of theology, just as the
facts of nature are the contents of the natural sciences. It is also assumed that the
relation of these biblical facts to each other, the principles involved in them, the
laws which determine them, are in the facts themselves and are to be deduced from
the facts of nature. In neither case are the principles derived from the mind and
imposed upon the facts, but equally in both departments, the principles or laws are
deduced from the facts and recognized by the mind.

Theology*

If the views presented in the preceding chapter be correct, the question, What is
Theology? is already answered. If natural science be concerned with the facts and
laws of nature, theology is concerned with the facts and the principles of the Bible.
If the object of the one be to arrange and systematize the facts of the external
world, and to ascertain the laws by which they are determined; the object of the
other is to systematize the facts of the Bible, and ascertain the principles or general
truths which those facts involve. And as the order in which the facts of nature are
arranged cannot be determined arbitrarily, but by the nature of the facts themselves, so it is with the facts of the Bible. The parts of any organic whole have a
natural relation which cannot with impunity be ignored or changed. The parts of a

*Chapter 2, *Systematic Theology.*

watch, or of any other piece of mechanism, must be normally arranged or it will be in confusion and worthless. All the parts of a plant or animal are disposed to answer a given end and are mutually dependent. We cannot put the roots of a tree in the place of the branches or the teeth of an animal in the place of its feet. So the facts of science arrange themselves. They are not arranged by the naturalist. His business is simply to ascertain what the arrangement given in the nature of the facts is. If he makes a mistake, his system is false, and to a greater or less degree valueless. The same is obviously true with regard to the facts or truths of the Bible. They cannot be held in isolation, nor will they admit of any and every arrangement the theologian may choose to assign them. They bear a natural relation to each other which cannot be overlooked or perverted without the facts themselves being perverted. If the facts of Scripture are what Augustinians believe them to be, then the Augustinian system is the only possible system of theology. If those facts be what Romanists or Remonstrants [i.e., Arminians] take them to be, then their system is the only true one. It is important that the theologian should know his place. He is not master of the situation. He can no more construct a system of theology to suit his fancy than the astronomer can adjust the mechanism of the heavens according to his own good pleasure. As the facts of astronomy arrange themselves in a certain order and will admit of no other, so it is with the facts of theology. Theology, therefore, is the exhibition of the facts of Scripture in their proper order and relation, with the principles or general truths involved in the facts themselves, and which pervade and harmonize the whole.

It follows, also, from this view of the subject, that as the Bible contains one class of facts or truths which are not elsewhere revealed, and another class which, although more clearly made known in the Scriptures than anywhere else, are, nevertheless, so far revealed in nature as to be deducible therefrom, theology is properly distinguished as natural and revealed. The former is concerned with the facts of nature so far as they reveal God and our relation to Him, and the latter with the facts of Scripture. This distinction, which in one view is important, in another, is of little consequence, inasmuch as all that nature teaches concerning God and our duties is more fully authoritatively revealed in his Word.

9

The Scriptures Are the Word of God
1841

When the publications committee of the American Sunday School Union felt the need in the late 1830s for a brief text describing simply the doctrines of Scripture, they turned to Charles Hodge. The result was *The Way of Life,* a nontechnical work that over the years has probably been more widely read than anything Hodge ever wrote. A. A. Hodge described the work in glowing terms that many others have since echoed: "the book is eminently luminous; its characteristic attribute is light suffused with love."[1] *The Way of Life* is important for an analysis of the Princeton Theology because of its approach to Scripture. Hodge here treats the Bible as self-authenticating and is not troubled as his predecessor and successor were by the need to demonstrate its truthfulness. A full analysis of Princeton's apologetic must take into account the reasoning of this work (as well as those discussions mentioned in the introduction to Selection 6) before rushing to conclusions about the "rationalistic" or "scholastic" character of the Princeton Theology. *The Way of Life* was published by the American Sunday School Union in 1841. It was immediately reprinted in England by the London Religious Tract Society. It was eventually translated into several other languages, including Hindustani. And it continues in print today. The excerpt which follows is from Chapter 1, "The Scriptures Are the Word of God," Sections I ("The internal evidence of the Divine origin of the Scriptures") and II ("The internal evidence of their Divine origin is the proper ground of faith in the Scriptures"), as published by the Banner of Truth Trust (London, 1959), pp. 11–16, 24–25.

IT OFTEN HAPPENS that those who hear the gospel doubt whether it is really the word of God. Having been taught from infancy to regard it as a Divine revelation and knowing no sufficient reason for rejecting it, they yield a general assent to its claims. There are times, however, when they would gladly be more fully assured that the Bible is not a cunningly devised fable. They think if that point was absolutely certain, they would at once submit to all the gospel requires.

Such doubts do not arise from any deficiency in the evidence of the Divine

---

1. A. A. Hodge, *Life of Charles Hodge,* p. 325, with pp. 324–331 on the composition and favorable reception of this work.

authority of the Scriptures; nor would they be removed by any increase of that evidence. They have their origin in the state of the heart. The most important of all the evidences of Christianity can never be properly appreciated unless the heart be right in the sight of God. The same exhibition of truth which produces unwavering conviction in one mind leaves another in a state of doubt or unbelief. And the same mind often passes rapidly, though rationally, from a state of scepticism to that of faith, without any change in the mere external evidence presented to it.

No amount of mere external evidence can produce genuine faith. The Israelites, who had seen a long succession of wonders in the land of Egypt, who had passed through the divided waters of the Red Sea, who were daily receiving by miracle food from heaven, who had trembled at the manifestations of the Divine majesty on Mount Sinai, within sight of that mountain made a golden calf their god. The men who saw the miracles of Christ performed almost daily in their presence, cried out, "Crucify him! Crucify him!" Hence our Saviour said, that those who hear not "Moses and the prophets, neither will they be persuaded though one rose from the dead." We may confidently conclude, therefore, that those who now believe not the gospel, would not be persuaded had they seen all the miracles which Christ performed.

It is important that the attention of the doubting should be directed to the fact that their want of faith is to be attributed to their own moral state, and not to any deficiency in the evidence of the truth. . . .

To make the testimony of others to the truth of Christianity the ground of faith, is inadmissible, for two obvious reasons. In the first place, as already intimated, it is not sufficiently extensive. The obligation to believe rests on multitudes to whom that testimony is not addressed. In the second place, it is entirely inadequate. The great mass of men cannot be required to believe, on the testimony of the learned few, a religion which is to control their conduct in this world, and to decide their destiny in the next. Besides, learned men testify on behalf of the Koran as well as in favour of the Bible. That, therefore, cannot be an adequate ground of faith which may be urged in support of error as well as of truth. To require the common people to be able to see why the testimony of learned Christians may safely be relied upon while that of learned Mussulmans should be rejected, is to require of them a task as severe as the examination of the historical evidences of Christianity. There is, therefore, no way of justifying the universal, immediate, and authoritative demand which the Bible makes on our faith, except by admitting that it contains within itself the proofs of its Divine origin. . . .

It is . . . the positive internal evidence of a Divine origin which gives power and authority to the claims of the Bible. This evidence consists mainly in its perfect holiness, in the correspondence between all its statements respecting God, man, redemption, and a future state, and all our own right judgements, reasonable apprehensions, and personal experience. When the mind is enlightened to see this holiness; when it perceives how exactly the rule of duty prescribed in the Word of God agrees with that enforced by conscience; how the account which it gives of human nature coincides with human experience; how fully it meets our whole case; when it feels how powerfully the truths there presented operate to purify, console, and sustain the soul—the belief of the Scriptures is a necessary consequence. The idea that such a book is a lie and a forgery involves a contradiction. The human mind is so constituted that it cannot refuse to assent to evidence, when clearly perceived. We cannot withhold our confidence from a man whose moral excellence is plainly, variously, and constantly manifested. We cannot see and feel his goodness, and yet believe him to be an impostor or deceiver. In like manner, we cannot see the excellence of the Scriptures, and yet believe them to be one enormous falsehood. The Bible claims to be the Word of God; it speaks in his name, it assumes his authority. How can these claims be false and yet the Bible so holy? How can falsehood be an element of perfect excellence? The only possible way of shaking our confidence in the competent testimony of a man is to show that he is not a good man. If his goodness is admitted, confidence in his word cannot be withheld, and especially when all he says finds its confirmation in our own experience and commends itself to our conscience and judgment. Thus also it is impossible that we should discern the excellence of the Scriptures and feel their correspondence with our experience and necessities, and yet suppose them to be untrue. . . .

It is, therefore, plainly the doctrine of the Scriptures themselves that the Word of God is to be believed because of the authority or command of God manifesting itself therein in a manner analogous to the exhibition of his perfections in the works of nature. If, as Paul teaches us, the eternal power and Godhead are so clearly manifested by the things that are made that even the heathen are without excuse; and if their unbelief is ascribed not to the want of evidence but to their not liking to retain God in their knowledge, we need not wonder that the far clearer manifestation of the Divine perfections made in the Scripture should be the ground of a more imperative command to believe.

It is the experience of true Christians in all ages and nations that their faith is founded on the spiritual apprehension and experience of the power of the truth. There are multitudes of such Christians, who if asked why they believe the Scriptures to be the Word of God might find it difficult to give an answer, whose faith is nevertheless both strong and rational. They are conscious of its grounds, though they may not be able to state them. They have the witness in themselves and know that they believe, not because others believe, or because learned men have proved certain facts which establish the truth of Christianity. They believe in Christ for the same reason that they believe in God; and they believe in God because they see his glory, and feel his authority and power.

If, then, the truth of God contains in its own nature a revelation of Divine excellence, the sin of unbelief is a very great sin. Not to have faith in God when clearly revealed is the highest offence which a creature can commit against its Creator. . . .

10

Inspiration
1857

The generation before the Civil War witnessed the first flourishing of modern biblical scholarship in the United States. In New England especially, critical concepts imported from Germany received careful attention. Orthodox Congregationalists like Moses Stuart and conservative Unitarians like Andrews Norton generally resisted any retreat from traditional beliefs in the Bible's infallibility and inspiration, even as they paid serious attention to Europeans who did. But more daring critics, like Transcendentalist Theodore Parker, were willing to affirm that the Bible must be treated like every other "historical phenomenon . . . entirely subject to the laws of historical inquiry."[1] Parker, for example, whose works on Scripture first appeared in the 1840s, accepted the multiple authorship of the Pentateuch and late dates for many Old Testament books; he also questioned the reliability of miracle stories in both Testaments.

Closer to the theological mainstream, the work of Horace Bushnell raised more immediate questions about traditional views of Scripture. Bushnell, a Congregationalist pastor in Hartford, Connecticut, published a "Preliminary Dissertation on the Nature of Language" as an introduction to his 1849 work, *God in Christ,* in which he questioned correspondence views of language.[2] Speech or writing about ultimate reality, which Bushnell called "intelligent discourse," provided only hints, momentary glimpses, or veiled symbols of the truth. In making these assertions Bushnell was introducing into an American context the kind of thinking which Schleiermacher had earlier provided in Germany and Samuel Taylor Coleridge in England. When applied to Scripture, these ideas undercut the biblical literalism, and even more, the belief in the propositional character of truth that was so much a part of the Princeton Theology as well as of many other theological positions in America.

Charles Hodge had handled Bushnell's *God in Christ* severely when it first appeared ("Bushnell's Discourses," BRPR, 21 [April 1849], 259–298). He conceded that Bushnell's observations on language were correct—"that there are two great departments of language, the physical and intellectual, or proper and

---

1. Quoted in Jerry Wayne Brown, *The Rise of Biblical Criticism in America, 1800–1870: The New England Scholars* (Middletown, Conn.: Wesleyan University Press, 1969), p. 166. This entire book provides an excellent general survey of American biblical criticism during Hodge's lifetime.

2. See ibid., pp. 177–179. Bushnell's "Dissertation on the Nature of Language" is reprinted, with helpful notes, in Ahlstrom, *Theology in America,* pp. 317–370.

figurative, the language of sensation and the language of thought" ("Bushnell's Discourses," p. 265). But he chastised Bushnell for exaggerating this distinction. If Bushnell is correct, Hodge asserted, "there can be no revelation from God to men, except to the imagination and the feelings, none to the reason" (p. 266). Hodge, as a creedal Calvinist and a pupil of Archibald Alexander, could not tolerate Bushnell's romantic imprecision. For him the Bible remained an intelligible word of actual revelation.

Hodge's uneasiness with Bushnell's ideas on language and his awareness of New England's dabbling in biblical higher criticism provided the backdrop for his 1857 article on the inspiration of the Scriptures. The immediate occasion was his commendation of a work by William Lee of Trinity College, Dublin, entitled *The Inspiration of Holy Scripture, its Nature and Proof.* Ideas latent in Alexander's teaching on Scripture are here sharpened and made explicit. The Bible is trustworthy because it is God's word, inspired by the Holy Spirit and attested by Jesus. Scripture does not arise from a mechanical process of dictation but from the Holy Spirit's active superintendence of the human author. The result "is the communication or the record of truth." The truth of the Bible, moreover, will never contradict truth which we discover in other realms of inquiry (Hodge mentions astronomy and geology). Hodge is not impressed with those who find errors in the Bible, for he feels these can be ascribed to scribal mistakes in copying the text or to our own impatient ignorance.

The 1857 essay set out most of the principles and made most of the qualifying statements that reappeared in the more famous 1881 article by A. A. Hodge and Warfield on the same subject (Selection 19). The two later Princetonians refined and clarified the elder Hodge's thinking, but did not deviate measurably from it, except in the reduced emphasis which they placed on the internal testimony of the Holy Spirit as the strongest demonstration of Scripture's truthfulness. Their careful definition of terms like *inspired, infallible, without error*—terms which have meant much to evangelicals in the twentieth century—drew heavily on Charles Hodge's exposition in this essay. Selections here are from "Inspiration," BRPR, 29 (October 1857), 660-661, 668-670, 672-678, 682-684, 686-687. Many of these themes reappear in ST, I: 151-190.

H APPILY THE BELIEF of the inspiration of the Scriptures is so connected with faith in Christ that the latter in a measure necessitates the former. A man can hardly believe that Jesus is the Son of God, and worship him as such, without regarding as the word of God the volume which reveals his glory; which treats of his person and work from its first page to its last sentence; which predicted his advent four thousand years before his manifestation in the flesh; which, centuries before his birth, described his glory as though it was an object of sight, and his life and death as though they had already occurred. To such a believer the assumption that the Scriptures are the work of man is as preposterous as the assumption that man made the sun. Nor can any such believer read the discourses of our Lord, and hear him say that the Scriptures cannot be broken, that heaven and earth may pass away but one jot of the law cannot fail until all be fulfilled, that David spoke in the Spirit; he cannot hear his command, "Search the Scriptures, for they testify of me," without sharing in his conviction that the Scriptures are infallible. When a man becomes a true Christian, when he is made a partaker of the precious faith of God's elect, what is it that he believes? The scriptural answer to that question is, he believes the record which God has given of his Son. And where is that record? In every part of the Bible, directly or indirectly, from Genesis to Revelation.

Faith therefore in Christ involves faith in the Scriptures as the word of God, and faith in the Scriptures as the word of God is faith in their plenary inspiration. That is, it is the persuasion that they are not the product of the fallible intellect of man but of the infallible intellect of God. This faith, as the apostle teaches us, is not founded on reason, i.e., on arguments addressed to the understanding, nor is it induced by persuasive words addressed to the feelings, but it rests in the demonstration of the Spirit. This demonstration is internal. It does not consist in the outward array of evidence, but in a supernatural illumination imparting spiritual discernment, so that its subjects have no need of external teaching, but this anointing teacheth them what is truth. . . .

The infallibility consequent on inspiration was limited to the nature of the object to be accomplished. As that object was the communication, orally and by writing, of the will of God (i.e., of what God willed to be communicated and recorded as his word), inspired men were infallible only in that work. Infallibility did not become a personal attribute so that the sacred writers could not err in judgment or conduct in the ordinary affairs of life. Inspiration did not cure their ignorance, nor preserve them from error, except in their official work and while acting as the spokesmen of God. . . . All that is in the New Testament is in the Old but it was not fully understood until expounded and unfolded by the prophets and apostles of the new dispensation. And much contained in the New Testament has a fulness of meaning which the apostles themselves little imagined. They were ignorant of many things and were as liable to error or ignorance beyond the limits of their official teaching as other men. An inspired man could not, indeed, err in his instruction on any subject. He could not teach by inspiration that the earth is the centre of our system, or that the sun, moon, and stars are mere satellites of our globe, but such may have been his own conviction. Inspiration did not elevate him in secular knowledge above the age in which he lived; it only, so far as secular and scientific truths are concerned, preserved him from *teaching* error. The indications are abundant and conclusive that the sacred writers shared in all the current opinions of the generation to which they belonged. To them the heavens were solid, and the earth a plane; the sun moved from east to west over their heads. Whatever the ancient Hebrews thought of the constitution of the universe, of the laws and operations of nature, of the constitution of man, of the influence of unseen spirits, was no part of the faith of the sacred writers. The latter were not rendered by their inspiration one whit wiser than the former in relation to any such points. We may therefore hold that the Bible is in the strictest sense the word of God, and infallible in all its parts, and yet admit the ignorance and errors of the sacred writers as men. It was only as sacred writers they were infallible. . . .

Inspiration did not destroy the conscious self-control of its subjects. Inspired men were not thrown into a state of ecstasy in which their understandings were in abeyance and they were led to give utterance to words of which they knew not the import. They were not carried away to speak or write, as it were, in spite of themselves, as was the case with the utterers of heathen oracles or those possessed with evil spirits. The spirits of the prophets were subject to the prophets. The influence under which they spoke may not have revealed itself to their consciousness any more than the renewing and sanctifying influences of the Spirit are matters of consciousness to those who experience them. From the beginning to the end of the Bible there is constant evidence of the calm self-control of the sacred writers. They all wrote and spoke as men in the full possession of their faculties, just as men of their age and circumstances might be expected to speak and write. It is, therefore, a perversion of the common doctrine to represent it as reducing the inspired penmen into mere machines, as though they were guided by an influence which destroyed or superseded their own activity. If the Spirit of God can mingle itself with the elements of human action and render it certain that a man will repent and believe and persevere in holiness without interfering with his consciousness or liberty, why may not that same Spirit guide the mental operations of a man so that he shall speak or write without error and still be perfectly self-controlled and free? . . .

The guidance of the Spirit extended to the words no less than to the thoughts of the sacred writers. The prophets not only constantly say, "Thus saith the Lord," and the apostle not only affirms that he used "words taught by the Spirit," but it arises from the very nature of inspiration as actually exhibited in the sacred volume that the guidance of the Spirit extended to the words employed. If inspiration were only an elevation of the natural powers analogous to the stimulus of passion or the excitement of enthusiasm, then indeed, both thoughts and words would be due to the writer's own mind, and inspiration would lose its divine character and value. But if (as it actually reveals itself in Scripture), it is a supernatural control exerted by the Holy Spirit over the minds of its subjects, it must of necessity include the language which they use. In no other way could there be any effectual control over the thoughts expressed. The end to be accomplished is the communication or the record of truth. That communication or record is made in human language; unless the language is determined by the Spirit, the communication after all is human and not divine. In the historical portions of Scripture there is little for inspiration to accomplish beyond the proper selection of the materials and accuracy of statement; and if the Spirit left the mode of such to the uninfluenced mind of the writer, then the whole end to be accomplished failed. There is nothing on this hypothesis to distinguish the scriptural histories from the narratives of ordinary men. Again, in those instance in which the revelations to be recorded were objectively made, as in the discourses of our Lord, the only office of inspiration, the only thing which could distinguish the record of those discourses made by an apostle from a report made by any other auditor would be the infallible correctness of the report, and this, of course, involves the propriety and fitness of the language used to convey the thoughts to be communicated. To deny, in such cases, the control of the Spirit over the words of the sacred writer is to deny inspiration altogether. . . .

There is another obvious fact which proves that the sacred writers employed words "taught by the Holy Ghost." In many cases the appeal is made to a single word, or the argument is made to rest upon the form of expression. In many instances, indeed, the apostles in quoting the Old Testament content themselves with giving the sense without regarding the language of the original, but they often rest the force of the passage quoted upon the very words employed. They argue from the titles given to the Messiah; they make the very language of the ancient prophets the foundation of their conclusions, and Paul rests his exposition of an ancient prediction on the use of the singular (seed) instead of the plural (seeds). The view, therefore, everywhere presented in the New Testament of the inspiration of the ancient prophets, supposes them to be under the guidance of the Holy Spirit in the selection of the words which they employ. . . .

It has already been remarked that verbal inspiration does not suppose anything mechanical. It does not make the writer a machine. It is not a process of dictation, as when a language unknown to the penman is employed. The writer retains his consciousness and self-control; he may be unconscious of the influence of which he is subject; he speaks or writes as freely and as characteristically as though he were entirely uninfluenced by the Spirit of God. . . . If then the providential and the spiritual agency of God may control human action and leave the agent free, why may not the Spirit of God, as the spirit of inspiration, guide the mental operations of the sacred writers so that while they are unconscious of his power, they yet speak as they are moved by the Holy Ghost? It is a mere popular misconception with which, however, even scholars are often chargeable, which supposes that verbal inspiration implies such a dictation as supersedes the free selection of his words on the part of the sacred writer. It is a fundamental principle of scriptural theology that a man may be infallibly guided in his free acts. . . . Verbal inspiration, therefore, or that influence of the Spirit which controlled the sacred writers in the selection of their words, allowed them perfect freedom within the limits of truth. They were kept from error and guided to the use of words which expressed the mind of the Spirit, but within these limits they were free to use such language and to narrate such circumstances as suited their own taste or purposes. To adduce the evidence of this freedom, and consequent diversity in the sacred writers, as an argument against verbal inspiration, as is done even by distinguished writers, only betrays ignorance of the doctrine which they profess to oppose. . . .

It is not only natural and according to analogy that there should be difficulties connected with this doctrine, but the marvel is that they are not a hundred-fold greater. Let any man bring the case before his mind. Infallibility, or absolute freedom from error, is claimed for a book containing sixty-six distinct productions, on all subjects of history, of law, of religion, of morals; embracing poetry, prophecy, doctrinal and practical discourses, covering the whole of man's present necessities and future destiny, written by about forty different men, at intervals more or less distant, during fifteen hundred years. If this is a human production, if written by uninspired men, its claim to infallibility could be disproved to the conviction of an idiot. It must contain evidence of human imbecility, ignorance, and error, so overwhelming as to put to silence and cover with shame the most illiterate and bigoted advocate of its divine origin. Instead, however, of any such overwhelming evidence against the infallibility of the Bible, the difficulties are so minute as to escape the notice of ordinary intelligence. They must be sought as with a microscope and picked out with the most delicate forceps of criticism. One writer says that on a certain occasion twenty-four thousand persons were slain; another, a thousand years after, says there were twenty-three thousand; one evangelist says the inscription on the cross was, "The King of the Jews;" another says it was, "This is the King of the Jews." Are not these objections pitiful? And yet they are seriously adduced by able and learned men. We do not say that there are not other objections, and some of a more serious kind; but we do say that, considering the nature of the claim, these difficulties are miraculously small. That is, it is a miracle they are not greater. Let it be remembered that the Bible was written before the birth of science, that it touches on all departments of human knowledge; it speaks of the sun, moon, and stars, of the earth, air, and ocean, of the origin, constitution, and destiny of man; yet, what has science or philosophy to say against the Bible? It is true, when astronomy first began to unfold the mechanism of the universe there was great triumph among infidels, and great alarm among believers, at the apparent conflict between science and the Scriptures. But how stands the case now? The universe is revealed to its profoundest depths and the Bible is found to harmonize with all its new discovered wonders. No man now pretends that there is a word in the Bible, from Genesis to Revelation, inconsistent with the highest results of astronomy. Geology has of late asserted her claims and there are the same exultations and the same alarms. But any one who has attended to the progress of this new science must be blind indeed not to see that geology will soon be found side by side with astronomy in obsequiously bearing up the queenly train of God's majestic word. . . .

A very large proportion of the objections to the common doctrine of inspiration is founded on misapprehension of its nature. It is assumed that if the Bible is the word of God there can be no human element about it, no diversity of style, no evidence of different mental peculiarities, no variety in the narratives of the same event, no greater amplitude in one case than in another, no presenting the same event or the same truth under different aspects or relations. . . . Now, as the church doctrine of inspiration is that the Spirit guides each man in the use of his own peculiar faculties and powers, whether he be Greek or Hebrew, gentle or simple, learned or unlearned, infant or adult, such objections as the above are wide of the mark. . . .

Much the most serious difficulties which the advocate of the doctrine of inspiration has to encounter arise from the real or apparent inconsistencies, contradictions, and inaccuracies of the sacred volume. With regard to this class of objections, we would repeat a remark already made, viz., that the cases of contradiction or inconsistencies are, considering the age and character of the different books constituting the Bible, wonderfully few and trivial. Secondly, these inconsistencies do not concern matters of doctrine or duty, but numbers, dates, and historical details. Thirdly, in many cases the contradictions are merely apparent and readily admit of being fairly reconciled. Fourthly, with regard to those which cannot be satisfactorily explained it is rational to confess our ignorance, but irrational to assume that what we cannot explain is inexplicable. There are so many errors of transcription in the text of Scripture, such obscurity as to matters necessary to elucidate these ancient records, so little is known of contemporary history, that a man's faith in the divinity of the Bible must be small indeed if it be shaken because he cannot harmonize the conflicting dates and numbers in Kings and Chronicles. We are perfectly willing to let these difficulties remain and to allow the objectors to make the most of them. They can no more shake the faith of a Christian than the unsolved perturbations of the orbit of a comet shake the astronomer's confidence in the law of gravitation. . . .

11

Geology and the Bible
1872

The Princeton stake in science was always very great. In the first place, the Princeton theologians affirmed the unity of truth. The world, its natural laws, and divine revelation were all results of God's activity and thus, in principle, could not be inconsistent with each other. But these theologians had another reason to follow scientific developments closely, since they defined theology in explicitly scientific terms. A proper theologian approached his "facts" objectively, he collected them and arranged them like a morphologist, and he put them together inductively by building general positions from an accumulation of particulars (Selection 8). The Bible was the supreme repository of facts for the theologian, but the natural world also constituted an assemblage of facts. The first came from God through revelation, the second from God through creation. It was thus imperative—to preserve both a general conception of truth and a particular approach to Scripture—that the results of theological enterprise and of natural science complement each other.

American theologians who held such beliefs had been given a start ("staggered" as Hodge puts it below) when geologists early in the nineteenth century began to posit an immense age for the earth.[1] The shock came from the manifest discrepancy between such conclusions (resting on an inductive approach to facts gathered through geological inquiry) and the settled conviction that the earth was only about six thousand years old (resting on an inductive approach to the facts expressed in the genealogies of Genesis). Although some American theologians, like Moses Stuart of Andover Seminary,[2] refused to give way to the new geological interpretation, the Princeton theologians found no difficulty in making the necessary adjustment. "The Church," Hodge had written in 1859, "is willing to meet men of science on equal terms. . . . The church will stand by her convictions founded on something surer than consciousness, even the power of

1. On this development and its implications for theology, see John C. Greene, "Science and Religion," pp. 50-69, in *The Rise of Adventism,* ed. Edwin Scott Gaustad (New York: Harper & Row, 1974); Bozeman, *Protestants in an Age of Science,* pp. 95-97 and *passim;* Herbert Hovenkamp, *Science and Religion in America 1800-1860* (Philadelphia: University of Pennsylvania Press, 1978); and on similar developments in astronomy, Ronald L. Numbers, *Creation by Natural Law: Laplace's Nebular Hypothesis in American Thought* (Seattle: University of Washington Press, 1977), especially pp. 88-104.
2. On Stuart's Common Sense Philosophy and biblical literalism, see George M. Marsden, "Everyone One's Own Interpreter? The Bible, Science, and Authority in Mid-Nineteenth-Century America," in *The Bible in America,* pp. 92-93.

God, (I Cor. 2:5), and let science prove what facts it can, assured that God in nature can never contradict God in the Bible and in the hearts of his people." In that same essay, Hodge even conceded that "the church . . . is willing that the Bible should be interpreted under the guidance of the facts of science." So, if a heliocentric solar system or an ancient earth can be established as fact, the church will modify its theories concerning scriptural facts to accommodate those findings. The key, however, remained for Hodge the "real difference between facts and theories, the former, and not the latter, are authoritative" ("The Unity of Mankind," BRPR 31 [January 1859]: 106-7). Interpretations of the Bible may bow to the facts of science, but the facts of Scripture may never give way to mere theories of science.

Hodge expounded upon this accommodation between biblical and geological facts in a full section of his *Systematic Theology*. He was pleased that better interpretations of Scripture had emerged under the guidance of geological facts; he could even affirm that scriptural facts had anticipated the facts of modern earth science. So far as geology was concerned, the harmony of natural and special revelation prevailed, and the scientific nature of theology was preserved. Already by 1872, however, Hodge was troubled about another scientific proposal, this one from Charles Darwin, where the harmonies of revelation and creation were being put to a more stringent test (Selection 12). The excerpt below is from ST, I: 570-571, 573-574.

T HE GEOLOGICAL OBJECTIONS to the Mosaic record are apparently the most serious. According to the commonly received chronology, our globe has existed only a few thousand years. According to geologists, it must have existed for countless ages. And again, according to the generally received interpretation of the first chapter of Genesis, the process of creation was completed in six days, whereas geology teaches that it must have been in progress through periods of time which cannot be computed.

Admitting the facts to be as geologists would have us to believe, two methods of reconciling the Mosaic account with those facts have been adopted. First, some understand the first verse to refer to the original creation of the matter of the universe in the indefinite past, and what follows to refer to the last reorganizing change in the state of our earth to fit it for the habitation of man. Second, the word day as used throughout the chapter is understood of geological periods of indefinite duration.

In favour of this latter view it is urged that the word day is used in Scripture in many different senses; sometimes for the time the sun is above the horizon; sometimes for a period of twenty-four hours; sometimes for a year, as in Lev. 25:29, Judges 17:10, and often elsewhere; sometimes for an indefinite period, as in the phrases, "the day of your calamity," "the day of salvation," "the day of the Lord," "the day of judgment." And in this account of the creation it is used for the period of light in antithesis to night; for the separate periods in the progress of creation;

and then, ch. 2:4, for the whole period: "In the day that the LORD God made the earth and the heavens."

It is of course admitted that taking this account by itself, it would be most natural to understand the word in its ordinary sense; but if that sense brings the Mosaic account into conflict with facts and another sense avoids such conflict, then it is obligatory on us to adopt that other. Now it is urged that if the word "day" be taken in the sense of "an indefinite period of time," a sense which it undoubtedly has in other parts of Scripture, there is not only no discrepancy between the Mosaic account of the creation and the assumed facts of geology, but there is a most marvelous coincidence between them. [Hodge then cites the work of James Dana of Yale and Arnold Guyot of Princeton, geologists who align geological history with the progression found in the creation account of Genesis 1.] Professor Dana of Yale and Professor Guyot of Princeton belong to the first rank of scientific naturalists; and the friends of the Bible owe them a debt of gratitude for their able vindication of the sacred record.

As the Bible is of God, it is certain that there can be no conflict between the teachings of the Scriptures and the facts of science. It is not with facts but with theories, believers have to contend. Many such theories have from time to time been presented, apparently or really inconsistent with the Bible. But these theories have either proved to be false or to harmonize with the Word of God, properly interpreted. The Church has been forced more than once to alter her interpretation of the Bible to accommodate the discoveries of science. But this has been done without doing any violence to the Scriptures or in any degree impairing their authority. Such change, however, cannot be effected without a struggle. It is impossible that our mode of understanding the Bible should not be determined by our views of the subjects of which it treats. So long as men believed that the earth was the centre of our system, the sun its satellite, and the stars its ornamentation, they of necessity understood the Bible in accordance with that hypothesis. But when it was discovered that the earth was only one of the smaller satellites of the sun and that the stars were worlds, then faith, although at first staggered, soon grew strong enough to take it all in and rejoice to find that the Bible, and the Bible alone of all ancient books, was in full accord with these stupendous revelations of science. And if it should be proved that the creation was a process continued through countless ages, and that the Bible alone of all the books of antiquity recognized the fact, then, as Professor Dana says, the idea of its being of human origin would become "utterly incomprehensible."

12

What Is Darwinism?
1874

Charles Hodge paid early attention to Charles Darwin's theories and their implications for Christian faith. In 1862, only three years after the publication of *The Origin of Species,* Hodge devoted a lengthy footnote to what he called "this interesting work." Darwin's theories, which set out to prove "that there is no such thing as permanence in the species of natural history," were not convincing, Hodge felt, because of "the stupendous absurdity of his conclusions"—that all life proceeded from a very few original forms ("Diversity of Species in the Human Race," BRPR, 34 [July 1862], 461 n.). Darwin's appeal, however, did not decline, and Hodge, after attacking him in the ST (II: 12-24), devoted an entire book to the subject which appeared in 1874, his own seventy-seventh year.

This volume, which the definitive study of religious reactions to Darwin has called "a perceptive and even-tempered (albeit logic-chopping) analysis of the Darwinian theory and its implication,"[1] set forth its case with force and clarity. "Darwinism," according to Hodge, involved belief in three things: evolution, natural selection as the vehicle of evolution, and "by far the most important," a denial of design in nature. Hodge himself rejected all three. He found the first and second objectionable because he could not square them with the "facts" of Scripture as expressed in the early chapters of Genesis, even though he acknowledged that perhaps others could. His weightiest objection was to Darwin's third contention, since Hodge saw everywhere in Scripture and in the world manifest testimonies to God's providential design of nature. This sense of divine design was not only one of the great truths of Scripture, it was also one of the most intractable assumptions of human thought, and hence a *prima facie* proof for God's existence.

It is one of the more interesting features of the Princeton Theology that A. A. Hodge and Warfield, who would make much more of such proofs for God's

---

1. James R. Moore, *The Post-Darwinian Controversies: A Study of the Protestant Struggle to Come to Terms with Darwin in Great Britain and America 1870-1900* (Cambridge: Cambridge University Press, 1979), p. 204, with pp. 193-216 on Hodge's general position. This excellent book provides essential background for modern discussions of creation and evolution. A perceptive discussion concerning Hodge's objection to Darwin is also found in John Dillenberger, *Protestant Thought and Natural Science: A Historical Study* (Nashville: Abingdon, 1960), pp. 326-344. For a more general picture, see Joseph E. Illick III, "The Reception of Darwinism at the Theological Seminary and the College at Princeton, New Jersey," *Journal of the Presbyterian Historical Society,* 38 (September 1960), 152-165, and (December 1960), 234-243.

existence than Charles Hodge, had little difficulty accommodating Darwin's "facts" to the "facts" of Scripture (Selections 20, 27). Both of these later theologians accepted the possibility of broad evolution, while denying that evolution necessarily involved a repudiation of design in nature. In any event, we see in Charles Hodge's respect for Darwin as a naturalist and in his successors' ability to reconcile important aspects of Darwin's thought with biblical faith the continued Princeton desire to pursue theology with an ear to science and science within the bounds of theology. The following is from Charles Hodge, *What Is Darwinism?* (New York: Scribners, Armstrong, and Company, 1874), pp. 1–7, 26–30, 40–44, 46–48, 52–53, 60, 71, 104, 141, 168–169, 173–177.

T HIS IS A QUESTION which needs an answer. Great confusion and diversity of opinion prevail as to the real views of the man whose writings have agitated the whole world, scientific and religious. If a man says he is a Darwinian, many understand him to avow himself virtually an atheist; while another understands him as saying that he adopts some harmless form of the doctrine of evolution. This is a great evil.

It is obviously useless to discuss any theory until we are agreed as to what that theory is. The question, therefore, What is Darwinism? must take precedence of all discussion of its merits.

The great fact of experience is that the universe exists. The great problem which has ever pressed upon the human mind is to account for its existence. What was its origin? To what causes are the changes we witness around us to be referred? As we are a part of the universe, these questions concern ourselves. What are the origin, nature, and destiny of man? . . . Mr. Darwin undertakes to answer these questions. He proposes a solution of the problem which thus deeply concerns every living man. Darwinism is, therefore, a theory of the universe, at least so far as the living organisms on this earth are concerned.

The Scriptural Solution of the Problem of the Universe

That solution is stated in words equally simple and sublime: "In the beginning God created the heavens and the earth." We have here, first, the idea of God. The word *God* has in the Bible a definite meaning. It does not stand for an abstraction, for mere force, for law or ordered sequence. God is a spirit, and as we are spirits, we know from consciousness that God is, (1) A Substance; (2) That He is a person; and, therefore, a self-conscious, intelligent, voluntary agent. He can say I; we can address Him as Thou; we can speak of Him as He or Him. This idea of God pervades the Scriptures. It lies at the foundation of natural religion. It is involved in our religious consciousness. It enters essentially into our sense of moral obligation. It is inscribed ineffaceably in letters more or less legible on the heart of every human being. The man who is trying to be an atheist is trying to free himself from the laws of his being. He might as well try to free himself from liability to hunger or thirst.

The God of the Bible, then, is a spirit, infinite, eternal, and unchangeable in his being, wisdom, power, holiness, goodness, and truth. As every theory must begin with some postulate, this is the grand postulate with which the Bible begins. This is the first point.

The second point concerns the origin of the universe. It is not eternal either as to matter or form. It is not independent of God. It is not an evolution of his being. . . . He is extramundane as well as antemundane. The universe owes its existence to his will.

Thirdly, as to the nature of the universe; it is not a mere phenomenon. It is an entity, having real objective existence or actuality. This implies that matter is a substance endowed with certain properties, in virtue of which it is capable of acting and of being acted upon. These properties, being uniform and constant, are physical laws to which, as their proximate causes, all the phenomena of nature are to be referred.

Fourthly, although God is extramundane, He is nevertheless everywhere present. That presence is not only a presence of essence but also of knowledge and power. He upholds all things. He controls all physical causes, working through them, with them, and without them, as He sees fit. As we, in our limited spheres, can use physical causes to accomplish our purposes, so God everywhere and always cooperates with them to accomplish his infinitely wise and merciful designs.

Fifthly, man a part of the universe, is, according to the Scriptures, as concerns his body, of the earth. So far, he belongs to the animal kingdom. As to his soul, he is a child of God, who is declared to be the Father of the spirit of all men. God is a spirit, and we are spirits. We are, therefore, of the same nature with God. We are God-like; so that in knowing ourselves we know God. No man conscious of his manhood can be ignorant of his relationship to God as his Father. The truth of this theory of the universe rests, in the first place, so far as it has been correctly stated, on the infallible authority of the Word of God. In the second place, it is a satisfactory solution of the problem to be solved: (1) It accounts for the origin of the universe. (2) It accounts for all the universe contains and gives a satisfactory explanation of the marvellous contrivances which abound in living organisms, of the adaptations of these organisms to conditions external to themselves, and for those provisions for the future which on any other assumption are utterly inexplicable. (3) It is in conflict with no truth of reason and with no fact of experience. (4) The Scriptural doctrine accounts for the spiritual nature of man and meets all his spiritual necessities. It gives him an object of adoration, love, and confidence. It reveals the Being on whom his indestructible sense of responsibility terminates. The truth of this doctrine, therefore, rests not only on the authority of the Scriptures but on the very constitution of our nature. The Bible has little charity for those who reject it. It pronounces them to be either derationalized or demoralized, or both. . . .

Darwin does not speculate on the origin of the universe, on the nature of matter, or of force. He is simply a naturalist, a careful and laborious observer; skillful in his descriptions, and singularly candid in dealing with the difficulties in the way of his peculiar doctrine. He set before himself a single problem, namely, How are the fauna and flora of our earth to be accounted for? In the solution of this problem, he assumes:

1. The existence of matter, although he says little on the subject. Its existence, however, as a real entity, is everywhere taken for granted.

2. He assumes the efficiency of physical causes, showing no disposition to resolve them into mind-force, or into the efficiency of the First Cause.

3. He assumes also the existence of life in the form of one or more primordial germs. He does not adopt the theory of spontaneous generation. What life is he does not attempt to explain. . . .

4. To account for the existence of matter and life, Mr. Darwin admits a Creator. This is done explicitly and repeatedly. Nothing, however, is said of the nature of the Creator and of his relation to the world, further than is implied in the meaning of the word.

5. From the primordial germ or germs (Mr. Darwin seems to have settled down to the assumption of only one primordial germ), all living organisms, vegetable and animal, including man, on our globe, through all the stages of its history, have descended.

6. As growth, organization, and reproduction are the functions of physical life, as soon as the primordial germ began to live, it began to grow, to fashion organs, however simple, for its nourishment and increase, and for the reproduction, in some way of living forms like itself. How all living things on earth, including the endless variety of plants, and all the diversity of animals—insects, fishes, birds, the ichthyosaurus, the mastodon, the mammoth, and man—have descended from the primordial animalcule, he thinks, may be accounted for by the operation of the following natural laws, viz.—

First, the law of Heredity, or that by which like begets like. The offspring are like the parent.

Second, the law of Variation, that is, while the offspring are, in all essential characteristics, like their immediate progenitor, they nevertheless vary more or less within narrow limits, from their parent and from each other. Some of these variations are indifferent, some deteriorations, some improvements, that is, they are such as enable the plant or animal to exercise its functions to greater advantage.

Third, the law of Over Production. All plants and animals tend to increase in a geometrical ratio; and therefore tend to overrun enormously the means of support. . . . Hence of necessity arises a struggle for life. Only a few of the myriads born can possibly live.

Fourth, here comes in the law of Natural Selection, or the Survival of the Fittest. That is, if any individual of a given species of plant or animal happens to have a slight deviation from the normal type, favorable to its success in the struggle for life, it will survive. This variation, by the law of heredity, will be transmitted to its offspring, and by them again to theirs. Soon these favored ones gain the ascendency, and the less favored perish; and the modification becomes established in the species. After a time another and another of such favorable variations occur with like results. Thus very gradually, great changes of structure are introduced, and not only species, but genera, families, and orders, in the vegetable and animal world are produced. Mr. Darwin says he can set no limit to the changes of structure, habits, instincts, and intelligence which these simple laws in the course of millions or [billions] of centuries may bring into existence. He says, "we cannot comprehend what the figures 60,000,000 really imply, and during this, or perhaps a longer roll of years, the land and waters have everywhere teemed with living creatures, all exposed to the struggle for life, and undergoing change...." Years in this connection have no meaning. We might as well try to give the distance of the fixed stars in inches. As astronomers are obliged to take the diameter of the earth's orbit as the unit of space, so Darwinians are obliged to take a geological cycle as their unit of duration....

We have not yet reached the heart of Mr. Darwin's theory. The main idea of his system lies in the word "natural." He uses that word in two senses: first, as antithetical to the word "artificial." Men can produce very marked varieties as to structure and habits of animals. This is exemplified in the production of the different breeds of horses, cattle, sheep, and dogs; and specially, as Mr. Darwin seems to think, in the case of pigeons.... If then, he argues, man, in a comparatively short time, has by artificial selection produced all these varieties, what might be accomplished on the boundless scale of nature during the measureless ages of the geologic periods?

Secondly, he uses the word "natural" as antithetical to supernatural. Natural selection is a selection made by natural laws, working without intention and design. It is, therefore, opposed not only to artificial selection, which is made by the wisdom and skill of man to accomplish a given purpose, but also to supernatural selection, which means either a selection originally intended by a power higher than nature; or which is carried out by such power. In using the expression Natural Selection, Mr. Darwin intends to exclude design or final causes. All the change in structure, instinct, or intelligence, in the plants or animals, including man, descended from the primordial germ or animalcule, have been brought about by unintelligent physical causes. On this point he leaves us in no doubt. He defines nature to be "the aggregate action and product of natural laws; and laws are the sequence of events as ascertained by us...." It is affirmed that natural selection is the operation of natural laws, analogous to the action of gravitation and of chemical affinities. It is denied that it is a process originally designed, or guided by intelligence, such as the activity which foresees an end and consciously selects and controls the means of its accomplishment. Artificial selection, then, is an intelligent process; natural selection is not.

There are in the animal and vegetable worlds innumerable instances of at least apparent contrivance which have excited the admiration of men in all ages. There are three ways of accounting for them. The first is the Scriptural doctrine, namely, that God is a spirit, a personal, self-conscious, intelligent agent; that He is infinite, eternal, and unchangeable in his being and perfections; that He is ever present; that this presence is a presence of knowledge and power. In the external world there is always and everywhere indisputable evidence of the activity of two kinds of force: the one physical, the other mental. The physical belongs to matter and is due to the properties with which it has been endowed; the other is the everywhere present and everacting mind of God. To the latter are to be referred all the manifestations of design in nature, and the ordering of events in Providence. This doctrine does not ignore the efficiency of second causes; it simply asserts that God overrules and controls them. Thus the Psalmist says, "I am fearfully and wonderfully made.... My substance was not hid from thee, when I was made in secret, and curiously wrought . . . in the lower parts of the earth. Thine eyes did see my substance yet being imperfect; and in thy book all my members were written, which in continuance were fashioned, when as yet there were none of them...." He sends rain, frost, and snow. He controls the winds and the waves. He determines the casting of the lot, the flight of an arrow, and the falling of a sparrow. This universal and constant control of God is not only one of the most patent and pervading doctrines of the Bible, but it is one of the fundamental principles of even natural religion.

The second method of accounting for contrivances in nature admits that they were foreseen and purposed by God, and that He endowed matter with forces which He foresaw and intended should produce such results. But here his agency stops. He never interferes to guide the operation of physical causes. He does nothing to control the course of nature, or the events of history....

This banishing God from the world is simply intolerable, and, blessed be his name, impossible. An absent God who does nothing is, to us, no God. Christ brings God constantly near to us.... It may be said that Christ did not teach science. True, but He taught truth; and science, so called, when it comes in conflict with truth is what man is when he comes in conflict with God....

The third method of accounting for the contrivances manifested in the organs of plants and animals, is that which refers them to the blind operation of natural causes. They are not due to the continued cooperation and control of the divine mind, nor to the original purpose of God in the constitution of the universe. This is the doctrine of Materialists, and to this doctrine, we are sorry to say, Mr. Darwin, although himself a theist, has given in his adhesion. It is on this account the Materialists almost deify him.

From what has been said, it appears that Darwinism includes three distinct elements. First evolution, or the assumption that all organic forms, vegetable and animal, have been evolved or developed from one, or a few, primordial living germs; second, that this evolution has been effected by natural selection, or the survival of the fittest; and third, and by far the most important and only distinctive element of his theory, that this natural selection is without design, being conducted by unintelligent physical causes. Neither the first nor the second of these elements constitute Darwinism; nor do the two combined....

It is however neither evolution nor natural selection which give Darwinism its peculiar character and importance. It is that Darwin rejects all teleology, or the doctrine of final causes. He denies design in any of the organisms in the vegetable or animal world. He teaches that the eye was formed without any purpose of producing an organ of vision. . . . It is the distinctive doctrine of Mr. Darwin that species owe their origin, not to the original intention of the divine mind; not to special acts of creation calling new forms into existence at certain epochs; not to the constant and everywhere operative efficiency of God, guiding physical causes in the production of intended effects; but to the gradual accumulation of un-intended variations of structure and instinct, securing some advantage to their subjects. . . .

It would be absurd to say anything disrespectful of such a man as Mr. Darwin, and scarcely less absurd to indulge in any mere extravagance of language; yet we are expressing our own experience when we say that we regard Mr. Darwin's books the best refutation of Mr. Darwin's theory. He constantly shuts us up to the alterna-tive of believing that the eye is a work of design or the product of the unintended action of blind physical causes. To any ordinarily constituted mind, it is absolutely impossible to believe that it is not a work of design. . . .

That design implies an intelligent designer is a self-evident truth. Every man believes it; and no man can practically disbelieve it. Even those naturalists who theoretically deny it, if they find in a cave so simple a thing as a flint arrowhead, are as sure that it was made by a man as they are of their own existence. And yet they want us to believe that an eagle's eye is the product of blind natural causes. . . .

The words "evolution" and "Darwinism" are so often in this country, but not in Europe, used interchangeably, that it is conceivable that Dr. Peabody could retain his faith in God, and yet admit the doctrine of evolution. But it is not conceivable that any man should adopt the main element of Mr. Darwin's theory, viz., the denial of all final causes, and the assertion that since the first creation of matter and life God has left the universe to the control of unintelligent physical causes, so that all the phenomena of the plants and animals, all that is in man, and all that has ever happened on the earth is due to physical force, and yet retain his faith in Christ. On that theory, there have been no supernatural revelation, no miracles; Christ is not risen, and we are yet in our sins. . . .

It is conceded that a man may be an evolutionist and yet not be an atheist and may admit of design in nature. But we cannot see how the theory of evolution can be reconciled with the declarations of the Scriptures. Others may see it, and be able to reconcile their allegiance to science with their allegiance to the Bible. . . .

All the innumerable varieties of plants, all the countless forms of animals, with all their instincts and faculties, all the varieties of men with their intellectual endowments, and their moral and religious nature, have, according to Darwin, been evolved by the agency of the blind, unconscious laws of nature. . . . The grand and fatal objection to Darwinism is this exclusion of design in the origin of species or the production of living organisms. By design is meant the intelligent and volun-tary choice, application, and control of means appropriate to the accomplishment of that end. That design, therefore, implies intelligence, is involved in its very nature. . . . But in thus denying design in nature, these writers array against themselves the intuitive perception and irresistible convictions of all mankind—a barrier which no man has ever been able to surmount. . . .

The conclusion of the whole matter is that the denial of design in nature is virtually the denial of God. Mr. Darwin's theory does deny all design in nature, therefore, his theory is virtually atheistical; his theory, not he himself. He believes in a Creator. But when that Creator, millions on millions of ages ago, did something— called matter and a living germ into existence—and then abandoned the universe to itself to be controlled by chance and necessity, without any purpose on his part as to the result, or any intervention or guidance, then He is virtually consigned, so far as we are concerned, to non-existence. . . . This is the vital point. The denial of final causes is the formulative idea of Darwin's theory, and therefore no teleologist can be a Darwinian. . . .

We have thus arrived at the answer to our question, What is Darwinism? It is atheism. This does not mean, as before said, that Mr. Darwin himself and all who adopt his views are atheists; but it means that his theory is atheistic; that the exclusion of design from nature is, as Dr. Gray says,[2] tantamount to atheism.

2. Asa Gray (1810–1888) was a Harvard botanist who, while maintaining Christian faith and a belief in Scripture, also accepted major portions of Darwin's conclusions. See Moore, *Post-Darwinian Controversies*, pp. 269–280; and A. Hunter Dupree, *Asa Gray, 1810–1888* (Cambridge: Harvard University Press, 1959).

13

Advertisement for *Princeton Review*
1829

The first issue of the *Biblical Repertory and Theological Review* set this journal on a course from which it did not deviate so long as Charles Hodge was its editor. Although the name was changed to the *Biblical Repertory and Princeton Review* in 1837 to reflect more accurately its provenance, it did not change its purposes. For more than forty years the journal was Hodge's great forum to defend the faith and bring it to bear on the issues of the day.[1] Its "Advertisement," BRPR 1 (January 1829), underestimated the contention which would attend its efforts, but the determination to defend the truth as Hodge and his associates perceived it was clear to all. The following is from pp. iv–vi of that advertisement.

SEVERAL YEARS AGO the Professor of Biblical Literature in the Seminary at Princeton undertook to publish a quarterly journal (the Biblical Repertory), the exclusive object of which was to assist ministers and candidates in the criticism and interpretation of the Bible. Experience, however, has shown that the time has not yet arrived when a work of this kind can be adequately supported in our country. It was therefore thought expedient at the beginning of the present year to make a change in the character of this publication. It is intended hereafter to conduct it according to the following plan.

1. The original design of the work, instead of being wholly laid aside, is to be so modified as to adapt it to the use and benefit of all intelligent Christians. The Bible is the only source of authentic information on the doctrines and duties of Christianity. The Bible is about to be placed in every family in the nation.[2] The right of private judgment in this free country is unequivocally admitted. It is therefore of the utmost importance to afford to the people every possible facility for a right understanding of the divine oracles. To accomplish this is to be one of the primary objects of the Biblical Repertory in its present form.

---

1. On Hodge's service for the journal and the causes he defended in its pages, see BRPR, *Index Volume* (1870–71), II: 200–211; and A. A. Hodge, *Life of Charles Hodge*, pp. 99, 247–271, 332–343, 400–424.

2. Hodge is referring to the work of the country's various Bible Societies, which were indeed making great strides at placing a Bible in every American home.

2. Philosophy and literature in every age have exerted a powerful influence on religious sentiment and doctrine. This will be the case until the Bible shall have established a complete and universal supremacy, and men shall have learned to submit without reserve to Scripture, fairly interpreted. This work, then, in accomplishing its great purpose of assisting in forming right opinions on the meaning of the Bible, must bring under strict and impartial review the philosophy and literature of the time and show their influence, whether for good or evil, on biblical interpretation, systematic theology, and practical religion. In doing this, it will be necessary to detect and expose the error, common in every age, of founding religious doctrines on insulated passages and partial views of bible-truth, or forcing the Scriptures to a meaning which shall accord with philosophical theories.

3. The circumstances belonging to every age produce a tendency to some particular form of error, so as to make it the epidemic of the period. At one time men are disposed to be satisfied with a heartless and inactive orthodoxy. At another, religious action is represented as every thing, and its stimulus is substituted for those deep inward feelings which mark the character of thorough piety. It will be the business of this Journal carefully to notice and faithfully to exhibit dangers of this kind.

4. The history of religious doctrine and opinion will be given in the progress of the work as far as the nature of the case will admit; the revival of old and exploded doctrines will be noticed; and their effects on vital religion as clearly as possible exhibited.

5. The influence of different principles of ecclesiastical polity on piety, morals, literature, and civil institutions will form a subject for careful consideration.

6. It will be left for the monthly and weekly publications to communicate religious intelligence: but at the same time, the various enterprizes of Christian benevolence will be observed with the deepest attention and interest and sustained with all the zeal and talent which can be brought to aid the mighty cause. Especially the vast and growing importance of Sabbath Schools will be duly appreciated. The books employed in them will be strictly examined; and it will be reckoned a more valuable service to lend efficient aid in securing to these publications a suitable character, than to control, if that were possible, the literature and philosophy of the whole nation.

7. Such attention, however, as the limits of the work will permit, will be bestowed on the important interests of general knowledge; and select literary information will be given with every number.

8. The work is not designed to be controversial in its character, but to state temperately and mildly yet firmly and fearlessly, Bible truth in its whole extent.

14

Schaff's Protestantism

1845

From 1844 to 1849 the tiny seminary of the German Reformed Church at Mercersburg, Pennsylvania, witnessed one of the most remarkable flourishings in the history of American theology.[1] In 1840 John Williamson Nevin (1803-1886) had come to teach at Mercersburg after having studied at Princeton Seminary where he also taught as Hodge's substitute during the latter's journey to Europe, and after having served as an instructor in another Presbyterian seminary in Pittsburgh. Nevin was joined in 1844 by an immigrant from Germany, Philip Schaff[2] (1819-1893), who had participated in Germany's Protestant awakening in the 1830s and who had studied with Hodge's friends Tholuck, Neander, and Hengstenberg. Together the two produced a series of remarkable works over the next five years concerning the principles of theology and the situation of the church in America: Nevin's *The Anxious Bench* (2nd ed., 1844), which questioned the practices of revivalists like Charles Finney; Schaff's *The Principle of Protestantism* (1845), which called for a Protestant recovery of a high view of the church; Schaff's *What Is Church History?* (1846), which gave much more credit to the Catholic heritage of the church than American Protestants usually did; Nevin's *The Mystical Presence* (1846), which argued for a return to the Reformers' view of a "real spiritual presence" in the Lord's Supper; Nevin's *History and Genius of the Heidelberg Catechism* (1847), which offered a rationale for preferring sixteenth-century Protestantism over modern American "Puritanism"; Nevin's *The Church* (1847), which echoed Schaff's convictions about the essential place of formal ecclesiology for Christian life; and Nevin's *Anti-christ, or the Spirit of Sect and Schism* (1848), which decried the casual American attitude toward division and separation within the church.

In these works, and also a voluminous periodical production, the Mercersburg theologians were attempting to incorporate elements of German post-Kantian thought into traditional Reformed categories. While they drew upon Schleiermacher's insistence that the personal bond to Christ was the essence of the faith, they were influenced also by the conservative German reaction to

1. On Nevin, Schaff, and the Mercersburg School, see James Hastings Nichols, *Romanticism in American Theology: Nevin and Schaff at Mercersburg* (Chicago: University of Chicago Press, 1961); Nichols, ed., *The Mercersburg Theology* (New York: Oxford University Press, 1966); and Ahlstrom, *Theology in America*, pp. 371-426.

2. When this essay appeared, Hodge spelled Schaff's name with only one *f*, as Schaff himself did. Soon a second *f* was added, however, and this more common spelling is used here.

Schleiermacher as embodied in theologians like Neander and Hengstenberg. Both Nevin and Schaff felt keenly the need for a historical grasp of the church's development which fully appreciated the working of the Spirit in every age of the church. And they looked forward to the growth and expansion of the visible church—with its powerful preaching and, even more, its celebration of the Eucharist—as the harbinger of a new, divinely quickened humanity. However stimulating such ideas have proved to twentieth-century American theologians, in the nineteenth century the works from Mercersburg were too philosophical and too historical to make much of an impact on the American public at large. They were, however, noticed at Princeton.

Charles Hodge seemed to have been a friend of Nevin when the latter was his student and temporary replacement at Princeton. But as soon as Nevin began to speak with even qualified approval of Schleiermacher and German idealism, or to praise the virtues of the Roman Catholic past, Hodge leapt to the attack. As in his review of Schaff's *Principle of Protestantism,* reproduced below, Hodge was willing to grant to Mercersburg the necessity of maintaining the faith of the Reformation. But he utterly repudiated the Mercersburg argument that American Protestantism, even conservative American Presbyterianism, had deviated from Reformation norms through its acceptance of sectarianism, its rationalization of the Lord's Supper, and its minimization of the visible church. Hodge, it was clear, was stung by these charges, for he responded to Mercersburg assertions with a sharpness largely absent from his other polemics. His review below is cautious in its respect for Schaff but critical of Nevin's dalliance with German tendencies. His review of *The Mystical Presence* charged Nevin with rationalism, Romanism, and anti-Trinitarianism ("Doctrine of the Reformed Church on the Lord's Supper," BRPR, 20 [April 1848]; reprinted in *Essays and Reviews,* pp. 341-392).[3] When Schaff published a *History of the Apostolic Church* (1853), Hodge called it to account for being too Catholic and German and for containing a strong "anti-Protestant leaven." Hodge criticized Schaff particularly for his ties with Nevin: "Of the external circumstances which have tended to produce a suspicion of a Romanizing tendency on the part of Dr. Schaff, the most important is his association with Dr. Nevin. The latter gentleman has justly, as we think, forfeited entirely the confidence of the Protestant community" ("Dr. Schaff's Apostolic Church," BRPR, 26 [January 1854], 149, 151). Hodge repeated such attacks thereafter, as in 1860 when he accused Nevin of taking from Christianity "a present, personal Saviour . . . his righteousness . . . the blessed Spirit of God," as well as the true meaning of faith and regeneration ("What Is Christianity?" BRPR, 32 [January 1860], 160-161).

As Hodge read them, the Mercersburg theologians replaced objective truth with idealistic subjectivity, Anglo-American good sense with Teutonic mysticism, and a biblical view of the church with Roman Catholic pretensions.[4] Whatever

3. For a fine review of this dispute, see E. Brooks Holifield, "Mercersburg, Princeton, and the South: The Sacramental Controversy in the Nineteenth Century," *Journal of Presbyterian History,* 54 (Summer 1976), 238-257.

4. Nevin evidently felt keenly the weight of Hodge's attacks; see George H. Shriver, "Passages in Friendship: John W. Nevin to Charles Hodge, 1872," *Journal of Presbyterian History,* 58 (Summer 1980), 116-122.

one may make of Hodge's assertions, his debate with Mercersburg constituted one of the most consequential episodes within the history of Reformed faith during the nineteenth century. This selection presents the entirety of Hodge's essay, "Schaff's Protestantism," BRPR 17 (October 1845): 626-36.

T HE IMPORTANCE OF the subject of which this book treats, the ability which it displays, and the attention which it has excited, all claim for it an elaborate review. Such a review would be a very difficult task; one which we should not be ambitious to assume, even if circumstances beyond our control had not shut us up to the necessity of confining ourselves to this short notice.

It is a book not easy to understand, especially that part of it which has proceeded from the pen of Dr. Nevin. We have read the whole twice over and yet we are very far from being satisfied that we adequately comprehend its principles. This obscurity is no doubt due, in part, to the nature of the subject. Every thing that involves the nature of the church pertains to one of the most difficult departments of theology; one in which the indefiniteness of language almost unavoidably leads to more or less confusion. The obscurity, however, of which we complain, we are disposed to attribute in no small measure to the manner in which the subject is treated. The book is thoroughly German. The mode of thinking and the forms of expression are so unenglish that it is not easy for an American to enter into the views of the authors. German writers have many characteristic excellencies; but they have also some characteristic faults. They are seldom very intelligible. Their preference for the reason over the understanding leads them to eschew Begriffe, definite conceptions, and to abound in ideas, whose import and limits are indeterminate. It is hard, therefore, in many cases to tell precisely what they mean. This whole book is about the church, and yet we have tried in vain to find out what the authors mean by the church. Is it the body of professors? Or the body of true believers? or the two in inseparable union as one body? These are questions we cannot answer; and therefore we cannot tell what interpretation is to be put upon their language. If a writer speaks of man in such a way that his readers are at a loss to determine whether what he says is to be referred to the soul or to the body, or to the whole as a unit, they must be at a loss whether to assent or dissent. This is precisely the state of mind in which the perusal of this book has left us. This remark is intended to apply in a measure to the whole work, but more particularly to the introduction and appendix, which are by far the most difficult to understand.

The first point which Prof. Schaff endeavours to establish is that the Reformation was neither a revolution nor a restoration. It was neither a violent disruption from all that preceded it nor the return of the church to the state in which it had existed during any preceding century. As to both these points, we presume, he speaks the general sentiments of Protestants. The Middle Ages were no doubt pregnant with the Reformation; the church lived through all those ages, and

Protestantism was the revival through the word and Spirit of God, of a backslidden church, and not a new creation. It is also no doubt true that as in the case of an individual believer who is brought back from his declensions, and by the grace of God rendered more enlightened and stable than at any previous stage of his career, so the church of the Reformation was in a more advanced state than the church of the second or third centuries. No one would think of comparing the works of the Fathers with those of the Reformers as to enlightened, scriptural, and comprehensive views of the gospel.

When again Prof. Schaff speaks of the distinguishing principles of Protestantism, he follows the common method of evangelical theologians. Those principles are the doctrine of justification by faith and the supremacy of scripture as the rule of faith. The former is our continued protest against the error of a mediating church or priesthood. It is undoubledly the vital principle of Protestantism that God is now accessible to all men by Jesus Christ; that all who hear the gospel may come to Christ, and through him to God, receiving, in virtue of union with Christ by faith, the imputation of his righteousness for justification and the indwelling of his Spirit for sanctification. In this liberty of access lies the priesthood of all believers. And so long as this is asserted, do we protest against the great error of Rome that men can only come to God through the church or through the mediation of other men as priests, by whose ministrations alone the benefits of redemption can be applied to the soul. The reverse of this is true, and the reverse of this is Protestantism. We are in the church because we are in Christ, and not in Christ because we are in the church. The analysis and exposition which Prof. Schaff gives of this great doctrine of justification by faith alone is thoroughly evangelical. We commend it to our new school brethren as a mirror in which they may see the true principle of the Reformation, and thence learn how far they have lapsed towards Romanism in their denial or explaining away of the corruption of our nature by original sin, and in making justification mere pardon to the exclusion of the imputation of the righteousness of Christ. Our author, however, presents this doctrine too exclusively "in opposition to all Pelagian and Semi-Pelagian error." He does not present it sufficiently in its opposition to the doctrine of a mediating church which was historically its most prominent aspect. When the sinner asked, What must I do to be saved? the answer which the Spirit of God, and their own dear bought experience taught the Reformers to give, was: Believe in the Lord Jesus Christ and thou shalt be saved. That alone can save you; and that can and most certainly will. And by faith they meant, not mere assent, but, as Dr. Schaff says, a personal appropriation of the merits of Christ. That is all the sinner needs in order to secure his justification, and with that blessing sanctification and eternal life are inseparably connected. The answer given by Rome and "ecclesiasticism" in general to the momentous question, What must I do to be saved? is, Come to me, I have the merits of Christ; I have the Spirit; I have the custody of the blessings of redemption. Your own act of faith will do you little good; you can only come to Christ by me; I give you his merits and grace in baptism; and if you lose them, I alone can restore them by the sacrament of penance. It was in opposition to all this; it was as their protest against this, the very thing that made them Protestants, that the Reformers said, we are justified freely by faith alone. We need not your mediation, Christ is every where present. And we can and must, each one for himself, lay hold on him by faith, and we know that whosoever believes on him hath eternal life, though he has never heard of the church, or of a priest, or of the sacraments. It is this aspect of the doctrine of justification by faith alone which Prof. Schaff has failed to render prominent; and it is the *apparent* denial of this view of the subject by Dr. Nevin which forms the stumbling block presented in this book. It is this which gives his portion of the work the Puseyite[5] aspect which has created so much anxiety. We say "apparent denial," because we are not satisfied that it is any thing more than apparent. For while he speaks somewhat too contemptuously of those who make the turning point between us and Rome, the question, "whether salvation be an individual concern or something that comes wholly by the church"; p. 12, and says: "We are not Christians, each one by himself, but we become such through the church"; p. 200, still he pronounces "ecclesiasticism, as held by Rome and also by Oxford," a terrible error; and declares it would be treason to the gospel to reject "the position that religion is an individual interest, a strictly personal concern, a question between a man singly and his maker. He that believeth shall be saved; he that believeth not shall be damned." p. 12. We can only repeat what we have already said, as to our inability fully to comprehend his meaning on this point; and comfort ourselves with the conviction that it is impossible to hold the doctrine of justification by faith alone, as it is stated in this book, and yet mean by saying, "we become Christians through the church," what Puseyites mean by such expressions.

In the exposition given by Dr. Schaff of the formal principle of Protestantism, viz: that the scriptures are the only infallible rule of faith and practice, we in general concur. As the doctrine of justification by faith is the protest of the Reformed against the Romish doctrine of a mediating church so the assertion of the sole infallible authority of the written word of God is their protest against the doctrine of an inspired church to whose teaching we are obliged to bow. As the church, according to Rome, consists of all who profess the Christian religion and are subject to the Pope, the wisdom and teaching of that body consisting in great measure of unsanctified men is but another name for the wisdom and teaching of the world. But if by the church is meant the body of true believers in whom Christ dwells by his Spirit, and whom he leads to the knowledge of the truth, then indeed to differ from the church is a serious, and if on any essential doctrine, a fatal matter. It is by losing sight too much of this distinction that Prof. Schaff is led to attribute much more weight to the usages and opinions, i.e., to the traditions, of the visible church

5. Hodge is referring to the Oxford Movement in England, led by Edward B. Pusey (1800–1882), John Keble (1792–1866), and John Henry Newman (1801–1890). This Movement called for a return to Catholic principles in the Church of England. Newman eventually became a Catholic, while Pusey and Keble remained to lead the Anglo-Catholic party within Anglicanism. Hodge attacked the Oxford Movement on several occasions: "Oxford Tracts," BRPR, 10 (January 1838), 84–119; "Bishop Doane and the Oxford Tracts," BRPR, 13 (July 1841), 450–462; and "Theories of the Church," BRPR, 18 (January 1846), reprinted in *Essays and Reviews*, pp. 201–220.

than we think is due to them consistently with Protestant principle. This is a subject, however, on which we cannot dwell. We only wish to express our dissent from the obvious or apparent meaning of some of his remarks on tradition; which though we think they admit of a good sense, yet more naturally express one with which we cannot concur. We are more sensible of the difference of views between our author and the mass of his American readers, as to this point, from the conclusions to which his principles lead him than from the statement of those principles themselves. He condemns not only the more rigid Puritans, but most of the Reformed churches for repudiating the usages (ritual traditions) of the church, and commends the greater regard of the Lutherans for such traditions. In this respect he will find few American Protestants to agree with him.

The two great diseases of Protestantism our author represents to be Rationalism and Sectarism. He gives a historical sketch of the rise and progress of the former in Germany, and concludes with the expression of his conviction that "the most dangerous enemy with which we are threatened on theoretical ground, is not the catholicism of Rome, but the foe within our own borders; not the hierarchic papacy of the Vatican, but the worldly papacy of the subjective understanding; not the Concilium Tridentium, but the theology of unbelief, as proclaimed by a Rhoer, a Wegscheider, a Strauss, a Feuerbach, and others of the same stamp." This is a very natural view to be taken by a theologian born and educated in Germany, who has been accustomed to see comparatively little of the evils of Romanism, and before whose eyes the desolations wrought by Rationalism were constantly present. In itself considered, however, and in reference to the state of the church in America, we consider Romanism immeasurably more dangerous than infidelity. Not by any means, as some have said, a greater evil; but an evil more dangerous to Protestantism. This is only expressing our conviction that a false religion is more likely to spread than mere irreligion; and that the human mind has greater affinity for superstition than for infidelity.

The section relating to "Sectarism" we consider as more marred by false principles and false views of facts and of their historical relations than any other in the book. Here we think our author betrays erroneous principles as to the unity of the church, too much forgetting that it is a spiritual unity arising from the union of believers with Christ and from the indwelling of his Spirit; and which manifests itself in unity of faith, of love, and of communion. There is therefore more of real unity, more real brotherhood existing between the evangelical denominations of America than is to be found in the church of Rome, the church of England, or in the Reformed or Lutheran church of Germany. The true unity of the church is therefore, in a measure, independent of external ecclesiastical union. It is marred by all diversity of faith, all want of love, and by all refusal of intercommunion and fraternal subjection and intercourse; and is destroyed by the entire absence of any of these bonds. It is not, however, necessarily interrupted by separate ecclesiastical organizations or diversity as to modes of discipline and worship; uniformity and unity being very different things. We do not suppose that Dr. Schaff denies this, but he constantly speaks as though he regarded external union, that is, union secured and expressed by outward bonds, as far more essential to unity of the church than appears to us consistent with its true nature.

Again, his principles as to conformity and the preservation of outward union seem to us erroneous. He says, the Reformers had "they been permitted to preach the pure word of God with freedom, and to administer the sacraments according to Christ's appointment, would have remained in their original communion." He blames the Puritans for separating from the established church of England, and condemns the recent secession of the Free Church in Scotland. All this we think betrays very wrong notions as to the principles involved in such questions. Such separations are a duty which we owe to God and to the real unity of the church whenever unscriptural terms of communion are enjoined. If the Puritans, in order to their connexion with the church of England, were required to declare their "assent and consent" to all and every thing contained in the book of Common Prayer, then those who could not assent to the baptismal or burial service, or to the semi-deification of Charles I, were bound in conscience to separate from that church, and to protest against the schismatical principle of making such matters terms of Christian communion. The same remark may of course be applied to a multitude of other cases.

When our author says that sects have their origin in sinful ambition and pride, we think he is wrong as to the majority of cases, as far as evangelical sects are concerned.—They have much more commonly had their origin in the imposition, by those in authority, of unscriptural terms of communion. In many cases no doubt they have arisen from narrow-mindedness, and scrupulosity, but even in such cases, there is something to respect in the assertion of the supremacy of conscience. We miss in our author any definite conception of Sectarism, or what it is that constitutes a sect. Why are the Congregationalists, or Baptists any more a sect than the German Reformed, or the Episcopalians?

In the account given by Dr. Schaff of the Puritans of Cromwell, of the relation of the church in this country with the English Independents, we think he shows that he is from home. He is speaking of events, which as they did not occur in Germany, cannot be supposed to be so well understood by a scholar so thoroughly German. He betrays also the disadvantage under which he labours as a stranger when he comes to speak of the state of things in this country. The paragraph on p. 116 in which he speaks of the multiplication of sects in America is an extravagant exaggeration. It is easy to string together a number of names of religious parties, here and anywhere else, and not more here than in England, or even Germany, but what do they amount to? The vast mass of our population belong either to the Romish, the Episcopal, the Baptist, Methodist, Congregational, or Presbyterian churches, including in the last named the English, Dutch, and German Presbyterians. Beyond these, all other sects are made up of handfuls and these are to be found wherever there is liberty enough for what actually exists to make itself known.

We are not to be considered as apologists for "Sectarism" because we object to the exaggerated statements of the nature and extent of the evil given by our author. We admit that it is a very serious evil, and one which the friends of the church, in the true sense of the term, should endeavour to correct. What then are the means by which these two diseases of Protestantism, viz., Rationalism and Sectarism, are to be cured? To the answer of this question Dr. Schaff addresses himself in the latter part of his book.

He begins by saying that Puseyism is a well-meant, but mistaken effort to accomplish this cure. It is represented as a legitimate reaction from false or ultra-Protestantism; an attempt to cure Rationalism by subjecting the judgment of the individual to that of the church; and Sectarism, by merging all parties into the outward unity of established uniformity. There may be some truth in this genesis of Puseyism; but we are disposed to assign it a less honourable origin. We believe it had its birth in wrong views as to the nature of religion, and wrong principles as to the nature of the church. Prof. Schaff thinks its end legitimate, but its means mistaken. We think its end a mistaken one, and therefore its means illegitimate. Rationalism and Sectarism were not the real evils which it proposed to cure, but Protestantism itself, i.e., the gospel, salvation by grace, justification by faith, the worship of God in spirit and in truth, instead of outward forms or inward mysticism or superstitious reverence. The gospel is the great evil against which it is directed with consummate skill. We cannot therefore regard it as embodying any great truth. It is not the expression of the sense of need of Christian unity, in the proper meaning of the term, but rather of the desire to be religious and secure heaven by some means sanctioned by antiquity which does not include submission to the gospel.

What means then does our author propose for the cure of the diseases of Protestantism? "Historical Progress. Puseyism looks backward; we look forward. It looks toward Rome . . . We toward Jerusalem." Here comes in again the idea of the gradual development of Christianity with which the work commences. Not that Christianity admits of any improvement, but simply that it comes gradually to be better understood and more fully to pervade the church and the world. As the advanced Christian believes just what he believed when a babe in Christ, but apprehends it more justly and is more under its influence; so the church of the Reformation was in advance of the church of the third century, and the consummated church will be in advance of the church of the Reformation. In all this there is much truth. In the manner in which it is presented and in the exhibition of the means by which this development is to be carried on, there is a great deal that is due to the peculiar philosophical and historical training of the writer; much that we do not understand and much with which we cannot agree. And yet there is much that is healthful and encouraging. It is very plain from this brief analysis of the book before us that the apprehension that Dr. Nevin and Prof. Schaff are tending toward Puseyism, if by Puseyism be meant prelacy and Rome and what is necessarily connected with them, is altogether unfounded. It would be suicidal in them and entirely opposed to all their principles, to step out of the line "of historical development" to which they belong. They are in the Reformed church, that church is an immeasurable advance on the church of the Middle Ages; to go back to the ground which the Puseyites are endeavouring to regain, would, in their view, be for men to turn children. Their motto is Forward. What is the future they have figured for themselves and for the church, we cannot distinctly discern.

We confess we have not much faith in the means of progress on which these gentlemen seem to place their main reliance. German philosophy and German theology appear to be the great sources of their hopes, as far as human agency is concerned. We once heard a distinguished German professor say, "England and America are the hands of the church, Germany is the head. She must do the thinking, they the work." A division of labour with which we ought to be content, especially if our working does not depend upon our understanding their thinking. Prof. Schaff's book is imbued with the same idea of the relative vocations of the several portions of the church. "Germany is the proper home of Protestant theology." If we allude to German Rationalism, we are told "only an archangel can become a devil." To Germany therefore we must look for the impulse and the light to impel and guide this onward movement of the church. We are very ready to admit the great superiority of Germany in all that can be attained by research and concentrated labour. We admit too that the German mind is in some of its attributes favourably distinguished from the English and American, but we think Dr. Schaff not only estimates this superiority, but finds it, in some instances, in those very peculiarities where the advantage is on the other side. The Germans have never been celebrated for their ability to distinguish between the unknown and the unknowable, they cannot discern the limits of human knowledge; and by passing those limits they lose all the criteria of knowledge, and are unable to distinguish between truth and the phantoms of their creative imaginations. To our apprehension the willingness of the English mind to rest content within the sphere which God has assigned it; to submit to the laws of its nature, and to confide in the principles of belief impressed upon our constitution, without attempting either to question the legitimacy of those laws, or the conclusions to which they lead, is worth more as a means of attaining truth than all that mysterious "power of perceiving the supernatural, the infinite, the harmonious unity, the essence of things, the primal idea of the absolute," which is the peculiar excellence of our German brethren.

In order to decide what the church has to hope from German theology in securing the anticipated progress in divine knowledge, it would seem natural to inquire what that theology, since its revival, has actually accomplished. A question we are not competent to answer. On the one hand, we are disposed to hope that it has not done much in unsettling old landmarks, when we find such thoroughly evangelical exhibitions of the doctrine of justification as that given by Prof. Schaff, and when we see that the very best of the recent German theologians are precisely those who are most like the Reformers. On the other hand, we cannot repress our fears when we find that to those most imbued with this theology, every thing seems alike. Fichte, Schelling, Hegel, as philosophers; Daub, Schleiermacher, Marheinecke, as theologians, seem to be regarded as differing from each other, and differing from received standards, only as to their mode of presenting truth. When we express surprise that men who seem to deny a personal God, to deny sin, to deny the continued personal existence of the soul after death, should be referred to as substantially sound, we are told we do not understand these writers and therefore are not competent to form an opinion on the subject. The sufficiency of this answer we should feel bound to admit, were it not for two circumstances. First, we see the professed and thoroughly instructed disciples of these schools in Germany itself asserting that these philosophers do in fact teach what their words seem to imply, viz., that there is no God, no sin, no conscious existence hereafter. And secondly, when we hear some of the most highly educated and devout among the Germans themselves denouncing as an utter abomination those very systems and writers who are so much lauded in this country. Here then are two classes of men, neither of which can be summarily set down as destitute of the Anschauungsvermögen, the power of perceiving the absolute and infinite, who unite in condemning just what those among us most zealous for German philosophy and theology, unite in lauding. We confess that this, more than any thing else, far more than any confidence in our own limited knowledge of these systems and writers, makes us fear their influence. We are afraid of their confounding all the landmarks of truth, of leading men to see no difference between holiness and beauty, sin and defect, fate and providence, a self-conscious universe, and our Father who is in heaven.

While we say this from a deep conviction of its truth, we are not insensible either to the merits of this work or to the advantages which the author derives from his familiarity with the varied learning of his native country. The evangelical character of the leading doctrines of his book, the seriousness and warmth of feeling which pervade it, and the high order of ability which it displays, give ground to hope that Dr. Schaff will prove a blessing to the church and country of his adoption.

15

Finney's Lectures on Theology
1847

Charles Finney (1792–1875) was converted in 1821 in upstate New York and almost immediately began to preach as a revivalist.[1] His legal training, his self-confidence, and his great success as an itinerant preacher of conversion and personal righteousness all influenced the shape of his more formal theology. Charles Hodge had written against Finney as early as 1832 when, in an article entitled "The New Divinity Tried," he reviewed controversy in New England over revivalistic preaching. In that essay he chose to regard Finney as one who carried further the errors of New England's New Haven Theology.[2] To Hodge, the New Divinity, associated most prominently with Yale's Nathaniel William Taylor, mistakenly equated moral responsibility with individual capacity to choose God and the good. Hodge, as an Augustinian Calvinist, held that while people were not prevented from following God by any thing in their created nature, they did suffer a moral inability because of the bondage of sin. Hodge also felt that the New Divinity exalted its own ideas over Scripture. In 1832 he wrote that "the characteristic tendency" of Finney's preaching "is to keep the Holy Spirit and his influences out of view." As a consequence, "Christ and his cross are practically made of none effect," since everything is made to hang on the exercise of the individual's will ("The New Divinity Tried," BRPR 4 [April 1832]: 301).

By 1847, when Hodge came to review Finney's *Lectures on Systematic Theology,* embracing *Lectures on Moral Government, together with Atonement, Moral and Physical Depravity, Philosophical Theories, and Evidences of Regeneration,* his objections had intensified. Hodge contended that Finney's theology was really an exercise in specious deductive reasoning. He began with erroneous assumptions and spun these out with blatant disregard for Scripture and Christian experience. The result was a work "false as to its principles and at variance with Scripture, experience, and the common consciousness of men." Hodge is particularly offended that Finney adduced Scripture only as a support for propositions already deduced from his own reasoning. Finney in fact reasons precisely this way.[3] But in his defense it may be said that this volume represented

---

1. On Finney's life, see Sydney E. Ahlstrom, *A Religious History of the American People* (New Haven: Yale University Press, 1972), pp. 459–461; and *Memoirs of Rev. Charles G. Finney, Written by Himself* (1876; repr. ed., New York: AMS Press, 1973).

2. For a summary of the Princetonians' views of the New Divinity, see Warfield, Selection 31.

3. For example, early in the *Lectures,* Finney argued extensively that moral obligations

only part of the course in theology which he delivered at Oberlin College, which course may presumably have used Scripture more directly in its other parts.[4] Hodge would not have been impressed if it had, for he found Finney's willingness to move from ideas of moral government to conclusions concerning sin and salvation a fatal flaw that stood proper biblical theology on its head.

Two matters in Hodge's review require brief mention. Hodge criticizes Finney for confusing the terms *reason* and *understanding*. In the first half of the nineteenth century, when faculty psychology ruled the intellectual marketplace, much hung on such definitions. Hodge here takes *reason* to be the active human intelligence which is itself a source of knowledge. He regards *understanding* as a critical faculty which measures, sorts, and arranges information. In this review he calls Finney to task for approximating the Transcendentalists, who exalted *reason* into a nearly divine source of authority. But he also criticizes Finney for confusing *reason* and *understanding* under the ambiguous term *intelligence*. To complicate matters, Hodge himself defined these faculties somewhat differently in sт, I: 49–55. In spite of a confusing vocabulary, Hodge's point is still clear—Finney errs because he lets the activity of his own mind (however labeled) assume greater importance than the testimony of Scripture in deciding such crucial questions as the nature of freedom and human responsibility.

In making this objection, Hodge once again displayed his theological breadth. As in his lecture to theological students (Selection 6), Hodge constructs a broad and eclectic epistemology. Reason is important, but so are emotions and the conscience as well as the self-attesting Bible. The rationalistic strains present elsewhere in the Princeton Theology (e.g., Selections 3, 8, 17, 21; sт, I: 49–55) recede here, to be replaced by a view of truth that takes full cognizance of subjectivity. When faced with a truly rationalistic theologian, with one who brooks no exception to "common sense," Hodge seems to recoil from these same tendencies in his own thought, however freely they emerge when he battles mystical or romantic theologians like Nevin, Bushnell, or Edwards Amasa Park.

The following is the first part of Charles Hodge, "Finney's Lectures on Theology," BRPR, 19 (April 1847), and is taken from *Essays and Reviews*, pp. 245–258. The excerpt is a typical example of the close reasoning and dialectical logic which Hodge often brought to bear on his opponents.

T HIS IS IN more senses than one a remarkable book. It is to a degree very unusual an original work; it is the product of the author's own mind. The principles which he holds have indeed been held by others; and the conclusions at which he arrives had been reached before; but still it is abundantly evident that all the principles here advanced are adopted by the writer, not on authority, but on

---

pertain, in a strict sense, only to intentions. At the end of his reasoning he added, "The Bible everywhere either expressly or implicitly recognizes this truth." From the 1878 edition, ed. by J. H. Fairchild (Whittier, Calif.: Colporter Kemp, 1944; or Minneapolis: Bethany Fellowship, 1976), p. 23.
    4. Ibid., p. xi.

conviction, and that the conclusions presented have all been wrought out by himself and for himself. The work is therefore in a high degree logical. It is as hard to read as Euclid. Nothing can be omitted; nothing passed over slightly. The unhappy reader once committed to a perusal is obliged to go on, sentence by sentence, through the long concatenation. There is not one resting-place; not one lapse into amplification, or declamation, from beginning to the close. It is like one of those spiral staircases, which lead to the top of some high tower, without a landing from the base to the summit; which if a man has once ascended, he resolves never to do the like again. The author begins with certain postulates, or what he calls first truths of reason, and these he traces out with singular clearness and strength to their legitimate conclusions. We do not see that there is a break or a defective link in the whole chain. If you grant his principles, you have already granted his conclusions. Such a work must of course be reckless. Having committed himself to the guidance of the discursive understanding, which he sometimes calls the intelligence, and sometimes the reason, and to which he alone acknowledges any real allegiance, he pursues his remorseless course, regardless of any protest from other sources. The Scriptures are throughout recognized as a mere subordinate authority. They are allowed to come in and bear confirmatory testimony, but their place is altogether secondary. Even God himself is subordinate to "the intelligence"; his will can impose no obligation; it only discloses what is obligatory in its own nature and by the law of reason. There can be no positive laws, for nothing binds the conscience but the moral law, nothing is obligatory but what tends to the highest good, and as a means to that end, which must be chosen not out of regard for God, not for the sake of the moral excellence implied in it, but for its own sake as what alone has any intrinsic value. All virtue consists "in obedience to the moral law as revealed in the reason." P. 30. "Benevolence (i.e., virtue) is yielding the will up unreservedly to the demands of the intelligence." P. 275. Moral law "is the soul's idea or conception of that state of heart or life which is exactly suited to its nature and relations. It cannot be too distinctly understood that moral law is nothing more or less than the law of nature, that is, it is the rule imposed on us, not by the arbitrary will of any being, but by our own intelligence." P. 6. It is obligatory also upon every moral agent, entirely independent of the will of God. Their nature and relations being given and their intelligence being developed, moral law must be obligatory upon them, and it lies not in the option of any being to make it otherwise. "To pursue a course of conduct suited to their nature and relations, is necessarily and self-evidently obligatory, the willing or nilling of any being to the contrary notwithstanding." P. 5. As man's allegiance is to the universe—to being in general, and the rule of his obedience his own intelligence, God is reduced to the same category. He is "under moral law," he is bound to seek the highest good of being, and as the highest well-being of the universe demands moral government, and as God is best qualified, "it is his duty to govern." P. 19. "His conscience must demand it." P. 20. Our obligation, however, to obey him rests neither on our dependence, nor on his infinite superiority, but simply on "the intrinsic value of the interests to be secured by government, and conditionated upon the fact, that government is the necessary means or condition of securing that end." P. 24. God's right is therefore limited by its foundation, "by the fact, that thus far, and no further, government is necessary to the highest good of the universe. No legislation in heaven or earth—no enactment can impose obligation, except upon condition that such legislation is demanded by the highest good of the governor and the governed. Unnecessary legislation is invalid legislation. Unnecessary government is tyranny. It can in no case be founded in right." P. 24. The question is not what form of truth may be conveyed under these expressions; we quote them as exhibiting what we have called the recklessness of the writer; his tracing out his principles to conclusions which shock the ordinary sensibilities of Christians; which assume, to say the least, principles inconsistent with the nature of religion as presented in the Bible and as avowed by the vast body of the people of God. The Scriptures assume that our allegiance is to God, and not to being in general; that the foundation of our obligation to obey him is his infinite excellence, and not the necessity of obedience to the highest happiness of moral agents; and that the rule of our obedience is his will, and not "the soul's conception" of what is suited to our nature and relations. According to the doctrine of this book, there is no such thing as religion or the service of God as God. The universe has usurped his place as the supreme object of love; and reason, or "the intelligence," has fallen heir to his authority. A very slight modification in the form of statement would bring the doctrine of Mr. Finney into exact conformity to the doctrine of the modern German school which makes God but a name for the moral law or order of the universe, or reason in the abstract. It is in vain, however, to tell Mr. Finney that his conclusions shock the moral and religious consciousness; what right, he asks, has "the empirical consciousness" to be heard in the premises. "If the intelligence affirms it, it must be true or reason deceives us. But if the intelligence deceives in this, it may also in other things. If it fail us here, it fails us on the most important of all questions. If reason gives us false testimony, we can never know truth from error upon any moral subject; we certainly can never know what religion is, if the testimony of reason can be set aside. If the intelligence cannot be safely appealed to, how are we to know what the Bible means? for it is the only faculty by which we get at the truth of the oracles of God." P. 171.

Our object at present, however, is not to discuss principles, but to state the general character of this work. It is eminently logical, rationalistic, reckless, and confident. Conclusions at war with common faith of Christians are not only avowed without hesitation, but "sheer nonsense," "stark nonsense," "eminently nonsensical," are terms applied to doctrines which have ever held their place in the faith of God's people, and which will maintain their position undisturbed, long after this work is buried in oblivion. Men have other sources of knowledge than the understanding, the feeble flickering light burning in the midst of misty darkness. If deaf to the remonstrance of our moral nature, to the protests even of the emotional part of our constitution, we follow that light, it belongs to history and not to prophecy to record the issue. It really seems strange when the first sentence of his preface informs the reader that "the truths of the blessed gospel have been hidden under a false philosophy," that the author, instead of presenting those truths free from that false ingredient, should write a book which hardly pretends to be anything else than philosophy. The attempt to cure philosophy by philosophy is a homeopathic mode of treatment in which we have very little confidence. The gospel was intended for plain people. Its doctrines admit of being plainly stated. They imply indeed a certain psychology, and a certain moral system. The true and Christian method is to begin with the doctrines, and let them determine our philosophy, and not to begin with philosophy and allow it to give law to the doctrines. The title page of this book is not plainer than the fact that the doctrines which it inculcates are held, not on the authority of God speaking in his word, but on the authority of reason. They are almost without exception first proved, demonstrated as true, as the necessary sequences of admitted or assumed principles, before the Bible is so much as named. It is by profession a philosophy, or a philosophical demonstration of certain doctrines of morals and religion, and which might be admitted and adopted as true by a man who did not believe one word of the Scriptures, or who had never heard of their existence. The only doctrines which are assumed as facts, and not deduced from assumed premises, are the atonement as a fact, and the influence of the Holy Spirit on the mind, and as to the former its nature, design, and effect are all proved *a priori*;[5] and as to the latter the writer professes "to understand the philosophy of the Spirit's influence." P. 28. It is altogether a misnomer to call such a book "Lectures on Systematic Theology." It would give a far more definite idea of its character, to call it, "Lectures on Moral Law and Philosophy." Under the former title, we are authorized to expect a systematic exhibition of the doctrines of the Bible, as resting on the authority of a divine revelation; under the latter we should expect to find what is here presented, a regular evolution from certain radical principles of a code of moral laws. We wish it to be distinctly understood that we neither deny nor lightly estimate works of the kind just described. There can be no higher or more worthy subject of study, apart from the word of God, than the human soul and the laws which regulate its action and determine its obligations. Nor do we suppose that these subjects can ever be divorced from theology. They occupy so much ground in common that they never have been and never can be kept distinct. But still, it is very important that things should be called by their right names and not presented to the public for what they are not. Let moral philosophy be called moral philosophy and not Systematic Theology.

While we admit that the philosophical and theological element in any system of Christian doctrine cannot be kept distinct, it is of the last importance that they should be kept, as already remarked, in their proper relative position. There is a view of free agency and of the grounds and extent of moral obligation which is perfectly compatible with the doctrines of original sin, efficacious grace, and divine sovereignty; and there is another view of those subjects as obviously incompatible

---

5. By *a priori* reasoning, which he refers to later in this review as well, Hodge means conclusions about theological matters drawn from a process of thought *before* examining the "facts" of Scripture.

with these doctrines. There are two courses which a theologian may adopt. He may either turn to the Scriptures and ascertain whether those doctrines are really taught therein. If satisfied on that point, and especially if he experience through the teachings of the Holy Spirit their power on his own heart, if they become to him matters not merely of speculative belief but of experimental knowledge, he will be constrained to make his philosophy agree with his theology. He cannot consciously hold contradictory propositions, and must therefore make his convictions harmonize as far as he can; and those founded on the testimony of the Spirit will modify and control the conclusions to which his own understanding would lead him. Or, he may begin with his philosophy and determine what is true with regard to the nature of man and his responsibilities, and then turn to the Scriptures and force them into agreement with foregone conclusions. Every one in the slightest degree acquainted with the history of theology knows that this latter course has been adopted by errorists from the earliest ages to the present day. Our own age has witnessed what must be regarded as, on the whole, a very beneficial change in this respect. Rationalists, instead of coercing Scripture into agreement with their philosophy, have agreed to let each stand on its own foundation. The modern systems of theology proceeding from that school give first the doctrines as they are presented in the Bible, and then examine how far those doctrines agree with, and how far they contradict the teachings of philosophy, or—as they are commonly regarded—the deductions of reason. As soon as public sentiment allows of this course being pursued in this country, it will be a great relief to all concerned. We do not, however, mean to intimate that those who among ourselves pursue the opposite course and who draw out that system of moral and religious truth, as they sometimes express it, which every man has in the constitution of his own nature, before they go to the Bible for instruction, and whose system is therefore essentially rationalistic, are insincere in their professions of faith in the Bible. It is too familiar a fact to be doubted that if a man is previously convinced the Scriptures cannot teach certain doctrines, it is no difficult task to persuade himself that they do not in fact teach them. Still there is a right and a wrong method of studying and teaching theology; there is a healthful and unhealthful posture of mind to be preserved towards the word of God. And we confess that when we see a system of theology beginning with moral government, we take it for granted that the Bible is to be allowed only a very humble part in its construction.

There is one other general remark we would make on the work before us. We object not only to the method adopted, to the assumption that from a few postulates the whole science of religion can be deduced by a logical process, but to the mode in which the method has been carried out. As all truth is consistent; as some moral and religious truths are self-evident, and as all correct deductions from correct premises must themselves be correct, it is of course conceivable that an *a priori* system of morals and religion might be constructed which, as far as it went, would agree exactly with the infallible teachings of the Bible. But apart from the almost insurmountable difficulties in the way of the successful execution of such a task, and the comparatively slight authority that could be claimed for any such production, everything depends upon the manner in which the plan is executed. Now we object to Mr. Finney's mode of procedure that he adopts as first principles, the very points in dispute. He postulates what none but a limited class of his readers are prepared to concede. His whole groundwork, therefore, is defective. He has built his tower on contested ground. As a single example of this fundamental logical error, we refer to his confounding liberty and ability. In postulating the one, he postulates also the other. It is a conceded point that man is a free agent. The author therefore is authorized to lay down as one of his axioms that liberty is essential to moral agency; but he is not authorized to assume as an axiom that liberty and ability are identical. He defines free will to be "the power to choose in every instance, in accordance with moral obligation, or to refuse so to choose. This much," he adds, "must be included in free will, and I am not concerned to affirm anything more." P. 32. "To talk of inability to obey moral law, is to talk sheer nonsense." P. 4. Mr. Finney knows very well that he has thus taken for granted what has been denied by nine-tenths of all good men since the world began, and is still denied by no small portion of them as we verily hope and believe. This is a point that cannot be settled by a definition *ex cathedra*. He is guilty of a *petitio principii* [question begging] when he lays down as an axiom that liberty implies ability to obey moral law and consequently that responsibility is limited by ability. This is one of the assumptions on which his whole system depends; it is one of the hooks from which is strung his long concatenation of sequences. We deny the right of Mr. Finney to assume this definition of liberty as a "first truth of reason" because it lacks both the essential characteristics of such truths; it neither forces assent as soon as intelligibly stated, nor does it constitute a part of the instinctive (even if latent) faith of all mankind. On the contrary, it is intelligently denied, not only by theorists and philosophers, but by the great mass of ordinary men. It is one of the most familiar facts of consciousness that a sense of obligation is perfectly consistent with a conviction of entire inability. The evidence of this is impressed on the devotional language of all churches and ages, the hymns and prayers of all people recognize at once their guilt and helplessness, a conviction that they ought and that they cannot, and a consequent calling upon God for help. It is a dictum of philosophers, not of common people, "I ought, therefore, I can." To which every unsophisticated human heart, and especially every heart burdened with a sense of sin, replies, "I ought to be able, but I am not." Mr. Finney would doubtless say to such people, this is "sheer nonsense," it is all a false philosophy; no man is bound to do or to be what is not completely, and at all times, in his own power. This does not alter the case. Men still feel at once their obligation and their helplessness, and calling them fools for so doing will not destroy their painful conviction of their real condition. As the doctrine, the very opposite of Mr. Finney's assumed axiom, is thus deeply and indelibly impressed on the heart of man, so it is constantly asserted or assumed in Scripture. The Bible nowhere asserts the ability of fallen man to make himself holy; it in a multitude of places asserts just the reverse, and all the provisions and promises of grace, and all the prayers and thanksgivings for holiness recorded in the Scriptures, take for granted that men cannot make themselves holy.

This therefore has been and is the doctrine of every Christian church under the sun, unless that of Oberlin be an exception. There is no confession of the Greek, Romish, Lutheran, or Reformed churches in which this truth is not openly avowed. It was, says Neander, the radical principle of Pelagius's system that he assumed moral liberty to consist in the ability, at any moment, to choose between good and evil, or, as Mr. Finney expresses it, "in the power to choose, in every instance, in accordance with moral law." It is an undisputed historical fact that this view of liberty has not been adopted in the confession of any one denominational church in Christendom but is expressly repudiated by them all. We are not concerned, at present, to prove or disprove the correctness of this definition. Our only object is to show that Mr. Finney had no right to assume as an axiom or a first truth of reason, a doctrine which nine-tenths of all Christians intelligently and constantly reject. He himself tells us that "a first truth" is one "universally and necessarily assumed by all moral agents, their speculations to the contrary notwithstanding." Now it has rather too much the appearance of effrontery for any man to assert (in reference to any thing which relates to the common consciousness of men) that to be a truth universally and necessarily believed by all moral agents, which the vast majority of such agents as intelligent and as capable of interpreting their own consciousness as himself, openly and constantly deny. This is only one illustration of the objection to Mr. Finney's method, that he gratuitously assumes controverted points as first truths or axioms.

A second objection to his mode of executing his task is that he gives himself up to the exclusive guidance of the understanding. We do not mean that he neglects the Scriptures or makes them subordinate to reason. On that characteristic of his work we have already remarked. We now refer to the fact that it is not the informed and informing soul of man which he studies, and whence he deduces his principles and conclusions. He will listen to nothing but the understanding. He spurns what he calls the "empirical consciousness," and denies its right to bear any testimony in relation to what is truth. It is not easy indeed to determine by his definitions what he means by the intelligence to which he so constantly appeals and to which he ascribes such supremacy. He tells us at times that it includes Reason, Conscience, and Self-consciousness. Of Reason he says, it is the intuitive faculty or function of the intellect; that which gives us the knowledge of the absolute, the infinite, the perfect, the necessarily true. It postulates all the *a priori* truths of science. "Conscience is the faculty or function of the Intelligence that recognizes the conformity or disconformity of the heart or life to the moral law, as it lies revealed in the reason, and also awards praise to conformity, and blame to disconformity to that law." "Consciousness is the faculty or function of self-knowledge. It is the faculty that recognizes our own existence, mental actions and states, together with the attributes of liberty or necessity, belonging to those actions and states." To complete the view of his psychology, we must repeat his definition of the two other constituent faculties of our nature, viz.: the sensibility and will. The former "is the faculty or susceptibility of feeling. All sensation, desire, emotion, passion, pain, pleasure, and in short every kind and degree of feeling, as the term is commonly used, is a phenomenon of this faculty." The Will, as before stated, is defined to be the power to choose, in every instance, in accordance with the moral obligation, or to refuse so to choose. "The will is the voluntary power. In it resides the power of causality. As consciousness gives the affirmation that necessity is an attribute of the phenomena of the intellect and the sensibility, so it just as unequivocally gives the affirmation that liberty is an attribute of the phenomena of the will." "I am as conscious of being free in willing, as I am of not being free or voluntary in my feelings and intuitions."—P. 30, 32. Here is an analysis of the faculties of the soul in which the understanding finds no place. It is not included in the Intellect, for that is said to embrace only Reason, Conscience, and Consciousness; and Reason so defined as to distinguish it from the understanding. Here is Vernunft [reasoning], but where is the Verstand [understanding]? The fact is that Mr. Finney has for this once, and for once only, lapsed into transcendentalism. He has taken the definition of the Reason from Cousin or some other expounder of the modern philosophy, without remembering that according to that philosophy reason is something very different from the understanding.[6] This latter faculty has thus been dropped out of his catalogue. This, however, is only a momentary weakness. Mr. Finney is the last man in the world to be reproached with the sin of taking his doctrines at second hand from any school or individual. We do not find in this analysis, however, what we are searching for. The reader of this book perceives, on perusing the first page, that he is about to enter on a long and intricate path. He naturally wishes to know who is to be his guide. It is not Reason, as here defined; for that only gives him the point of departure, and tells him the bearing. Of course it is neither the susceptibility nor the will. What then is it? Why, under the new name of the Intelligence, it is the old faculty, familiar to all Englishmen and Americans as the understanding. Nothing more nor less. Not reason, in its transcendental sense, as the faculty for the absolute, but the discursive understanding. The ordinary New England faculty which calculates, perceives, compares, infers and judges. No man can read a dozen pages in any part of the book, without perceiving that it is the product of the speculative understanding, to the exclusion to a most wonderful degree, of every other faculty. This is its presiding genius. This is the organ which is "phrenologically"[7] developed most disproportionately in the head of the writer, and which gives character to his philosophy and theology. Now we earnestly protest against the competency of this guide. It does not belong to the understanding as described above and as it domineers in this book, to speak with authority on questions of religion and morals. It is not the informing faculty; nor can it be trusted as a guide. Let a man attempt to write a work on aesthetics, putting as Mr. Finney does, his mailed foot on the susceptibilities, not allowing them any voice in determining the principles of taste, and he will produce a work which no cultivated man could recognize as treating on

6. See the introduction to this Selection for a brief summary of Hodge's use of the terms "reason" and "understanding."

7. Phrenology was the "science," greatly in vogue during the 1840s, that sought to read character by analyzing the shape of, and bumps upon, the human head.

the subject. Every such man would say the writer had purposely put out the light in order to see by the sparks struck by his iron-bound feet. In like manner if any man undertakes the task of writing on morals and religion, unchecked and unguided by the emotional part of our nature, by the susceptibilities, the "empirical conscious-ness," he will most assuredly find the heart, conscience, and consciousness of all sane and good men against him. This task has been attempted long before Mr. Finney was born and with much the same results. The understanding, which has neither heart nor conscience, can speak on these subjects only as informed and guided by the moral and religious susceptibilities which are themselves the instinc-tive impulses of our higher nature. They belong to a far higher sphere than the speculative understanding, to the πνεῦμα [spirit] as distinguished from the ινοῦς [mind]; and are masters and not slaves. The understanding, if divorced from the other faculties, may demonstrate, just as it demonstrates that there is no external world, that there is no such thing as sin, or virtue, or good, or justice; what is that to the conscience? What becomes of all its syllogisms, when the sceptic comes to die? Are they unravelled and answered by the understanding? Or do they drop from its palsied hand the moment conscience affirms the truth? We consider it as the radical, fatal error of the "method" of this book that it is a mere work of the understanding: the heart, the susceptibilities, the conscience, are allowed no authority in deciding moral questions; which is as preposterous as it would be to write a mathematical treatise on poetry. The whole history of the church teems with illustrations of the fact that when men write on morals without being guided by the moral emotions; or on religion, uncontrolled by right religious feeling; they are capable of any extravagance of error. But such men say, as Mr. Finney does in a passage already quoted, if they do not follow the intelligence they have nothing else to follow; if reason gives false testimony or deceives them they can never know truth from error. This is all a mistake. It is not reason deceiving them, but the understanding making fools of them, as the apostle says, φάσκοντες εἶναι σοφοὶ ἐμωράνθησαν ["professing themselves to be wise, they became fools," Rom. 1:22]. This is no disparagement of the understanding. It is only saying that it is of no authority out of its legitimate sphere. It receives and gives light. It guides and is guided. It cannot be divorced from the other faculties, and act alone, and give the law to them as a separate power. Conscience is intelligent, feeling is intelligent, the soul is an intelligent and feeling agent, and not like a threefold cord, whose strands can be untwisted and taken apart. It is one indivisible substance whose activity is manifested under various forms but not through faculties as distinct from each other as the organ of sight is from that of hearing. Hence intelligence may be predicated of the susceptibilities and moral character of the acts of the intelligence. No emotion or mental passion or feeling, is a mere phenomenon of the susceptibil-ity. Is there no difference between feeling in a brute and feeling in a man? Nothing but error can result from this absolute divorce of one faculty of the soul from the others; and especially from setting the intelligence in a state of perfect isolation, and then making it, in that state, the law-giver of man.

If Mr. Finney will take the trouble to look into the books of casuistry common among Romanists or into works on what they call Moral Theology, he will be convinced that the most demoralizing of all studies is the study of morals under the exclusive guidance of the understanding. The Romish practice of confession has created a demand for the consideration of all possible cases of conscience and has led to the subjection of the soul to the scalpel of the moral anatomist, laying open to the cold eye of the "Intelligence" all the curious net-work of the feelings and emotions to be judged not by their nature but their relations. The body, when dead, may stand this; the living soul cannot. And hence no set of men have the moral sense so perverted as these same casuists. Jesuitism, theoretical and practical, is the product of this method of making the soul a mere anatomical subject for the understanding; and therefore stands as a lesson and a warning.

Apart then from the radical error of making theology a science to be deduced from certain primary principles, or first truths, we object to Mr. Finney's work that it assumes as axioms contested points of doctrine; and that it makes the mere understanding, as divorced from the other faculties, the law-giver and judge on all questions of moral and religious truth. The result is that he has produced a work, which though it exhibits singular ability for analysis and deduction, is false as to its principles and at variance with Scripture, experience, and the common consciousness of men. We feel on reading it just as a man feels who resigns himself to the arguments of an idealist who leads him step by step to the conclusion that there is no external world, that all things are nothing. Such a reader sees no flaw in the argument but feels no force in the conclusion. He knows it to be false, just as much after it has been *proved* to be true, as he did before. There is this difference between the cases, however. We are disposed to smile at the world of phantasms to which idealism leads us; but where the conclusions arrived at are such as are urged in this book, we feel that all true religion, the very essence and nature of piety, are at stake. It is not a question whether the world is real or phenomenal; but whether God or being is to be worshipped; whether sin is sin, and holiness is a good; whether religion consists in loving God for his divine excellence, or in purposing the happiness of moral agents; whether men are responsible for their feeling or only for their intentions; whether there is any other regeneration than a change of purpose or any possibility of salvation for the imperfectly sanctified. These and similar questions obviously concern the very vitals of Christianity, and if Mr. Finney is right, it is high time the church knew that religion is something essentially different from what has been commonly supposed.

16

Bushnell on Christian Nurture
1847

One of the most striking chapters in the history of the Princeton Theology was Hodge's approval in 1847 of a work by Horace Bushnell. Bushnell, as one who appreciated Schleiermacher and who strove to incorporate subjectivity into the Christian faith, stood far removed from Hodge on very many particulars of religion.[1] Two years later Hodge scored Bushnell's *God in Christ* for eviscerating the doctrine of the Trinity—"if rationalism is Dr. Bushnell's sword, mysticism is his shield" ("Bushnell's Discourses," BRPR 21 [April 1849]: 273). Two decades later Hodge attacked Bushnell's *The Vicarious Sacrifice,* which propounded a moral-influence view of the atonement, in even harsher terms—"Dr. Bushnell's theory, as it ignores or denies some of the plainest facts of the Bible and the most articulate declarations of the common consciousness of men, so it is destructive of practical religion" ("Bushnell on Vicarious Sacrifice," BRPR 38 [April 1866]: 191). Yet in 1847 Hodge was willing to commend, with careful qualifications, Bushnell's conception of Christian nurture.

Hodge did so because Bushnell's discussion of what is now referred to as Christian education comported so well with traditional Presbyterian concepts and because it seemed to contradict the drift of the New England theology. Hodge, like Bushnell, questioned the overreliance on revivalistic conversion that had become commonplace in America. Like Bushnell, Hodge believed in an organic relationship among the members of families, indeed among members of the whole human race. Precisely at this point Hodge felt that Bushnell (perhaps unwittingly) supported the Old School Presbyterians in their struggle against New England Congregationalists. If there is an organic union between parent and child, whereby God's saving mercies extended to the child before it was conscious of its own choices, may not we affirm the same for sin and its effects? Hodge had long struggled against the New England insistence that sin lay only in the sinner's explicit acts, not in the fallen nature. Yet the latter, Augustinian view was an essential part of Hodge's Calvinism, for it pointed to the need for God's sovereign grace in salvation. To the extent that Hodge felt Bushnell's organic picture of life pushed in that Augustinian direction, he was delighted. His only fear was that Bushnell's carping remarks about the old covenant theology indicated less approval of Augustinian-Calvinistic beliefs than the essay first

1. On Bushnell, see Barbara M. Cross, *Horace Bushnell: Minister to a Changing America* (Chicago: University of Chicago Press, 1958); and the excellent anthology edited by H. Shelton Smith, *Horace Bushnell* (New York: Oxford University Press, 1965).

suggested. Hodge's later reviews show that he felt those fears were justified. But his approval is striking, especially as it offered him the opportunity to comment on common American attitudes toward revival and conversion, to which he had at least some objections.

The selection is from Charles Hodge, "Bushnell on Christian Nurture," BRPR 19 (October 1847), as it appears in *Essays and Reviews*, pp. 303–6, 310–12, 319–25.

T HE LEADING IDEA of Dr. Bushnell's Discourses is organic as distinguished from individual life. Whatever may be thought of the expression or whatever may be the form in which it lies in his mind, it represents a great and obvious truth; a truth, which however novel it may appear to many of our New England brethren, is as familiar to Presbyterians as household words. Strange, and in our view distorted, as is the form in which this truth appears in Dr. Bushnell's book, and incongruous as are the elements with which it is combined, it still has power to give his Discourses very much of an "Old-school" cast, and to render them in a high degree attractive and hopeful in our estimation. Apart from the two great illustrations of this truth, the participation of the life of Adam by the whole race, and of the life of Christ by all believers, we see on every hand abundant evidence that every church, nation, and society, has a common life besides the life of its individual members. This is the reason why nothing of importance can occur in one part of the church without influencing all other parts. No new form of doctrine, no revival or decline of spiritual life can exhibit itself in New England that is not effective throughout the Presbyterian church. We as a body owe, in no small measure, our character as distinguished from other Presbyterian communities to our participation, so to speak, of the life of New England; and the New England churches are indebted, in like manner, for their character as distinguished from other Congregational bodies, to the influence of their Presbyterian brethren. No community can isolate itself. The subtle influence which pervades the whole permeates through every barrier, as little suspected and yet as effective as the magnetic or electric fluid in nature. This fact may be explained in a manner more or less obvious or profound according to our philosophy or disposition, but it cannot be denied, and should not be disregarded.

We are, therefore, not uninterested spectators of the changes going on in New England. They are changes in the body of which we are members and their effects for good or evil we must share. We are not therefore stepping out of our own sphere, or meddling with what does not concern us, in calling attention to Dr. Bushnell's book, and to the discussions to which it has given rise. . . .

The truths which give value to this publication, and from which we anticipated such favorable results, are principally the following: First, the fact that there is such a divinely constituted relation between the piety of parents and that of their children as to lay a scriptural foundation for a confident expectation in the use of the appointed means that the children of believers will become truly the children of God. We do not like the form in which Dr. Bushnell states this fact; much less, as we shall probably state more fully in the sequel, the mode in which he accounts for it; but the fact itself is most true and precious. It is founded on the express and repeated declaration and promise of God. He said to Abraham: I will establish my covenant between me and thee and thy seed after thee in their generations for an everlasting covenant, to be a God to thee, and to thy seed after thee. Gen. 17:7. In the New Testament the fact that the promises made to believers include their children was recognized from the very foundation of the Christian church. In the sermon delivered by Peter on the day of Pentecost, he said, the promise is to thee and to thy seed after thee. And Paul assures us even with regard to outcast Israel, the children are beloved for the father's sake. It is, therefore, true as might be much more fully proved that by divine appointment the children of believers are introduced into the covenant into which their parents enter with God, and that the promises of that covenant are made no less to the children than to the parents. He promises to be their God, to give them his Spirit, to renew their hearts, and to cause them to live....

A second truth prominently presented by our author is that parental nurture, or Christian training, is the great means for the salvation of the children of the church. We of course recognize the native depravity of children, the absolute necessity of their regeneration by the Holy Spirit, the inefficiency of all means of grace without the blessing of God. But what we think is plainly taught in Scripture, what is reasonable in itself, and confirmed by the experience of the church, is that early, assiduous, and faithful religious culture of the young, especially by believing parents, is the great means of their salvation. A child is born in a Christian family, its parents recognize it as belonging to God and included in his covenant. In full faith that the promise extends to their children as well as to themselves, they dedicate their child to him in baptism. From its earliest infancy it is the object of tender solicitude and the subject of many believing prayers. The spirit which reigns around it is the spirit, not of the world, but of true religion. The truth concerning God and Christ, the way of salvation and of duty, is inculcated from the beginning and as fast as it can be comprehended. The child is sedulously guarded as far as possible from all corrupting influence, and subject to those which tend to lead him to God. He is constantly taught that he stands in a peculiar relation to God, as being included in his covenant and baptized in his name; that he has in virtue of that relation a right to claim God as his Father, Christ as his Saviour, and the Holy Ghost as his sanctifier; and assured that God will recognize that claim and receive him as his child if he is faithful to his baptismal vows. The child thus trained grows up in the fear of God; his earliest experiences are more or less religious; he keeps aloof from open sins; strives to keep his conscience clear in the sight of God and to make the divine will the guide of his conduct. When he comes to maturity, the nature of the covenant of grace is fully explained to him, he intelligently and deliberately assents to it, publicly confesses himself to be a worshipper and follower of Christ, and acts consistently with his engagements. This is no fancy sketch. Such an experience is not uncommon in actual life. It is obvious that in such cases it must be difficult both for the person himself and for those around him to fix on the precise period when he passed from death unto life. And even in cases, where there is more of conflict, where the influence of early instruction has met with greater opposition, and where the change is more sudden and observable, the result, under God, is to be attributed to this parental training.

What we contend for then is that this is the appointed, the natural, the normal, and ordinary means by which the children of believers are made truly the children of God. And consequently this is the means which should be principally relied upon and employed, and that the saving conversion of our children should in this way be looked for and expected. It certainly has the sanction of God. He has appointed and commanded precisely this early assiduous and faithful training of the young. These words, saith the Lord, which I command you this day, shall be in thine hearts: and thou shalt teach them diligently unto thy children, and shalt talk of them when thou sittest in thy house, and when thou walkest by the way, and when thou liest down, and when thou risest up. Ye fathers, provoke not your children to wrath, but bring them up in the nurture and admonition of the Lord. As this method of religious training has the sanction of a divine command, so it has also the benefit of his special promise. Success in the use of this means is the very thing promised to parents in the covenant into which they are commanded to introduce their children. God, in saying that he will be their God, give them his Spirit, and renew their hearts, and in connecting this promise with the command to bring them up for him, does thereby engage to render such training effectual. Train up a child in the way he should go, and when he is old he will not depart from it, is moreover the express assurance of his word. There is also a natural adaptation in all means of God's appointment, to the end they are intended to accomplish. There is an appropriate connexion between sowing and reaping, between diligence and prosperity, truth and holiness, religious training and the religious life of children. If the occasional and promiscuous hearing of the word as preached is blessed to their conviction and conversion, why should not the early, personal, appropriate application of the same truth, aided by all the influence of natural affection, and the atmosphere of a pious home, be expected to be still more effective? How sensibly is a child's disposition and character moulded in other respects by parental example and teaching. How much greater, humanly speaking, is the advantage which a parent possesses than any preacher can have, in his constant intercourse with his child, in his hold on its confidence and love, and in the susceptibility to good impressions which belongs to the early period of life. Surely contact with the world, the influence of evil passions long indulged, of opposition to the truth, to the dictates of conscience, and the strivings of the Spirit, must harden the heart, and increase the difficulties of a sound conversion. In no part of his Discourses nor in his Argument in their defence is Dr. Bushnell so true or eloquent as in what he says of the natural power of parental influence, even before the development of reason in the child. . . .

We think it can hardly be doubted that many of the popular views of religion are one-sided and defective. On the one hand there are many who, influenced by the conviction of the supernatural character of religion, greatly neglect to avail themselves of the instrumentalities which God has appointed for its promotion. Others again resolve it all into a mere process of nature, or attribute everything to the power of the will. The former class lose confidence in the effect of religious training and seem to take it for granted that children must, or at least in all ordinary cases, will, grow up unconverted. They look upon conversion as something that can only be effected in a sudden and sensible manner; a work necessarily distinct to the consciousness of its subject and apparent to those around him. This conviction modifies their expectation, their conduct, their language, and their prayers. It affects to a very serious degree both parents and children, and as it arises from false, or at least imperfect views of the nature of religion, it of course tends to produce and perpetuate them. We see evidence of this mistake all around us, in every part of the country, and in every denomination of Christians. We see it in the disproportionate reliance placed on the proclamation of the gospel from the pulpit as almost the only means of conversion; and in the disposition to look upon revivals as the only hope of the church. If these seasons of special visitation are few or not remarkable in extent or power, religion is always represented as declining, the Spirit is said to have forsaken us, and all our efforts are directed to secure a return of these extraordinary manifestations of his presence.

We shall not, it is hoped, be suspected of denying or of undervaluing the importance either of the public preaching of the gospel or of revivals of religion. The former is a divine appointment which the experience of all ages has proved to be one of the most efficient means for the conversion of sinners and edification of saints. But it is not the only means of divine appointment; and as it regards the children of believers, it is not the first nor the ordinary means of their salvation, and therefore should not be so regarded to the neglect or undervaluing of religious parental training. Besides, public preaching is effective, as already remarked in all ordinary cases, just in proportion to the degree in which this early training has been enjoyed. As to revivals of religion, we mean by the term what is generally meant by it, and therefore it is not necessary to define it. We avow our full belief that the Spirit of God does at times accompany the means of grace with extraordinary power, so that many unrenewed men are brought to the saving knowledge of the truth, and a high degree of spiritual life is induced among the people of God. We believe also that such seasons have been among the most signal blessings of God to his church, from the day of Pentecost to our own times. We believe, moreover, that we are largely indebted for the religious life which we now enjoy to the great revivals which attended the preaching of Edwards, Whitefield, and the Tennents; and at a later period, of Davies, Smith, and others, in Virginia. What, however, we no less believe and feel constrained in conscience to say, is that a great and hurtful error has taken fast hold on the mind of the church on this subject. Many seem to regard these extraordinary seasons as the only means of promoting religion. So that if these fail, every thing fails. Others again, if they do not regard them as the only means for that end, still look upon them as the greatest and the best. They seem to regard this alternation of decline and revival as the normal condition of the church; as that which God intended and which we must look for; that the cause of Christ is to advance not by a growth analogous to the progress of spiritual life in the individual believer, but by sudden and violent paroxysms of exertion. We do not believe this because it is out of analogy with all God's dealings with men. Life in no form is thus fitful. It is not in accordance with the constitution which God has given us. Excitation, beyond a given standard, is unavoidably followed by a corresponding depression. This depression in religion is sinful, and therefore any thing which by the constitution of our nature necessarily leads to it is not a normal and proper condition. It may be highly useful, or even necessary, just as violent remedies are often the only means of saving life. But such remedies are not the ordinary and proper means of sustaining and promoting health. While, therefore, we believe that when the church has sunk into a low state, God does in mercy visit it with these extraordinary seasons of excitement, we do not believe that it is his will that we should rely upon them as the ordinary and most desirable means for the promotion of his kingdom. This conviction is confirmed by the experience of the church. These revivals are in a great measure, if we may so speak, an idiosyncrasy of our country. They are called *American* revivals. There is nothing American, however, in true religion. It is the same in its nature, and in its means of progress, in all parts of the world. Every one who has paid any attention to the subject has observed how much religious experience, or the form in which religion manifests itself, is determined by sectarian and national peculiarities. Moravian, Lutheran, Methodist, Presbyterian religion has each its peculiar characteristics. So has American, Scotch, and German religion. It is very easy to mistake what is thus sectional, arising from the peculiar opinions or circumstances of a church or people, for what is essential. Such peculiarities are due, in almost every instance, to something aside from the truth as given in the word of God, and consequently is so far spurious. The very fact, therefore, that these revivals are *American;* that they are in a great measure peculiar to the form of religion in this country; that the Spirit of God who dwells in all portions of his church and who manifests himself everywhere in the same way does not ordinarily carry on his work elsewhere by this means, should convince us that this is neither the common, nor the best, mode in which the cause of religion is to be advanced.

No one can fail to remark that this too exclusive dependence on revivals tends to produce a false or unscriptural form of religion. It makes excitement essential to the people, and leads them to think that piety consists in strong exercises of feelings, the nature of which it is difficult to determine. The ordinary means of grace become insipid or distasteful, and a state of things is easily induced in which even professors of religion become utterly remiss as to all social religious duties of an ordinary character. We have been told of parts of the church where the services of the sanctuary are generally neglected, but where the mere notice of a protracted meeting will at once fill the house with hearers who will come just as long as those meetings last and then fall back into their habitual apathy and neglect. How serious also is the lesson read to us by the history of revivals in this country, of their tendency to multiply false conversions and spurious religious experiences. It is surely not a healthful state of the church when nothing is done and nothing hoped for but in seasons when everything is thrown out of its natural state, and when the enemy has every advantage to pervert and corrupt the souls of men. Perhaps, however, the most deplorable result of the mistake we are now considering is the neglect which it necessarily induces of the divinely appointed means of careful Christian nurture. With many excellent ministers, men who have the interests of their people deeply at heart, it is so much a habit to rely on revivals as the means of their conversion that all other means are lost sight of. If religion is at low ebb in their congregations, they preach about a revival. They pray for it themselves and exhort others to do so also. The attention of pastor and people is directed to that one object. If they fail, they are chafed. The pastor gets discouraged; is disposed to blame his people, and the people to blame the pastor. And all the while, the great means of good may be entirely neglected. Family training of children and pastoral instruction of the young are almost entirely lost sight of. We have long felt and often expressed the conviction that this is one of the most serious evils in the present state of our churches. It is not confined to any one denomination. It is a state of things which has been gradually induced and is widely extended. It is, therefore, one of the great merits of Dr. Bushnell's book, in our estimation, that it directs attention to this very point, and brings prominently forward the defects of our religious views and habits, and points out the appropriate remedy, viz., family religion and Christian nurture.

There is a third feature of this little tract which gives it great interest and importance in our view. Dr. Bushnell cannot sustain his view of the intimate con-nexion between the religion of parents and that of their children without advancing doctrines which we regard as of great value, and which, according to his testimony and other sources of evidence, have been very much lost sight of, especially in New England.[2] The philosophy which teaches that happiness is the great end of creation; that all sin and virtue consist in voluntary acts; that moral character is not trans-missible but must be determined by the agent himself; that every man has power to determine and to change at will his own character or to make himself a new heart; has, as every one knows, extensively prevailed in this country. The obvious tendency and unavoidable effect of this philosophy has been to lower all the scriptural doc-trines concerning sin, holiness, regeneration, and the divine life. It represents every man as standing by himself, and of course denies any such union with Adam as involves the derivation of a corrupt nature from him. Divine influence and the indwelling of the Spirit dwindle down to little more than moral suasion. Union with Christ, as the source of righteousness and life, is left out of view. His work is regarded as scarcely more than a device to render the pardon of sin expedient, and to open the way to deal with men according to their conduct. Attention is turned from him as the ground of acceptance and source of strength, and everything made to depend on ourselves. The great question is, not what he is and what he has

2. Hodge here begins a catalogue of errors which he associated with the New England Theol-ogy of N. W. Taylor and associates.

done, but what is our state and what have we done? Religion is obviously some-thing very different, according to this view of the gospel, from what it is according to the evangelical scheme of doctrine. The pillars of this false and superficial sys-tem are overturned in Dr. Bushnell's book. He has discovered that "Goodness (holy virtue), or the production of goodness, is the supreme end of God." P. 34. "That virtue must be the product of separate and absolutely independent choice, is pure assumption." P. 31. He, on the contrary, asserts that "virtue is rather a state of being than an act or series of acts." P. 31. What mighty strides are here! "So glued," says he in his Argument, p. 39, "is our mental habit to the impression that religious charac-ter is wholly the result of choice in the individual, or if it be generated by a divine *ictus* [blow], preceded, of absolute necessity, by convictions and struggles which are possible only in the reflective age, that we cannot really conceive, when it is stated, the possibility that a child should be prepared for God by causes prior to his own will." "There was a truth," he says, Discourses p. 42, "an important truth, underlying the old doctrine of federal headship and original or imputed sin, though strangely misconceived, which we seem in our one-sided speculations to have quite lost sight of." Very true. But by whom has this important truth been more miscon-ceived, misrepresented, and derided than by Dr. Bushnell and his collaborators? "How can we hope," he asks, "to set ourselves in harmony with the Scriptures, in regard to family nurture, or household baptism, or any other subject, while our theories exclude or overlook precisely that which is the basis of all their teachings and appointments?" A question those must answer, who can. It is precisely this one-sided view of the nature and relation of man, this overlooking his real union with Adam and consequent participation of his nature and condemnation, that old-school men have been perpetually objecting to the speculations of New England. And we therefore rejoice to see any indication that the truth on this subject has begun to dawn on minds hitherto unconscious of its existence.

If, as Dr. Bushnell teaches, character may be derived from parents, if that char-acter may be formed prior to the will of the child; if the child is passive during this forming process, the period of its effectual calling, and emerges into his individual-ity "as one that is regenerated, quickened into spiritual life" (Argument, p. 32), then, of course, we shall hear no more of regeneration as necessarily the act of the subject of it, the decision of his own will; and then, too, the doctrine of the plenary ability of the sinner to change his heart must be given up. This latter doctrine is expressly repudiated. "The mind," says Dr. Bushnell, "has ideals revealed in itself that are even celestial, and it is the strongest of all proofs of its depravity that, when it would struggle up towards its own ideals, it cannot reach them, cannot, apart from God, even lift itself towards them." P. 26. How true, and yet how old is this! Again, "What do theologians understand by a fall and a bondage under the laws of evil, but evil, once entering a soul, becomes its master; so that it cannot deliver itself—therefore that a rescue must come, a redemption must be undertaken by a power transcending nature." P. 37. Here then we have the avowal of most important truths, truths which sound Presbyterians have ever held dear. Happiness is not the chief good; virtue does not consist entirely in acts, but is a state of being; men are not isolated individuals, each forming his own character by the energy of his will; moral character is transmissible, may be derived passively on the one hand by birth from Adam, and on the other, by regeneration; when sin enters the soul it is a bondage, from which it cannot deliver itself, redemption must come from God. These are comprehensive truths. Dr. Bushnell seems surprised at finding himself in the company into which such avowals introduce him. He endeavors to renounce such fellowship and to avenge himself by unwonted sneers at those to whose doctrines he is conscious of an approximation. This can be easily borne. He sees as yet men as trees walking. Whether he will come forward into clearer light or go back into thicker darkness, we cannot predict. There is much in his book which makes us fear the latter alternative. We hope and pray for the brighter issue. . . .

17

Theology of the Intellect
and of the Feelings

1850

Edwards Amasa Park (1808-1900) was the last of the New England theologians who self-consciously looked back to Jonathan Edwards for inspiration, and who yet felt at home with the modifications made in Edwards's theology by Timothy Dwight, Lyman Beecher, Nathaniel W. Taylor, and other representatives of nineteenth-century Congregationalism.[1] Park, himself a graduate of Andover Seminary, pastored briefly before beginning a teaching career at Andover that stretched from 1836 to 1881. He was closer to Jonathan Edwards than to Charles Finney on the supernatural character of regeneration, and he accepted more of an Augustinian view of human sinfulness than did his New England colleagues. Still, with them he denied the imputation of Adam's guilt, he asserted that sinfulness arises from our own acts of sin, he maintained N. W. Taylor's convictions about free agency (which were nearly the reverse of Edwards's), and he verged toward a moral influence view of the atonement. Although he stood on the conservative side of New England Congregationalism, the convictions he shared with them made him suspect to the Old School Presbyterians at Princeton.

When Park published a sermon titled, "The Theology of the Intellect and That of the Feelings," which he had delivered to Congregationalist ministers on May 30, 1850, Charles Hodge took immediate exception. The result was a lengthy exchange between Andover and Princeton which occupied considerable space in Park's *Bibliotheca Sacra* and Hodge's BRPR for the next 18 months.[2] The

---

1. On Park, see Foster, *The New England Theology,* pp. 471-540; and Anthony C. Cecil, *The Theological Development of Edwards Amasa Park, Last of the Consistent Calvinists* (Missoula, Mont.: Scholar's Press, 1974).

2. The major contributions were the following:

Park, "The Theology of the Intellect and That of the Feelings," *Bibliotheca Sacra,* 7 (July 1850), 533-569.

Hodge, "The Theology of the Intellect and That of the Feelings," BRPR, 22 (October 1850), 642-674; reprinted in *Essays and Reviews,* 539-569.

Park, "Remarks on the Princeton Review," *Bibliotheca Sacra,* 8 (January 1851), 135-180.

Hodge, "Prof. Park's Remarks on the Princeton Review," BRPR, 23 (April 1851), 306-347; reprinted in *Essays and Reviews,* pp. 571-611.

Park, "Unity and Diversities of Belief even on Imputed and Involuntary Sin: with comments on a Second Article in The Princeton Review," *Bibliotheca Sacra,* 8 (July 1851), 594-647.

Hodge, "Professor Park and the Princeton Review," BRPR, 23 (October 1851), 674-695; reprinted in *Essays and Reviews,* 613-633.

debate forced both Park and Hodge to clarify their respective positions as each advanced the claim to stand as the genuine heir of earlier Calvinism. For our purposes, however, it is sufficient to see how Hodge's first response to Park (presented below) allowed him to sum up a lifetime of polemical concerns. It gave him the chance to attack once again Schleiermacher, the drift of theology in New England, "Romanism," and subjective epistemology. It also let him defend again his conception of a proper philosophy, his belief in the truth-telling character of the Bible, and the tenets of Calvinism which New England theologians considered an embarrassment. Hodge's response, moreover, contained the fullest exposition found anywhere in his writing concerning the proper balance between objectivity and subjectivity, between thinking and emotion, in the Christian faith.[3] This essay was, in fact, the most complete and the most characteristic of his polemical essays. It stands today as a virtual recapitulation of his contribution to the Princeton Theology.

The essay, with its blend of exposition and commentary, is also a good example of Hodge's approach to polemics. Hodge does not always quote Park to the latter's advantage, but the full citations in Hodge's piece are an adequate reflection of Park's concern, which was to retain allegiance to Scripture without interpreting all of its teachings in the same terms.

As Hodge and Park battled each other throughout 1850 and 1851, they exhibited their opponents' weaknesses with telling force—Hodge hit home with his contention that one cannot have truth in feelings and error in intellect at the same time, Park with the argument that the Christian faith does not resolve itself as neatly into dogmatic categories as traditionally assumed. Yet insightful as the combatants were, they may have missed one important thing. They may not have realized how much the long-term intellectual prospects of Calvinism suffered at the spectacle of two of its theological giants—each calling himself a consistent Calvinist, each claiming the Bible for his own defense, each expressing his thoughts in the categories of Scottish Common Sense—engaged in such deadly combat. In 1850 when Hodge and Park began their debate there was not much Calvinism in America outside of Congregationalism and Presbyterianism.[4] By 1900, Park's Calvinism had largely vanished from Congregationalism, and by 1930 Hodge's occupied but a tiny corner of Presbyterianism. Many factors contributed to this decline. One of them may have been the overly precise scruples and overly sharp scalpels of its exponents.

This selection presents almost all of Charles Hodge, "The Theology of the Intellect and That of the Feelings," BRPR 22 (October 1850); from *Essays and Reviews*, pp. 539-40, 542-69.

T HE NORMAL AUTHORITY of the Scripture is one of the subjects about which at the present time the mind of the church is most seriously agitated.

---

3. Hodge, as we have seen, is occasionally more rationalistic (e.g., Selections 8, 10, 14), occasionally more subjective (e.g., Selections 6 and 9). His response to Finney (Selection 15) comes as close as any other major essay to reflecting the balance shown in this selection.

4. See Timothy L. Smith, *Revivalism and Social Reform in Mid-Nineteenth–Century America* (Nashville: Abingdon, 1957), pp. 15–33.

The old doctrine of the plenary inspiration, and consequent infallibility of the written word, is still held by the great body of believers. It is assailed, however, from various quarters and in different ways. Some of these assaults are from avowed enemies; some, from pretended friends; and others, from those who are sincere in thinking they are doing God service in making his word more pliant, so that it may accommodate itself the more readily not to science but to the theories of scientific men; not to philosophy but to the speculations of philosophers. The form of these attacks is constantly varying. The age of naked rationalism is almost over. That system is dying of a want of heart. Its dissolution is being hastened by the contempt even of the world. It is no longer the mode to make "common sense" the standard of all truth. Since the discovery of the *Anschauungsvermögen* [intuitive faculty] men see things in their essence. The intuitional consciousness has superseded the discursive understanding; and Rationalists have given place to Transcendentalists. In the hands of many of the latter, the Scriptures share the same fate which has overtaken the outward world. As the material is but the manifestation of the spiritual—so the facts and doctrines of the Bible are the mere forms of the spirit of Christianity; and if you have the spirit, it matters not what form it takes. These gifted ones, therefore, can afford to be very liberal. They see in Christianity, as in all things else, a manifestation of what is real. They pity, but can bear with, those who lay stress on the historical facts and doctrinal assertions of the Scriptures. They look on them as occupying a lower position, and as belonging to a receding period. Still men can have the substance in that form as well as in another. The misfortune is that they persist in considering the form to be the substance, or at least insepara- ble from it. They do not see that as the principle of vegetable life is as vigorous now as when it was expressed in forms extant only as fossils, and would continue unimpaired though the whole existing flora should perish; so Christianity would flourish uninjured, though the New Testament should turn out to be a fable.

This theory has more forms than one; and has many advocates who are not prepared to take it in its full results. Neither is it confined to Germany. With most of the productions of that teeming soil, it is in the process of transplanting. Shoots have been set out and assiduously watered in England and America which bid fair to live and bear fruit. The doctrine that "Christianity consists not in propositions—it is life in the soul,"[5] and a life independent of the propositions, of necessity super- sedes the authority, if not the necessity, of the Scriptures. This doctrine, variously modified, is one of the forms in which the word of God is made of none effect. . . .

Under the same general category must be classed the beautiful solo of Dr. Bushnell. He endeavored to seduce us from cleaving to the letter of the Scriptures by telling us the Bible was but a picture or poem; that we need as little to know its dogmas as the pigments of an artist; the aesthetic impression was the end designed, which was to be reached, not through the logical understanding, but the

---

5. Hodge's note: "Morell's *Philosophy of Religion*, p. 172." John Daniel Morell (1816–1891) was a British educational theorist who studied philosophy in Germany and who published *The Philoso- phy of Religion* in 1849, in which the influence of German idealism was strong.

imagination. It was not a creed men needed or about which they should contend. All creeds are ultimately alike. It is of no use however to score the notes of a dying swan, as the strain cannot be repeated, except by another swan in *articulo mortis* [moment of death]. Dr. Bushnell has had his predecessors. A friend of ours, when in Germany, had Schleiermacher's *Reden über die Religion*[6] put into his hands. When asked what he thought of those celebrated discourses, he modestly confessed he could not understand them. "Understand them!" said his friend, "that is not the point. Did you not feel them?"

We are sincerely sorry to be obliged to speak of Professor Park's sermon, which was listened to with unbounded admiration, and the fame of which has gone through the land, as inimicable to the proper authority of the word of God. But if it is right in him to publish such an attack on doctrines long held sacred, it must be right in those who believe those doctrines to raise their protest against it. We are far from supposing that the author regards his theory as subversive of the authority of the Bible. He has obviously adopted it as a convenient way of getting rid of certain doctrines which stand out far too prominently in Scripture and are too deeply impressed on the hearts of God's people, to allow of their being denied. It must be conceded that they are in the Bible. To reconcile this concession with their rejection, he proposes the distinction between the theology of feeling and that of the intellect. There are two modes of apprehending and presenting truth. The one by logical consciousness (to use the convenient nomenclature of the day) that it may be understood; the other by the intuitional consciousness, that it may be felt. These modes do not necessarily agree; they may often conflict, so that what is true in the one may be false in the other. If an assertion of Scripture commends itself to our reason, we refer it to the theology of the intellect and admit its truth. If it clashes with any of our preconceived opinions, we can refer it to the theology of the feelings and deny its truth for the intellect. In this way, it is obvious any unpalatable doctrine may be got rid of, but no less obviously at the expense of the authority of the word of God. There is another advantage of this theory of which the Professor probably did not think. It enables a man to profess his faith in doctrines which he does not believe. Dr. Bushnell could sign any creed by help of that chemistry of thought which makes all creeds alike. Professor Park's theory will allow a man to assert contradictory propositions. If asked, Do you believe that Christ satisfied the justice of God? he can say, yes, for it is true of his feelings; and he can say, no, because it is false to his intellect. A judicious use of this method will carry a man a great way. This whole discourse, we think, will strike the reader as a set of variations on the old theme, "What is true in religion is false in philosophy": and the "tearful German," of whom our author speaks, who said: "In my heart I am Christian, while in my head I am a philosopher," might find great comfort in the doctrine here propounded. He might learn that his condition instead of a morbid, was, in fact, the normal one; as what is true to the feelings is often false to the intellect.

6. Schleiermacher published his *Reden* (*Religion: Speeches to Its Cultured Despisers*) in 1799. This work described religion as "a sense and taste for the infinite," it depreciated the value of dogma, and it exalted intuition and feeling.

We propose to give a brief analysis of this sermon, and then, in as few words as possible, endeavor to estimate its character.

The sermon is founded upon Gen. 6:6, and 1 Sam. 15:29. In the former passage it is said, "It repented the Lord"; and in the latter, God—"is not a man, that he should repent." Here are two assertions in direct conflict, God repented and God cannot repent. Both must be true. But how are they to be reconciled? The sermon proposes to give the answer, and to show how the same proposition may be both affirmed and denied. Our author begins by telling us of a father who, in teaching astronomy to his child, produced a false impression by presenting the truth; while the mother produced a correct impression by teaching error.[7] This, if it means anything to the purpose, is rather ominous as a commencement. A right impression is the end to be aimed at in all instruction; and, if the principle implied in this illustration be correct, we must discard the fundamental maxim in religion, "Truth is in order to holiness," and assume that error is better adapted to that purpose; a principle on which Romanists have for ages acted in their crass misrepresentations of divine things in order to impress the minds of the people.

But we must proceed with our analysis. "The theology of the intellect," we are told, "conforms to the laws, subserves the wants, and secures the approval of our intuitive and deductive powers. It includes the decisions of the judgment, of the perceptive part of conscience and taste, indeed of all the faculties which are essential to the reasoning process. It is the theology of speculation, and therefore comprehends the truth just as it is, unmodified by excitements of feeling. It is received as accurate not in its spirit only, but in its letter also." P. 534. It demands evidence. It prefers general to individual statements, the abstract to the concrete, the literal to the figurative. Its aim is not to be impressive, but intelligible and defensible. For example, it affirms "that he who united in his person a human body, a human soul, and a divine spirit, expired on the cross, but it does not originate the phrase that the soul expired, nor that.'God, the mighty Maker, died.'" "It would never suggest the unqualified remark that Christ has fully paid the debt of sinners, for it declares that this debt may be justly claimed from them; nor that he suffered the whole punishment which they deserve, for it teaches that this punishment may still be righteously inflicted on themselves; nor that he has entirely satisfied the law, for it insists that the demands of the law are yet in force." It gives origin to "no metaphor so bold, and so liable to disfigure our idea of the divine equity as that Heaven imputes the crime of one man to millions of his descendants, and then imputes their myriad sins to him who was harmless and undefiled." "It is suited not for eloquent appeals, but for calm controversial treatises and bodies of divinity; not so well for the

---

7. Hodge is perhaps guilty of misconstruing Park's intent here. Park's actual words were as follows, from pp. 533–534 of "Theology of the Intellect": "I have heard of a father who endeavored to teach his children a system of astronomy in precise philosophical language, and although he uttered nothing but the truth, they learned from him nothing but falsehood. I have also heard of a mother who, with a woman's tact, so exhibited the general features of astronomical science that although her statements were technically erroneous, they still made upon her children a better impression, and one more nearly right than would have been made by a more accurate style."

hymn-book as for the catechism; not so well for the liturgy as for the creed."
P. 535.

We must pause here for a moment. It so happens that all the illustrations which our author gives of modes of expression which the theology of the intellect would not adopt, are the products of that theology. They are the language of speculation, of theory, of the intellect, as distinguished from the feelings—that Christ bore our punishment; that he satisfied the law; that Adam's sin is imputed to us, and our sins to Christ, are all generalizations of the intellect; they are summations of the manifold and diversified representations of Scripture; they are abstract propositions embodying the truth presented in the figures, facts, and didactic assertions found in the sacred writing. It would be impossible to pick out of the whole range of theological statements any which are less impassioned, or which are more purely addressed to the intellect. They have been framed for the very purpose of being "intelligible and defensible." They answer every criterion the author himself proposes for distinguishing the language of the intellect from that of the feeling. Accordingly, these are the precise representations given in catechisms, in calm controversial treatises and bodies of divinity for strictly didactic purposes. They are found in the accurately worded and carefully balanced confessions of faith, designed to state with all possible precision the intellectual propositions to be received as true. These are the very representations, moreover, which have been held up to reproach as "theoretical," as "philosophy" introduced into the Bible. Whether they are correct or incorrect, is not now the question. What we assert is that if there be any such thing as the theology of the intellect; any propositions framed for the purpose of satisfying the demands of the intelligence; any purely abstract and didactic formulae, these are they. Yet Professor Park, simply because he does not recognize them as true, puts them under the category of feeling, and represents them as passionate expressions designed not to be intelligible but impressive; addressed not to the intellect but to the emotions!

The theology of the feelings is declared to be the form of belief which is suggested by, and adapted to, the wants of the well-trained heart. It is embraced as involving the substance of truth, although, when literally interpreted, it may or may not be false. It studies not the exact proportions of doctrine, but gives special prominence to those features which are thought to be most grateful to the sensibilities. It insists not on dialectical argument, but receives whatever the healthy affections crave. P. 535. It sacrifices abstract remarks to visible and tangible images. It is satisfied with vague, indefinite representations. P. 536. For example, instead of saying God can do all things which are the objects of power, it says, He spake and it was done. Instead of saying that the providence of God comprehends all events; it says, "The children of men put their trust under the cover of Jehovah's wings." To keep back the Jews from the vices and idolatry of their neighbors, it plied them with a stern theology which represented God as jealous and angry, and armed with bow, arrows, and glittering sword. But when they needed a soothing influence, they were told that "the Lord feedeth his flock like a shepherd." It represents Christians as united to their Lord as the branch to the vine, or the members to the head; but it does not mean to have these endearing words metamorphosed into an intellectual theory of our oneness with Christ, for with another end in view it teaches that he is distinct from us, as a captain from his soldiers. The free theology of the feelings is ill-fitted for didactic or controversial treatises or doctrinal standards. Anything, everything can be proved from the writings of those addicted to its use, because they indite sentences congenial with an excited heart, but false as expressions of deliberate opinion. P. 537. This is the theology of and for our sensitive nature, of and for the normal emotion, affection, passion. It is, moreover, permanent. Ancient philosophy has perished, ancient poetry is as fresh as ever. So the theology of reason changes, theory chases theory, "but the theology of the heart, letting the minor accuracies go for the sake of holding strongly upon the substance of doctrine, need not always accommodate itself to scientific changes, but may often use its old statements, even if, when literally understood, they be incorrect, and it thus abides permanent as are the main impressions of the truth." P. 539.

We must again pause in our analysis. If there be any such thing as the theology of the feeling as distinct from that of the intellect, the passages cited above neither prove nor illustrate it. Our author represents the feelings as expressing themselves in figures, and demanding "visible and tangible images." We question the correctness of this statement. The highest language of emotion is generally simple. Nothing satisfies the mind when under great excitement but literal or perfectly intelligible expressions. Then is not the time for rhetorical phrases. There is a lower state of feeling, a placid calmness which delights in poetic imagery, which at once satisfies the feelings and excites the imagination and thus becomes the vehicle of moral and aesthetic emotions combined. The emotions of terror and sublimity also, as they are commonly excited through the imagination, naturally clothe themselves in imaginative language. But the moral, religious, and social affections, when strongly moved, commonly demand the simplest form of utterance. "Holy, Holy, Holy is the Lord of Hosts," is the language of seraphic devotion, yet what more simple! "The loving kindness of the Lord is over all his works," is surely as much the language of feeling, and tends as directly to excite gratitude and confidence, as saying, "The Lord is my shepherd." The most pathetic lamentation upon record is that of David over his son Absalom, which is indeed, an apostrophe, but nothing can be freer from tropical expression. How simple, also, is the language of penitence as recorded in the Bible. "God be merciful to me a sinner!" "Against thee, thee only have I sinned and done this evil in thy sight." "Behold I am vile, what shall I answer thee?" "O my God! I am ashamed, and blush to lift up my face to thee my God."

Admitting, however, that figurative language is the usual vehicle of emotion, this affords no foundation for the distinction between the theology of feeling and the theology of the intellect—the one vague and inaccurate, the other precise and exact. For, in the first place, figurative language is just as definite in its meaning and just as intelligible as the most literal. After the church had been struggling for centuries to find language sufficiently precise to express distinctly its consciousness respecting the person of Christ, it adopted the figurative language of the

Athanasian creed, "God of God, Light of Light, Begotten, and not made." Calling
God our shepherd presents as definite an idea to the mind as the most literal form
of expression. To say that God is angry, or jealous, expresses as clearly the truth that
his nature is opposed to sin, as the most abstract terms could do. We have here no
evidence of two kinds of theology, the one affirming what the other denies; the one
true to the feelings and false to the intellect, and the reverse. The two passages on
which this sermon is founded, chosen for the purpose of illustrating this theory,
might be selected to show that it is without foundation. The declarations, "God
repented," and "God cannot repent," do not belong to different categories; the one is
not the language of feeling and the other of the intelligence; the one does not affirm
what the other denies. Both are figurative. Both are intelligible. The one, in its
connection, expresses God's disapprobation of sin, the other, his immutability. The
one addresses the sensibilities as much as the other; and the one is as much
directed to the intellect as the other. To found two conflicting kinds of theology on
such passages as these, is as unreasonable as it would be to build two systems of
anthropology on the verbally contradictory propositions constantly used about
men. We say a man is a lion, and we say he is not a quadruped. Do these assertions
require a new theory of psychology, or even a new theory of interpretation in order
to bring them into harmony? Figurative language, when interpreted literally, will of
course express what is false to the intellect; but it will in that case be no less false to
the taste and to the feelings.

Such language, when interpreted according to established usage, and made to
mean what it was intended to express, is not only definite in its import, but it never
expresses what is false to the intellect. The feelings demand truth in their object;
and no utterance is natural or effective as the language of emotion which does not
satisfy the understanding. Saying God repents; that he is jealous; that he is our
shepherd; that men hide under the shadow of his wings; are true to the intelligence
in the precise sense in which they are true to the feelings; and it is only so far as they
are true to the former that they are effective or appropriate for the latter. It is
because calling God our shepherd presents the idea of a person exercising a kind
care over us, that it has power to move the affections. If it presented any conception
inconsistent with the truth, it would grate on the feelings as much as it would
offend the intellect. We object, therefore, to our author's exposition of his doctrine,
first, because much that he cites as the language of feeling is incorrectly cited; and
secondly, because, granting his premises, his conclusion does not follow. A third
objection is, that he is perfectly arbitrary in the application of his theory. Because
figurative language is not to be interpreted literally, the Socinian[8] infers that all that
is said in Scripture in reference to the sacrificial nature of Christ's death is to be
understood as expressing nothing more than the truth that he died for the benefit
of others. When the patriot dies for his country; or a mother wears herself out in
the service of her child, we are wont to say they sacrifice themselves for the object
of their affection. This deceives no one. It expresses the simple truth that they died

8. On Socinianism, see above, Selection 4, note 4.

for the good of others. Whether this is all that the Scriptures mean when they call Christ a sacrifice is not to be determined by settling the general principle that figures are not to be interpreted according to the letter. That is conceded. But figures have a meaning which is not to be explained away at pleasure. Professor Park would object to this exposition of the design of Christ's death, not by insisting that figurative language is to be interpreted literally, but by showing that these figures are designed to teach more than the Socinian is willing to admit. In like manner we say that if we were disposed to admit the distinction between the theology of the feelings and that of the intellect, as equivalent to that between figurative and literal language, or, as our author says, between poetry and prose, we should still object to his application of his principle. He is just as arbitrary in explaining away the scriptural representations of original sin, of the satisfaction of divine justice by the sacrifice of Christ, as the Socinian is in the application of his principle. He just as obviously violates the established laws of language, and just as plainly substitutes the speculations of his own mind for the teachings of the word of God. Entirely irrespective, therefore, of the validity of our author's theory, we object to this sermon that it discards, as the language of emotion, historical, didactic, argumentative statements, and in short, everything he is not willing to receive, as far as appears, for no other reason and by no other rule than his own repugnance to what is thus presented.

Having considered some of the differences between the emotive and intellectual theology, the author adverts to the influence which the one exerts over the other. And first the theology of the intellect illustrates and vivifies itself by that of the feelings. We must add a body, he says, to the soul of a doctrine, whenever we would make it palpable and enlivening. The whole doctrine of the spiritual world is one that requires to be rendered tangible by embodiment. An intellectual view is too general to be embraced by the feelings. They are balked with the notion of a spaceless, formless existence, continuing between death and the resurrection, p. 540.

In the second place, the theology of the intellect enlarges and improves that of the feelings, and is also enlarged and improved by it. The more extensive and accurate are our views of literal truth, so much the more numerous and salutary are the forms which it may assume for enlisting the affections. It is a tendency of pietism to undervalue the human intellect for the sake of exalting the affections, as if the reason had fallen deeper than the will. It cannot be a pious act to underrate those powers which are given by him who made the soul in his image. We must speculate. The heart is famished by an idle intellect. When fed by an enquiring mind, it is enlivened, and reaches out for an expanded faith.

The theology of reason not only amends and amplifies that of the affections, it is also improved and enlarged by it. When a feeling is constitutional and cannot but be approved, it furnishes data to the intellect by means of which it may add new materials to its dogmatic system. The doctrines which concentrate in and around a vicarious atonement are so fitted to the appetences of a sanctified heart, as to gain the favor of the logician, precisely as the coincidence of some geological or astronomical theories with the phenomena of the earth or sky is part of the syllogism which has these theories for its conclusion. The fact that the faithful in all ages concur in one substance of belief is a proof of the correctness of their faith. The church is not infallible in her bodies of divinity, nor her creeds, nor catechisms, nor any logical formula; but underneath all there lies a grand substance of doctrine around which the feelings of all reverent men cling ever and everywhere, and which must be right, for it is precisely adjusted to the soul, and the soul was made for it. These universal feelings provide a test for our faith. Whenever our representations fail to accord with those feelings, something must be wrong. "Our sensitive nature is sometimes a kind of instinct which anticipates many truths, incites the mind to search for them, intimates the process of investigation, and remains unsatisfied" until it finds the object towards which it gropes its way.

But while the theology of reason derives aid from the impulses of emotion, it maintains its ascendancy over them. In all investigations for truth, the intellect must be the authoritative power, employing the sensibilities as indices of right doctrine, but surveying and superintending them from its commanding elevation, pp. 543–46.

In the third place, the theology of the intellect explains that of the feeling into essential agreement with all the constitutional demands of the soul. It does this by collecting all the discordant representations which the heart allows, and eliciting the one self-consistent principle which underlies them. The Bible represents the heart sometimes as needing to be purified by God, sometimes as able to purify itself, &c., &c. These expressions, literally understood, are dissonant. The intellect educes light from these repugnant phrases, and reconciles them into the doctrine, "that *the character of our race needs an essential transformation by an interposed influence of God,*" p. 547. Certainly a very genteel way of expressing the matter, which need offend no one, Jew or Gentile, Augustin or Pelagius.[9] All may say that much, and make it mean more or less at pleasure. If such is the sublimation to which the theology of the intellect is to subject the doctrines of the Bible, they will soon be dissipated into thin air.

Another illustration is borrowed from "the heart's phrases" respecting its ability. Sometimes the man of God longs to abase himself, and exclaims without one modifying word: "I am too frail for my responsibilities, and have no power to do what is required of me." At another time he says: "I know thee, that thou art not a hard master, exacting of me duties which I have no power to discharge, but thou attemperest thy law to my strength, and at no time imposest upon me a heavier burden than thou at that very time makest me able to bear." The reason seeks out some principle to reconcile these and similar contradictions, and finds it, as Professor Park thinks, in the doctrine that man with no extraordinary aid from divine

9. Pelagius and Augustine debated the question of human ability and God's sovereign grace in the first decades of the fifth century. Under Augustine's urging, the church declared as heresy Pelagius's conviction that people had natural and moral ability to do good. But it did not follow Augustine completely in his belief that individuals were completely lost in their sin until and unless they were rescued by God's all-sovereign grace.

grace, is fully set in those wayward preferences which are an abuse of his freedom. His unvaried wrong choices imply a full, unremitted natural power of choosing right. The emotive theology, therefore, when it affirms this power is correct both in matter and style; but when it denies this power, it uses the language of emphasis, of impression, of intensity; it means the certainty of wrong preference by declaring the inability of right; and in its vivid use of *cannot* for *will not* is accurate in substance but not in form, p. 549.[10]

It is to be remembered that it is not the language of excited, fanatical, fallible men that our author undertakes thus to eviscerate, but the formal didactic assertions of the inspired writers. We can hardly think that he can himself be blind to the nature of the process which he here indicates. The Bible plainly, not in impassioned language but in the most direct terms, asserts the inability of men to certain acts necessary to their salvation. It explains the nature, and teaches the origin of that inability. This doctrine, however, is in conflict, not with other assertions of Scripture, for there are no counter statements, but with a peculiar theory of responsibility, which the author adopts; and therefore, all the expressions of this truth are to be set down to irrational feeling which does not understand itself. Thus a doctrine which is found in the symbols of all churches, Latin, Lutheran, and Reformed, is explained out of the Bible, and the most vapid formula of Pelagianism (viz. that present strength to moral and spiritual duties is the measure of obligation), put in its place. The author has surely forgot what a few pages before he said of the informing nature of Christian consciousness. If there is one thing which that consciousness teaches all Christians more clearly than anything else, it is their helplessness, their inability to do what reason, conscience, and God require, in the plain unsophisticated sense of the word *inability*. And we venture to say that no Christian ever used *from the heart*, such language as Professor Park puts into the "good man's" mouth, about his power to do all that God requires. Such is not the language of the heart, but of a head made light by too much theorizing. Give us, by all means, the theology of the heart in preference to the theology of the intellect. We would a thousandfold rather take our faith from Professor Park's feelings than from what he miscalls his reason, but which is in fact the fragments of a philosophy that was, but is not.

His fourth remark is that the theology of the intellect and that of the feeling tend to keep each other within the sphere for which they were respectively designed, and in which they are fitted to improve the character. When an intellectual

10. Park's assertions on pp. 548–549 of his essay, which Hodge quotes and paraphrases here, concern the much debated matter of human free will. Park feels that when Scripture says people *cannot* do good that this is the theology of the feelings, for common sense tells the intellect that we do in fact retain a freedom to choose good *or* evil. Hodge, as an Augustinian, is offended because he feels the Bible means pretty much what it says when it uses words like *cannot* to describe human motivation. See Foster, *New England Theology*, pp. 526–531, on Park's view of freedom and conversion. As Foster notes, Park was closer to Jonathan Edwards and Augustine on the will than was N. W. Taylor, but Hodge evidently did not think that it was necessary or useful to draw distinctions between shades of New England error.

statement is transferred to the province of emotion, it often appears chilling, lifeless; and when a passionate phrase is transferred to the dogmatic province, it often appears grotesque, unintelligible, absurd. To illustrate this point he refers to the declaration in reference to the bread and wine in the eucharist. "This is my body, this is my blood." To excited feelings such language is appropriate, but no sooner are these phrases transmuted into utterances of intellectual judgments than they become absurd. So the lamentation: "Behold I was shapen in iniquity, and in sin did my mother conceive me," is natural and proper as an expression of penitential feelings. But if seized by a theorist to straighten out into the dogma that man is blamable before he chooses to do wrong, deserving of punishment for the involuntary nature which he has never consented to gratify, really sinful before we actually sin, then all is confusion.

Here again a plain doctrine of the Bible, incorporated in all Christian creeds, inwrought into all Christian experience, is rejected in deference to the theory that all sin consists in acts; a theory which ninety-nine hundredths of all good men utterly repudiate; a theory which never has had a standing in the symbols of any Christian church, a clear proof that it is in conflict with the common consciousness of believers. Because the doctrine here discarded finds expression in a penitential psalm is surely no proof that it is not a doctrine of Scripture. Thomas's passionate exclamation at the feet of his risen Saviour, "My Lord and my God," is no proof that the divinity of Christ belongs to the theology of feeling and is to be rejected by the reason. It is because such doctrines are didactically taught in the Bible and presented as articles of faith that they work themselves into the heart, and find expression in its most passionate language. The doctrine of innate sinful depravity does not rest on certain poetic phrases, it is assumed and accounted for it; it is implicated in the doctrines of redemption, regeneration, and baptism; it is sustained by arguments from analogy, experience, and consciousness; it is part and parcel of the universal faith of Christendom, and its rejection, on the score that passionate phrases are not to be interpreted by the letter, is as glaring an example of subjecting Scripture to theory as the history of interpretation affords.

In the conclusion of his discourse, our author represents the confusion of the two kinds of theology which he endeavors to discriminate as a great source of evil. "Grave errors," he says, "have arisen from so simple a cause as that of confounding poetry with prose." Is it not a still more dangerous mistake to turn prose into poetry? What doctrine of the Scriptures have Rationalists, by that simple process, failed to explain away? What do they make of the ascription of divine names and attributes to Christ, but eastern metaphor and hyperbole? How do they explain the worship paid to him on earth and in heaven, but as the language of passion which the intellect repudiates? The fact is that poetry and prose have their fixed rules of interpretation, and there is no danger of mistaking the one for the other, nor are they ever so mistaken, where there is a disposition humbly to receive the truth they teach.

"In the Bible," says our author, "there are pleasing hints of many things which were never designed to be doctrines, such as the literal and proper necessity of the will, passive and physical sin, baptismal regeneration, clerical absolution, the literal imputation of guilt to the innocent, transubstantiation, eternal generation and procession. In that graceful volume, these metaphors (?) bloom as the flowers of the field; *there* they toil not neither do they spin. But the schoolman has transplanted them to the rude exposure of logic, there they are frozen up, their juices evaporated, and their withered leaves are preserved as specimens of that which in its rightful place surpassed the glory of the wisest sage." P. 558. It would be a pity to throw the veil of comment over the self-evidencing light of such a sentence. Its animus is self-revealing.

A more cheering inference from the doctrine of his sermon our author finds in the revelation it affords of "the identity in the essence of many systems which are run in scientific or aesthetic moulds unlike each other." There are, indeed, kinds of theology which cannot be reconciled with each other. There is a life, a soul, a vitalizing spirit of truth, which must never be relinquished for the sake of peace, even with an angel. "There is," as we rejoice to hear our author say, "a line of separation which cannot be crossed, between those systems which insert, and those which omit the doctrine of justification by faith in the sacrifice of Jesus. This is the doctrine which blends in itself the theology of intellect and feeling and which can no more be struck out from the moral than the sun from the planetary system. Here the mind and the heart, like justice and mercy, meet and embrace each other; and here is found the specific and ineffaceable difference between the gospel and every other system. But among those who admit the atoning death of Christ as the organic principle of their faith, there are differences, some of them more important, but many far less important than they seem to be. One man prefers a theology of the judgment; a second, that of the imagination; a third, that of the heart; one adjusts his faith to a lymphatic, another to a sanguine, and still another to a choleric temperament. Yet the subject matter of these heterogeneous configurations may often be one and the same, having for its nucleus the same cross, with the formative influence of which all is safe." P. 559. But what in the midst of all these diversities becomes of God's word? Is that so multiform and heterogeneous in its teaching? Or is the rule of faith after all subjective, a man's temperament and preferences? It is obvious, first, that the Scriptures teach one definite form of faith to which it is the duty and for the spiritual interests of every man to conform his faith, and every departure from which is evil and tends to evil. Secondly, that there is doubtless far more agreement in the apprehension, and inward experience of the doctrines of the Bible than in the outward expression of them; so that sincere Christians agree much more nearly in their faith than they do in their professions. Thirdly, that this is no proof that diversities of doctrinal propositions are matters of small moment; or that we may make light of all differences which do not affect the very fundamentals of the gospel. Truth and holiness are most intimately related. The one produces and promotes the other. What injures the one, injures also the other. Paul warns all teachers against building, even on the true foundation, with wood, hay, and stubble. He reminds them that God's temple is sacred; that it cannot be injured with impunity, and that those who inculcate error instead of truth, will, in the great day, suffer loss, though they may themselves be saved as by fire. It will avail them little to say that their temperament was lymphatic, sanguine, or choleric; that they conceived of truth themselves and presented it to others in a manner suited to their idiosyncrasies. They were sent to teach God's word, and not their own fancies. The temple of God, which temple is the church, is not to be built up by rubbish.

When we began to write, we intended to furnish an analysis of this discourse before making any remarks on the views which it presents. We have been seduced, however, into giving expression to most of what we had to say in the form of comment on the successive heads of the sermon. We shall, therefore, not trespass much longer on the reader's patience. There are two points to which it has been our object to direct attention. First, the theory here propounded, and secondly, the application which the author makes of his principle.

As to the theory itself, it seems to us to be founded on a wrong psychology. Whatever doctrine the writer may actually hold as to the nature of the soul, his thoughts and language are evidently framed on the assumption of a much greater distinction between the cognitive and emotional faculties in man than actually exists. The very idea of a theology of feeling as distinct from that of the intellect seems to take for granted that there are two percipient principles in the soul. The one sees a proposition to be true, the other sees it to be false. The one adopts symbols to express its apprehensions; the other is precise and prosaic in its language. We know, indeed, that the author would repudiate this statement and deny that he held to any such dualism in the soul. We do not charge him with any theoretic conviction of this sort. We only say that this undue dissevering the human faculties underlies his whole doctrine and is implied in the theory which he has advanced. Both Scripture and consciousness teach that the soul is a unit; that its activity is one life. The one rational soul apprehends, feels, and determines. It is not one faculty that apprehends, another that feels, and another that determines. Nor can you separate in the complex states of mind of which we are every moment conscious, the feeling from the cognition. From the very nature of affection in a rational being, the intellectual apprehension of its object is essential to its existence. You cannot eliminate the intellectual element and leave the feeling. The latter is but an attribute of the former, as much as form or color is an attribute of bodies. It is impossible, therefore, that what is true to the feelings should be false to the intellect. It is impossible that a man should have the feeling (i.e., the consciousness) of inability to change his own heart, and yet the conviction that he has the requisite power. The mind cannot exist in contradictory states at the same time. Men may indeed pass from one state to another. They may sometimes speak under the influence of actual experience; and sometimes under the guidance of a speculative theory; and such utterances may be in direct conflict. But then the contradiction is real and not merely apparent. The intellectual conviction expressed in the one state is the direct reverse of that expressed in the other. These are the vacillations of fallible men whose unstable judgments are determined by the varying conditions of their minds. We have known men educated under the influence of a sceptical philosophy who have become sincere Christians. Their conversion was, of course, a supernatural process, involving a change of faith as well as feeling. But as this change was not effected by a scientific refutation of their former opinions, but by the demonstration of the Spirit revealing to them the truth and power of the gospel; when the hearts of such men grow cold, their former sceptical views rise before them in all their logical consistence, and demand assent to their truth which for the time is reluctantly yielded, though under a solemn protest of the conscience. When the Spirit returns revealing Christ, these demons of doubt vanish and leave the soul rejoicing in the faith. These states cannot co-exist. The one is not a state of feeling; the other of cognition. Both are not true; the one when judged by one standard; and the other, by another. They are opposite and contradictory. The one affirms what the other denies. One must be false. A poor, fallible man driven about by the waves may thus give utterance to different theologies under different states of mind; but the difference, as just stated, is that between truth and falsehood. Nothing of this kind can be admitted with regard to the sacred penmen, and therefore, this change to which uninspired men may be subject in their apprehension and expression of religious truth cannot be attributed to those who spoke as they were moved by the Holy Spirit.

The changes just referred to are therefore something very different from those for which our author contends, and consequently the occurrence of such changes in the experience of men is no proof of the correctness of his theory; neither do they show that the mind is not one percipient, feeling, and willing agent. The point which we wish now to urge is that the theory of Professor Park assumes a greater difference in the faculties of the soul than actually exists. From its individuality and unity it follows that all its affections suppose a cognition of their appropriate objects, and that such cognition is an intellectual exercise and must be conformed to the laws of the intelligence; and consequently in those complex states of mind to which our author refers as illustrating the origin of the theology of feeling, the rational element is that very cognition by the intellect which belongs to the other form of theology. Besides, it is to be remembered that although in the apprehension of speculative truths, as in mathematics, for example, the cognition is purely an intellectual exercise, but when the object is an aesthetic or moral truth the apprehension is of necessity complex. There is no such thing as a purely intellectual cognition of a moral truth. It is the exercise of a moral nature; it implies moral sensibility. It of necessity involves feeling to a greater or less degree. It is the cognition of a being sensitive to moral distinctions, and without that sensibility there can be no such cognition. To separate these two elements therefore is impossible, and to place them in collision is a contradiction. A man can no more think an object to be cold which he feels to be warm, or to be beautiful which he sees to be deformed, than he can apprehend it as false and feel it to be true. It contradicts the laws of our nature as well as all experience to say that the feelings apprehend Christ as suffering the penalty of the law in our stead, while the intellect pronounces such apprehension to be false. You might as well say that we feel a thing to be good while we see it to be sinful, or feel it to be pleasant while we know it to be the reverse.

Professor Park's whole theory is founded upon the assumption that such contradictions actually exist. It supposes not different modes of activity, but different percipient agencies in the soul. It assumes not that the soul can perceive one way at one time and another way at another time, which all admit, but that the feelings perceive in one way and the intellect in another; the one seeing a thing as true while the other sees it to be false. It is important to note the distinction between the different judgments which we form of the same object, in different states of mind, and the theory of this discourse. The distinction is two-fold. The diverse successive judgments of which we are conscious are different intellectual cognitions, and not different modes of apprehending the same object by different faculties—the feelings and the intellect. For example, if a man judges at one time Christianity to be true, and at another that it is false, it would be absurd to say that it is true to his feelings and false to his intellect. The fact is, at one time he sees the evidence of the truth of the gospel and assents to it. At others, his mind is so occupied by objections that he cannot believe. This is a very common occurrence. A man in health and fond of philosophic speculations may get his mind in a state of complete scepticism. When death approaches, or when he is convinced of sin, he is a firm believer. Or at one time the doctrines of man's dependence, of God's sovereignty, and the like, are seen and felt to be true; at another, they are seen and felt to be false; that is, the mind rejects them with conviction and emotion. In all such cases of different judgments we have different intellectual apprehensions as well as different feelings. It is not that a proposition is true to the intellect and false to the feelings, or the reverse; but at one time it is true to the intellect and at another false to the same faculty. This, which is a familiar fact of consciousness, is, we apprehend, very different from Professor Park's doctrine. The second distinction is this. According to our author these conflicting apprehensions are equally true. It is true to the feelings that Christ satisfied divine justice; that we have a sinful nature; that we are unable of ourselves to repent and believe the gospel, but all these propositions are false to the intellect. He therefore can reconcile it with his views that good men, and even the inspired writers, should sometimes affirm and sometimes deny these and similar propositions. We maintain that such propositions are irreconcilable. The one judgment is true and the other false. Both can never be uttered under the guidance of the Spirit. He cannot lead the sinner to feel his helplessness, and inspire Paul to deny it; much less can he inspire men sometimes to assert, and sometimes to deny the same thing. When the mind passes, as we all know it repeatedly does, from the disbelief to the belief of those and other doctrines, it is a real change in its cognitions as well as in its feelings—a change which implies fallibility and error, and which therefore can have no place in the Bible, and can furnish no rule of interpreting its language, or the language of Christian experience. To make the distinction between Professor Park's theory and the common doctrine on this subject the more apparent, we call attention to their different results. He teaches that the theology of feelings which apprehends and expresses truth in forms which the intellect cannot sanction is appropriate to the Hymn Book and the Liturgy. He assumes that forms of devotion which are designed to express religious feeling may properly contain much that the intelligence rejects as false. He condemns those critics who "are ready to exclude from our psalms and hymns all such stanzas as are not accurate expressions of dogmatic truth." In opposition to this view, we maintain that the feelings demand truth, *i.e.*, truth which satisfies the intellect in the appropriation and expression of their object. The form in which that truth is expressed may be figurative but it must have the sanction of the understanding. The least suspicion of falsehood destroys the feeling. The soul cannot feel towards Christ as God if it regards him as merely a man. It cannot feel towards him as a sacrifice if it believes he died simply as a martyr. In short, it cannot believe what it knows to be a lie, or apprehend an object as false and yet feel towards it as true. Let it be assumed that a man is convinced that ability is necessary to responsibility; that sin cannot be imputed to the innocent; that Christ did not satisfy divine justice, then no genuine religious feeling can find expression in such forms of speech. Professor Park says on this principle he must believe that God actually came from Teman, and the Holy One from Mount Paran; that he really rode upon a chariot, &c.[11] This indicates a most extraordinary confusion of mind. Is there no difference between the figurative expression of what is true and the assertion of what is false? The phrase that "God came from Teman," or, "He made the clouds his chariot," when interpreted according to the established laws of language, expresses a truth. The phrases "Christ took upon him our guilt," "he satisfied divine justice," &c., &c., when interpreted by the same laws express, as our author thinks, what is false. Is there then no difference between these cases? Professor Park evidently confounds two things which are as distinct as day and night; viz.: a metaphor and a falsehood—a figurative expression and a doctrinal untruth. Because the one is allowable, he pleads for the other also. Because I may express the truth that Christ was a sacrifice by calling him the Lamb of God who bears the sin of the world—I may, in solemn acts of worship, so address him without believing in his sacrificial death at all! All religious language false to the intellect is profane to the feelings and a mockery of God. That such is the dictate of Christian consciousness is plain from the fact that the Hymn Book or Liturgy of no church contains doctrines contrary to the creed of such church. We challenge Professor Park to produce from the hymns used by Presbyterians a single phrase inconsistent with the Westminster Confession. If one such could be found, its inaccuracy as an expression "of dogmatic truth" would be universally regarded as a sufficient reason for its repudiation. Men may no more sing falsehood to God than speak it in the pulpit, or profess it in a creed. In the early part of his discourse our author says, the intellect does not originate the phrase "God, the mighty maker, died." This he attributes to the feelings as a passionate expression, designed to be impressive rather than intelligible. This, therefore, we presume he would adduce as an example of doctrinal inaccuracy in the language of devotion. A moment's reflection, however, is sufficient to show that instead of this phrase being forced on the intellect by the feelings, it has to be

11. Hodge is referring to Habakkuk 3:3—"God came from Teman, and the Holy One from Mount Paran. Selah."

defended by the intellect at the bar of the feelings. The latter at first recoil from it. It is not until its strict doctrinal propriety is apprehended by the intelligence that the feelings acquiesce in its use and open themselves to the impression of the awful truth which it contains. An attempt was actually made, on the score of taste, to exclude that phrase from our hymn book. But its restoration was demanded by the public sentiment of the church on the score of doctrinal fidelity. It was seen to be of importance to assert the truth that he, the person who died upon the cross, was "God, the mighty Maker, the Lord of glory, the Prince of Life," for on this truth depends the whole value of his death. In all cases, therefore, we maintain that the religious feelings demand truth and repudiate falsehood. They cannot express themselves under forms which the intelligence rejects, for those feelings themselves are the intelligence in a certain state, and not some distinct percipient agent.

Here, as before remarked, is the radical error of our author's theory. It supposes in fact two conflicting intelligences in man; the one seeing a thing to be true and the other seeing it to be false, and yet both seeing correctly from its own position and for its own object. We have endeavored to show that there is no such dualism in the soul, and therefore no foundation for two such systems of conflicting theologies as this theory supposes. The familiar fact that men sometimes regard a doctrine as true and sometimes look upon it as false; that they have conflicting judgments, and give utterances to inconsistent declarations, we maintain is no proof of a theology of the feelings as distinct from that of the intellect. These vacillating judgments are really contradictory apprehensions of the intellect, one of which must be false, and therefore to attribute them to the sacred writers, under the plea that they sometimes spoke to be impressive, and sometimes to be intelligible, is to destroy their authority; and to use in worship expressions which the intellect pronounces doctrinally untrue is repudiated by the whole Christian church as profane. If we wish to get the real faith of a people, that faith on which they live, in which intellect and heart alike acquiesce, go to their hymns and forms of devotion. There they are sincere. There they speak what they know to be true; and there consequently their true creed is to be found.

Having endeavored to show that Professor Park finds no foundation for his theory in the constitution of our nature or in those familiar changes of views and feelings, in varying states of mind, of which all are conscious, we wish to say further that this theory finds no support in the different modes in which the mind looks on truth for different purposes. Sometimes a given proposition, or the truth which it contains, is contemplated merely in its relation to the reason. Its import, its verity, its consistency with the standard of judgment, is all that the mind regards. Sometimes it contemplates the logical relations of that with other truths; and sometimes it is the moral excellence of truth which is the object of attention. When the mind addresses itself to the contemplation of truth, its posture and its subjective state will vary according to the object it has in view. But neither the truth itself nor the apprehension of it as truth suffers any change. It is not seen now as true, and now as false; or true to the feelings and false to the reason, but one and the same truth is viewed for different purposes. When, for example, we open the Bible and turn to any particular passage, we may examine it to ascertain its meaning; or having determined its import, we may contemplate the truth it contains in its moral aspects and in its relation to ourselves. These are different mental operations, and the state of mind which they suppose or induce must of course be different. Every Christian is familiar with fact. He knows what it is to contemplate the divine perfections for the purpose of understanding them, and to meditate on them to appreciate their excellence and feel their power. He sometimes is called on to form a clear idea of what the Bible teaches of the constitution of Christ's person or the nature of his work; but much more frequently his mind turns towards the Son of God clothed in our nature, to behold his glory, to rejoice in his divine excellence, and amazing condescension and love. In all such cases, the intellectual apprehension is the same. It is the very truth and the very same form of that truth which is arrived at, by a careful exegesis, which is the subject of devout mediation. A Christian does not understand the Bible in one way when he reads it as a critic, and in another way when he reads for spiritual edification. His thoughts of God and Christ when endeavoring to discover the truth revealed concerning them are the same as when he is engaged in acts of worship. Nay more, the clearer and more extended this speculative knowledge, the brighter and more undisturbed is the spiritual vision, *other things being equal.* One man may indeed be a better theologian but a less devout Christian than another; but the devout Christian is only the more devout with every increase in the clearness and consistency of his intellectual apprehensions. It may be further admitted that the language of speculation is different from the language of emotion; that the terms employed in defining a theological truth are not always those which would be naturally employed in setting forth that truth as the object of the affections. But these representations are always consistent. All hymns to Christ express precisely the same doctrine concerning his person that is found in the Athanasian creed. The same remarks may be made in reference to all departments of theology. The doctrines concerning the condition of men by nature; of their relation to Adam; of their redemption through Christ; of the work of God's Spirit; may be examined either to be understood or to be felt. But in every case it is the truth as understood that is felt. The understanding does not take one view and the feelings a different; the former does not pronounce for plenary power, and the latter for helplessness; the one does not assert that all sin consists in acts, and the other affirm the sinfulness of the heart; the one does not look on Christ as merely teaching by his death that sin is an evil, and the other behold him as bearing our sins in his own body on the tree.

This subject admits of abundant illustration, did our limits allow of a protracted discussion. A man may look over a tract of country and his inward state will vary with his object. He may contemplate it in reference to its agricultural advantages, or in regard to its topography, or its geological formation, or he may view it as a landscape. Another may gaze on a picture, or on any other work of art, as a critic, to ascertain the sources of the effect produced, or simply to enjoy it as an object of beauty. He may listen to a strain of music to note the varying intervals, the succession of chords and the like, or merely to receive the pleasurable impression of the sounds. In all these cases the object contemplated is the same—the intellectual apprehension is the same, and though the terms which he employs as an agriculturalist or a geologist or a critic may differ from those which he uses to give expression to his emotions, there can be no contrariety. He cannot apprehend the same region to be barren and yet fertile, the same picture to be beautiful and yet discordant. His intellect cannot make one report, and his feeling an opposite one. It is thus with regard to divine truth. It may be viewed in order to be understood, or in order to be felt. We may come to the contemplation of it as theologians or as Christians, and our inward state will vary with our object but there will be no contrariety in our apprehensions or in their expression.

The points of difference between the views expressed in the foregoing paragraph and the theory of this discourse are two. First, Professor Park makes the perceptions themselves to vary, so that what appears true to the feelings is apprehended as false by the intellect. Secondly, he says that the expression of these different perceptions is, or may be, contradictory. Hence there may be, and actually are, two theologies, the one affirming, the other denying; the one teaching sound old school orthodoxy, the other, any form of new school divinity that suits the reigning fashion in philosophy. We maintain on the contrary that there is perfect consistency between the intellectual apprehension of truth when viewed in order to be understood and when contemplated in order to be felt; and that however different the language employed on these different occasions, there can be no contradiction. There cannot therefore be two conflicting theologies; but on the contrary, the theology of the feeling is the theology of the intellect in all its accuracy of thought and expression.

There is still another view of this subject, so extensive and important that we hesitate even to allude to it in the conclusion of this article. What is the true relation between feeling and knowledge in matters of religion? The discussion of this question might properly be made to cover the whole ground embraced in this discourse. This is really the point which Professor Park's subject called upon him to elucidate, but which he has only incidentally referred to. We have already endeavored to show that this relation is not such as his theory assumes. It does not admit of contradiction between the two. There cannot be two conflicting theologies, one of the feeling and another of the intellect. But if these principles cannot be in conflict, what is the relation between them? Are they independent, as rationalism supposes, which allows feeling no place in determining our faith? Or is the intellect determined by the feelings, so that the province of the former is only to act as the interpreter of the latter? Or are the feelings determined by the intellect, so that the intellectual apprehension decides the nature of the affection? These are questions upon which we cannot now enter. It appears very evident to us that neither the first nor the second of the views here intimated has any support either from Scripture or experience. The intellect and feelings are not independent, nor is the former the mere interpreter of the latter. This is becoming a very current opinion and has been adopted in all its length from Schleiermacher by Morell. Knowledge or truth objectively revealed, is, according to this theory of a very subordinate importance. We have certain religious feelings: to develop the contents of those feelings is the province of the intelligence, so that theology is but the intellectual forms in which the religious consciousness expresses itself. The standard of truth is, therefore, nothing objective but this inward feeling. Any doctrine which can be shown to be the legitimate expression of an innate religious feeling is true—and any which is assumed to have a different origin, or to be foreign to the religious consciousness, is to be rejected.

What the Scriptures teach on this subject is, as it seems to us, in few words, simply this. In the first place, agreeably to what has already been said, the Bible never recognizes that broad distinction between the intellect and the feelings which is so often made by metaphysicians. It regards the soul as a perceiving and feeling individual subsistence whose cognitions and affections are not exercises of distinct faculties, but complex states of one and the same subject. It never predicates depravity or holiness of the feelings as distinct from the intelligence, or of the latter as distinct from the former. The moral state of the soul is always represented as affecting its cognitions as well as its affections. In popular language, the understanding is darkened as well as the heart depraved. In the second place, the Scriptures as clearly teach that holiness is necessary to the perception of holiness. In other words, that the things of the Spirit must be spiritually discerned; that the unrenewed have not this discernment, and therefore, they cannot know the things which are freely given to us of God, i.e., the things which he has graciously revealed in this word. They may have that apprehension of them which an uncultivated ear has of complicated musical sounds, or an untutored eye of a work of art. Much in the object is perceived, but much is not discerned, and that which remains unseen is precisely that which gives to these objects their peculiar excellence and power. Thirdly, the Bible further teaches that no mere change of the feelings is adequate to secure this spiritual discernment; but on the contrary, in the order of nature and of experience, the discernment precedes the change of the affections, just as the perception of beauty precedes the answering aesthetic emotion. The eyes must be opened in order to see wondrous things out of the law of God. The glory of God, as it shines in the face of Jesus Christ, must be revealed, before the corresponding affections of admiration, love, and confidence rise in the heart. This illumination is represented as the peculiar work of the Spirit. The knowledge consequent on this illumination is declared to be eternal life. It is the highest form of the activity of the soul. It is the vision of God and of the things of God, now seen indeed as through a glass darkly. This knowledge is the intuition not merely of the truth, but also of the excellence of spiritual objects. It is common to all the people of God, given to each in his measure, but producing in all a conviction and love of the same great truths.

If this be a correct exhibition of Scriptural teaching on this subject, it follows first that the feelings are not independent of the intellect, or the intellect of the feelings, so that the one may be unholy and the other indifferent; or so that the one is uninfluenced by the other. It must also follow that the feelings do not determine the intelligence, as though the latter in matters of religion was the mere exponent of the former. The truth is not given in the feelings and discovered and unfolded by the intellect. The truth is objectively presented in the word; and is by the Spirit revealed in its excellence to the intelligence, and thus the feelings are produced as necessary attributes, or adjuncts of spiritual cognition. This is not "the light system." We do not hold that the heart is changed by the mere objective presentation of the truth. The intellect and heart are not two distinct faculties to be separately affected or separately renewed. There is a divine operation of which the whole soul is the subject. The consequence of the change thus effected is the intuition of the truth and glory of the things of God. If this representation be correct, there must be the most perfect harmony between the feelings and the intellect; they cannot see with different eyes, or utter discordant language. What is true to the one, must be true to the other; what is good in the estimation of the one, must be good also to the other. Language which satisfies the reason in the expression of truth must convey the precise idea which is embraced in the glowing cognition which constitutes religious feeling; and all the utterances of emotion must justify themselves at the bar of the intellect as expressing truth before they can be sanctioned as vehicles of the religious affections. The relation then between feeling and knowledge, as assumed in Scripture and proved by experience, is utterly inconsistent with the theory of this discourse which represents them in perpetual conflict; the one affirming our nature to be sinful, the other denying it; the one teaching the doctrine of inability, the other that of plenary power; the one craving a real vicarious punishment of sin, the other teaching that a symbolical atonement is all that is needed; the one pouring forth its fervent misconceptions in acts of devotion, and the other whispering all that must be taken *cum grano salis*.

We have now endeavored to show that there is no foundation for Professor Park's theory in the use of figurative language as the expression of emotion; nor in those conflicting judgements which the mind forms of truth in its different conditions; nor in the different states of mind consequent on contemplation of truth for different objects; nor in what the Scriptures and experience teach concerning the relation between the feelings and intellect. We have further endeavored to show that this theory is destructive of the authority of the Bible because it attributes to the sacred writers conflicting and irreconcilable representations. Even should we admit that the feelings and the intellect have different apprehensions and adopt different modes of expression, yet as the feelings of the sacred writers were excited, as well as their cognitions determined by the Holy Spirit, the two must be in perfect harmony. In unrenewed, or imperfectly sanctified, uninspired men, there might be on the hypothesis assumed, this conflict between feeling and knowledge, but to attribute such contradictions to the Scriptures is to deny their inspiration. Besides this, the practical operation of a theory which supposes that so large a part of the Bible is to be set aside as inexact because the language of passion must be to subject its teachings to the opinion and prejudices of the reader. No adequate criteria are given for discriminating between the language of feeling and that of the intellect. Every one is left to his own discretion in making the distinction, and the use of this discretion, regulated by no fixed rules of language, is of course determined by caprice or taste.

But even if our objections to the theory of this discourse be deemed unsound, the arbitrary application which the author makes of his principles would be enough to condemn them. We have seen that he attributes to the feeling the most abstract propositions of scientific theology, that he does not discriminate between mere figurative language and the language of emotion; that he adopts or rejects the representations of the Bible at pleasure, or as they happen to coincide with, or contradict his preconceived opinions. That a sentence of condemnation passed on all men for the sin of one man; that men are by nature the children of wrath; that without Christ we can do nothing; that he hath redeemed us from the curse of the law by being made a curse for us; that men are not merely pardoned but justified; are represented as bold metaphors, impressive, but not intelligible, true to the feelings, but false to the reason.

It will be a matter of deep regret to many to find Professor Park, with his captivating talents and commanding influence, arrayed against the doctrines repudiated in this discourse; and many more will lament that he should have prepared a weapon which may be used against one doctrine as easily as another. Our consolation is that however keen may be the edge or bright the polish of that weapon, it has so little substance, it must be shivered into atoms with the first blow it strikes against those sturdy trees which have stood for ages in the garden of the Lord and whose leaves have been for the healing of the nations.

Archibald Alexander Hodge
1823–1886

18

Outlines of Theology
1878

The brief excerpts which follow from the second edition of A. A. Hodge's popular *Outlines of Theology* show how much he was his father's son. Charles Hodge, though dead, yet spoke clearly so long as A. A. Hodge held the chair of theology at Princeton. The *Outlines* show the same fidelity to the Bible, the same commitment to Calvinism, the same beliefs about theology as a science, the same convictions about "facts," and the same belief in the harmony of science and Scripture. As his other works, like *Popular Lectures on Theological Themes,* attested, A. A. Hodge was more the popularizer and less the discursive theologian than his father. Yet he was a careful thinker who clarified and advanced Charles Hodge's ideas. In the selection below we see a distillation of his father's views on theological method, a refinement of his views on inspiration, and a confident restatement of his convictions on the unity of scientific and biblical knowledge.

The preparation of a second, expanded edition of *Outlines of Theology* coincided with A. A. Hodge's arrival at Princeton Seminary to take up duties in 1877 as the associate professor of didactic and polemic theology. The first edition had appeared in 1860 while Hodge was still a minister in Fredericksburg, Virginia.[1] The first edition took its structure from a list of questions which Charles Hodge had expounded to his theology class in 1845 and 1846. A. A. Hodge had modified and augmented these to a limited extent, yet he acknowledged that "I have attempted little more . . . than to abridge my father's lectures."[2] In their use of the question and answer format both father and son followed the example of Turretin, whose *Institutes* had employed that device with great effect. By the time the second edition appeared, A. A. Hodge had been active for fourteen years as a seminary professor. He was thus able to incorporate more of his own thinking into the volume, which appeared with 50 percent more material than the first edition. Still, it is not too much to say that even this second edition presents a clearer picture of what Charles Hodge's students heard from him in the 1840s than can be provided even by his *Systematic Theology.*

This selection is from A. A. Hodge, *Outlines of Theology,* rev. ed. (New York: Robert Carter and Brothers, 1878), pp. 15-16, 75-77, 245-48.

1. On Hodge's preaching career, see C. A. Salmond, *Princetoniana. Charles and A. A. Hodge: With Class and Table Talk of Hodge the Younger* (Edinburgh: Oliphant, Anderson & Ferrier, 1888), pp. 73-77.
2. A. A. Hodge, "Preface to First Edition," *Outlines of Theology* (rev. ed., New York: Robert Carter and Brothers, 1878), p. 7.

Christian Theology; its Several Branches; and Their Relation to Other Departments of Human Knowledge.*

1. What is Religion? And what Theology in its Christian sense?

Religion, in its most general sense, is the sum of the relations which man sustains to God, and comprises the truths, the experiences, actions, and institutions which correspond to or grow out of those relations.

Theology, in its most general sense, is the science of religion.

The Christian religion is that body of truths, experiences, actions, and institutions which are determined by the revelation supernaturally presented in the Christian Scriptures. Christian Theology is the scientific determination, interpretation, and defence of those Scriptures, together with the history of the manner in which the truths it reveals have been understood, and the duties they impose have been performed by all Christians in all ages.

2. What is Theological Encyclopaedia? And what Theological Methodology?

Theological Encyclopaedia, from the Greek ἐγκυκλοπαιδεία (the whole circle of general education), presents to the student the entire circle of the special sciences devoted to the discovery, elucidation, and defence of the contents of the supernatural revelation contained in the Christian Scriptures, and aims to present these sciences in those organic relations which are determined by their actual genesis and inmost nature.

Theological Methodology is the science of theological method. As each department of human inquiry demands a mode of treatment peculiar to itself; and as even each subdivision of each general department demands its own special modifications of treatment, so theological methodology provides for the scientific determination of the true method, general and special, of pursuing the theological sciences. And this includes two distinct categories: (a) The methods proper to the original investigation and construction of the several sciences, and (b) the methods proper to elementary instruction in the same.

All this should be accompanied with critical and historical information, and direction as to the use of the vast literature with which these sciences are illustrated.

3. How far is the scientific arrangement of all the theological sciences possible? And on what account is the attempt desirable?

Such an arrangement can approach perfection only in proportion as these sciences themselves approach their final and absolute form. At present every such attempt must be only more or less an approximation to an ideal unattainable in the present state of knowledge in this life. Every separate attempt also must depend for its comparative success upon the comparative justness of the general theological

*Chapter 1, Outlines of Theology.

principles upon which it is based. It is evident that those who make Reason, and those who make the inspired Church, and those who make the inspired Scriptures the source and standard of all divine knowledge, must severally configure the theological sciences to the different foundations on which they are made to stand.

The point of view adopted in this book is the evangelical and specifically the Calvinistic or Augustinian one, assuming the following fundamental principles: 1st. The inspired Scriptures are the sole, and an infallible standard of all religious knowledge. 2d. Christ and his work is the centre around which all Christian theology is brought into order. 3d. The salvation brought to light in the gospel is supernatural and of FREE GRACE. 4th. All religious knowledge has a *practical end.* The theological sciences, instead of being absolute ends in themselves, find their noblest purpose and effect in the advancement of personal holiness, the more efficient service of our fellow men, and THE GREATER GLORY OF GOD.

The advantages of such a grouping of the theological sciences are obvious and great. The relations of all truths are determined by their nature, whence it follows that their nature is revealed by an exhibition of their relations. Such an exhibition will also tend to widen the mental horizon of the student, to incite him to breadth of culture, and prevent him from unduly exalting or exclusively cultivating any one special branch, and thus from perverting it by regarding it out of its natural limitations and dependencies.

The Inspiration of the Bible*

20. What objection to the doctrine of Plenary Inspiration is drawn from the alleged fact that "discrepancies" exist in the Scriptural Text? And how is this objection to be answered?

It is objected that the sacred text contains numerous statements which are inconsistent with other statements made in some part of Scripture itself, or with some certainly ascertained facts of history or of science.

It is obvious that such a state of facts, even if it could be proved to exist, would not, in opposition to the abundant positive evidence above adduced,[3] avail to disprove the claim that the Scriptures are to some extent and in some degree the product of divine inspiration. The force of the objection would depend essentially upon the number and character of the instances of discrepancy actually proved to exist, and would bear not upon the fact of inspiration, but upon its nature and degree and extent.

The fact of the actual existence of any such "discrepancies," it is evident, can be determined only by the careful examination of each alleged case separately. This examination belongs to the departments of Biblical Criticism and Exegesis. The

*Chapter 4, *Outlines of Theology.*
3. Hodge cited this evidence in a section entitled, "The Proof of the Church Doctrine of Inspiration," ibid., pp. 69–75. Many of these arguments reappeared in Hodge and Warfield's work on Scripture in 1881 (Selection 19).

following considerations, however, are evidently well-grounded, and sufficient to allay all apprehension on the subject.

1st. The Church has never held the verbal infallibility of our translations, nor the perfect accuracy of the copies of the original Hebrew and Greek Scriptures now possessed by us. These copies confessedly contain many "discrepancies" resulting from frequent transcription. It is, nevertheless, the unanimous testimony of Christian scholars, that while these variations embarrass the interpretation of many details, they neither involve the loss nor abate the evidence of a single essential fact or doctrine of Christianity. And it is moreover reassuring to know that believing criticism, by the discovery and collation of more ancient and accurate copies, is constantly advancing the Church to the possession of a more perfect text of the original Scriptures than she has enjoyed since the apostolic age.

2d. The Church has asserted absolute infallibility only of the original autograph copies of the Scriptures as they came from the hands of their inspired writers. And even of these she has not asserted infinite knowledge, but only absolute infallibility in stating the matters designed to be asserted. A "discrepancy," therefore, in the sense in which the new critics affirm and the Church denies its existence, is a form of statement existing in the original text of the Hebrew and Greek Scriptures evidently designed to assert as true that which is in plain irreconcilable contradiction to other statements existing in some other portions of the same original text of Scripture, or to some other certainly ascertained element of human knowledge. A "discrepancy" fulfilling in every particular this definition must be proved to exist, or the Church's doctrine of plenary verbal inspiration remains unaffected.

3d. It is beyond question that in the light of all that the Scriptures themselves assert or disclose as to the nature and the extent of the divine influence controlling their genesis, and as to their authority over man's conscience and life as the voice of God, the existence of any such "discrepancies" as above defined is a violent improbability. Those who assert the existence of one or more of them must bring them out, and prove to the community of competent judges that all the elements of the above definition meet in each alleged instance, not probably merely, but beyond the possibility of doubt. The *onus probandi* [burden of proof] rests exclusively on them.

4th. But observe that this is for them a very difficult task to perform, one in any instance indeed hardly possible. For to make good their point against the vast presumptions opposed to it, they must prove over and over again in the case of each alleged discrepancy each of the following points: (1) That the alleged discrepant statement certainly occurred in the veritable autograph copy of the inspired writing containing it. (2) That their interpretation of the statement, which occasions the discrepancy, is the only possible one, the one it was certainly to bear. The difficulty of this will be apprehended when we estimate the inherent obscurity of ancient narratives, unchronological, and fragmentary, with a background and surroundings of almost unrelieved darkness. This condition of things which so often puzzles the interpreter and prevents the apologist from proving the harmony of the narrative, with equal force baffles all the ingenious efforts of the rationalistic critic to demonstrate the "discrepancy." Yet this he must do, or the presumption will remain that it does not exist. (3) He must also prove that the facts of science or of history or the Scriptural statements with which the statement in question is asserted to be inconsistent, are real facts or real parts of the autograph text of canonical Scripture; and that the sense in which they are found to be inconsistent with the statement in question is the only sense they can rationally bear. (4) When the reality of the opposing facts or statements is determined and their true interpretation is ascertained, then it must in conclusion be shown not only that they appear inconsistent, nor merely that their reconciliation is impossible in our present state of knowledge, but that they are in themselves essentially incapable of being reconciled.

5th. Finally it is sufficient for the present purpose to point to the fact that no single case of "discrepancy" as above defined has been so proved to exist as to secure the recognition of the community of believing scholars. Difficulties in interpretation and apparently irreconcilable statements exist, but no "discrepancy" has been proved. Advancing knowledge removes some difficulties and discovers others. It is in the highest degree probable that perfect knowledge would remove all.

The Creation of the World*

20. What is the present attitude of Geological science in relation to the Mosaic Record of creation?

The results of modern geological science clearly establish the conclusions: (a) That the elementary materials of which the world is composed existed an indefinitely great number of ages ago. (b) That the world has been providentially brought to its present state by a gradual progression through many widely contrasted physical conditions and through long intervals of time. (c) That it has successively been inhabited by many different orders of organized beings, each in turn adapted to the physical conditions of the globe in its successive stages, and generally marked in each stage by an advancing scale of organization from the more elementary to the more complex and more perfect forms. (d) That man completes the pyramid of creation, the most perfect, and the last formed of all the inhabitants of the world. The only difficulty in adjusting these results with the Mosaic Record of creation is found in matters of detail, in which the true sense of the inspired record is obscure, and the conclusions of the science are immature. Therefore all such detailed adjustments as that attempted by Hugh Miller in his "Testimony of the Rocks" have failed. As to the relation of the findings of science with respect to the antiquity of man to Biblical Chronology see below, Chapter 16.[4] In general, however, there is a most remarkable agreement between the Mosaic Record and the results of Geology as to the following principal points. The Record agrees with the science in teaching: (a) The creation of the elements in the remote

*Chapter 12, *Outlines of Theology.*
4. Ibid., pp. 297–298, where Hodge leans toward an old age for the earth.

past. (b) The intermediate existence of chaos. (c) The advance of the earth through various changes to its present physical condition. (d) The successive creations of different genera and species of organized beings—the vegetable before the animal—the lower forms before the higher forms—in adaptation to the improving condition of the earth—and man last of all.

If we remember when and where and for what purpose this Record was produced, and compare it with all other ancient or medieval cosmogonies, this wonderful agreement with the last results of modern science will be felt to contribute essentially to the evidences of its divine origin. It is certainly, even when read subject to the most searching modern criticism, seen to be amply sufficient for the end intended as a general introduction to the history of Redemption which, although rooted in creation, is henceforward carried on as a system of supernatural revelation and influences.

21. State the several principles which should always be borne in mind in considering questions involving an apparent conflict of science and revelation.

1st. God's works and God's word are equally revelations from him. They are consequently both alike true and both alike sacred and to be treated with reverence. It is absolutely impossible that when they are both adequately interpreted they can come into conflict. Jealousy on either part is treason to the Author and Lord of both.

2d. Science, or the interpretation of God's works, is therefore a legitimate and obligatory department of human study. It has rights which must be respected and its duties which it must observe. It is the right of every science to pursue the investigation of its own branch according to its own legitimate methods. We can not require of the chemist that he should pursue the methods of the philologist, nor of the geologist that he should go to history, either profane or sacred, for his facts.[5] It is the duty of the students of every science to keep within its province, to recognize the fact that it is only one department of the vast empire of truth, and to respect alike all orders of truth, historical and inspired as well as scientific; mental and spiritual as well as material.

3d. It follows as a practical consequence from the narrowness of the human faculties that men confined to particular branches of inquiry acquire special habits of thought and associations of ideas peculiar to their line, by which they are apt to measure and judge the whole world of truth. Thus the man of science misinterprets and then becomes jealous of the theologian, and the theologian misinterprets and becomes jealous of the man of science. This is narrowness, not superior knowledge; weakness, not strength.

4th. Science is only the human interpretation of God's works; it is always

---

5. This line of reasoning concerning the proper boundaries of the various sciences reappeared frequently in Warfield's work, as, for example, in his review of Andrew White's *History of the Warfare of Science with Theology in Christendom,* in *Presbyterian and Reformed Review* 36 (July 1898): 510–12.

imperfect and makes many mistakes. Biblical interpreters are also liable to mistakes and should never assert the absolute identity of their interpretations of the Bible with the mind of God.

5th. All sciences in their crude condition have been thought to be in conflict with Scripture. But as they have approached perfection, they have been all found to be perfectly consistent with it. Sometimes it is the science which is amended into harmony with the views of the theologian. Sometimes it is the views of the theologians which are amended into harmony with perfected and demonstrated science, e.g., the instance of the universal and now grateful acceptance by the church of the once abhorred Copernican system.

6th. In the case of many sciences, as eminently of Geology, the time has not yet come to attempt an adjustment between their conclusions and revelation. Like contemporaneous history in its relation to prophecy, Geology in its relation to the Mosaic Record of creation is *in transitu.* Its conclusions are not yet mature. When geologists are agreed among themselves, when all the accessible facts of the science are observed, analyzed, and classified, and when Generalization has done its perfect work, and when all of its results are finished and finally fixed as part of the intellectual heritage of man forever, then the adjustment between science and revelation will stand self-revealed, and science will be seen to support and illustrate, instead of oppose, the written word of God.

7th. There are hence two opposite tendencies which equally damage the cause of religion and manifest the weakness of the faith of its professed friends. *The first* is the weak acceptance of every hostile conclusion of scientific speculators as certainly true; the constant confession of the inferiority of the light of revelation to the light of nature, and of the certainty of the conclusions of Biblical exegesis and Christian theology to that of the results of modern science; the constant attempt to accommodate the interpretation of the Bible, like a nose of wax, to every new phase assumed by the current interpretations of nature. *The second and opposite* is that of jealously suspecting all the findings of science as probable offences against the dignity of revelation, and of impatiently attacking even those passing phases of imperfect science which for the time appear to be inconsistent with our own opinions. Standing upon the rock of divine truth. PERFECT FAITH, as well as perfect love, CASTETH OUT ALL FEAR. All things are ours, whether the natural or the supernatural, whether science or revelation.

19

Inspiration (with Warfield)

1881

As Jerry Wayne Brown has shown, the first American efforts to engage in critical study of the Bible, which occurred before the Civil War, did not "take."[1] Most American theologians, in the older denominations as well as in the newest sects, continued to accept the Scriptures with full, if undifferentiated, confidence in their saving power and revealed truth. After the Civil War, however, critical assumptions that were by then commonplace in Europe began to exert a larger influence in America.[2] The Bible, it was argued, was more like other ancient books than the orthodox had believed. It deserved no extraordinary treatment, except as an unusual record of ancient religious experiences. Such views created particular distress at Princeton Seminary, where theology depended entirely on a sure, accurate, and reliable Scripture.

It is not surprising, then, that Princeton theologians were among the leaders in rebutting the claims of the new higher criticism. Charles Hodge had done so in 1857 (Selection 10) and in his *Systematic Theology* (I: 151-190). Yet even in the systematics from the 1870s the elder Hodge concentrated his defense against the foes of his youth, principally Schleiermacher and the Catholics. It remained for his son, and for Warfield, to take the full measure of new criticism and to restate in the modern world the traditional Princeton doctrine of Scripture. Their joint effort in 1881, reproduced in part below, was the fullest early effort in that direction. A. A. Hodge used that essay to recapitulate some of the arguments from the two editions of his *Outlines of Theology* (see Selection 18), but he and Warfield also went much further in the detail and precision with which they stated their case.

The article refines Charles Hodge's 1857 insistence on the verbal character of inspiration. It clarifies what he had said in defense of Biblical "accuracy," as opposed to what A. A. Hodge here calls the modern sense of "exactness." It also reaffirms the traditional Princeton belief in the harmony of science and Scripture. The 1881 essay does place greater weight, in its section called "Presuppositions," on the need to demonstrate Scripture's truthfulness than was Charles Hodge's custom. And it makes more of the fact that inspiration and the consequent errorlessness of the Bible apply, when strictly defined, only to the original

1. Brown, *The Rise of Biblical Criticism in America.*
2. For a perceptive overview of this development, see Wacker, "The Demise of Biblical Civilization," in *The Bible in America*, pp. 121-138.

autographs of the Bible, that is, to the texts as penned by the biblical writers themselves.

The essay sparked controversy in the 1880s, and it has also been a source of contention in very recent years. A. A. Hodge, the conservative Presbyterian, and Charles Briggs, representing those more inclined to modern views, had founded the *Presbyterian Review* in 1880 as a way to keep theological channels open among the various elements in the denomination. The journal's first number described itself as an "enterprise, which seeks to combine all the varied interests and sections of our Presbyterian Church in order to secure a Review that will truly represent it by a strong, hearty, steady, and thorough advocacy of Presbyterian principles."[3] Yet before the year was out, Briggs and Hodge were corresponding about the need to present opinions on Scripture with moderation and caution.[4] Nevertheless, when B. B. Warfield, then a young professor of New Testament at Western Seminary, proposed an essay to defend a traditional position, Hodge was quick to join him in the effort. The result was the paper, "Inspiration," which was followed rapidly by seven other weighty essays in the *Presbyterian Review* on the general subject of biblical inspiration and more specific questions of biblical criticism.[5] The eight articles that appeared from 1881 to 1883 were evenly divided between conservative and progressive viewpoints. But differences within Presbyterianism over Scripture were now out in the open. And the battle was joined which led, first, to Briggs's exit from the

3. A. A. Hodge and Charles Briggs, "The Idea and Aim of the Presbyterian Review," *Presbyterian Review,* 1 (January 1880): 3.

4. See Loetscher, *Broadening Church,* pp. 29-30; and Balmer, "The Old Princeton Doctrine of Inspiration," pp. 18-21, for the circumstances surrounding the publication of the essay.

5. On the essay and its effects, see Loetscher, *Broadening Church,* pp. 30-32; and Marsden, *Fundamentalism and American Culture,* pp. 113-15. For a full discussion of this essay, its doctrine of the Bible, and the place of the essay in the Princeton tradition, see the introduction, notes, and appendices provided by Roger R. Nicole for the recent republication of *Inspiration* (Grand Rapids: Baker, 1979). The eight essays of 1881-1883, as cited by Nicole, *Inspiration,* pp. xii-xiii, were as follows:

a) Hodge and Warfield, "Inspiration," *Presbyterian Review,* 2 (April 1881), 225-260.
b) Briggs, "Critical Theories of the Sacred Scriptures in Relation to their Inspiration," ibid., 2 (1881), 550-579.
c) William Henry Green, "Professor W. Robertson Smith on the Pentateuch," ibid., 3 (1882), 108-156.
d) Henry Preserved Smith, "The Critical Theories of Julius Wellhausen," ibid., 3 (1882), 357-388.
e) Samuel I. Curtiss, "Delitzsch on the Origin and Composition of the Pentateuch," ibid., 3 (1882), 553-588.
f) Willis J. Beecher, "The Logical Methods of Professor Kuenan," ibid., 3 (1882), 701-731.
g) Briggs, "A Critical Study of the History of Higher Criticism with Special Reference to the Pentateuch," ibid., 4 (1883), 69-130.
h) Francis L. Patton, "The Dogmatic Aspect of Pentateuchal Criticism," ibid., 4 (1883), 341-410.

Articles a, c, f, and h stood on the conservative side; articles b, d, e, and g were more open to modern criticism, though with considerable caution.

denomination in 1893, and then, after a passage of years, to the demise of the Princeton Theology itself within the main body of American Presbyterians.[6]

In more recent years, controversy has once again centered on the 1881 essay. Some have spoken of the article, especially its stress on the original autographs of Scripture, as a defensive innovation that cut Hodge and Warfield off from the mainstream of church teaching on Scripture.[7] Others have responded that the essay did no more than restate the doctrine on Scripture which was traditional at Princeton and many other places in a form appropriate for the new critical questions.[8] In this modern debate, those who (like myself) are at least generally satisfied with the 1881 essay usually exonerate Hodge and Warfield of any damaging innovation, while those who are not regard it as a serious misstep.

The selection below presents approximately the first half of the essay. A. A. Hodge was responsible for the introduction and for the sections labeled "Presuppositions," "The Genesis of Scripture," and "Statement of the Doctrine," while Warfield was the author of those labeled "Proof of the Doctrine" and "Legitimate Presumptions."[9] The remaining half of the essay carried Warfield's discussion entitled "Critical Objections Tried," which defended the Protestant canon, the accuracy of biblical statements, the internal harmony of Scripture, and the New Testament use of the Old. Warfield expanded on the arguments in this last half of the essay several times during his career. Selections 23, 24, and 25 provide examples of that work.

The essay appeared first in the *Presbyterian Review* 2 (April 1881): 225–60. It was reprinted that same year as a pamphlet by the Presbyterian Board of Publication in Philadelphia. The following is from the republication of that pamphlet in Archibald A. Hodge and Benjamin B. Warfield, *Inspiration*, intro. Roger R. Nicole (Grand Rapids: Baker, 1979), pp. 5–37.

THE WORD "INSPIRATION," as applied to the Holy Scriptures, has gradually acquired a specific technical meaning independent of its etymology. At first this word, in the sense of "God-Breathed," was used to express the entire agency of God in producing that divine element which distinguished Scripture from all other writings. It was used in a sense comprehensive of supernatural revelation, while the immense range of providential and gracious divine activities concerning the genesis of the word of God in human language was practically

6. See Loetscher, *Broadening Church*, especially pp. 48–62; and Ahlstrom, *Religious History*, pp. 813–814.

7. See Sandeen, *Roots of Fundamentalism*, pp. 125–131; and Rogers and McKim, *Authority and Interpretation of the Bible*, pp. 298–310.

8. See Balmer, "The Old Princeton Doctrine of Inspiration," and "Princetonians and Scripture: A Reconsideration"; Woodbridge, "Biblical Authority," pp. 205–208; and Gerstner, "Warfield's Case for Biblical Inerrancy."

9. On the division of responsibility, see Nicole, *Inspiration*, p. xii; and Loetscher, *Broadening Church*, pp. 31, 162n16.

overlooked. But Christian scholars have come to see that this divine element, which penetrates and glorifies Scripture at every point, has entered and become incorporated with it in very various ways, natural, supernatural and gracious, through long courses of providential leading, as well as by direct suggestion—through the spontaneous action of the souls of the sacred writers, as well as by controlling influences from without. It is important that distinguishable ideas should be connoted by distinct terms, and that the terms themselves should be fixed in a definite sense. Thus we have come to distinguish sharply between Revelation, which is the frequent, and Inspiration, which is the constant, attribute of all the thoughts and statements of Scripture, and between the problem of the genesis of Scripture on the one hand, which includes historic processes and the concurrence of natural and supernatural forces, and must account for all the phenomena of Scripture, and the mere fact of inspiration on the other hand, or the superintendence by God of the writers in the entire process of their writing, which accounts for nothing whatever but the absolute infallibility of the record in which the revelation, once generated, appears in the original autograph. It will be observed that we intentionally avoid applying to this inspiration the predicate "influence." It summoned, on occasion, a great variety of influences, but its essence was superintendence. This superintendence attended the entire process of the genesis of Scripture, and particularly the process of the final composition of the record. It interfered with no spontaneous natural agencies, which were, in themselves, producing results conformable to the mind of the Holy Spirit. On occasion it summoned all needed divine influences and suggestions, and it sealed the entire record and all its elements, however generated, with the imprimatur of God, sending it to us as his Word.

The importance of limiting the word "inspiration" to a definite and never-varying sense, and one which is shown, by the facts of the case, to be applicable equally to every part of Scripture, is self-evident, and is emphasized by the embarrassment which is continually recurring in the discussions of this subject, arising sometimes from the wide, and sometimes from the various, senses in which this term is used by different parties. The history of theology is full of parallel instances, in which terms of the highest import have come to be accepted in a more fixed and narrow sense than they bore at first either in scriptural or early ecclesiastical usage, and with only a remote relation to their etymology; as, for instance, Regeneration, Sacrament, etc.

Presuppositions

From this definition of the term it is evident that instead of being, in the order of thought, the first religious truth which we embrace, upon which, subsequently, the entire fabric of true religion rests, it is the last and crowning attribute of those sacred books from which we derive our religious knowledge. Very many religious and historical truths must be established before we come to the question of inspiration; as, for instance, the being and moral government of God, the fallen condition of man, the fact of a redemptive scheme, the general historical truth of the

Scriptures, and the validity and authority of the revelation of God's will, which they contain—i.e., the general truth of Christianity and its doctrines. Hence it follows that while the inspiration of the Scriptures is true, and, being true, is a principle fundamental to the adequate interpretation of Scripture, it nevertheless is not in the first instance a principle fundamental to the truth of the Christian religion. In dealing with skeptics it is not proper to begin with the evidence which immediately establishes inspiration, but we should first establish theism, then the historical credibility of the Scriptures, and then the divine origin of Christianity. Nor should we ever allow it to be believed that the truth of Christianity depends upon any doctrine of inspiration whatever. Revelation came in large part before the record of it, and the Christian Church before the New-Testament Scriptures. Inspiration can have no meaning if Christianity is not true, but Christianity would be true and divine—and, being so, would stand—even if God had not been pleased to give us, in addition to his revelation of saving truth, an infallible record of that revelation absolutely errorless by means of inspiration.[10]

In the second place, it is also evident that our conception of revelation and its methods must be conditioned upon our general views of God's relation to the world, and his methods of influencing the souls of men. The only really dangerous opposition to the Church doctrine of inspiration comes either directly or indirectly, but always ultimately, from some false view of God's relation to the world, of his methods of working, and of the possibility of a supernatural agency penetrating and altering the course of a natural process. But the whole genius of Christianity, all of its essential and most characteristic doctrines, presuppose the immanence of God in all his creatures, and his concurrence with them in all of their spontaneous activities. In him, as an active, intelligent Spirit, we all live and move and have our being. He governs all his creatures and all their actions, working in men even to will and spontaneously to do his good pleasure. The currents, thus, of the divine activities do not only flow around us, conditioning or controlling our action from without, but they nonetheless flow within the inner current of our personal lives, confluent with our spontaneous self-movements, and contributing to the effects whatever properties God may see fit that they shall have.

There is also a real logical and ideal, if not a physical continuity between all the various provinces and methods of God's working: providence and grace, the natural and the supernatural, all constitute one system in the execution of one plan. All these agents and all these methods are so perfectly adjusted in the plan of God that not one interferes with any other, and all are so adjusted and controlled that each works perfectly, according to the law of its own nature, and yet all together infallibly bring about the result God designs. In this case that design is a record without error of the facts and doctrines he had commissioned his servants to teach.

10. Warfield also echoed this sentiment later, as in 1893, "The Real Problem of Inspiration," wbbw, I: 209: "Let it not be said that . . . we found the whole Christian system upon the doctrine of plenary inspiration. We found the whole Christian system on the doctrine of plenary inspiration as little as we found it upon the doctrine of angelic existences."

Of the manner in which God may inform and direct a free intelligence without violating its laws we have a familiar analogy in Nature in the relation of instinct to free intelligence. Intelligence is personal, and involves self-consciousness and liberty. Instinct is impersonal, unconscious, and not free. Both exist alike in man, with whom intelligence predominates, and in the higher animals with whom instinct predominates. In every case the instinct of the creature is the intelligence of the Creator working through the creature's spontaneity, informing and directing, yet never violating any of the laws of his free intelligence. And in Nature we can trace this all the way from the instinct of the bee, which works mechanically, to the magic play of the aesthetic instincts, which largely constitute the genius of a great artist. We are not absurdly attempting to draw a parallel between natural instinct and supernatural inspiration. But the illustration is good simply to show that as a matter of fact God does prompt from within the spontaneous activities of his intelligent creatures, leading them by unerring means to ends imperfectly discerned by themselves; and that this activity of God, as in instinct or other wise, does not in any wise reveal itself, either in consciousness or in the character of the action to which it prompts, as interfering with the personal attributes or the free rational activities of the creature.

The Genesis of Scripture

We allude here to this wide and as yet imperfectly explored subject only for the purpose of distinctly setting apart the various problems it presents, and isolating the specific point of inspiration with which we, as well as the Church in general, are more particularly interested. All parties of believers admit that this genesis of Holy Scripture was the result of the co-operation, in various ways, of the agency of men and the agency of God.

The human agency, both in the histories out of which the Scriptures sprang, and in their immediate composition and inscription, is everywhere apparent, and gives substance and form to the entire collection of writings. It is not merely in the matter of verbal expression or literary composition that the personal idiosyncrasies of each author are freely manifested by the untrammeled play of all his faculties, but the very substance of what they write is evidently for the most part the product of their own mental and spiritual activities. This is true except in that comparatively small element of the whole body of sacred writing in which the human authors simply report the word of God objectively communicated, or, as in some of the prophecies, they wrote by divine dictation. As the general characteristic of all their work, each writer was put to that special part of the general work for which he alone was adapted by his original endowments, education, special information, and providential position. Each drew from the stores of his own original information, from the contributions of other men, and from all other natural sources. Each sought knowledge, like all other authors, from the use of his own natural faculties of thought and feeling, of intuition and of logical inference, of memory and imagination, and of religious experience. Each gave evidence of his own special limitations of knowledge and mental power, and of his personal defects as well as of his powers. Each wrote upon a definite occasion, under special historically grouped circumstances, from his own standpoint in the progressively unfolded plan of redemption, and each made his own special contribution to the fabric of God's word.

The divine agency, although originating in a different source, yet emerges into the effect very much through the same channels. The Scriptures have been generated, as the plan of redemption has been evolved, through an historic process. From the beginning God has dealt with man in the concrete, by self-manifestations and transactions. The revelation proceeds from facts to ideas, and has been gradually unfolded as the preparation for the execution of the work of redemption has advanced through its successive stages. The general providence unfolding this plan has always been divine, yet has also been largely natural in its method, while specially directed to its ends, and at the same time surcharged along portions of its line, especially at the beginning and at great crises, with the supernatural, as a cloud is surcharged with electricity. There were divine voices, appearances, covenants, supernatural communications and interventions—the introduction of new institutions, and their growth under special providential conditions. The prophet of God was sent with special revelations and authority at particular junctures to gather and interpret the lessons of the past, and to add to them lessons springing out of the providential conditions of the present. The Scriptures were generated through sixteen centuries of this divinely-regulated concurrence of God and man, of the natural and the supernatural, of reason and revelation, of providence and grace. They are an organism consisting of many parts, each adjusted to all the rest, as the "many members" to the "one body." Each sacred writer was by God specially formed, endowed, educated, providentially conditioned, and then supplied with knowledge naturally, supernaturally, or spiritually conveyed, so that he, and he alone, could, and freely would, produce his allotted part. Thus God predetermined all the matter and form of the several books largely by the formation and training of the several authors, as an organist determines the character of his music as much when he builds his organ and when he tunes his pipes as when he plays his keys. Each writer also is put providentially at the very point of view in the general progress of revelation to which his part assigns him. He inherits all the contributions of the past. He is brought into place and set to work at definite providential junctures, the occasion affording him object and motive, giving form to the writing God appoints him to execute.

The Bible, moreover, being a work of the Spirit for spiritual ends, each writer was prepared precisely for his part in the work by the personal dealings of the Holy Spirit with his soul. Spiritual illumination is very different from either revelation or inspiration, and yet it had, under the providence of God, a large share in the genesis of Scripture, contributing to it a portion of that divine element which makes it the word of God. The Psalms are divinely-inspired records of the religious experience of their writers, and are by God himself authoritatively set forth as typical and exemplary for all men for ever. Paul and John and Peter largely drew upon the resources and followed the lines of their own personal religious experience in the intuitional or the logical development of their doctrine; and their experience had, of course, been previously divinely determined for that very purpose. And in determining their religious experience God so far forth determined their contributions to Scripture. And he furnished each of the sacred writers, in addition to that which came to him through natural channels, all the knowledge needed for his appointed task, either by vision, suggestion, dictation, or elevation of faculty, or otherwise, according to his will. The natural knowledge came from all sources, as traditions, documents, testimonies, personal observations, and recollection—by means also of intuitions, logical processes of thought, feeling, experience, etc.; and yet all were alike under the general direction of God's providence. The supernatural knowledge became confluent with the natural in a manner which violated no law of reason or of freedom. And throughout the whole of his work the Holy Spirit was present, causing his energies to flow into the spontaneous exercises of the writer's faculties, elevating and directing where need be, and everywhere securing the errorless expression in language of the thought designed by God. This last element is what we call "Inspiration."

In all this process, except in a small element of prophecy, it is evident that as the sacred writers were free and active in their thinking and in the expression of their thoughts, so they were conscious of what they were doing, of what their words meant, and of the design of their utterance. Yet even then, it is no less evident that they all, like other free instruments of Providence, "builded better than they knew." The meanings of their words, the bearing of the principles they taught, of the facts they narrated, and the relation of their own part to the great organism of divine revelation, while luminous to their own consciousness, yet reached out into infinitely wider horizons than those penetrated by any thought of theirs.

Statement of the Doctrine

During the entire history of Christian theology the word "Inspiration" has been used to express either some or all of the activities of God co-operating with its human authors in the genesis of Holy Scripture. We prefer to use it in the single sense of God's continued work of superintendence, by which, his providential, gracious, and supernatural contributions having been presupposed, he presided over the sacred writers in their entire work of writing, with the design and effect of rendering that writing an errorless record of the matters he designed them to communicate, and hence constituting the entire volume in all its parts the word of God to us.

While we have restricted the word "Inspiration" to a narrower sphere than that in which it has been used by many in the past, nevertheless we are certain that the above statement of the divine origin and infallibility of Scripture accurately expresses the faith of the Christian Church from the first. Still, several points remain to be more particularly considered, concerning which some difference of opinion at present prevails.

First. Is it proper to call this inspiration "plenary"? This word, which has often been made the occasion of strife, is in itself indefinite, and its use contributes nothing either to the precision or the emphasis of the definition. The word means simply "full," "complete," perfectly adequate for the attainment of the end designed, whatever that might have been. There ought not to be on any side any hesitancy to affirm this of the books of the Bible.

Second. Can this inspiration be properly said to be "verbal"? The objection to the application of this predicate to inspiration is urged upon three distinct grounds:

(1) We believe that the great majority of those who object to the affirmation that inspiration is verbal are impelled thereto by a feeling, more or less definite, that the phrase implies that inspiration is, in its essence, a process of verbal dictation, or that, at least in some way, the revelation of the thought or the inspiration of the writer was by means of the control which God exercised over his words. And there is the more excuse for this misapprehension because of the extremely mechanical conceptions of inspiration maintained by many former advocates of the use of this term "verbal." This view, however, we repudiate as earnestly as any of those who object to the language in question. At the present time the advocates of the strictest doctrine of inspiration in insisting that it is verbal do not mean that in any way the thoughts were inspired by means of the words, but simply that the divine superintendence, which we call inspiration, extended to the verbal expression of the thoughts of the sacred writers, as well as to the thoughts themselves, and that hence the Bible, considered as a record, an utterance in words of a divine revelation, is the word of God to us. Hence, in all the affirmations of Scripture of every kind there is no more error in the words of the original autographs than in the thoughts they were chosen to express. The thoughts and words are both alike human, and therefore subject to human limitations, but the divine superintendence and guarantee extend to the one as much as the other.

(2) There are others who, while insisting as strongly as any upon the presence of the divine element in Scripture, developed through special providences and gracious dealings, religious experiences and mental processes, in the very manner we have just set forth under the head of the "Genesis of Scripture," yet substantially deny what we have here called "inspiration." They retain the word "inspiration," but signify by it the divine element in the revelation, or providential or gracious dealing aforesaid, and they believe that the sacred writers, having been divinely helped to certain knowledge, were left to the natural limitations and fallibility incidental to their human and personal characters, alike in their thinking out their several narrations and expositions of divine truth, and in their reduction of them to writing. This view gives up the whole matter of the immediate divine authorship of the Bible as the word of God, and its infallibility and authority as a rule of faith and practice. We have only the several versions of God's revelations as rendered mentally and verbally, more or less adequately, yet always imperfectly, by the different sacred writers. This class of objectors are, of course, self-consistent in rejecting verbal inspiration in any sense. But this view is not consistent either with the claims of Scripture, the consciousness of Christians, or the historic doctrine of the Church.

(3) There are others who maintain that the Scriptures have been certainly inspired so far forth as to constitute them in all their parts, and as a whole, an infallible and divinely-authoritative rule of faith and practice, and yet hold that, while the thoughts of the sacred writers concerning doctrine and duty were inspired and errorless, their language was of purely human suggestion, and more or less accurate. The question as to whether the elements of Scripture relating to the course of Nature and to the events of history are without error will be considered below: it is sufficient to say under the present head that it is self-evident that, just as far as the thoughts of Scripture relating to any element or topic whatsoever are inspired, the words in which those thoughts are expressed must be inspired also. Every element of Scripture, whether doctrine or history, of which God has guaranteed the infallibility, must be infallible in its verbal expression. No matter how in other respects generated, the Scriptures are a product of human thought, and every process of human thought involves language. "The slightest consideration will show that words are as essential to intellectual processes as they are to mutual intercourse.... Thoughts are wedded to words as necessarily as soul to body. Without it the mysteries unveiled before the eyes of the seer would be confused shadows; with it, they are made clear lessons for human life."[11]

Besides this, the Scriptures are a *record* of divine revelations, and as such consist of words; and as far as the record is inspired at all, and as far as it is in any element infallible, its inspiration must reach to its words. Infallible thought must be definite thought, and definite thought implies words. But if God could have rendered the thoughts of the apostles regarding doctrine and duty infallibly correct without words, and then left them to convey it to us in their own language, we should be left to precisely that amount of certainty for the foundation of our faith as is guaranteed by the natural competency of the human authors, and neither more nor less. There would be no divine guarantee whatever. The human medium would everywhere interpose its fallibility between God and us. Besides, most believers admit that some of the prophetical parts of Scripture were verbally dictated. It was, moreover, promised that the apostles should speak as the Spirit gave them utterance. "The word of God came unto the prophet." The Church has always held, as expressed by the Helvetic Confession, II [1566], "that the canonical Scriptures *are the word of God."* Paul claims that the Holy Spirit superintended and guaranteed his words as well as his thoughts (1 Cor. 2:13). The things of the Spirit we teach "not in the words which man's wisdom teacheth, but which the Holy Ghost teacheth" (συγκρίνοντες), combining spiritual things with spiritual—i.e., spiritual thoughts with spiritual words.

It is evident, therefore, that it is not clearness of thought which inclines any of the advocates of a real inspiration of the Holy Scriptures to deny that it extends to the words. Whatever discrepancies or other human limitations may attach to the

11. Hodge's note: "Canon Westcott's *Introduction to the Study of the Gospels,* 5th edition: Introduction, pp. 14, 15." Brooke Foss Westcott (1825–1901), one of the great Anglican churchmen and biblical scholars of the nineteenth century, published the first edition of this work in 1860.

sacred record, *the line* (of inspired or not inspired, of infallible or fallible) *can never rationally be drawn between the thoughts and the words of Scripture.*

Third. It is asked again: In what way and to what extent, is the doctrine of inspiration dependent upon the supposed results of modern criticism as to the dates, authors, sources, and modes of composition of the several books? To us the following answer appears to be well founded, and to set the limits within which the Church doctrine of inspiration is in equilibrium with the results of modern criticism fairly and certainly:

The doctrine of inspiration, in its essence—and, consequently, in all its forms—presupposes a supernatural revelation and a supernatural providential guidance entering into and determining the genesis of Scripture from the beginning. Every naturalistic theory, therefore, of the evolution of Scripture, however disguised, is necessarily opposed to any true version of the catholic doctrine of inspiration. It is also a well-known matter of fact that Christ himself is the ultimate witness on whose testimony the Scriptures, as well as their doctrinal contents, rest. We receive the Old Testament just as Christ handed it to us, and on his authority. And we receive as belonging to the New Testament all, and only those, books which an apostolically-instructed age testifies to have been produced by the apostles or their companions—i.e., by the men whom Christ commissioned, and to whom he promised infallibility in teaching. It is evident, therefore, that every supposed conclusion of critical investigation which denies the apostolical origin of a New Testament book or the truth of any part of Christ's testimony in relation to the Old Testament and its contents, or which is inconsistent with the absolute truthfulness of any affirmation of any book so authenticated, must be inconsistent with the true doctrine of inspiration. On the other hand, the defenders of the strictest doctrine of inspiration should cheerfully acknowledge that theories as to the authors, dates, sources, and modes of composition of the several books which are not plainly inconsistent with the testimony of Christ or his apostles as to the Old Testament, or with the apostolic origin of the books of the New Testament, or with the absolute truthfulness of any of the affirmations of these books so authenticated, cannot in the least invalidate the evidence or pervert the meaning of the historical doctrine of inspiration.

Fourth. The real point at issue between the more strict and the more lax views of inspiration maintained by believing scholars remains to be stated. It is claimed, and admitted equally on both sides, that the great design and effect of inspiration is to render the Sacred Scriptures in all their parts a divinely infallible and authoritative rule of faith and practice, and hence that in all their elements of thought and expression, concerned in the great purpose of conveying to men a revelation of spiritual doctrine or duty, the Scriptures are absolutely infallible. But if this be so, it is argued by the more liberal school of Christian scholars that this admitted fact is not inconsistent with other facts which they claim are matters of their personal observation: to wit, that in certain elements of Scripture which are purely incidental to their great end of teaching spiritual truth, such as history, natural history, ethnology, archaeology, geography, natural science, and philosophy, they, like all the best human writings of their age, are while for the most part reliable, yet limited by inaccuracies and discrepancies. While this is maintained, it is generally at the same time affirmed that when compared with other books of the same antiquity these inaccuracies and discrepancies of the Bible are inconsiderable in number, and always of secondary importance, in no degree invalidating the great attribute of Scripture—its absolute infallibility and its divine authority as a rule of faith and practice.

The writers of this article are sincerely convinced of the perfect soundness of the great catholic doctrine of biblical inspiration—i.e., that the Scriptures not only contain, but ARE, THE WORD OF GOD, and hence that all their elements and all their affirmations are absolutely errorless and binding the faith and obedience of men. Nevertheless, we admit that the question between ourselves and the advocates of the view just stated is one of fact, to be decided only by an exhaustive and impartial examination of all the sources of evidence—i.e., the claims and the phenomena of the Scriptures themselves. There will undoubtedly be found upon the surface many apparent affirmations presumably inconsistent with the present teachings of science, with facts of history or with other statements of the sacred books themselves. Such apparent inconsistencies and collisions with other sources of information are to be expected in imperfect copies of ancient writings, from the fact that the original reading may have been lost, or that we may fail to realize the point of view of the author, or that we are destitute of the circumstantial knowledge which would fill up and harmonize the record. Besides, the human forms of knowledge by which the critics test the accuracy of Scripture are themselves subject to error. In view of all the facts known to us, we affirm that a candid inspection of all the ascertained phenomena of the original text of Scripture will leave unmodified the ancient faith of the Church. In all their real affirmations these books are without error.

It must be remembered that it is not claimed that the Scriptures, any more than their authors, are omniscient. The information they convey is in the form of human thought, and limited on all sides. They were not designed to teach philosophy, science, or human history as such. They were not designed to furnish an infallible system of speculative theology. They are written in human languages, whose words, inflection, constructions, and idioms bear everywhere indelible traces of human error. The record itself furnishes evidence that the writers were in large measure dependent for their knowledge upon sources and methods in themselves fallible, and that their personal knowledge and judgments were in many matters hesitating and defective, or even wrong. Nevertheless, the historical faith of the Church has always been that all the affirmations of Scripture of all kinds, whether of spiritual doctrine or duty, or of physical or historical fact, or of psychological or philosophical principle, are without any error when the *ipsissima verba* of the original autographs are ascertained and interpreted in their natural and intended sense. There is a vast difference between exactness of statement, which includes an exhaustive rendering of details, an absolute literalness, which the Scriptures never profess, and accuracy, on the other hand, which secures a correct statement of facts or principles intended to be affirmed. It is this accuracy, and this alone, as distinct from exactness, which the Church doctrine maintains of every affirmation in the original text of Scripture without exception. Every statement accurately corresponds to truth just as far forth as affirmed.

Proof of the Doctrine

We of course do not propose to exhibit this evidence in this article. We wish merely to refresh the memory of our readers with respect to its copiousness, variety, and cogency.

First. The New Testament writers continually assert of the Scriptures of the Old Testament, and of the several books which constitute it, that they ARE THE WORD OF GOD. What their writers said, God said. Christ sent out the apostles with the promise of the Holy Ghost, and declared that in hearing them, men would hear him. The apostles themselves claimed to speak as the prophets of God and with plenary authority in his name binding all consciences. And while they did so God endorsed their teaching *and their claims* with signs and wonders and divers miracles. These claims are a universal and inseparable characteristic of every part of Scripture.

Second. Although composed by different human authors on various subjects and occasions, under all possible varieties of providential conditions, in two languages, through sixteen centuries of time, yet they evidently constitute one system, all their parts minutely correlated, the whole unfolding a single purpose, and thus giving indubitable evidence of the controlling presence of a divine intelligence from first to last.

Third. It is true that the Scriptures were not designed to teach philosophy, science, or ethnology, or human history as such, and therefore they are not to be studied primarily as sources of information on these subjects. Yet all these elements are unavoidably incidentally involved in the statements of Scripture. Many of these, because of defective knowledge or interpretation upon our part, present points of apparent confusion or error. Yet the outstanding fact is that the general conformableness of the sacred books to modern knowledge in all these departments is purely miraculous. If these books, which originated in an obscure province of the ancient world, be compared with the most enlightened cosmogonies or philosophies or histories of the same or immediately subsequent centuries, their comparative freedom even from apparent error is amazing. Who prevented the sacred writers from falling into the wholesale and radical mistakes which were necessarily incidental to their position as mere men? The fact that at this date scientists of the rank of Faraday and Henry, of Dana, of Guyot and Dawson, maintain that there is no real conflict between the really ascertained facts of science and the first two chapters of Genesis, rightly interpreted, of itself demonstrates that a supernatural intelligence must have directed the writing of those chapters. This, of course, proves that the scientific element of Scripture, as well as the doctrinal, was within the scope of inspiration. And this argument is every day acquiring greater force from the results of the critical study of Scripture, and from advanced knowledge in every department of history and science which continually tend to solve difficulties and to lessen the number of apparent discrepancies.

Fourth. The moral and spiritual character of the revelation which the Scriptures convey of God, of the person of Christ, of the plan of redemption, and of the law of absolute righteousness, and the power which the very words of the record, as well as the truths they express, have exercised over the noblest men and over nations and races for centuries—this is the characteristic self-demonstration of the word of God and has sufficed to maintain the unabated catholicity of the strict doctrine of inspiration through all change of time and in spite of all opposition.

Fifth. This doctrine of the inspiration of Scripture, in all its elements and parts, has always been the doctrine of the Church. Dr. Westcott has proved this by a copious catena of quotations from Ante-Nicene Fathers in Appendix B to his *Introduction to the Study of the Gospels.* He quotes Clemens Romanus as saying that the Scriptures are "the true utterances of the Holy Ghost." He quotes Tertullian as saying that these books are "the writings and the words of God," and Cyprian as saying that the "gospel cannot stand in part and fall in part," and Clement of Alexandria to the effect that the foundations of our faith "we have received from God through the Scriptures," of which not one tittle shall pass away without being accomplished, "for the mouth of the Lord the Holy Spirit spake it." Dr. Westcott quotes Origen as teaching that the Scriptures are without error, since "they were accurately written by the co-operation of the Holy Ghost," and that the words of Paul are the words of God.

The Roman Church (Can. Conc. Trid., Sess. IV. [Council of Trent, 1545]] says, "God is the author of both" Testaments. The Second Helvetic Confession [1566] represents the whole Protestant Reformation in saying (Ch. I.): "The canonical Scriptures are the true word of God," for "God continues to speak to us through the Holy Scriptures." The Westminster Confession [1646] says: "It pleased the Lord at sundry times and in divers manners to reveal himself and to declare his will unto his Church, and afterward . . . to commit the same wholly unto writing." It declares that the Scriptures are in such a sense given by inspiration that they possess a divine authority, and that "God is their author," and they "are the WORD OF GOD."

It is not questionable that the great historic churches have held these creed definitions in the sense of affirming the errorless infallibility of the word. This is everywhere shown by the way in which all the great bodies of Protestant theologians have handled Scripture in their commentaries, systems of theology, catechisms, and sermons. And this has always been pre-eminently characteristic of epochs and agents of reformation and revival. All the great world-moving men, as Luther, Calvin, Knox, Wesley, Whitfield and Chalmers, and proportionately those most like them, have so handled the divine word. Even if the more lax doctrine has the suffrage of many scholars, or even if it be true, it is nevertheless certain that hitherto in nineteen centuries it has never been held by men who also possessed the secret of using the word of God like a hammer or like a fire.

Legitimate Presumptions

In testing this question by a critical investigation of the phenomena of Scripture, it is evident that the stricter view, which denies the existence of errors, discrepancies, or inaccurate statements in Scripture, has the presumption in its favor, and that the *onus probandi* [burden of proof] rests upon the advocates of the other view. The latter may fairly be required to furnish positive and conclusive evidence in each alleged instance of error until the presumption has been turned over to the other side. The *prima facie* evidence of the claims of Scripture is assuredly all in favor of an errorless infallibility of all scriptural affirmations. This has been from the first the general faith of the historical Church and of the Bible-loving, spiritual people of God. The very letter of the word has been proved from ancient times to be a tremendous power in human life.

It is a question also of infinite importance. If the new views are untrue, they threaten not only to shake the confidence of men in the Scriptures, but the very Scriptures themselves as an objective ground of faith. We have seen that the Holy Spirit has, as a matter of fact, preserved the sacred writers to a degree unparalleled elsewhere in literature from error in the departments of philosophy and science. Who then shall determine the limit of that preserving influence? We have seen that in God's plan doctrine grows out of history, and that redemption itself was wrought out in human history. If, then, the inspiration of the sacred writers did not embrace the department of history, or only of sacred and not of profane history, who shall set the limit and define what is of the essence of faith and what the uncertain accident? It would assuredly appear that, as no organism can be stronger than its weakest part, if error be found in any one element or in any class of statements, certainty as to any portion could rise no higher than belongs to that exercise of human reason to which it will be left to discriminate the infallible from the fallible.

The critical investigation must be made, and we must abide by the result when it is unquestionably reached. But surely it must be carried on with infinite humility and teachableness, and with prayer for the constant guidance of the gracious Spirit. The signs of success will never be presumption, an evident sense of intellectual superiority, or a want of sympathy with the spiritual Church of all ages or with the painful confusion of God's humble people of the present.

With these presumptions and in this spirit let it (1) be proved that each alleged discrepant statement certainly occurred in the original autograph of the sacred book in which it is said to be found. (2) Let it be proved that the interpretation which occasions the apparent discrepancy is the one which the passage was evidently intended to bear. It is not sufficient to show a difficulty which may spring out of our defective knowledge of the circumstances. The true meaning must be definitely and certainly ascertained, and then shown to be irreconcilable with other known truth. (3) Let it be proved that the true sense of some part of the original autograph is directly and necessarily inconsistent with some certainly-known fact of history or truth of science, or some other statement of Scripture certainly ascertained and interpreted. We believe that it can be shown that this has never yet been successfully done in the case of one single alleged instance of error in the WORD OF GOD. . . .

20

Theism and Evolution

1886

Although A. A. Hodge never repudiated his father's objections to Darwin's philosophy—that nature evolves through mechanisms of blind chance—he did strike a truce with Darwin's empirical findings—that nature evolves. In 1880, less than two years after his father's death, Hodge could write, "We have no sympathy with those who maintain that scientific theories of evolution are necessarily atheistic." Yet at that same time he hastened to take note of "the essential logical incongruousness of evolution and theistic philosophy."[1] Six years later, while still keeping options open, he nonetheless came closer to approving scientists who made use of evolution. This broader approval did stress the boundaries beyond which evolutionary theories became anti-Christian speculation. Evolution must not pretend to fathom "origins, or causes, or final ends," nor to exclude "design, providence, grace, or miracles." If it does overstep these bounds, then it deserves the label given it by "Dr. Charles Hodge" as "atheistic." Yet if it avoids these excesses, it must be accepted as a potentially useful hypothesis for explaining natural development.

Hodge thus took the necessary step toward maintaining traditional Princeton beliefs in the unity of science and Christianity. Unlike his father, he could accept "facts" from evolutionary science. Like his father, he resisted atheistic interpretations of evolutionary speculation. With these assertions, A. A. Hodge reaffirmed in the age of Darwin the unity of truth and the general value of scientific method as his father and Alexander had done in the age of Newton.

The following is from A. A. Hodge's "Introduction" to Joseph S. Van Dyke,[2] *Theism and Evolution* (New York: A. C. Armstrong & Son, 1886), pp. xv–xxii.[3]

1. A. A. Hodge, Review of Asa Gray's *Natural Science and Religion* (1880), in *Presbyterian Review*, 1 (July 1880), 586, 588.

2. Joseph Smith Van Dyke (1832–1915) was a graduate of Princeton College (1857) and Princeton Seminary (1861), and a pastor of the Second Presbyterian Church of Cranbury, New Jersey, when he published this book. In 1884 he had received a D. D. degree from Princeton College where another Calvinistic evolutionist, James McCosh, was president. See *Biographical Catalogue*, p. 220.

3. On Hodge's introduction and Van Dyke's cautious discussion (which included the assertion that "progressive development is not necessarily hostile to theism, nor to any statement contained in Scripture," p. 41), see Moore, *Post-Darwinian Controversies*, pp. 241–45.

S INCE THE APPEARANCE of Charles Darwin's great work, *The Origin of Species,* the general doctrine of evolution in one or other of its many forms, has been very generally accepted by scientists as representing the view they have come to take of the operations of nature. This general conception of evolution is as old as human speculation, but it has only now been associated with accurate scientific methods, as a working hypothesis, and its truth supposed to be verified by actual proof. It is typified by the gradual growth under proper conditions of the chicken out of the egg; of the tree out of the seed; of the foetus out of the germ; of the man out of the babe; and the solar systems, with their suns, planets, and satellites in various stages of consolidation and refrigeration, out of the original nebula, "without form and void," to which Scripture as well as Science traces back the birth of the material universe. The things that are proceed out of the things that were, and in turn give birth to the things that are to be, in unbroken continuity and imperceptible transitions, through the operation of natural laws. This is the very meaning of the old familiar term "Nature," that which is born, and that which gives birth. The *natura naturans,* the present equilibrium of the universe, producing the in-coming equilibrium of the universe, or the *natura naturata.*

Mere science has nothing to do with origins, or causes, or final ends. It is concerned only with phenomena and their fixed relations in time and space. It is obvious that in this definite view of the range of science, the phenomena of the physical world at least do present in their ceaseless succession the appearance which the evolutionist describes. The solar system is passing before our eyes through constant changes. The sun as it grows cooler is becoming more like Jupiter, Jupiter more like the earth, and the earth more like the moon. The earth and its zones are passing without interruption along a line of graduated change to which the fauna and flora of all continents are continually being adjusted. The various species of plants and animals rise from the simplest to the most complex in an ideal order, and new permanent varieties spring up before our eyes out of the unity of ancient species under new physical conditions. The human race itself has been differentiated into innumerable varieties by means of differences of climate, and social conditions, and the like, and all these changes are progressing in unbroken continuity through our own age into the future, just as they have through all past stages of human history.

The scientific doctrine of evolution emphasizes this view of the succession of phenomena, and applies it as a hypothetical law, or working hypothesis, in every department of scientific investigation; to the inorganic kingdom as cosmical evolution; to the kingdom of life alike vegetable and animal; to the origination of species as well as that of varieties and of individuals; to the kingdom of mind, to account for the origin of ideas and laws of thought; and to the kingdom of social and political life as traced in the origin and progress of human societies.

Now when strictly confined to the legitimate limits of pure science, that is, to the scientific account of phenomena and their laws of co-existence and of succession, this doctrine of evolution is not antagonistic to our faith as either theists or christians. It is only when this theory assumes to be a philosophy, or becomes associated with a philosophy supplying the ideas, the causes, and the final ends which give a rational account of the facts collected, that it can challenge our interest as christians, or threaten our faith. Evolution as connected with a materialistic philosophy will, of course, as are all phrases of materialism, be inconsistent with natural theism and revealed religion. The same is equally true if the theory of evolution is worked out on a basis of pantheism. If evolution is itself erected into a complete philosophy, and be put to the magical task of tracing the growth of all things out of nothing, and of a rational and all-comprehensive system of knowledge out of agnostic premises, then of course the result must be equally fatal to human reason and to christian faith. If again, progress along the entire line of biological advance is explained wholly on the hypothesis of an all-directioned variation, and the selection of special forms by an accidental environment (the precise position of Darwin), then certainly the universe and its order is referred to Chance, teleology is impossible, theism stripped of its most effective evidence, and therefore Dr. Charles Hodge was abundantly justified in indicating this phase of evolution as atheistic. Moreover, a theory of evolution which refuses to coalesce for any reason with spiritual views of man and God and their relations, which admits of the possibility of no interruption at any time or for any end; of no influence of any active agents exterior to the limited group of natural agents subject to the test of experiment, and hence of quantitative determination, will of course lead to a denial of the supernatural, and render prayer a delusion and all religion superstitious.

But it is evident that any doctrine of evolution which intelligently recognizes the plain facts of man's spiritual nature, his reason, conscience, and free-will, will equally recognize the same attributes as the property of God. Evolution considered as the plan of an infinitely wise Person and executed under the control of His everywhere present energies can never be irreligious; can never exclude design, providence, grace, or miracles. Hence we repeat that what christians have cause to consider with apprehension is not evolution as a working hypothesis of science dealing with facts, but evolution as a philosophical speculation professing to account for the origin, causes, and ends of all things. Science owes its special authority to its close adherence to facts capable of verification. But the philosophy of evolution has nothing to distinguish it from the great multitude of transient speculations which for thousands of years have been broken on the eternal facts of man's spiritual nature like the tides of the sea are broken upon the granite rock of the coast. The claim for finality and of superior authority put forth by this philosophy is simply absurd. But the conduct of some weak christian apologists who hasten with super-serviceable zeal to abate the claims of revelation, and to adjust the doctrines of christianity to the demands of the passing mode of thinking of the hour, surpasses all else in absurdity. It is inconsistent with honest faith to fear any possible outcome of genuine scientific progress. True science leads only to the truth, and all truth is congruous with true religion. We should heartily bid science Godspeed. Since our religion is true, matured science can only confirm and illume it. We have nothing to fear from the ultimate results of the doctrine of evolution as a factor in science. For the same reason it is not becoming the christian faith for its representatives to show haste in bringing forth crude schemes for reconciling our time-tested interpretations of Scripture with the transient interpretations of nature presented by science in its hypothetical stage.

In the meantime, while we wait, it will suffice to indicate certain boundary lines which the scientific doctrine of evolution must not pass; and the passing of which can alone be rightly regarded as a *casus belli* by the christian church.

Every rational doctrine of evolution must recognize its own limitations, and presuppose a creative and rational basis on which it rests. The evolving agencies and the laws of their evolution must necessarily precede and can never be accounted for by the process of the evolution itself.

A true doctrine of evolution can never violate the fundamental laws of human thought. The universal causal judgment affirms that every new thing coming into being must have been preceded by a cause adequate to account rationally for its existence. No possible evolution of molecular mechanics can account for the origin of life, nor for the peculiar properties of living beings, such as organic form, or function, reproduction, heredity, and the like. Much less can such a cause account for the origin of sensation, consciousness, instinct, or intelligence.

Much less can any doctrine really scientific pretend to account for the origination of the higher reason of man, and especially for his conscience and its imperial dictates, by any evolution from preceding non-rational or non-moral existence. The new facts are not composites resulting from the synthesis of pre-existing elements. They are ultimate, incapable of analysis, essentially distinct, and they could have been introduced into the glow of natural evolution only by an immediate act of God, as a new thread is shot by the hand of the weaver into a rapidly evolving web of cloth. Hence it follows that no true doctrine of evolution can pretend to account on its own principles alone for the origin of man, nor for his fall, nor for the great central epoch-making stages of his redemption. The soul of man stands in such marked contrast with all that precedes it as to be evidently a new creation, and its advent introduces a new era. Hence the facts recorded in the Scriptures as to the creation of Adam and the formation of Eve are not inconsistent with the analogy of truth, and must be recognized as historically true. The character of man sets him forth evidently as subject to a law of entirely different grade than that which has been operating in the previous history of the world. New relations are sustained and a new order of events introduced. Henceforth no doctrine of evolution can be tenable which does not make room for a moral government and a redemptive providence, including miracles and the Incarnation of God, and the gracious operations of the Holy Ghost.

It is not intended in all that has been said to express any opinion as to the truth of evolution in any of its forms, but only to indicate the limits, on the respective sides of which christians, as such, can have no controversy, or no truce.

Dr. Van Dyke has already acquired an enviable reputation as a successful author. He is able, learned, and thoroughly sound in his philosophical and theological principles. The present work is on a subject of universal interest and of vital importance, and is the result of very wide reading and of mature reflection. It is not intended for men of science, but for that large circle of general readers who are interested in such questions. The object is to allay unwarranted fears on the part of christians, and to warn careless speculators of the limits beyond which it is unsafe to go. The undersigned has accepted the honor of contributing this Introduction, not because he agrees with all the positions assumed by the author, but because he sympathizes with his general purpose and believes the work adapted to be generally useful. The writer of the Introduction, as far as he differs from the author, would have preferred a more imperative affirmation of the limits beyond which science cannot rationally pass, nor pass without conflict with christianity. This however does not prevent his sincere hope that the book may be greatly blessed in its destined end of confirming true philosophy and revealed religion, and in promoting peace between the men of knowledge and the men of faith.

Benjamin Breckinridge Warfield
1851–1921

21

The Idea of Systematic Theology

1896

When B. B. Warfield was called to Princeton Seminary in 1887 as A. A. Hodge's successor in the chair of theology, he chose to speak at his inaugural on "The Idea of Systematic Theology Considered as a Science." This address was published immediately.[1] But Warfield continued to reflect on the subject and published in 1896 an expanded version of the essay, which is substantially reproduced below.

The essay was in many ways the capstone to Princeton's seventy-five years of reflection on the nature of the theological enterprise. Warfield gathered up the sentiments of his predecessors concerning the scientific character of theology, and presented them in an elegant, measured, and finished form. "Systematic theology . . . is a science, and is to be conceived as a science and treated as a science."[2] It is a science with God as its object and Scripture as its authority. Useful as other forms of God's revelation may be (conscience, nature, religious experience), the fulness of God's revelation in the Bible "all but supersedes their necessity." Scriptural revelation, moreover, conveys "facts" which the various subdivisions of theology (exegesis, biblical theology, historical theology) work up for the use of the systematician. Systematic theology progresses as science progresses, inch by inch, line by line, with each generation building on the foundation of the one before. Finally, to know mentally the facts of good theology and to feel them religiously is to be a Christian. In all these assertions, Warfield refined positions that had already become hallmarks of the Princeton Theology.

But Warfield's discussion of systematic theology also represented, if not a new chapter, at least several new emphases at Princeton. For one thing, the essay lacked the emphasis which especially Charles Hodge had placed on religious experience. Warfield did believe that theology had its proper end in the stirring of heart, will, and emotion. And he occasionally recognized the importance of subjective predispositions for the faith.[3] Yet he expressed his central

1. *The Idea of Systematic Theology Considered as a Science* (New York: Randolph, 1888). The indispensable guide to Warfield's voluminous writings is John E. Meeter and Roger Nicole, *A Bibliography of Benjamin Breckinridge Warfield* (Nutley, N.J.: Presbyterian and Reformed, 1974).

2. Warfield repeated his thoughts on this same subject in an essay for the *Bible Student,* January 1900; "Theology as a Science," ssww, II: 207-212.

3. See especially, "On Faith in its Psychological Aspects," 1911, in wввw, IX: 313-342, particularly pp. 325-329, 341. For a full treatment of Warfield's beliefs concerning piety and religious experience, see Hoffecker, *Piety and the Princeton Theologians,* pp. 95-155.

convictions on this issue toward the end of the essay reproduced below: "The character of our religion is, in a word, determined by the character of our theology." Alexander and the two Hodges would have applauded, but Charles Hodge also could say, as he did in 1829, that "opinions on moral and religious subjects depend mainly on the state of the moral and religious feelings" (Selection 6). With Warfield the subjective side of the faith, while not absent entirely, occupies a less prominent place than it did for his predecessors.

In his inaugural and its expanded version Warfield also placed a renewed emphasis on the apologetic foundation of the faith. More like Alexander than Charles Hodge, Warfield was convinced, as he puts it here, that "philosophical apologetics is . . . presupposed in and underlies the structure of scientific theology." Again, "Apologetical theology prepares the way for all theology by establishing its necessary presuppositions without which no theology is possible—the existence and essential nature of God, the religious nature of man which enables him to receive a revelation from God, the possibility of a revelation and its actual realization in the Scriptures." With these words we find ourselves back more with Alexander, who would prove Scripture and then use it (Selection 4), than with Hodge, who often downplayed rational argumentation (Selection 6). For his part, Warfield maintained a belief in the great value of apologetics throughout his career. In one of his clearest statements on the subject, he enlisted Thomas Aquinas in support of the conviction

> that though faith be a moral act and the gift of God, it is yet formally conviction passing into confidence; and that all forms of conviction must rest on evidence as their ground, and it is not faith but reason which investigates the nature and validity of this ground. . . . We believe in Christ because it is rational to believe in Him. . . . Of course mere reasoning cannot make a Christian; but that is not because faith is not the result of evidence, but because a dead soul cannot respond to evidence. The action of the Holy Spirit in giving faith is not apart from evidence, but along with evidence ("Apologetics," 1908, in wbbw, IX: 15).[4]

This conviction set Warfield against modern "rationalists" (e.g., "The Latest Phase of Historical Rationalism," 1895, in wbbw, IX: 585-645, on Albrecht Ritschl and A. C. McGiffert), against the evangelical advocates of the direct activity of the Holy Spirit (e.g., "The 'Higher Life' Movement," 1918-1919, in wbbw, VIII: 463-558), and even against Reformed leaders from the Netherlands (Selection 29).

This selection includes the full argument, with scholarly references deleted, of B. B. Warfield, "The Idea of Systematic Theology," *Presbyterian and Reformed Review,* 7 (April 1896); as found in wbbw, Vol. IX: *Studies in Theology,* pp. 49-87.

Marsden, *Fundamentalism and American Culture,* pp. 114-116, captures well the Common Sense convictions which encouraged such a high view of reason in Warfield.

4. Warfield's works are filled with his own persuasive apologetical efforts. For a particularly revealing expression of his confidence in such work, from early in his career, see "Christian Evidences: How Affected by Recent Criticism," 1888, in ssww, II: 124-131.

T HE TERM "SYSTEMATIC THEOLOGY" has long been in somewhat general use, especially in America, to designate one of the theological disciplines. And, on the whole, it appears to be a sufficiently exact designation of this discipline. . . .

What is meant by calling this discipline "Systematic Theology" is not that it deals with its material in a systematic or methodical way, and the other disciplines do not; but that it presents its material in the form of a system. Other disciplines may use a chronological, a historical, or some other method: this discipline must needs employ a systematic, that is to say, a philosophical or scientific method. It might be equally well designated, therefore, "Philosophical Theology," or "Scientific Theology." But we should not by the adoption of one of these terms escape the ambiguities which are charged against the term "Systematic Theology." Other theological disciplines may also claim to be philosophical or scientific. If exegesis should be systematic, it should also be scientific. If history should be methodical, it should also be philosophical. An additional ambiguity would also be brought to these terms from their popular usage. There would be danger that "Philosophical Theology" should be misapprehended as theology dominated by some philosophical system. There would be a similar danger that "Scientific Theology" should be misunderstood as theology reduced to an empirical science, or dependent upon an "experimental method." Nevertheless these terms also would fairly describe what we mean by "Systematic Theology." They too would discriminate it from its sister disciplines, as the philosophical discipline which investigates from the philosophical standpoint the matter with which all the disciplines deal. And they would keep clearly before our minds the main fact in the case, namely, that Systematic Theology, as distinguished from its sister disciplines, is a science, and is to be conceived as a science and treated as a science.

The two designations, "Philosophical Theology" and "Scientific Theology," are practically synonyms. But they differ in their connotation as the terms "philosophy" and "science" differ. The distinction between these terms in a reference like the present would seem to be that between the whole and one of its parts. Philosophy is the *scientia scientiarum.* What a science does for a division of knowledge, that philosophy essays to do for a mass of knowledge. A science reduces a section of our knowledge to order and harmony: philosophy reduces the sciences to order and harmony. Accordingly there are many sciences, and but one philosophy. . . . To call "Systematic Theology" "Philosophical Theology" or "Scientific Theology" would therefore be all one in essential meaning. Only when we call it "Philosophical Theology," we should be conceiving it as a science among the sciences and should have our eye upon its place in the universal sum of knowledge: while when we call it "Scientific Theology," our mind should be occupied with it in itself, as it were in isolation, and with the proper mode of dealing with its material. In either case we are affirming that it deals with its material as an organizable system of knowledge; that it deals with it from the philosophical point of view; that it is, in other words, in its essential nature a science.

It is possible that the implications of this determination are not always fully realized. When we have made the simple assertion of "Systematic Theology" that it is in its essential nature a science, we have already determined most of the vexing questions which arise concerning it in a formal point of view. In this single predicate is implicitly included a series of affirmations, which, when taken together, will give us a rather clear conception not only of what Systematic Theology is, but also of what it deals with, whence it obtains its material, and for what purpose it exists.

I. First of all, then, let us observe that to say that Systematic Theology is a science is to deny that it is a historical discipline, and to affirm that it seeks to discover not what has been or is held to be true, but what is ideally true; in other words, it is to declare that it deals with absolute truth and aims at organizing into a concatenated system all the truth in its sphere. Geology is a science, and on that very account there cannot be two geologies; its matter is all the well-authenticated facts in its sphere, and its aim is to digest all these facts into one all-comprehending system. There may be rival psychologies which fill the world with vain jangling; but they do not strive together in order that they may obtain the right to exist side by side in equal validity, but in strenuous effort to supplant and supersede one another: there can be but one true science of mind. In like manner, just because theology is a science there can be but one theology. This all-embracing system will brook no rival in its sphere, and there can be two theologies only at the cost of one or both of them being imperfect, incomplete, false. It is because theology, in accordance with a somewhat prevalent point of view, is often looked upon as a historical rather than a scientific discipline, that it is so frequently spoken of and defined as if it were but one of many similar schemes of thought. There is no doubt such a thing as Christian theology as distinguished from Buddhist theology or Mohammedan theology; and men may study it as the theological implication of Christianity considered as one of the world's religions. But when studied from this point of view, it forms a section of a historical discipline and furnishes its share of facts for a history of religions; on the data supplied by which a science or philosophy of religion may in turn be based. We may also, no doubt, speak of the Pelagian and Augustinian theologies, or of the Calvinistic and Arminian theologies; but, again, we are speaking as historians and from a historical point of view. The Pelagian and Augustinian theologies are not two coordinate sciences of theology; they are rival theologies. If one is true, just so far the other is false, and there is but one theology. This we may identify, as an empirical fact, with either or neither; but it is at all events one, inclusive of all theological truth and exclusive of all else as false or not germane to the subject. . . .

II. There is much more than this included, however, in calling theology a science. For the very existence of any science, three things are presupposed: (1) the reality of its subject-matter; (2) the capacity of the human mind to apprehend, receive into itself, and rationalize this subject-matter; and (3) some medium of communication by which the subject-matter is brought before the mind and presented to it for apprehension. There could be no astronomy, for example, if there were no heavenly bodies. And though the heavenly bodies existed, there could still be no science of them were there no mind to apprehend them. Facts do not make a science; even facts as apprehended do not make a science; they must be not only apprehended, but also so far comprehended as to be rationalized and thus combined into a correlated system. The mind brings to every science somewhat which, though included in the facts, is not derived from the facts considered in themselves alone, as isolated data, or even as data perceived in some sort of relation to one another. Though they be thus known, science is not yet; and is not born save through the efforts of the mind in subsuming the facts under its own intuitions and forms of thought. No mind is satisfied with a bare cognition of facts: its very constitution forces it on to a restless energy until it succeeds in working these facts not only into a network of correlated relations among themselves, but also into a rational body of thought correlated to itself and its necessary modes of thinking. The condition of science, then, is that the facts which fall within its scope shall be such as stand in relation not only to our faculties, so that they may be apprehended; but also to our mental constitution, so that they may be so far understood as to be rationalized and wrought into a system relative to our thinking. . . .

Like all other sciences, therefore, theology, for its very existence as a science, presupposes the objective reality of the subject-matter with which it deals; the subjective capacity of the human mind so far to understand this subject-matter as to be able to subsume it under the forms of its thinking and to rationalize it into not only a comprehensive, but also a comprehensible whole; and the existence of trustworthy media of communication by which the subject-matter is brought to the mind and presented before it for perception and understanding. That is to say: (1) The affirmation that theology is a science presupposes the affirmation that God is, and that He has relation to His creatures. Were there no God, there could be no theology; nor could there be a theology if, though He existed, He existed out of relation with His creatures. The whole body of philosophical apologetics is, therefore, presupposed in and underlies the structure of scientific theology. (2) The affirmation that theology is a science presupposes the affirmation that man has a religious nature, that is, a nature capable of understanding not only that God is, but also, to some extent, what He is; not only that He stands in relation with His creatures, but also what those relations are. Had man no religious nature he might, indeed, apprehend certain facts concerning God, but he could not so understand Him in His relations to man as to be able to respond to those facts in a true and sympathetic embrace. The total product of the great science of religion, which investigates the nature and workings of this element in man's mental constitution, is therefore presupposed in and underlies the structure of scientific theology. (3) The affirmation that theology is a science presupposes the affirmation that there are media of communication by which God and divine things are brought before the minds of men, that they may perceive them and, in perceiving, understand them. In other words, when we affirm that theology is a science, we affirm not only the reality of God's existence and our capacity so far to understand Him, but we affirm that He has made Himself known to us—we affirm the objective reality of a revelation. Were there no revelation of God to man, our capacity to understand Him would lie dormant and unawakened: and though He really existed it would be to us as if He were not. There would be a God to be known and a mind to know Him; but theology would be as impossible as if there were neither the one nor the other. Not only, then, philosophical, but also the whole mass of historical apologetics by which the reality of revelation and its embodiment in the Scriptures are vindicated, is presupposed in and underlies the structure of scientific theology.

III. In thus developing the implications of calling theology a science, we have already gone far towards determining our exact conception of what theology is. We have in effect, for example, settled our definition of theology. A science is defined from its subject-matter; and the subject-matter of theology is God in His nature and in His relations with His creatures. Theology is therefore that science which treats of God and of the relations between God and the universe. To this definition most theologians have actually come. And those who define theology as "the science of God," mean the term God in a broad sense as inclusive also of His relations; while others exhibit their sense of the need of this inclusiveness by calling it "the science of God and of divine things"; while still others speak of it, more loosely, as "the science of the supernatural." These definitions fail rather in precision of language than in correctness of conception.

Others, however, go astray in the conception itself. Thus theologians of the school of Schleiermacher usually derive their definition from the sources rather than the subject-matter of the science—and so speak of theology as "the science of faith" or the like; a thoroughly unscientific procedure, even though our view of the sources be complete and unexceptionable, which is certainly not the case with this school. Quite as confusing is it to define theology, as is very currently done and often as an outgrowth of this same subjective tendency, as "the science of religion," or even—pressing to its greatest extreme the historical conception, which as often underlies this type of definition—as "the science of the Christian religion." Theology and religion are parallel products of the same body of facts in divers spheres; the one in the sphere of thought and the other in the sphere of life. And the definition of theology as "the science of religion" thus confounds the product of the facts concerning God and His relations with His creatures working through the hearts and lives of men, with those facts themselves; and consequently, whenever strictly understood, bases theology not on the facts of the divine revelation, but on the facts of the religious life. This leads ultimately to a confusion of the two distinct disciplines of theology, the subject-matter of which is objective, and the science of religion, the subject-matter of which is subjective; with the effect of lowering the data of theology to the level of the aspirations and imaginings of man's own heart. Wherever this definition is found, either a subjective conception of theology, which reduces it to a branch of psychology, may be suspected; or else a historical conception of it, a conception of "Christian theology" as one of the many theologies of the world, parallel with, even if unspeakably truer than, the others with which it is classed and in conjunction with which it furnishes us with a full account of religion. When so conceived, it is natural to take a step further and permit the methodology of the science, as well as its idea, to be determined by its distinguishing element: thus theology, in contradiction to its very name, becomes Christocentric. No doubt "Christian theology," as a historical discipline, is Christocentric; it is by its doctrine of redemption that it is differentiated from all the other theologies that the world has known. But theology as a science is and must be theocentric. So soon as we firmly grasp it from the scientific point of view, we see that there can be but one science of God and of His relations to His universe, and we no longer seek a point of discrimination but rather a center of development; and we quickly see that there can be but one center about which so comprehensive a subject-matter can be organized—the conception of God. He that hath seen Christ, has beyond doubt seen the Father; but it is one thing to make Christ the center of theology so far as He is one with God, and another thing to organize all theology around Him as the theanthropos [God-man] and in His specifically theanthropic work.

IV. Not only, however, is our definition of theology thus set for us: we have also determined in advance our conception of its sources. We have already made use of the term "revelation," to designate the medium by which the facts concerning God and His relations to His creatures are brought before men's minds, and so made the subject-matter of a possible science. The word accurately describes the condition of all knowledge of God. If God be a person, it follows by stringent necessity, that He can be known only so far as He reveals or expresses Himself. And it is but the converse of this, that if there be no revelation, there can be no knowledge, and, of course, no systematized knowledge or science of God. Our reaching up to Him in thought and inference is possible only because He condescends to make Himself intelligible to us, to speak to us through work or word, to reveal Himself. We hazard nothing, therefore, in saying that, as the condition of all theology is a revealed God, so, without limitation, the sole source of theology is revelation.

In so speaking, however, we have no thought of doubting that God's revelation of Himself is "in divers manners." We have no desire to deny that He has never left man without witness of His eternal power and Godhead, or that He has multiplied the manifestations of Himself in nature and providence and grace, so that every generation has had abiding and unmistakable evidence that He is, that He is the good God, and that He is a God who marketh iniquity. Under the broad skirts of the term "revelation," every method of manifesting Himself which God uses in communicating knowledge of His being and attributes may find shelter for itself— whether it be through those visible things of nature whereby His invisible things are clearly seen, or through the constitution of the human mind with its causal judgment indelibly stamped upon it, or through that voice of God that we call conscience, which proclaims His moral law within us, or through His providence in which He makes bare His arm for the government of the nations, or through the exercises of His grace, our experience under the tutelage of the Holy Ghost—or whether it be through the open visions of His prophets, the divinely-breathed pages of His written Word, the divine life of the Word Himself. How God reveals Himself—in what divers manners He makes Himself known to His creatures—is thus the subsequent question, by raising which we distribute the one source of theology, revelation, into the various methods of revelation, each of which brings us true knowledge of God, and all of which must be taken account of in building our knowledge into one all-comprehending system. It is the accepted method of theology to infer that the God that made the eye must Himself see; that the God who sovereignly distributes His favors in the secular world may be sovereign in grace too; that the heart that condemns itself but repeats the condemnation of the greater God; that the songs of joy in which the Christian's happy soul voices its sense of God's gratuitous mercy are valid evidence that God has really dealt graciously with it. It is with no reserve that we accept all these sources of knowledge of God—nature, providence, Christian experience—as true and valid sources, the well-authenticated data yielded by which are to be received by us as revelations of God, and as such to be placed alongside of the revelations in the written Word and wrought with them into one system. As a matter of fact, theologians have always so dealt with them; and doubtless they always will so deal with them.

But to perceive, as all must perceive, that every method by which God manifests Himself, is, so far as this manifestation can be clearly interpreted, a source of knowledge of Him, and must, therefore, be taken account of in framing all our knowledge of Him into one organic whole, is far from allowing that there are no differences among these various manifestations—in the amount of revelation they give, the clearness of their message, the ease and certainty with which they may be interpreted, or the importance of the special truths which they are fitted to convey. Far rather is it *à priori* likely that if there are "divers manners" in which God has revealed Himself, He has not revealed precisely the same message through each; that these "divers manners" correspond also to divers messages of divers degrees of importance, delivered with divers degrees of clearness. And the mere fact that He has included in these "divers manners" a copious revelation in a written Word, delivered with an authenticating accompaniment of signs and miracles, proved by recorded prophecies with their recorded fulfillments, and pressed, with the greatest solemnity, upon the attention and consciences of men as the very Word of the Living God, who has by it made all the wisdom of men foolishness; nay, proclaimed as containing within itself the formulation of His truth, the proclamation of His law, the discovery of His plan of salvation: this mere fact, I say, would itself and prior to all comparison, raise an overwhelming presumption that all the others of "the divers manners" of God's revelation were insufficient for the purposes for which revelation is given, whether on account of defect in the amount of their communication or insufficiency of attestation or uncertainty of interpretation or fatal onesidedness in the character of the revelation they are adapted to give.

We need not be surprised, therefore, that on actual examination, such imperfections are found undeniably to attach to all forms of what we may, for the sake of discrimination, speak of as mere manifestations of God; and that thus the revelation of God in His written Word—in which are included the only authentic records of the revelation of Him through the incarnate Word—is easily shown not only to be incomparably superior to all other manifestations of Him in the fullness, richness, and clearness of its communications, but also to contain the sole discovery of much that it is most important for the soul to know as to its state and destiny, and of much that is most precious in our whole body of theological knowledge. The superior lucidity of this revelation makes it the norm of interpretation for what is revealed so much more darkly through the other methods of manifestation. The glorious character of the discoveries made in it throws all other manifestations into comparative shadow. The amazing fullness of its disclosures renders what they can tell us of little relative value. And its absolute completeness for the needs of man, taking up and reiteratingly repeating in the clearest of language all that can be wrung from their sometimes enigmatic indications, and then adding to this a vast body of still more momentous truth undiscoverable through them, all but supersedes their necessity. With the fullest recognition of the validity of all the knowledge of God and His ways with men, which can be obtained through the manifestations of His power and divinity in nature and history and grace; and the frankest allowance that the written Word is given, not to destroy the manifestations of God, but to fulfill them; the theologian must yet refuse to give these sources of knowledge a place alongside of the written Word, in any other sense than that he gladly admits that they, alike with it, but in unspeakably lower measure, do tell us of God. And nothing can be a clearer indication of a decadent theology or of a decaying faith than a tendency to neglect the Word in favor of some one or of all of the lesser sources of theological truth, as fountains from which to draw our knowledge of divine things. This were to prefer the flickering rays of a taper to the blazing light of the sun; to elect to draw our water from a muddy run rather than to dip it from the broad bosom of the pure fountain itself.

Nevertheless, men have often sought to still the cravings of their souls with a purely natural theology; and there are men today who prefer to derive their knowledge of what God is and what He will do for man from an analysis of the implications of their own religious feelings: not staying to consider that nature, "red in tooth and claw with ravin," [sic] can but direct our eyes to the God of law, whose deadly letter kills; or that our feelings must needs point us to the God of our imperfect apprehensions or of our unsanctified desires—not to the God that is, so much as to the God that we would fain should be. The natural result of resting on the revelations of nature is despair; while the inevitable end of making our appeal to even the Christian heart is to make for ourselves refuges of lies in which there is neither truth nor safety. We may, indeed, admit that it is valid reasoning to infer from the nature of the Christian life what are the modes of God's activities towards His children: to see, for instance, in conviction of sin and the sudden peace of the new-born soul, God's hand in slaying that He may make alive, His almighty power in raising the spiritually dead. But how easy to overstep the limits of valid inference; and, forgetting that it is the body of Christian truth known and assimilated that determines the type of Christian experience, confuse in our inferences what is from man with what is from God, and condition and limit our theology by the undeveloped Christian thought of the man or his times. The interpretation of the data included in what we have learned to call "the Christian consciousness," whether of the individual or of the Church at large, is a process so delicate, so liable to error, so inevitably swayed to this side or that by the currents that flow up and down in the soul, that probably few satisfactory inferences could be drawn from it, had we not the norm of Christian experience and its dogmatic implications recorded for us in the perspicuous pages of the written Word. But even were we to suppose that the interpretation was easy and secure, and that we had before us, in an infallible formulation, all the implications of the religious experience of all the men who have ever known Christ, we have no reason to believe that the whole body of facts thus obtained would suffice to give us a complete theology. After all, we know in part and we feel in part; it is only when that which is perfect shall appear that we shall know or experience all that Christ has in store for us. With the fullest acceptance, therefore, of the data of the theology of the feelings, no less than of natural theology, when their results are validly obtained and sufficiently authenticated as trustworthy, as divinely revealed facts which must be wrought into our system, it remains nevertheless true that we should be confined to a meager and doubtful theology were these data not confirmed, reinforced, and supplemented by the surer and fuller revelations of Scripture; and that the Holy Scriptures are the source of theology in not only a degree, but also a sense in which nothing else is.[5]

There may be a theology without the Scriptures—a theology of nature, gathered by painful, and slow, and sometimes doubtful processes from what man sees around him in external nature and the course of history, and what he sees within him of nature and of grace. In like manner there may be and has been an astronomy of nature, gathered by man in his natural state without help from aught but his naked eyes, as he watched in the fields by night. But what is this astronomy of nature to the astronomy that has become possible through the wonderful appliances of our observatories? The Word of God is to theology as, but vastly more than, these instruments are to astronomy. It is the instrument which so far increases the possibilities of the science as to revolutionize it and to place it upon a height from which it can never more descend. What would be thought of the deluded man, who, discarding the new methods of research, should insist on acquiring all the astronomy which he would admit, from the unaided observation of his own myopic and astigmatic eyes? Much more deluded is he who, neglecting the instrument of God's Word written, would confine his admissions of theological truth to what he could discover from the broken lights that play upon external nature, and the faint gleams of a dying or even a slowly reviving light, which arises in his own sinful soul. Ah, no! The telescope first made a real science of astronomy possible: and the Scriptures form the only sufficing source of theology.

V. Under such a conception of its nature and sources, we are led to consider the place of Systematic Theology among the other theological disciplines as well as among the other sciences in general. Without encroaching upon the details of

---

5. The uneasiness which Warfield displays here concerning religious experience as a mode of revelation reappeared often in his career; see WBBW, VII and VIII (*Perfectionism Part One, Perfectionism Part Two*).

Theological Encyclopedia,[6] we may adopt here the usual fourfold distribution of the theological disciplines into the Exegetical, the Historical, the Systematic, and the Practical, with only the correction of prefixing to them a fifth department of Apologetical Theology. The place of Systematic Theology in this distribution is determined by its relation to the preceding disciplines, of which it is the crown and head. Apologetical Theology prepares the way for all theology by establishing its necessary presuppositions without which no theology is possible—the existence and essential nature of God, the religious nature of man which enables him to receive a revelation from God, the possibility of a revelation and its actual realization in the Scriptures. It thus places the Scriptures in our hands for investigation and study. Exegetical Theology receives these inspired writings from the hands of Apologetics, and investigates their meaning; presenting us with a body of detailed and substantiated results, culminating in a series of organized systems of Biblical History, Biblical Ethics, Biblical Theology, and the like, which provide material for further use in the more advanced disciplines. Historical Theology investigates the progressive realization of Christianity in the lives, hearts, worship, and thought of men, issuing not only in a full account of the history of Christianity, but also in a body of facts which come into use in the more advanced disciplines, especially in the way of the manifold experiments that have been made during the ages in Christian organization, worship, living, and creed-building, as well as of the sifted results of the reasoned thinking and deep experience of Christian truth during the whole past. Systematic Theology does not fail to strike its roots deeply into this matter furnished by Historical Theology; it knows how to profit by the experience of all past generations in their efforts to understand and define, to systematize and defend revealed truth; and it thinks of nothing so little as lightly to discard the conquests of so many hard-fought fields. It therefore gladly utilizes all the material that Historical Theology brings it, accounting it, indeed, the very precipitate of the Christian consciousness of the past; but it does not use it crudely, or at first hand for itself, but accepts it as investigated, explained, and made available by the sister discipline of Historical Theology which alone can understand it or draw from it its true lessons. It certainly does not find in it its chief or primary source, and its relation to Historical Theology is, in consequence, far less close than that in which it stands to Exegetical Theology which is its true and especial handmaid. The independence of Exegetical Theology is seen in the fact that it does its work wholly without thought or anxiety as to the use that is to be made of its results; and that it furnishes a vastly larger body of data than can be utilized by any one discipline. It provides a body of historical, ethical, liturgic, ecclesiastical facts, as well as a body of theological facts. But so far as its theological facts are concerned, it provides them chiefly that they may be used by Systematic Theology as material out of which to build its system.

6. In A. A. Hodge's definition (Selection 18), Theological Encyclopedia "presents to the student the entire circle of the special sciences devoted to the discovery, elucidation and defence of the contents of the supernatural revelation contained in the Christian Scriptures, and aims to present these sciences in those organic relations which are determined by their actual genesis and inmost nature."

This is not to forget the claims of Biblical Theology. It is rather to emphasize its value, and to afford occasion for explaining its true place in the encyclopedia, and its true relations on the one side to Exegetical Theology, and on the other to Systematics—a matter which appears to be even yet imperfectly understood in some quarters. Biblical Theology is not a section of Historical Theology, although it must be studied in a historical spirit, and has a historical face; it is rather the ripest fruit of Exegetics, and Exegetics has not performed its full task until its scattered results in the way of theological data are gathered up into a full and articulated system of Biblical Theology. It is to be hoped that the time will come when no commentary will be considered complete until the capstone is placed upon its fabric by closing chapters gathering up into systematized exhibits the unsystematized results of the continuous exegesis of the text, in the spheres of history, ethics, theology, and the like. The task of Biblical Theology, in a word, is the task of coordinating the scattered results of continuous exegesis into a concatenated whole, whether with reference to a single book of Scripture or to a body of related books or to the whole Scriptural fabric.[7] Its chief object is not to find differences of conception between the various writers, though some recent students of the subject seem to think this is so much their duty, that when they cannot find differences they make them. It is to reproduce the theological thought of each writer or group of writers in the form in which it lay in their own minds, so that we may be enabled to look at all their theological statements at their angle, and to understand all their deliverances as modified and conditioned by their own point of view. Its exegetical value lies just in this circumstance that it is only when we have thus concatenated an author's theological statements into a whole, that we can be sure that we understand them as he understood them in detail. A light is inevitably thrown back from Biblical Theology upon the separate theological deliverances as they occur in the text, such as subtly colors them, and often for the first time, gives them to us in their true setting, and thus enables us to guard against perverting them when we adapt them to our use. This is a noble function, and could students of Biblical Theology only firmly grasp it, once for all, as their task, it would prevent this important science from being brought into contempt through a tendency to exaggerate differences in form of statement into divergences of view, and so to force the deliverances of each book into a strange and unnatural combination, in the effort to vindicate a function for this discipline.

The relation of Biblical Theology to Systematic Theology is based on a true view of its function. Systematic Theology is not founded on the direct and primary results of the exegetical process; it is founded on the final and complete results of exegesis as exhibited in Biblical Theology. Not exegesis itself, then, but Biblical Theology, provides the material for Systematics. Biblical Theology is not, then, a rival of Systematics; it is not even a parallel product of the same body of facts, provided by exegesis; it is the basis and source of Systematics. Systematic Theology

---

7. It is for the absence of such integrative efforts concerning Scripture that Warfield would later criticize fundamentalist leaders; see Selection 28.

is not a concatenation of the scattered theological data furnished by the exegetic process; it is the combination of the already concatenated data given to it by Biblical Theology. It uses the individual data furnished by exegesis, in a word, not crudely, not independently for itself, but only after these data have been worked up into Biblical Theology and have received from it their final coloring and subtlest shades of meaning—in other words, only in their true sense, and after Exegetics has said its last word upon them. Just as we shall attain our finest and truest conception of the person and work of Christ, not by crudely trying to combine the scattered details of His life and teaching as given in our four Gospels into one patchwork life and account of His teaching; but far more rationally and far more successfully by first catching Matthew's full conception of Jesus, and then Mark's, and then Luke's, and then John's, and combining these four conceptions into one rounded whole: so we gain our truest Systematics not by at once working together the separate dogmatic statements in the Scriptures, but by combining them in their due order and proportion as they stand in the various theologies of the Scriptures. Thus we are enabled to view the future whole not only in its parts, but in the several combinations of the parts; and, looking at it from every side, to obtain a true conception of its solidity and strength, and to avoid all exaggeration or falsification of the details in giving them place in the completed structure. And thus we do not make our theology according to our own pattern, as a mosaic, out of the fragments of the Biblical teaching; but rather look out from ourselves upon it as a great prospect, framed out of the mountains and plains of the theologies of the Scriptures and strive to attain a point of view from which we can bring the whole landscape into our field of sight.

From this point of view, we find no difficulty in understanding the relation in which the several disciplines stand to one another with respect to their contents. The material that Systematics draws from other than Biblical sources may be here left momentarily out of account. The actual contents of the theological results of the exegetic process, of Biblical Theology, and of Systematics, with this limitation, may be said to be the same. The immediate work of exegesis may be compared to the work of a recruiting officer: it draws out from the mass of mankind the men who are to constitute the army. Biblical Theology organizes these men into companies and regiments and corps, arranged in marching order and accoutered for service. Systematic Theology combines these companies and regiments and corps into an army—a single and unitary whole, determined by its own all-pervasive principle. It, too, is composed of men—the same men which were recruited by Exegetics; but it is composed of these men, not as individuals merely, but in their due relations to other men of their companies and regiments and corps. The simile is far from a perfect one; but it may illustrate the mutual relations of the disciplines, and also, perhaps, suggest the historical element that attaches to Biblical Theology, and the element of all-inclusive systematization which is inseparable from Systematic Theology. It is just this element, determining the spirit and therefore the methods of Systematic Theology, which, along with its greater inclusiveness, discriminates it from all forms of Biblical Theology, the spirit of which is purely historical.

VI. The place that theology, as the scientific presentation of all the facts that are known concerning God and His relations, claims for itself within the circle of the sciences is an equally high one with that which it claims among the theological disciplines. Whether we consider the topics which it treats, in their dignity, their excellence, their grandeur; or the certainty with which its data can be determined; or the completeness with which its principles have been ascertained and its details classified; or the usefulness and importance of its discoveries: it is as far out of all comparison above all other sciences as the eternal health and destiny of the soul are of more value than this fleeting life in this world. It is not so above them, however, as not to be also a constituent member of the closely interrelated and mutually interacting organism of the sciences. There is no one of them all which is not, in some measure, touched and affected by it, or which is not in some measure included in it. As all nature, whether mental or material, may be conceived of as only the mode in which God manifests Himself, every science which investigates nature and ascertains its laws is occupied with the discovery of the modes of the divine action, and as such might be considered a branch of theology. And, on the other hand, as all nature, whether mental or material, owes its existence to God, every science which investigates nature and ascertains its laws, depends for its foundation upon that science which would make known what God is and what the relations are in which He stands to the work of His hands and in which they stand to Him; and must borrow from it those conceptions through which alone the material with which it deals can find its explanation or receive its proper significance.

Theology, thus, enters into the structure of every other science. Its closest relations are, no doubt, with the highest of the other sciences, ethics. Any discussion of our duty to God must rest on a knowledge of our relation to Him; and much of our duty to man is undiscoverable, save through knowledge of our common relation to the one God and Father of all, and one Lord the Redeemer of all, and one Spirit the Sanctifier of all—all of which it is the function of theology to supply. This fact is, of course, not fatal to the existence of a natural ethics; but an ethics independent of theological conceptions would be a meager thing indeed, while the theology of the Scriptural revelation for the first time affords a basis for ethical investigation at once broad enough and sure enough to raise that science to its true dignity. Accordingly, a purely natural ethics has always been an incomplete ethics even relatively to the less developed forms of ethics resting on a revealed basis. . . .

We must not, however, on the ground of this intimacy of relation, confound the two sciences of theology and ethics. Something like it in kind and approaching it in degree exists between theology and every other science, no one of which is so independent of it as not to touch and be touched by it. Something of theology is implicated in all metaphysics and physics alike. It alone can determine the origin of either matter or mind, or of the mystic powers that have been granted to them. It alone can explain the nature of second causes and set the boundaries to their efficiency. It alone is competent to declare the meaning of the ineradicable persuasion of the human mind that its reason is right reason, its processes trustworthy, its intuitions true. All science without God is mutilated science, and no account of a single branch of knowledge can ever be complete until it is pushed back to find its completion and ground in Him. . . .

It is thus as true of sciences as it is of creatures that in Him they all live and move and have their being. The science of Him and His relations is the necessary ground of all science. All speculation takes us back to Him; all inquiry presupposes Him; and every phase of science consciously or unconsciously rests at every step on the science that makes Him known. Theology, thus, as the science which treats of God, lies at the root of all sciences. It is true enough that each could exist without it, in a sense and in some degree; but through it alone can any one of them reach its true dignity. Herein we see not only the proof of its greatness, but also the assurance of its permanence. . . .

It is only in theology, therefore, that the other sciences find their completion. Theology, formally speaking, is accordingly the apex of the pyramid of the sciences by which the structure is perfected. Its relation to the other sciences is, thus, in this broader sphere quite analogous to its relation to the other branches of the theological encyclopedia in that narrower sphere. All other sciences are subsidiary to it, and it builds its fabric out of material supplied by them. Theology is the science which deals with the facts concerning God and His relations with the universe. Such facts include all the facts of nature and history: and it is the very function of the several sciences to supply these facts in scientific, that is, thoroughly comprehended form. Scientific theology thus stands at the head of the sciences as well as at the head of the theological disciplines. The several sciences deal each with its own material in an independent spirit and supply a multitude of results not immediately useful to theology. But so far as their results stand related to questions with which theology deals, they exist only to serve her. . . .

It would seem to be a mistake . . . to conceive of scientific theology as the immediate and direct synthesis of the three sources—Natural Theology, Biblical Theology, and Comparative Theology—so that it would be considered the product in like degree or even in similar manner of the three. All three furnish data for the completed structure; but if what has been said in an earlier connection has any validity, Natural and Comparative Theology should stand in a somewhat different relation to Scientific Theology from that which Biblical Theology occupies—a relation not less organic indeed, but certainly less direct. The true representation seems to be that Scientific Theology is related to the natural and historical sciences, not immediately and independently for itself, but only indirectly, that is, through the mediation of the preliminary theological discipline of Apologetics. The work of Apologetics in its three branches of Philosophical, Psychological, and Historical, results not only in presenting the Bible to the theological student, but also in presenting to him God, Religion, and Christianity. And in so doing, it supplies him with the total material of Natural and Comparative Theology as well as with the foundation on which exegesis is to raise the structure of Biblical Theology. The materials thus provided Scientific Theology utilizes, just as it utilizes the results of exegesis through Biblical Theology, and the results of the age-long life of men under Christianity through Historical Theology. Scientific Theology rests, therefore, most directly on the results of Biblical exegesis as provided in Biblical Theology; but avails itself likewise of all the material furnished by all the preceding disciplines, and, in the results of Apologetics as found in Natural Theology and Comparative Theology, of all the data bearing on its problems, supplied by all the sciences. But it does not make its direct appeal crudely and independently to these sciences, any more than to exegesis and Christian history, but as it receives the one set of results from the hands of Exegetics and Historics, so it receives the others from the hand of Apologetics.[8] Systematic Theology is fundamentally one of the theological disciplines, and bears immediate relation only to its sister disciplines; it is only through them that it reaches further out and sets its roots in more remote sources of information.

VII. The interpretation of a written document, intended to convey a plain message, is infinitely easier than the interpretation of the teaching embodied in facts themselves. It is therefore that systematic treatises on the several sciences are written. Theology has, therefore, an immense advantage over all other sciences, inasmuch as it is more an inductive study of facts conveyed in a written revelation than an inductive study of facts as conveyed in life. It was, consequently, the first-born of the sciences. It was the first to reach relative completeness. And it is today in a state far nearer perfection than any other science. This is not, however, to deny that it is a progressive science. In exactly the same sense in which any other science is progressive, this is progressive. It is not meant that new revelations are to be expected of truth which has not been before within the reach of man. There is a vast difference between the progress of a science and increase in its material. All the facts of psychology, for instance, have been in existence so long as mind itself has existed; and the progress of this science has been dependent on the progressive discovery, understanding, and systematization of these facts. All the facts of theology have, in like manner, been within the reach of man for nearly two millenniums; and the progress of theology is dependent on men's progress in gathering, defining, mentally assimilating, and organizing these facts into a correlated system. So long as revelation was not completed, the progressive character of theology was secured

8. Warfield's note: It may be useful to seek to give a rough graphic representation of the relations of Systematic Theology as thus far outlined:

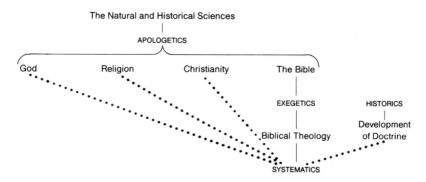

The Natural and Historical Sciences
|
APOLOGETICS

God   Religion   Christianity   The Bible
|
EXEGETICS   HISTORICS
| |
Development
Biblical Theology   of Doctrine
|
SYSTEMATICS

by the progress in revelation itself. And since the close of the canon of Scripture, the intellectual realization and definition of the doctrines revealed in it, in relation to one another, have been, as a mere matter of fact, a slow but ever advancing process.

The affirmation that theology has been a progressive science is no more, then, than to assert that it is a science that has had a history—and a history which can be and should be genetically traced and presented. First, the objective side of Christian truth was developed: pressed on the one side by the crass monotheism of the Jews and on the other by the coarse polytheism of the heathen, and urged on by its own internal need of comprehending the sources of its life, Christian theology first searched the Scriptures that it might understand the nature and modes of existence of its God and the person of its divine Redeemer. Then, more and more conscious of itself, it more and more fully wrought out from those same Scriptures a guarded expression of the subjective side of its faith; until through throes and conflicts it has built up the system which we all inherit. Thus the body of Christian truth has come down to us in the form of an organic growth; and we can conceive of the completed structure as the ripened fruit of the ages, as truly as we can think of it as the perfected result of the exegetical discipline. As it has come into our possession by this historic process, there is no reason that we can assign why it should not continue to make for itself a history. We do not expect the history of theology to close in our own day. However nearly completed our realization of the body of truth may seem to us to be; however certain it is that the great outlines are already securely laid and most of the details soundly discovered and arranged; no one will assert that every detail is as yet perfected, and we are all living in the confidence so admirably expressed by old John Robinson, "that God hath more truth yet to break forth from His holy Word." Just because God gives us the truth in single threads which we must weave into the reticulated texture, all the threads are always within our reach, but the finished texture is ever and will ever continue to be before us until we dare affirm that there is no truth in the Word which we have not perfectly apprehended, and no relation of these truths as revealed which we have not perfectly understood, and no possibility in clearness of presentation which we have not attained.

The conditions of progress in theology are clearly discernible from its nature as a science. The progressive men in any science are the men who stand firmly on the basis of the already ascertained truth. The condition of progress in building the structures of those great cathedrals whose splendid piles glorify the history of art in the Middle Ages was that each succeeding generation should build upon the foundations laid by its predecessor. If each architect had begun by destroying what had been accomplished by his forerunners, no cathedral would ever have been raised. The railroad is pushed across the continent by the simple process of laying each rail at the end of the line already laid. The prerequisite of all progress is a clear discrimination which as frankly accepts the limitations set by the truth already discovered, as it rejects the false and bad. Construction is not destruction; neither is it the outcome of destruction. There are abuses no doubt to be reformed; errors to correct; falsehoods to cut away. But the history of progress in every science and no less in theology, is a story of impulses given, corrected, and assimilated. And when they have been once corrected and assimilated, these truths are to remain accepted. It is then time for another impulse, and the condition of all further progress is to place ourselves in this well-marked line of growth. Astronomy, for example, has had such a history; and there are now some indisputable truths in astronomy, as, for instance, the rotundity of the earth and the central place of the sun in our system. I do not say that these truths are undisputed; probably nothing is any more undisputed in astronomy, or any other science, than in theology. At all events he who wishes, may read the elaborate arguments of the "Zetetic" philosophers, as they love to call themselves, who in this year of grace are striving to prove that the earth is flat and occupies the center of our system. Quite in the same spirit, there are "Zetetic" theologians who strive with similar zeal and acuteness to overturn the established basal truths of theology—which, however, can nevermore be shaken; and we should give about as much ear to them in the one science as in the other. It is utter folly to suppose that progress can be made otherwise than by placing ourselves in the line of progress; and if the temple of God's truth is ever to be completely built, we must not spend our efforts in digging at the foundations which have been securely laid in the distant past, but must rather give our best efforts to rounding the arches, carving the capitals, and fitting in the fretted roof. What if it is not ours to lay foundations? Let us rejoice that that work has been done! Happy are we if our God will permit us to bring a single capstone into place. This fabric is not a house of cards to be built and blown down again a hundred times a day, as the amusement of our idle hours: it is a miracle of art to which all ages and lands bring their varied tribute. The subtle Greek laid the foundations; the law-loving Roman raised high the walls; and all the perspicuity of France and ideality of Germany and systematization of Holland and deep sobriety of Britain have been expended in perfecting the structure; and so it grows.

We have heard much in these last days of the phrase "progressive orthodoxy," and in somewhat strange connections. Nevertheless, the phrase itself is not an inapt description of the building of this theological house. Let us assert that the history of theology has been and ever must be a progressive orthodoxy. But let us equally loudly assert that progressive orthodoxy and retrogressive heterodoxy can scarcely be convertible terms. Progressive orthodoxy implies that first of all we are orthodox, and secondly that we are progressively orthodox, that is, that we are ever growing more and more orthodox as more and more truth is being established. This has been and must be the history of the advance of every science, and not less, among them, of the science of theology. Justin Martyr, champion of the orthodoxy of his day, held a theory of the intertrinitarian relationship which became heterodoxy after the Council of Nicea; the ever struggling Christologies of the earlier ages were forever set aside by the Chalcedon Fathers; Augustine determined for all time the doctrine of grace, Anselm the doctrine of the atonement, Luther the doctrine of forensic justification. In any progressive science, the amount of departure from accepted truth which is possible to the sound thinker becomes thus ever less and less, in proportion as investigation and study result in the progressive establishment of an ever increasing number of facts. The physician who would bring back today the medicine of Galen would be no more mad than the theologian who would revive the theology of Clement of Alexandria. Both were men of light and leading in their time; but their time is past, and it is the privilege of the child of today to know a sounder physic and a sounder theology than the giants of that far past yesterday could attain. It is of the very essence of our position at the end of the ages that we are ever more and more hedged around with ascertained facts, the discovery and establishment of which constitute the very essence of progress. Progress brings increasing limitation, just because it brings increasing knowledge. And as the orthodox man is he that teaches no other doctrine than that which has been established as true, the progressively orthodox man is he who is quick to perceive, admit, and condition all his reasoning by all the truth down to the latest, which has been established as true.

VIII. When we speak of progress our eyes are set upon a goal. And in calling theology a progressive science we unavoidably raise the inquiry, what the end and purpose is towards an ever increasing fitness to secure which it is continually growing. Its own completeness and perfecting as a science—as a department of knowledge—is naturally the proximate goal towards which every science tends. And when we consider the surpassing glory of the subject-matter with which theology deals, it would appear that if ever science existed for its own sake, this might surely be true of this science. The truths concerning God and His relations are above all comparison, in themselves the most worthy of all truths of study and examination. Yet we must vindicate a further goal for the advance of theology and thus contend for it that it is an eminently practical science. The contemplation and exhibition of Christianity as truth is far from the end of the matter. This truth is specially communicated by God for a purpose, for which it is admirably adapted. That purpose is to save and sanctify the soul. And the discovery, study, and systematization of the truth is in order that, firmly grasping it and thoroughly comprehending it in all its reciprocal relations, we may be able to make the most efficient use of it for its holy purpose. Well worth our most laborious study, then, as it is, for its own sake as mere truth, it becomes not only absorbingly interesting, but inexpressibly precious to us when we bear in mind that the truth with which we thus deal constitutes, as a whole, the engrafted Word that is able to save our souls. The task of thoroughly exploring the pages of revelation, soundly gathering from them their treasures of theological teaching, and carefully fitting these into their due places in a system whereby they may be preserved from misunderstanding, perversion, and misuse, and given a new power to convince the understanding, move the heart, and quicken the will, becomes thus a holy duty to our own and our brothers' souls as well as an eager pleasure of our intellectual nature.

That the knowledge of the truth is an essential prerequisite to the production of those graces and the building up of those elements of a sanctified character for the production of which each truth is especially adapted, probably few will deny: but surely it is equally true that the clearer, fuller, and more discriminating this knowledge is, the more certainly and richly will it produce its appropriate effect; and in this is found a most complete vindication of the duty of systematizing the separate elements of truth into a single soundly concatenated whole by which the essential nature of each is made as clear as it can be made to human apprehension. It is not a matter of indifference, then, how we apprehend and systematize this truth. On the contrary, if we misconceive it in its parts or in its relations, not only do our views of truth become confused and erroneous, but also our religious life becomes dwarfed or contorted. The character of our religion is, in a word, determined by the character of our theology: and thus the task of the systematic theologian is to see that the relations in which the separate truths actually stand are rightly conceived, in order that they may exert their rightful influence on the development of the religious life. As no truth is so insignificant as to have no place in the development of our religious life, so no truth is so unimportant that we dare neglect it or deal deceitfully with it in adjusting it into our system. We are smitten with a deadly fear on the one side, lest by fitting them into a system of our own devising, we cut from them just the angles by which they were intended to lay hold of the hearts of men: but on the other side, we are filled with a holy confidence that, by allowing them to frame themselves into their own system as indicated by their own natures—as the stones in Solomon's temple were cut each for its place—we shall make each available for all men, for just the place in the saving process for which it was divinely framed and divinely given.

These theoretical considerations are greatly strengthened by the historical fact that throughout all the ages every advance in the scientific statement of theological truth has been made in response to a practical demand, and has been made in a distinctly practical interest. We wholly misconceive the facts if we imagine that the development of systematic theology has been the work of cold, scholastic recluses, intent only upon intellectual subtleties. It has been the work of the best heart of the whole Church driving on and utilizing in its practical interests, the best brain. . . .

If such be the value and use of doctrine, the systematic theologian is preeminently a preacher of the gospel; and the end of his work is obviously not merely the logical arrangement of the truths which come under his hand, but the moving of men, through their power, to love God with all their hearts and their neighbors as themselves; to choose their portion with the Saviour of their souls; to find and hold Him precious; and to recognize and yield to the sweet influences of the Holy Spirit whom He has sent. With such truth as this he will not dare to deal in a cold and merely scientific spirit, but will justly and necessarily permit its preciousness and its practical destination to determine the spirit in which he handles it, and to awaken the reverential love with which alone he should investigate its reciprocal relations. For this he needs to be suffused at all times with a sense of the unspeakable worth of the revelation which lies before him as the source of his material, and with the personal bearings of its separate truths on his own heart and life; he needs to have had and to be having a full, rich, and deep religious experience of the great doctrines with which he deals; he needs to be living close to his God, to be resting always on the bosom of his Redeemer, to be filled at all times with the manifest influences of the Holy Spirit. The student of systematic theology needs a very sensitive religious nature, a most thoroughly consecrated heart, and an outpouring of the Holy Ghost upon him, such as will fill him with that spiritual discernment without which all native intellect is in vain. He needs to be not merely a student, not merely a thinker, not merely a systematizer, not merely a teacher—he needs to be like the beloved disciple himself in the highest, truest, and holiest sense, a divine.

22

The Religious Life
of Theological Students
1911

Although Warfield, in Francis L. Patton's words, was nearly "a recluse," who did not preach often outside of Princeton or participate in church boards and courts, he did take his responsibilities as a teacher very seriously.[1] He was diligent in the instruction of his students during the week, and like the Hodges and Alexander before him, he also directed the Sunday afternoon "conferences" where, perhaps with a touch more formality than his predecessors, he expounded upon piety from the Scriptures (see the sermons from these exercises gathered in *Faith and Life*, 1916). When Warfield was called upon to address the seminary students in the fall of 1911, he thus was prepared with further words of advice. The address advocated the characteristic Princeton association between learning and piety. And it called students to be faithful in their duties as students, in their performance of public worship, and in the exercise of private devotion. It took its place as part of a venerable genre (see Selection 6 for comparison). The address testifies that even Warfield, the most rational of the Princeton theologians, never thought of theology except as a liturgical, as well as an intellectual, exercise.

The address was given October 4, 1911, and is taken from sssww, I: 411–412, 414–416, 418–419, 422, 424–425.

I AM ASKED TO speak to you on the religious life of the student of theology. I approach the subject with some trepidation. I think it the most important subject which can engage our thought. You will not suspect me, in saying this, to be depreciating the importance of the intellectual preparation of the student for the ministry. The importance of the intellectual preparation of the student for the ministry is the reason of the existence of our Theological Seminaries. Say what you will, do what you will, the ministry is a "learned profession"; and the man without learning, no matter with what other gifts he may be endowed, is unfit for its duties.

1. Francis L. Patton, "Benjamin Breckinridge Warfield," *Princeton Theological Review,* 19 (July 1921), 371. Of Warfield, Patton said in this memorial, p. 370: "He was pre-eminently a scholar and lived among his books." Patton also praised Warfield highly as an instructor of seminarians, pp. 381–385.

But learning, though indispensable, is not the most indispensable thing for a minister. . . . A minister must be learned, on pain of being utterly incompetent for his work. But before and above being learned, a minister must be godly.

Nothing could be more fatal, however, than to set these two things over against one another. Recruiting officers do not dispute whether it is better for soldiers to have a right leg or a left leg: soldiers should have both legs. Sometimes we hear it said that ten minutes on your knees will give you a truer, deeper, more operative knowledge of God than ten hours over your books. "What!" is the appropriate response, "than ten hours over your books, on your knees?" Why should you turn from God when you turn to your books, or feel that you must turn from your books in order to turn to God? If learning and devotion are as antagonistic as that, then the intellectual life is in itself accursed, and there can be no question of a religious life for a student, even of theology. The mere fact that he is a student inhibits religion for him. That I am asked to speak to you on the religious life of the student of theology proceeds on the recognition of the absurdity of such antitheses. You are students of theology; and, just because you are students of theology, it is understood that you are religious men—especially religious men, to whom the cultivation of your religious life is a matter of the profoundest concern—of such concern that you will wish above all things to be warned of the dangers that may assail your religious life, and be pointed to the means by which you may strengthen and enlarge it. In your case there can be no "either-or" here—either a student or a man of God. You must be both. . . .

Now as students of theology your vocation is to study theology; and to study it diligently, in accordance with the apostolic injunction: "Whatsoever ye do, do it heartily, as to the Lord." It is precisely for this that you are students of theology; this is your "next duty," and the neglect of duty is not a fruitful religious exercise. Dr. Charles Hodge, in his delightful autobiographical notes, tells of Philip Lindsay, the most popular professor in the Princeton College of his day—a man sought by nearly every college in the Central States for its presidency—that "he told our class that we would find that one of the best preparations for death was a thorough knowledge of the Greek grammar." "This," comments Dr. Hodge, in his quaint fashion, "was his way of telling us that we ought to do our duty." Certainly, every man who aspires to be a religious man must begin by doing his duty, his obvious duty, his daily task, the particular work which lies before him to do at this particular time and place. If this work happens to be studying, then his religious life depends on nothing more fundamentally than on just studying. You might as well talk of a father who neglects his parental duties, of a son who fails in all the obligations of filial piety, of an artisan who systematically skimps his work and turns in a bad job, of a workman who is nothing better than an eye-servant, being religious men as of a student who does not study being a religious man. It cannot be: you cannot build up a religious life except you begin by performing faithfully your simple daily duties. It is not the question whether you like these duties. You may think of your studies what you please. You may consider that you are singing precisely of them when you sing of "e'en servile labors," and of "the meanest work." But you must faithfully give yourselves to your studies, if you wish to be religious men. No religious character can be built up on the foundation of neglected duty.

There is certainly something wrong with the religious life of a theological student who does not study. But it does not quite follow that therefore everything is right with his religious life if he does study. It is possible to study—even to study theology—in an entirely secular spirit. I said a little while ago that what religion does is to send a man to his work with an added quality of devotion. In saying that, I meant the word "devotion" to be taken in both its senses—in the sense of "zealous application," and in the sense of "a religious exercise," as the Standard Dictionary phrases the two definitions. A truly religious man will study anything which it becomes his duty to study with "devotion" in both of these senses. That is what his religion does for him: it makes him do his duty, do it thoroughly, do it "in the Lord." But in the case of many branches of study, there is nothing in the topics studied which tends directly to feed the religious life, or to set in movement the religious emotions, or to call out specifically religious reactions. If we study them "in the Lord," that is only because we do it "for his sake," in the principle which makes "sweeping a room" an act of worship. With theology it is not so. In all its branches alike theology has as its unique end to make God known: the student of theology is brought by his daily task into the presence of God, and is kept there. Can a religious man stand in the presence of God, and not worship? It is possible, I have said, to study even theology in a purely secular spirit. But surely that is possible only for an irreligious man, or at least for an unreligious man. And here I place in your hands at once a touchstone by which you may discern your religious state, and an instrument for the quickening of your religious life. Do you prosecute your daily tasks as students of theology as "religious exercises"? If you do not, look to yourselves: it is surely not all right with the spiritual condition of that man who can busy himself daily with divine things, with a cold and impassive heart. If you do, rejoice. But in any case, see that you do! And that you may have done in the past, for the future make all your theological studies "religious exercises." This is the great rule for a rich and wholesome religious life in a theological student. Put your heart into your studies; do not merely occupy your mind with them, but put your heart into them. They bring you daily and hourly into the very presence of God; his ways, his dealing with men, the infinite majesty of his Being form their very subject-matter. Put the shoes from off your feet in this holy presence! . . .

Needful as common worship is, however, for men at large, the need of it for men at large is as nothing compared with its needfulness for a body of young men situated as you are. You are gathered together here for a religious purpose, in preparation for the highest religious service which can be performed by men—the guidance of others in the religious life; and shall you have everything else in common except worship? You are gathered together here, separated from your homes and all that home means; from the churches in which you have been brought up, and all that church fellowship means; from all the powerful natural influences of social religion—and shall you not yourselves form a religious community, with its own organic religious life and religious expression? I say it deliberately, that a body of young men, living apart in a community-life, as you are and must be living, cannot maintain a healthy, full, rich religious life individually, unless they are giving organic expression to their religious life as a community in frequent stated diets of common worship. Nothing can take the place of this common organic worship of the community as a community, at its stated seasons, and as a regular function of the corporate life of the community. Without it you cease to be a religious community and lack that support and stay, that incitement and spur, that comes to the individual from the organic life of the community of which he forms a part.

In my own mind, I am quite clear that in an institution like this the whole body of students should come together, both morning and evening, every day, for common prayer; and should join twice on every Sabbath in formal worship. Without at least this much common worship I do not think the institution can preserve its character as a distinctively religious institution—an institution whose institutional life is primarily a religious one. And I do not think that the individual students gathered here can, with less full expression of the organic religious life of the institution, preserve the high level of religious life on which, as students of theology, they ought to live. You will observe that I am not merely exhorting you "to go to church." "Going to church" is in any case good. But what I am exhorting you to do is to go to your own church—to give your presence and active religious participation to every stated meeting for worship of the institution as an institution. Thus you will do your part to give to the institution an organic religious life, and you will draw out from the organic religious life of the institution a support and inspiration for your own personal religious life which you can get nowhere else, and which you cannot afford to miss—if, that is, you have a care to your religious quickening and growth. To be an active member of a living religious body is the condition of healthy religious functioning. . . .

But not even with the most assiduous use of the corporate expressions of the religious life of the community have you reached the foundation-stone of your piety. That is to be found, of course, in your closets, or rather in your hearts, in your private religious exercises, and in your intimate religious aspirations. You are here as theological students; and if you would be religious men, you must do your duty as theological students; you must find daily nourishment for your religious life in your theological studies; you must enter fully into the organic religious life of the community of which you form a part. But to do all this you must keep the fires of religious life burning brightly in your heart; in the inmost core of your being, you must be men of God. Time would fail me, if I undertook to outline with any fulness the method of the devout life. Every soul seeking God honestly and earnestly finds him, and, in finding him, finds the way to him. One hint I may give you, particularly adapted to you as students for the ministry: Keep always before your mind the greatness of your calling, that is to say, these two things: the immensity of the task before you, the infinitude of the resources at your disposal. I think it has not been idly said, that if we face the tremendous difficulty of the work before us, it will certainly throw us back upon our knees; and if we worthily gauge the power of the gospel committed to us, that will certainly keep us on our knees. I am led to single out this particular consideration, because it seems to me that we have fallen upon an age in which we very greatly need to recall ourselves to the seriousness of life and its issues, and to the seriousness of our calling as ministers to life....

There is no mistake more terrible than to suppose that activity in Christian work can take the place of depth of Christian affections.

This is the reason why many good men are shaking their heads a little today over a tendency which they fancy they see increasing among our younger Christian workers to restless activity at the apparent expense of depth of spiritual culture. Activity, of course, is good: surely in the cause of the Lord we should run and not be weary. But not when it is substituted for inner religious strength. We cannot get along without our Marthas. But what shall we do when, through all the length and breadth of the land, we shall search in vain for a Mary? Of course the Marys will be as little admired by the Marthas today as of yore. "Lord," cried Martha, "dost thou not care that my sister hath left me to serve alone?" And from that time to this the cry has continually gone up against the Marys that they waste the precious ointment which might have been given to the poor, when they pour it out to God, and are idle when they sit at the Master's feet. A minister, high in the esteem of the churches, is even quoted as declaring—not confessing, mind you, but publishing abroad as something in which he gloried—that he has long since ceased to pray: he *works*. "Work and pray" is no longer, it seems, to be the motto of at least ministerial life. It is to be all work and no praying; the only prayer that is prevailing, we are told, with the same cynicism with which we are told that God is on the side of the largest battalions—is just work. You will say this is an extreme case. Thank God, it is. But in the tendencies of our modern life, which all make for ceaseless—I had almost said thoughtless, meaningless—activity, have a care that it does not become your case; or that your case—even now—may not have at least some resemblance to it. Do you pray? How much do you pray? How much do you love to pray? What place in your life does the "still hour" alone with God take?

I am sure that if you once get a true glimpse of what the ministry of the cross is, for which you are preparing, and of what you, as men preparing for this ministry, should be, you will pray, Lord, who is sufficient for these things, your heart will cry; and your whole soul will be wrung with the petition: Lord, make me sufficient for these things. Old Cotton Mather wrote a great little book once, to serve as a guide to students for the ministry. The not very happy title which he gave it is *Manductio ad Ministerium* [Food for the Ministry]. But by a stroke of genius he added a sub-title which is more significant. And this is the sub-title he added: *The angels preparing to sound the trumpets.* That is what Cotton Mather calls you, students for the ministry: the angels, preparing to sound the trumpets! Take the name to yourselves, and live up to it. Give your days and nights to living up to it! And then, perhaps, when you come to sound the trumpets the note will be pure and clear and strong, and perchance may pierce even to the grave and wake the dead.

23

The Inerrancy
of the Original Autographs
1893

The modern evangelical may be excused a sense of *déjà vu* upon reading Warfield's various writings on the nature of biblical authority, for the terms he debated and the issues with which he struggled remain to this day the center of controversy among theologically conservative Protestants. Warfield, never retreating from the high and carefully nuanced view of scriptural authority spelled out in 1881 with A. A. Hodge (Selection 19), defended, expanded, and clarified that view in many works thereafter.[1] Warfield's immediate concern in the 1880s and 1890s was the Presbyterian Church, but he never lost sight of the larger issues that transcended the turmoils of his own denomination.

Debate concerning the Bible within the Presbyterian Church of the United States of America (Northern) had been growing throughout the 1880s.[2] During the 1890s three of the most well known "progressive" Presbyterians—Charles A. Briggs, Henry Preserved Smith, and Arthur Cushman McGiffert—were expelled from or left the denomination, in no small measure because of their more liberal views of Scripture. The issues, then as now, were both simple and complex. Virtually all leaders in the church pledged themselves simply to believe in the Bible and its message of salvation. Vast disagreement, however, existed on the meaning of both "belief" and "the Bible." In this heated situation Warfield labored to achieve three goals—(1) to clarify the significance of the Bible's own statements about itself, (2) to clarify exactly what was at issue and what was not, and (3) to clarify precisely what the orthodox stance affirmed and what it did not. His contribution to the 1881 essay, "Inspiration," and several subsequent exegetical studies (including Selection 25) attempted the first task. An entire series of occasional works (including the essay below and Selection 24) attempted the second and third.[3]

In the following selection, Warfield attempted to counter objections raised against two terms that had become part of the conservative position, "inerrancy"

1. See the eighty-three writings cited by Roger R. Nicole in Appendix 3, "Warfield on Scripture: A Chronological Bibliography," *Inspiration*, pp. 83–90.
2. See Loetscher, *Broadening Church*, pp. 18–74; and Marsden, *Fundamentalism and American Culture*, pp. 116–118.
3. Many of Warfield's most important works on this general subject are found in WBBW, I (*Revelation and Inspiration*).

and "original autographs." In so doing he hoped to reaffirm the trustworthiness and authority of the Bible, while countering some of the connotations that more liberal writers had read in these terms. As part of the discussion, Warfield affirmed that the writers of the Westminster Confession (1646), while not using the same terms, had possessed the same convictions as those who in the 1890s wished to speak of inerrant original autographs.[4]

The following is the entirety of B. B. Warfield, "The Inerrancy of the Original Autographs," *The Independent,* March 23, 1893; from SSWW, II: 580–587.

O<small>UR LORD AND</small> his apostles looked upon the entire truthfulness and utter trustworthiness of that body of writings which they called "Scripture," as so fully guaranteed by the inspiration of God that they could appeal to them confidently in all their statements of whatever kind as absolutely true; adduce their deliverances on whatever subject with a simple "it is written," as the end of all strife; and treat them generally in a manner which clearly exhibits that in their view "Scripture says" was equivalent to "God says."

Following this example and teaching, the Westminster Confession of Faith calls "all the books of the Old and New Testament," in their entirety, "Holy Scripture or the Word of God written" (1.2), "all which," it affirms, "are given by inspiration of God," who is "the author thereof," being himself "truth itself" (1.4). Accordingly, it declares all these "books of the Old and New Testament," in their entirety, to be "of infallible truth and divine authority" (1.5), and asserts that "a Christian believeth to be true whatsoever is revealed in the Word, for the authority of God himself speaking therein" (14.2). For the further clearing of difficulties, the Confession distinguishes between translations of Scripture and the originals, and with reference to the originals between the transmitted and the original text (1.8). Of translations, it declares that they competently transmit the Word of God for all practical purposes. Of the transmitted text, it affirms that it has been providentially kept so pure as to retain full authoritativeness in all controversies of religion. Of the original text, it asserts that it was "immediately inspired of God"—a technical term in common theological use at the time, by which the idea of divine authorship, in the highest sense of the word, is conveyed. To this original text alone, therefore, it is to be understood, are attributed, in their fullest sense, the various "qualities" of Scripture which are ascribed to it in the Confession, on the ground of its being the Word of God—such as divine authority, perfection, perspicuity, entire trustworthiness, and the like.

Efforts are at present being made to undermine the historical truthfulness of the

4. The most recent full treatment of this subject, Rogers, *Scripture in the Westminster Confession,* sees more differences between the Westminster divines and Warfield on the character of inspiration than did Warfield in his own considerable studies of the topic: "The Westminster Doctrine of Holy Scriptures," 1893, WBBW, VI: 155–257; and "The Doctrine of Inspiration of the Westminster Divines," 1894, WBBW, VI: 261–333.

Scriptural history, in the interests of a school of criticism whose view of the historical development of religious usages and doctrines in Israel is not accordant with that of the Biblical writers. The Presbyterian Church has thus been forced, under the constitutional provision of its Form of Government (12.5), to remind the churches of its communion of their confessional doctrine of Scripture, which is being attacked and endangered by this advocacy of a historically untrustworthy Bible. In the course of the controversy which has arisen, the phrase which has been placed at the head of this article has somehow been forced to the front, and a strong effort is being made to make it appear the sole "bone of contention." This is not at all the case. The present controversy concerns something much more vital than the bare "inerrancy" of the Scriptures, whether in the copies or in the "autographs." It concerns the trustworthiness of the Bible in its express declarations, and in the fundamental conceptions of its writers as to the course of the history of God's dealings with his people. It concerns, in a word, the authority of the Biblical representations concerning the nature of revealed religion, and the mode and course of its revelation. The issue raised is whether we are to look upon the Bible as containing a divinely guaranteed and wholly trustworthy account of God's redemptive revelation, and the course of his gracious dealings with his people; or as merely a mass of more or less trustworthy materials out of which we are to sift the facts in order to put together a trustworthy account of God's redemptive revelation and the course of his dealings with his people. It is of the greatest importance that the Presbyterian Church should not permit its attention to be distracted from this serious issue.

Nevertheless, although the phrase "the inerrancy of the original autographs" is not an altogether happy one to express the doctrine of the Scriptures as given by God, yet it is intended to express this doctrine, and does, in its own way, sharply affirm it; and the strenuous opposition to it which has arisen, has its roots in doubt or denial of this Scriptural and Confessional doctrine. It is important here too, therefore, that the true issue should not be permitted to be confused by the skillful manipulation of a mere phrase. It has therefore seemed proper to call attention to some of the curiosities of the recent controversial use of this phrase with a view to keeping the real issue clear.

It is certainly a curiosity of the controversial use of a phrase, to see the Church's *limitation* of her affirmation of the absolute truth and trustworthiness of the Scriptures in all their declarations, to those Scriptures "as they came from God," represented as an additional strain upon faith. Would these controversialists have the Church affirm the absolute truth of scribes' slips and printers' errors? If we were to take some of them "at the foot of the letter," they would seem to represent it as easier to believe in the infallibility of compositors and proofreaders than the infallibility of God. Everybody knows that no book was ever printed, much less hand-copied, into which some errors did not intrude in the process; and as we do not hold the author responsible for these in an ordinary book, neither ought we to hold God responsible for them in this extraordinary book which we call the Bible. It is *the Bible* that we declare to be "of infallible truth"—the Bible that God gave us, not the corruptions and slips which scribes and printers have given us, some of which are in every copy. Yet a recent writer, with a great show of solemnity, calls upon the Presbyterian Church for "a frank and full disavowal," "of any intention to make the inerrancy of the original autographs (as distinguished from *the Bible as it is*) a test of orthodoxy."[5] But what is it that distinguishes "the Bible as it is" from the original autographs? Just scribes' corruptions and printers' errors; nothing else. And so this controversialist would have the Church "frankly and fully" disavow attaching more inerrancy to the Word of God, given by inspiration to men, than to the errors and corruptions of careless or bungling scribes and printers! Taken literally, this demand would amount to a strong asseveration of the utter untrustworthiness of the Bible.

It is another curiosity of the controversial use of a phrase to find the Church's careful definition of the complete truth and trustworthiness of the Scriptures as belonging, as a matter of course, only to the genuine text of Scripture, represented as an appeal from the actually existing texts of Scripture to a lost autograph—as if it were the autographic *codex* and not the autographic *text* that is in question.[6] Thus, we have heard a vast deal, of late, of "the first manuscripts of the Bible which no living man has ever seen," of "Scriptures that have disappeared forever," of "original autographs which have vanished," concerning the contents of which these controversialists are willing to declare, with the emphasis of italics, that they know nothing, that no man knows anything, and that they are perfectly contented with their ignorance. Now, again, if this were to be taken literally, it would amount to a strong asseveration that the Bible, as God gave it to men, is lost beyond recovery; and that men are shut up, therefore, to the use of Bibles so hopelessly corrupted that it is impossible now to say what was in the original autographs and what not! In proportion as we draw back from this contention—which is fortunately as absurd as it is extreme—in that proportion do we affirm that we have the autographic text; that not only we but all men may see it if they will; and that God has not permitted the Bible to become so hopelessly corrupt that its restoration to its original text is impossible. As a matter of fact, the great body of the Bible is, in its autographic text, in the worst copies of the original texts in circulation; practically the whole of it is in its autographic text in the best texts in circulation; and he who will may today read the autographic text in large stretches of Scripture without legitimate doubt, and, in the New Testament at least, may know precisely at what rarely occurring points, and to what not very great extent, doubts as to the genuineness of the text are still

5. Warfield's note: "Dr. Henry Van Dyke of New York in *The Bible as It Is.*" Henry van Dyke (1852–1933) was a Princeton Seminary graduate (1877) who defended Charles Briggs and other progressive leaders in the Presbyterian Church. This work, a printed sermon, was published in 1893 by Wm. C. Martin, New York. It attacked belief in "the inerrancy of the original autographs of Holy Scripture," at least when used as a test for orthodoxy.

6. Warfield is contrasting the actual material on which the words were written (codex) with the actual words thereupon (text). As he sees the matter, it is entirely possible to speak of having an "autographic text," even if the "autographic codex" is lost.

possible. If our controversial brethren could only disabuse their minds of the phantom of an autographic *codex*, which their excitement has raised (and which, apart from their excited vision "no living man has ever seen"), they might possibly see with the Church that genuine text of Scripture which is "by the singular care and providence of God" still preserved to us, and might agree with the Church that it is to it alone that authority and trustworthiness and utter truthfulness are to be ascribed.

Another curiosity of controversy is found in the representation that the Church, in affirming the entire truthfulness and trustworthiness of the genuine text of Scripture, asserts that this text is wholly free from all those difficulties and apparent discrepancies which we find in "the Scriptures as we have them." Of course the Church has never made such an assertion. That some of the difficulties and apparent discrepancies in current texts disappear on the restoration of the true text of Scripture is undoubtedly true. That all the difficulties and apparent discrepancies in current texts of Scripture are matters of textual corruption, and not, rather, often of historical or other ignorance on our part, no sane man ever asserted. We must not, indeed, confuse real discrepancies and *apparent* discrepancies,[7] quoting Dr. Charles Hodge's confession of his inability "to account for" [ST 1:170] some of the difficulties of the Bible, to justify our implication that they may very easily be accounted for—viz., as natural human errors in the genuine text of Scripture. The Church does indeed affirm that the genuine text of Scripture is free from real discrepancies and errors; but she does not assert that the genuine text of Scripture is free from those apparent discrepancies and other difficulties, on the ground of which, imperfectly investigated, the errancy of the Bible is usually affirmed. The Church recognizes her duty to preserve the text of "the Scriptures of truth" committed to her keeping pure, and to transmit it pure to future generations; it is only that text that she trusts, and only on it will she hang the credit of her teachings. But she does not expect to be freed from the duty of studying this text, or from the duty of defending it against the assaults of unbelief. It would be a miraculously perfect text indeed with which imperfectly informed men could not find fault.

Still another curiosity of the present controversy is found in the constant asseveration which we hear about us, that the distinction drawn by the Presbyterian Church between the genuine text of Scripture and the current and more or less corrupt texts in general circulation, is something new. This is a rather serious arraignment of the common sense of the whole series of preceding generations. What! Are we to believe that no man until our wonderful nineteenth century ever had acumen enough to detect a printer's error or to realize the liability of hand-copied manuscripts to occasional corruption? Are we really to believe that the happy possessors of "the Wicked Bible" held "thou shall commit adultery" to be as divinely "inerrant" as the genuine text of the seventh commandment—on the ground that the "inerrancy of the original autographs of the Holy Scriptures" must not be asserted "as distinguished from the Holy Scriptures which we now possess"?

---

7. Warfield's note: "As Dr. Van Dyke and others do."

Or, that those who read in their copies at 1 Cor. 15:51 (as the possessors of one edition did), "we shall not all sleep, but we shall all be hanged," would violently defend "the Bible as it is" against the claims of the genuine text? Of course, every man of common sense from the beginning of the world has recognized the difference between the genuine text and the errors of transmission, and has attached his confidence to the former in rejection of the latter.

Richard Baxter was speaking no more for himself than for his whole age, and all the ages before him, when he defended the present position of the Presbyterian Church with such direct statements as these: "All that the holy writers have recorded is true (and no falsehood in the Scriptures but what is from the error of scribes and translators)"; "No error or contradiction is in it, but what is in some copies, by failure of preservers, transcribers, printers, and translators"; and many more passages of the same purport. In exactly similar manner Calvin and Luther repeatedly assign special difficulties to the corrupt form of transmitted Scripture as distinguished from the genuine text—no doubt sometimes without sufficient warrant; but that is so far from being the question that it is an additional evidence of their full recognition of the distinction in discussion. The Fathers, because they were dependent on manuscript (as distinct from printed) texts, in which corruption was unavoidably greater, were even more free in assuming that difficulties which they could not explain were due to corruption of text, rather than to lack of insight on their part, and much more rather than to aboriginal error in Scripture. Augustine's statement fairly represents the judgment of the Patristic Age: "I have learned to defer this respect and honor to the canonical books of Scripture alone, that I most firmly believe that no one of their authors has committed any error in writing. And if in their writings I am perplexed by anything which seems to me contrary to truth, I do not doubt that it is nothing else than either the manuscript is corrupt, or that the translator has not followed what was said, or that I have myself failed to understand it."

From these facts alone, it is already apparent how seriously erroneous it is to say, as has been recently said, that the Westminster divines never "thought of the original manuscripts of the Bible as distinct from the copies in their possession." They could not help thinking of them. I fancy I see John Lightfoot's face, on someone making that remark to *him*, just after he had risen from the composition—say of his *Harmony, Chronicle, and Order of the New Testament*.[8] And I should vastly like to read his account of the remark and of his answer to it, as he might write it to one of his friends—say to "the great Mr. Selden, the learnedest man upon the earth," or to "the all-learned Mr. Wheelocke, to whom nothing is too difficult or unattainable," or to "the admirable Dr. Usher, the magazine of all manner of literature and knowledge"—who was just then helping Walton in the preparation of his

8. The individuals mentioned in this paragraph were among those who helped write the Westminster Confession or their contemporaries. For Warfield's own assessment of their work, see the writings mentioned in note 4.

great polyglot. I should like to see how such a remark would affect Samuel Rutherford, while the ink was still wet on the pages of his controversy with John Goodwin
on the very point of the relation of the inspired autographs to the uninspired but
providentially cared-for transmission. Why, this was the burning question as to the
Scriptures in the Westminster age. Nobody in that circle doubted the plenary
inspiration and absolute errorlessness of the genuine text; the question in discussion was in what sense and to what extent could there be posited a divine
superintendence of the transmission, and how far could the current copies and
translations be depended on as vehicles of the Word of God. The Westminster men
took high ground in this controversy; and their writings are full of the echoes of it.

It is, therefore, thoroughly misleading to represent the distinction made in the
Westminster Confession between the *immediate inspiration* of the original text of
Scripture and the *providential* supervision of the transmission as either accidental
or meaningless. The historical doubt really is not whether it may not mean less than
is now attributed to it, but whether it must mean more. And the declaration of the
Presbyterian Church that her Standards teach that "the inspired Word as it came
from God is without error," is a simple affirmation of the obvious meaning of those
Standards, and certainly is accordant with the teachings of the Bible and within the
limits of common sense.

24

The Divine and Human in the Bible
1894

While Presbyterians in the early 1890s pondered whether to revise the West-minster Confession and struggled toward a decision on Charles Briggs, Warfield drove his pen furiously to defend a conservative view of Scripture.[1] One of the forty-one essays, articles, reviews, and booklets which he published on this subject during the years 1891 to 1895 was the following essay on the divine and human in Scripture.[2] Warfield wanted friends and opponents alike to have a clear conception of his, and the Princeton Seminary, view of the Bible's inspiration. Warfield forswore all views of mechanical dictation, even as he attacked liberals for overemphasizing the Bible's human character at the expense of the divine. The essay attempts, in other words, to state clearly what the orthodox view, as Warfield understood it, did and did not affirm.

It appeared as "The Divine and Human in the Bible," in *The Presbyterian Journal*, May 3, 1894, and is reprinted here from SSWW, II: 542-48. The essay offers a good example of Warfield's capacity to bring his immense learning to bear on an issue presented to a lay audience.

T HERE IS PROBABLY no problem more prominently before the minds of Bible students of today than the one which concerns the relation between the divine and human elements in the Bible. Recent discussion of the authenticity, authorship, integrity, structure of the several Biblical books, has called men's attention, as possibly it has never before been called, to the human element in the Bible. Even those who were accustomed to look upon their Bible as simply divine, never once thinking of the human agents through whom the divine Spirit spoke, have had their eyes opened to the fact that the Scriptures are human writings, written by men, and bearing the traces of their human origin on their very face. In many minds the questions have become quite pressing: How are the two factors, the divine and the human, to be conceived as related to each other in the act of inspiration? And, how are the two consequent elements in the product, the divine and the human, to be conceived as related to each other in the Scriptures?

1. See Loetscher, *Broadening Church*, pp. 39–73.
2. Nicole, "Warfield on Scripture," pp. 84–87.

It would be a mistake to suppose such questions as these of little practical importance. It is true enough that Christian men are more concerned with the effects of inspiration than with its nature or mode. But men will not rest in their belief in effects which are not congruous with their conception of the nature and mode of inspiration. Inadequate or positively false conceptions of the nature and mode of inspiration are being continually suggested, and wherever they are in any degree accepted, they bring forth their natural fruit in a modified view of the effects of inspiration. Men are continually striving to be rid of the effects which are ascribed to inspiration in the Scriptures and the formularies of the Church, on the plea that inspiration is not to be so conceived as to require these effects. The question of how inspiration is to be conceived having been thus raised, it becomes of very serious importance to go at least so far into it as to exhibit the untenableness of those theories which, when accepted, wholly overthrow the Biblical conception of the effects of inspiration. It is a matter, then, of importance, and not merely of curious interest, to ask, how are the two factors, the divine and human, to be conceived to be related to each other in the act of inspiration? And how are the two consequent elements in the Bible, the divine and human, to be conceived to be related to each other in the product of inspiration?

1. In the first place, we may be sure that they are not properly conceived when one factor or element is so exaggeratingly emphasized as to exclude the other altogether.

At one time there arose in the Church, under the impulse of zeal to assert and safeguard the divinity of Scripture, a tendency toward so emphasizing the divine element as to exclude the human. The human writers of Scripture were conceived as mere implements in the hands of the Holy Ghost, by which (rather than through whom) he wrote the Scriptures. Men were not content to call the human authors of Scripture merely the penmen, the amanuenses of the Holy Spirit, but represented them as simply his pens. Inspiration, in this view, was conceived as a simple act of dictation; and it was denied that the human writers contributed any quality to the product, unless, indeed, it might be their hand-writing. This properly so-called mechanical theory of inspiration was taught by a number of seventeenth century divines in all Protestant communions alike—by Quenstedt, Calov, Hollaz, among the Lutherans; by Heidegger and Buxtorf, among the Reformed; by Richard Hooker, among the Anglicans; and by John White among the Puritans. The obvious marks of human authorship in the Biblical books, however, prevented it from becoming dominant in its extreme form. Recognition of these marks of human authorship—as for example, differences in vocabulary, style, and the like—was recognition of a human element in the Bible; and involved so far the substitution of a theory of co-authorship by God and man for the Scriptures, in the place of the strict theory of the sole divine authorship. In this form alone has the theory of dictation persisted in the Church; and in this form it no longer belongs to the class of theories under discussion. Probably no one today so emphasizes the divine element in Scripture as to exclude the human altogether.

The opposite fault, however, is exceedingly common today. Nothing, indeed, is more common than such theories of the origin and nature of the Scriptures as exclude the divine factor and element altogether, and make them purely human in both origin and character. Historically, this mode of thought is an outgrowth of Rationalism; but it takes every form which is required by a change of philosophical basis. A Hegelian, like Dr. Whiton, adapts himself to it as readily as a Deist; a mystic like R. F. Horton as readily as a vulgar Rationalist. The modes of statement given to it are very various, but they all agree in holding the Bible to be a purely human book. They differ only as to whether there has been any divine preparation for the book at all, or if this be allowed, whether this divine preparation included a revelation which men have recorded in this book, or whether it was only gracious or indeed only providential. The book market is flooded at present with treatises teaching this hopelessly one-sided theory. Dr. Washington Gladden's *Who Wrote the Bible?* is a very crude instance in point. To him God had the same sort of care over the production of the Bible that he has over the growth of an old apple tree. Dr. John DeWitt's recent book *What Is Inspiration?* is another crude instance. According to him the prophet was left to express himself in human language "as well as he could." A slightly higher conception is taken by T. George Rooke in his *Inspiration and Other Lectures;* and a higher one still by a recent German writer, Leonard Staehlin, who thinks that God specifically prepared the Biblical writers for their task, but left them, when prepared, to execute their task in a manner so "free" as to be without continued divine guidance. Throughout all these modifications the germinal conception persists that it was man and man alone who made the Bible; and that it is, therefore, a purely human book, although it may contain a human report of divine deeds and words.

2. We may be equally sure that the relation of the divine and human in inspiration and in the Bible is not properly conceived when they are thought of as elements in the Bible lying over against each other, so that where one enters the other is pushed out.

This hopelessly crude conception seems to have become extraordinarily common of recent years. It is this point of view which underlies the remark, now heard very frequently, that the human element in the Bible is coming to be recognized as larger than we had supposed—with the implication that, therefore, the divine element must be acknowledged to be smaller than we had supposed. Even so thoughtful a writer as Dr. Sanday falls into this mode of speech: "The tendency of the last 50 or 100 years of investigation," he tells us, "is to make it appear that this human element is larger than had been supposed." So, too, Prof. Kirkpatrick says: "In the origin of Scripture there has been a large human element, larger than there was at one time supposed." The underlying conception is that what is human cannot also be divine, and that wherever the human enters there the divine disappears. Thus Dr. Sanday speaks of his thesis as an apparent contention "for an encroachment of the human element upon the divine," and Dr. G. T. Ladd even speaks of the chief difficulty in the matter being the determination of "the exact place where the divine meets the human and is limited by it."[3]

---

3. Warfield is quoting from William Sanday (1843–1920), English New Testament scholar, *The*

On such a conception it is easy to see that every discovery of a human trait in Scripture is a disproving of the divinity of Scripture. If, then, it be discovered that the whole fabric of the Bible is human—as assuredly is true—men who start with this conception in mind must end with denying of the whole fabric of the Bible that it is divine. As a preliminary stage we shall expect to meet with efforts to go through the Bible and anxiously to separate the divine and human elements. And if these elements are really so related to one another that when one enters the other is pushed out, this task will not seem a hopeless one. We may be warned, as Dr. Sanday does warn us, that it is "a mistake to attempt to draw a hard and fast line between the two elements." Men will feel that, on this conception of their relation to each other, it is a greater mistake not to make such an attempt. How shall we consent to leave confused such very diverse elements? We need not be surprised, therefore, that men like Horton and Gess have made the attempt. Nor need we at least, who perceive the folly of the underlying conception of the mechanical relation of the two elements to each other, feel surprised over the destructive nature of their results. They do not fail to find the human element entering almost everywhere, and therefore the divine element almost nowhere.

3. Justice is done to neither factor of inspiration and to neither element in the Bible, the human or the divine, by any other conception of the mode of inspiration except that of *concursus*, or by any other conception of the Bible except that which conceives of it as a divine-human book in which every word is at once divine and human.

The philosophical basis of this conception is the Christian idea of God as immanent as well as transcendent in the modes of his activity. Its idea of the mode of the divine activity in inspiration is in analogy with the divine modes of activity in other spheres—in providence, and in grace wherein we work out our own salvation with fear and trembling, knowing that it is God who is working in us both the willing and the doing according to his own good pleasure. The Biblical basis of it is found in the constant Scriptural representation of the divine and human co-authorship of the Biblical commandments and enunciations of truth; as well as in the constant Scriptural ascription of Bible passages to both the divine and the human authors, and in the constant Scriptural recognition of Scripture as both divine and human in quality and character.

The fundamental principle of this conception is that the whole of Scripture is the product of divine activities which enter it, however, not by superseding the activities of the human authors, but confluently with them; so that the Scriptures are the joint product of divine and human activities, both of which penetrate them at every point, working harmoniously together to the production of a writing which is not divine here and human there, but at once divine and human in every part,

---

Oracles of God (1891), p. 161; Alexander Francis Kirkpatrick (1849–1940), English Old Testament scholar, *The Divine Library of the Old Testament* (1891), p. 53; and George T. Ladd (1842–1921), Congregational theologian from New England, *What is the Bible?* (1888), p. 437. Warfield does not provide citations for the other quotations in this essay.

every word and every particular. According to this conception, therefore, the whole Bible is recognized as human, the free product of human effort in every part and word. And at the same time, the whole Bible is recognized as divine, the Word of God, his utterances, of which he is in the truest sense the Author.

The human and divine factors in inspiration are conceived of as flowing confluently and harmoniously to the production of a common product. And the two elements are conceived of in the Scriptures as the inseparable constituents of one single and uncompounded product. Of every word of Scripture is it to be affirmed, in turn, that it is God's word and that it is man's word. All the qualities of divinity and of humanity are to be sought and may be found in every portion and element of the Scripture; while, on the other hand, no quality inconsistent with either divinity or humanity can be found in any portion or element of Scripture.

On this conception, therefore, for the first time full justice is done to both elements of Scripture. Neither is denied because the other is recognized. And neither is limited to certain portions of Scripture that place may be made for the other, nor is either allowed to encroach upon the other. As full justice is done to the human element as is done by those who deny that there is any divine element in the Bible; for of every word in the Bible, it is asserted that it has been conceived in a human mind and written by a human hand. As full justice is done to the divine element as is done by those who deny that there is any human element in the Bible; for of every word in the Bible it is asserted that it is inspired by God, and has been written under the direct and immediate guidance of the Holy Spirit. And full justice being done to both elements in the Bible, full justice is done also to human needs. "The Bible," says Dr. Westcott, "is authoritative, for it is the Word of God; it is intelligible, for it is the word of man." Because it is the word of man in every part and element, it comes home to our hearts. Because it is the word of God in every part and element, it is our constant law and guide.

25

Inspiration
1915

Although the Scottish theologian James Orr held a somewhat broader view of biblical inspiration than Warfield, he nonetheless invited his American Presbyterian friend to contribute the article "Inspiration" to his *International Standard Bible Encyclopedia*.[1] Excerpts from that article, one of Warfield's most complete treatments of the subject, appear below. The article was marked by the painstaking attention to the Bible's own phrases that Warfield had displayed in 1881,[2] and on many occasions thereafter. It presents Warfield's reasoning at its sharpest and his scholarship at its fullest. Over thirty years had passed since Warfield had proposed an essay on the same theme to A. A. Hodge, but his commitment to the high view of inspiration and its effects had not wavered. It may also be said that this essay preserved unbroken the historic Princeton insistence on scriptural inspiration that Alexander first laid out in 1812 (Selection 4).

The article, "Inspiration," appeared first in *The International Standard Bible Encyclopedia* (Chicago: Howard-Severance, 1915), III: 1473-1483; the excerpts here are from wbbw, Vol. I: *Revelation and Inspiration*, pp. 77-79, 81, 84-86, 89-90, 95-97, 100-104. Some of Warfield's discussion of key texts is omitted, even while the biblical references remain, in order to indicate which passages Warfield felt were most crucial to the discussion.

T HE WORD "INSPIRE" and its derivatives seem to have come into Middle English from the French, and have been employed from the first (early in the fourteenth century) in a considerable number of significations, physical and metaphorical, secular and religious. The derivatives have been multiplied and their applications extended during the procession of the years, until they have acquired a very wide and varied use. Underlying all their use, however, is the constant implication of an influence from without, producing in its object movements and effects beyond its native, or at least its ordinary powers. The noun "inspiration," although already in use in the fourteenth century, seems not to occur in any but a theological

1. For a brief summary of Orr's views, see Rogers and McKim, *Authority and Interpretation of the Bible*, pp. 385-388.
2. A. A. Hodge and Warfield, *Inspiration*, ed. Nicole, pp. 37-71.

sense until late in the sixteenth century. The specifically theological sense of all these terms is governed, of course, by their usage in Latin theology; and this rests ultimately on their employment in the Latin Bible. In the Vulgate Latin Bible the verb *inspiro* (Gen. 2:7; Wisd. 15:11; Ecclus. 4:12; 2 Tim. 3:16; 2 Pet. 1:21) and the noun *inspiratio* (2 Sam. 22:16; Job 32:8; Ps. 17:16; Acts 17:25) both occur four or five times in somewhat diverse applications. In the development of a theological nomenclature, however, they have acquired (along with other less frequent applications) a technical sense with reference to the Biblical writers or the Biblical books. The Biblical books are called inspired as the Divinely determined products of inspired men; the Biblical writers are called inspired as breathed into by the Holy Spirit, so that the product of their activities transcends human powers and becomes Divinely authoritative. Inspiration is, therefore, usually defined as a supernatural influence exerted on the sacred writers by the Spirit of God, by virtue of which their writings are given Divine trustworthiness.

Meanwhile, for English-speaking men, these terms have virtually ceased to be Biblical terms. They naturally passed from the Latin Vulgate into the English versions made from it (most fully into the Rheims-Douay: Job 32:8; Wisd. 15:11; Ecclus. 4:12; 2 Tim. 3:16; 2 Pet. 1:21). But in the development of the English Bible they have found ever-decreasing place. In the English versions of the Apocrypha (both Authorized Version and Revised Version) "inspired" is retained in Wisd. 15:11; but in the canonical books the nominal form alone occurs in the Authorized Version and that only twice: Job 32:8, "But there is a spirit in man: and the inspiration of the Almighty giveth them understanding"; and 2 Tim. 3:16, "All scripture is given by inspiration of God, and is profitable for doctrine, for reproof, for correction, for instruction in righteousness." The Revised Version removes the former of these instances, substituting "breath" for "inspiration"; and alters the latter so as to read: "Every scripture inspired of God is also profitable for teaching, for reproof, for correction, for instruction which is in righteousness," with a marginal alternative in the form of, "Every scripture is inspired of God and profitable," etc. The word "inspiration" thus disappears from the English Bible, and the word "inspired" is left in only once, and then, let it be added, by a distinct and even misleading mistranslation.

For the Greek word in this passage—θεόπνευστος, *theopneustos*—very distinctly does not mean "inspired of God." This phrase is rather the rendering of the Latin, *divinitus inspirata,* restored from the Wyclif ("Al Scripture of God ynspyrid is. . . .") and Rhemish ("All Scripture inspired of God is. . . .") versions of the Vulgate. The Greek word does not even mean, as the Authorized Version translates it, "given by inspiration of God," although that rendering (inherited from Tindale: "All Scripture given by inspiration of God is. . . ." and its successors; cf. Geneva: "The whole Scripture is given by inspiration of God and is. . . .") has at least to say for itself that it is a somewhat clumsy, perhaps, but not misleading, paraphrase of the Greek term in the theological language of the day. The Greek term has, however, nothing to say of *in*spiring or of *in*spiration: it speaks only of a "spiring" or "spiration." What it says of Scripture is, not that it is "breathed into by God" or is the product of the Divine "inbreathing" into its human authors, but that it is breathed out by God,

"God-breathed," the product of the creative breath of God. In a word, what is declared by this fundamental passage is simply that the Scriptures are a Divine product, without any indication of how God has operated in producing them. No term could have been chosen, however, which would have more emphatically asserted the Divine production of Scripture than that which is here employed. The "Breath of God" is in Scripture just the symbol of His almighty power, the bearer of His creative word. "By the Word of Jehovah," we read in the significant parallel of Ps. 33:6, "were the heavens made; and all the host of them by the breath of his mouth." And it is particularly where the operations of God are energetic that this term (whether רוּחַ, rūaḥ, or נְשָׁמָה, neshāmāh) is employed to designate them—God's breath is the irresistible outflow of His power. When Paul declared, then, that "every scripture," or "all scripture" is the product of the Divine breath, "is God-breathed," he asserts with as much energy as he could employ that Scripture is the product of a specifically Divine operation.

(1) 2 Tim. 3:16. . . .

(2) 2 Pet. 1:19–21. . . .

(3) Jn. 10:34f: How far the supreme trustworthiness of Scripture, thus asserted, extends may be conveyed to us by a passage in one of Our Lord's discourses recorded by John (Jn. 10:34–35). The Jews, offended by Jesus' "making himself God," were in the act to stone Him, when He defended Himself thus: "Is it not written in your law, I said, Ye are gods? If he called them gods, unto whom the word of God came (and the scripture cannot be broken), say ye of him, whom the Father sanctified [margin "consecrated"] and sent into the world, Thou blasphemest; because I said, I am the Son of God?" It may be thought that this defence is inadequate. It certainly is incomplete: Jesus made Himself God (Jn. 10:33) in a far higher sense than that in which "Ye are gods" was said of those "unto whom the word of God came": He had just declared in unmistakable terms, "I and the Father are one." But it was quite sufficient for the immediate end in view—to repel the technical charge of blasphemy based on His making Himself God: it is not blasphemy to call one God in any sense in which he may fitly receive that designation; and certainly if it is not blasphemy to call such men as those spoken of in the passage of Scripture adduced gods, because of their official functions, it cannot be blasphemy to call Him God whom the Father consecrated and sent into the world. The point for us to note, however, is merely that Jesus' defence takes the form of an appeal to Scripture; and it is important to observe how He makes this appeal. In the first place, He adduces the Scriptures as law: "Is it not written in your law?" He demands. The passage of Scripture which He adduces is not written in that portion of Scripture which was more specifically called "the Law," that is to say, the Penta-teuch; nor in any portion of Scripture of formally legal contents. It is written in the Book of Psalms; and in a particular psalm which is as far as possible from present-ing the external characteristic of legal enactment (Ps. 82:6). When Jesus adduces this passage, then, as written in the "law" of the Jews, He does it, not because it stands in this psalm, but because it is a part of Scripture at large. In other words, He here ascribes legal authority to the entirety of Scripture, in accordance with a

conception common enough among the Jews (cf. Jn. 12:34), and finding expression in the New Testament occasionally, both on the lips of Jesus Himself, and in the writings of the apostles. Thus, on a later occasion (Jn. 15:25), Jesus declares that it is written in the "law" of the Jews, "They hated me without a cause," a clause found in Ps. 35:19. And Paul assigns passages both from the Psalms and from Isaiah to "the Law" (1 Cor. 14:21; Rom. 3:19), and can write such a sentence as this (Gal. 4:21 f): "Tell me, ye that desire to be under the law, do ye not hear the law? For it is written. . . ." quoting from the narrative of Genesis. We have seen[3] that the entirety of Scripture was conceived as "prophecy"; we now see that the entirety of Scripture was also conceived as "law": these three terms, the law, prophecy, Scripture, were indeed, materially, strict synonyms, as our present passage itself advises us, by varying the formula of adduction in contiguous verses from "law" to "scripture." And what is thus implied in the manner in which Scripture is adduced, is immediately afterward spoken out in the most explicit language, because it forms an essential element in Our Lord's defence. It might have been enough to say simply, "Is it not written in your law?" But Our Lord, determined to drive His appeal to Scripture home, sharpens the point to the utmost by adding with the highest emphasis: "and the scripture cannot be broken." This is the reason why it is worthwhile to appeal to what is "written in the law," because "the scripture cannot be broken." The word "broken" here is the common one for breaking the law, or the Sabbath, or the like (Jn. 5:18; 7:23; Mt. 5:19), and the meaning of the declaration is that it is impossible for the Scripture to be annulled, its authority to be withstood, or denied. The movement of thought is to the effect that, because it is impossible for the Scripture—the term is perfectly general and witnesses to the unitary character of Scripture (it is all, for the purpose in hand, of a piece)—to be withstood, therefore this particular Scripture which is cited must be taken as of irrefragable authority. What we have here is, therefore, the strongest possible assertion of the indefectible authority of Scripture; precisely what is true of Scripture is that it "cannot be broken." Now, what is the particular thing in Scripture, for the confirmation of which the indefectible authority of Scripture is thus invoked? It is one of its most casual clauses—more than that, the very form of its expression in one of its most casual clauses. This means, of course, that in the Saviour's view the indefectible authority of Scripture attaches to the very form of expression of its most casual clauses. It belongs to Scripture through and through, down to its most minute particulars, that it is of indefectible authority. . . .

Thus clear is it that Jesus' occasional adduction of Scripture as an authoritative document rests on an ascription of it to God as its author. His testimony is that whatever stands written in Scripture is a word of God. Nor can we evacuate this testimony of its force on the plea that it represents Jesus only in the days of His flesh, when He may be supposed to have reflected merely the opinions of His day and generation. The view of Scripture He announces was, no doubt, the view of His day and generation as well as His own view. But there is no reason to doubt that it

---

3. Warfield had established this in his discussion of II Peter 1:19–21 which was omitted above.

was held by Him, not because it was the current view, but because, in His Divine-human knowledge, He knew it to be true; for, even in His humiliation, He is the faithful and true witness. And in any event we should bear in mind that this was the view of the resurrected as well as of the humiliated Christ. It was after He had suffered and had risen again in the power of His Divine life that He pronounced those foolish and slow of heart who do not believe all that stands written in all the Scriptures (Lk. 24:25); and that He laid down the simple "Thus it is written" as the sufficient ground of confident belief (Lk. 24:46). Nor can we explain away Jesus' testimony to the Divine trustworthiness of Scripture by interpreting it as not His own, but that of His followers, placed on His lips in their reports of His words. Not only is it too constant, minute, intimate, and in part, incidental, and therefore, as it were, hidden, to admit of this interpretation; but it so pervades all our channels of information concerning Jesus' teaching as to make it certain that it comes actually from Him. It belongs not only to the Jesus of our evangelical records but as well to the Jesus of the earlier sources which underlie our evangelical records, as anyone may assure himself by observing the instances in which Jesus adduces the Scriptures as Divinely authoritative that are recorded in more than one of the Gospels (e.g. "It is written," Mt. 4:4,7,10 [Lk. 4:4,8,10]; Mt. 11:10 [Lk. 7:27]; Mt. 21:13 [Lk. 19:46; Mk. 11:17]; Mt. 26:31 [Mk. 14:21]; "the scripture" or "the scriptures," Mt. 19:4 [Mk. 10:9]; Mt. 21:42 [Mk. 12:10; Lk. 20:17]; Mt. 22:29 [Mk. 12:24; Lk. 20:37]; Mt. 26:56 [Mk. 14:49; Lk. 24:44]). These passages alone would suffice to make clear to us the testimony of Jesus to Scripture as in all its parts and declarations Divinely authoritative. . . .

So, too, when the New Testament writers quoted Scripture there was no need to say whose word it was: that lay beyond question in every mind. This usage, accordingly, is a specially striking intimation of the vivid sense which the New Testament writers had of the Divine origin of the Scriptures, and means that in citing them they were acutely conscious that they were citing immediate words of God. How completely the Scriptures were to them just the word of God may be illustrated by a passage like Gal. 3:16: "He saith not, And to seeds, as of many; but as of one, And to thy seed, which is Christ." We have seen Our Lord hanging an argument on the very words of Scripture (Jn. 10:34); elsewhere His reasoning depends on the particular tense (Mt. 22:32) or word (Mt. 22:43) used in Scripture. Here Paul's argument rests similarly on a grammatical form. No doubt it is the grammatical form of the word which God is recorded as having spoken to Abraham that is in question. But Paul knows what grammatical form God employed in speaking to Abraham only as the Scriptures have transmitted it to him; and, as we have seen, in citing the words of God and the words of Scripture he was not accustomed to make any distinction between them. It is probably the Scriptural word, therefore, which he has here in mind: though, of course, it is possible that what he here witnesses to is rather the detailed trustworthiness of the Scriptural record than its direct divinity—if we can separate two things which apparently were not separated in Paul's mind. This much we can at least say without straining, that the designation of Scripture as "scripture" and its citation by the formula, "It is written," attest primarily its indefectible authority; the designation of it as "oracles" and the adduction of it by the formula,

"It says," attest primarily its immediate divinity. Its authority rests on its divinity and its divinity expresses itself in its trustworthiness; and the New Testament writers in all their use of it treat it as what they declare it to be—a God-breathed document, which, because God-breathed, as through and through trustworthy in all its assertions, authoritative in all its declaration, and down to its last particular, the very word of God, His "oracles."

That the Scriptures are throughout a Divine book, created by the Divine energy and speaking in their every part with Divine authority directly to the heart of the readers, is the fundamental fact concerning them which is witnessed by Christ and the sacred writers to whom we owe the New Testament. But the strength and constancy with which they bear witness to this primary fact do not prevent their recognizing by the side of it that the Scriptures have come into being by the agency of men. It would be inexact to say that they recognize a human element in Scripture: they do not parcel Scripture out, assigning portions of it, or elements in it, respectively to God and man. In their view the whole of Scripture in all its parts and in all its elements, down to the least minutiae, in form of expression as well as in substance of teaching, is from God; but the whole of it has been given by God through the instrumentality of men. There is, therefore, in their view, not, indeed, a human element or ingredient in Scripture, and much less human divisions or sections of Scripture, but a human side or aspect to Scripture; and they do not fail to give full recognition to this human side or aspect. In one of the primary passages which has already been before us, their conception is given, if somewhat broad and very succinct, yet clear expression. No "prophecy," Peter tells us (2 Pet. 1:21), "ever came by the will of man; *but as borne by the Holy Ghost,* men spake from God." Here the whole initiative is assigned to God, and such complete control of the human agents that the product is truly God's work. The men who speak in this "prophecy of scripture" speak not of themselves or out of themselves, but from "God": they speak only as they are "borne by the Holy Ghost." But it is they, after all, who speak. Scripture is the product of man, but only of man speaking from God and under such a control of the Holy Spirit as that in their speaking they are "borne" by Him. The conception obviously is that the Scriptures have been given by the instrumentality of men; and this conception finds repeated incidental expression throughout the New Testament. . . .

So soon, however, as we seriously endeavor to form for ourselves a clear conception of the precise nature of the Divine action in this "breathing out" of the Scriptures—this "bearing" of the writers of the Scriptures to their appointed goal of the production of a book of Divine trustworthiness and indefectible authority—we become acutely aware of a more deeply lying and much wider problem, apart from which this one of inspiration, technically so called, cannot be profitably considered. This is the general problem of the origin of the Scriptures and the part of God in all that complex of processes by the interaction of which these books, which we call the sacred Scriptures, with all their peculiarities, and all their qualities of whatever sort, have been brought into being. For, of course, these books were not produced suddenly, by some miraculous act—handed down complete out of heaven, as the phrase goes; but, like all other products of time, are the ultimate effect of many processes cooperating through long periods. There is to be considered, for instance, the preparation of the material which forms the subject-matter of these books: in a sacred history, say, for example, to be narrated; or in a religious experience which may serve as a norm for record; or in a logical elaboration of the contents of revelation which may be placed at the service of God's people; or in the progressive revelation of Divine truth itself, supplying their culminating contents. And there is the preparation of the men to write these books to be considered, a preparation physical, intellectual, spiritual, which must have attended them throughout their whole lives, and, indeed, must have had its beginning in their remote ancestors, and the effect of which was to bring the right men to the right places at the right times, with the right endowments, impulses, acquirements, to write just the books which were designed for them. When "inspiration," technically so called, is superinduced on lines of preparation like these, it takes on quite a different aspect from that which it bears when it is thought of as an isolated action of the Divine Spirit operating out of all relation to historical processes. Representations are sometimes made as if, when God wished to produce sacred books which would incorporate His will—a series of letters like those of Paul, for example—He was reduced to the necessity of going down to earth and painfully scrutinizing the men He found there, seeking anxiously for the one who, on the whole, promised best for His purpose; and then violently forcing the material He wished expressed through him, against his natural bent, and with as little loss from his recalcitrant characteristics as possible. Of course, nothing of the sort took place. If God wished to give His people a series of letters like Paul's, He prepared a Paul to write them, and the Paul He brought to the task was a Paul who spontaneously would write just such letters.

If we bear this in mind, we shall know what estimate to place upon the common representation to the effect that the human characteristics of the writers must, and in point of fact do, condition and qualify the writings produced by them, the implication being that, therefore, we cannot get from man a pure word of God. As light that passes through the colored glass of a cathedral window, we are told, is light from heaven, but is stained by the tints of the glass through which it passes: so any word of God which is passed through the mind and soul of a man must come out discolored by the personality through which it is given, and just to that degree ceases to be the pure word of God. But what if this personality has itself been formed by God into precisely the personality it is, for the express purpose of communicating to the word given through it just the coloring which it gives it? What if the colors of the stained-glass window have been designed by the architect for the express purpose of giving to the light that floods the cathedral precisely the tone and quality it receives from them? What if the word of God that comes to His people is framed by God into the word of God it is, precisely by means of the qualities of the men formed by Him for the purpose through which it is given? When we think of God the Lord giving by His Spirit a body of authoritative Scriptures to His people, we must remember that He is the God of providence and of grace as well as of revelation and inspiration, and that He holds all the lines of preparation as fully under His direction as He does the specific operation which we call technically, in the narrow sense, by the name of "inspiration." The production of the Scriptures is, in point of fact, a long process, in the course of which numerous and very varied Divine activities are involved, providential, gracious, miraculous, all of which must be taken into account in any attempt to explain the relation of God to the production of Scripture. When they are all taken into account we can no longer wonder that the resultant Scriptures are constantly spoken of as the pure word of God. We wonder, rather, that an additional operation of God—what we call specifically "inspiration," in its technical sense—was thought necessary. Consider, for example, how a piece of sacred history—say the Book of Chronicles, or the great historical work, Gospel and Acts, of Luke—is brought to the writing. There is first of all the preparation of the history to be written: God the Lord leads the sequence of occurrences through the development He has designed for them that they may convey their lessons to His people: a "teleological" or "aetiological" character is inherent in the very course of events. Then He prepares a man, by birth, training, experience, gifts of grace, and, if need be, of revelation, capable of appreciating this historical development and eager to search it out, thrilling in all his being with its lessons and bent upon making them clear and effective to others. When, then, by His providence, God sets this man to work on the writing of this history, will there not be spontaneously written by him the history which it was Divinely intended should be written? Or consider how a psalmist would be prepared to put into moving verse a piece of normative religious experience: how he would be born with just the right quality of religious sensibility, of parents through whom he should receive just the right hereditary bent, and from whom he should get precisely the right religious example and training, in circumstances of life in which his religious tendencies should be developed precisely on right lines; how he would be brought through just the right experiences to quicken in him the precise emotions he would be called upon to express, and finally would be placed in precisely the exigencies which would call out their expression. Or consider the providential preparation of a writer of a didactic epistle—by means of which he should be given the intellectual breadth and acuteness, and be trained in habitudes of reasoning, and placed in the situations which would call out precisely the argumentative presentation of Christian truth which was required of him. When we give due place in our thoughts to the universality of the providential government of God, to the minuteness and completeness of its sway, and to its invariable efficacy, we may be inclined to ask what is needed beyond this mere providential government to secure the production of sacred books which should be in every detail absolutely accordant with the Divine will.

The answer is, Nothing is needed beyond mere providence to secure such books—provided only that it does not lie in the Divine purpose that these books should possess qualities which rise above the powers of men to produce, even under the most complete Divine guidance. For providence is guidance; and guidance can bring one only so far as his own power can carry him. If heights are to be scaled above man's native power to achieve, then something more than guidance, however effective, is necessary. This is the reason for the superinduction, at the end of the long process of the production of Scripture, of the additional Divine operation which we call technically "inspiration." By it, the Spirit of God, flowing confluently in with the providentially and graciously determined work of men, spontaneously producing under the Divine directions the writings appointed to them, gives the product a Divine quality unattainable by human powers alone. Thus these books become not merely the word of godly men, but the immediate word of God Himself, speaking directly as such to the minds and hearts of every reader. The value of "inspiration" emerges, thus, as twofold. It gives to the books written under its "bearing" a quality which is truly superhuman; a trustworthiness, an authority, a searchingness, a profundity, a profitableness which is altogether Divine. And it speaks this Divine word immediately to each reader's heart and conscience; so that he does not require to make his way to God, painfully, perhaps even uncertainly, through the words of His servant, the human instruments in writing the Scriptures, but can listen directly to the Divine voice itself speaking immediately in the Scriptural word to him. . . .

26

The Antiquity and Unity of the Human Race

1911

As a young man B. B. Warfield had shown a great interest in science. When he became a theologian, he did not set aside that interest but rather nurtured it as a complement to his professional endeavors. In the course of his wide scientific reading, he brought to a conclusion A. A. Hodge's earlier efforts to make peace between the Princeton Theology and modern science. Eventually Warfield took special pains to transcend the antithesis which Charles Hodge had perceived between creation and evolution. He wrote in 1911 (as part of the following selection), "'evolution' cannot act as a substitute for creation, but at best can supply only a theory of the method of the divine providence." Evolution, that is, was one of the possible "interpretations" for the "facts" of nature which did not violate the "facts" of Scripture. In the essay below Warfield discusses the age and unity of humankind. His reading of the Bible has convinced him that "the question of the antiquity of man has of itself no theological significance." The genealogies of Genesis should not be taken as chronologies. Warfield, "as an interested spectator," hypothesized that humans had existed on the earth for only 10,000 to 20,000 years. Yet he had passed beyond the stage where such questions were of any theological significance. It was very different with the question of the unity of mankind. On this matter Warfield believed with Charles Hodge ("The Unity of Mankind," BRPR 31 [January 1859]: 103-48) that Scripture absolutely could not tolerate theories hypothesizing plural origins for humanity.

The following is from B. B. Warfield, "On the Antiquity and the Unity of the Human Race," *Princeton Theological Review,* 9 (January 1911); as taken from WBBW, Vol. IX: *Studies in Theology,* pp. 235-238, 245, 251-252.

T HE FUNDAMENTAL ASSERTION of the Biblical doctrine of the origin of man is that he owes his being to a creative act of God. Subsidiary questions growing out of this fundamental assertion, however, have been thrown from time to time into great prominence, as the changing forms of current anthropological speculation have seemed to press on this or that element in, or corollary from, the Biblical teaching. The most important of these subsidiary questions has concerned the method of the divine procedure in creating man. Discussion of this question became acute on the publication of Charles Darwin's treatise on the "Origin of Species" in 1859, and can never sink again into rest until it is thoroughly understood in all quarters that "evolution" cannot act as a substitute for creation, but at best can supply only a theory of the method of the divine providence. Closely connected with this discussion of the mode of origination of man, has been the discussion of two further questions, both older than the Darwinian theory, to one of which it gave, however, a new impulse, while it has well-nigh destroyed all interest in the other. These are the questions of the Antiquity of Man and the Unity of the Human Race, to both of which a large historical interest attaches, though neither of them can be said to be burning questions of today.

The question of the antiquity of man has of itself no theological significance. It is to theology, as such, a matter of entire indifference how long man has existed on earth. It is only because of the contrast which has been drawn between the short period which seems to be allotted to human history in the Biblical narrative, and the tremendously long periods which certain schools of scientific speculation have assigned to the duration of human life on earth, that theology has become interested in the topic at all. There was thus created the appearance of a conflict between the Biblical statements and the findings of scientific investigators, and it became the duty of theologians to investigate the matter. The asserted conflict proves, however, to be entirely factitious. The Bible does not assign a brief span to human history: this is done only by a particular mode of interpreting the Biblical data, which is found on examination to rest on no solid basis. Science does not demand an inordinate period for the life of human beings on earth: this is done only by a particular school of speculative theorizers, the validity of whose demands on time exact investigators are more and more chary of allowing. As the real state of the case has become better understood the problem has therefore tended to disappear from theological discussion, till now it is pretty well understood that theology as such has no interest in it.

It must be confessed, indeed, that the impression is readily taken from a *prima facie* view of the Biblical record of the course of human history, that the human race is of comparatively recent origin. It has been the usual supposition of simple Bible readers, therefore, that the Biblical data allow for the duration of the life of the human race on earth only a paltry six thousand years or so: and this supposition has become fixed in formal chronological schemes which have become traditional and have even been given a place in the margins of our Bibles to supply the chronological framework of the Scriptural narrative. The most influential of these chronological schemes is that which was worked out by Archbishop Ussher in his "Annales Veteri et Novi Testamenti" (1650–1654), and it is this scheme which has found a place in the margin of the Authorized English Version of the Bible since 1701. According to it the creation of the world is assigned to the year 4004 B.C. (Ussher's own dating was 4138 B.C.); while according to the calculation of Petau (in his "Rationarium Temporum"), the most influential rival scheme, it is assigned to

the year 3983 B.C. On a more careful scrutiny of the data on which these calculations rest, however, they are found not to supply a satisfactory basis for the constitution of a definite chronological scheme. These data consist largely, and at the
crucial points solely, of genealogical tables; and nothing can be clearer than that it
is precarious in the highest degree to draw chronological inferences from genealogical tables.

For the period from Abraham down we have, indeed, in addition to somewhat
minute genealogical records, the combined evidence of such so-called "long-dates"
as those of I Kings 6:1, Gal. 3:17, and several precise statements concerning the
duration of definite shorter periods, together with whatever aid it may be possible
to derive from a certain amount of contemporary extra-Biblical data. For the
length of this period there is no difficulty, therefore, in reaching an entirely satisfactory general estimate. But for the whole space of time before Abraham, we are
dependent entirely on inferences drawn from the genealogies recorded in the fifth
and eleventh chapters of Genesis. And if the Scriptural genealogies supply no solid
basis for chronological inferences, it is clear that we are left without Scriptural data
for forming an estimate of the duration of these ages. For aught we know they may
have been of immense length.

The general fact that the genealogies of Scripture were not constructed for a
chronological purpose and lend themselves ill to employment as a basis for chronological calculations has been repeatedly shown very fully; but perhaps by no one
more thoroughly than by Dr. William Henry Green in an illuminating article published in the *Bibliotheca Sacra* for April, 1890.[1] These genealogies must be esteemed
trustworthy for the purposes for which they are recorded; but they cannot safely be
pressed into use for other purposes for which they were not intended, and for
which they are not adapted. In particular, it is clear that the genealogical purposes
for which the genealogies were given, did not require a complete record of all the
generations through which the descent of the persons to whom they are assigned
runs; but only an adequate indication of the particular line through which the
descent in question comes. Accordingly it is found on examination that the genealogies of Scripture are freely compressed for all sorts of purposes; and that it can
seldom be confidently affirmed that they contain a complete record of the whole
series of generations, while it is often obvious that a very large number are omitted.
There is no reason inherent in the nature of the Scriptural genealogies why a
genealogy of ten recorded links, as each of those in Genesis 6 and 11 is, may not
represent an actual descent of a hundred or a thousand or ten thousand links. The
point established by the table is not that these are all the links which intervened
between the beginning and the closing names, but that this is the line of descent
through which one traces back to or down to the other.

1. William Henry Green, "Primeval Chronology," *Bibliotheca Sacra*, 47 (April 1890): 285–303.
Green concluded, after an examination of the various Old Testament genealogies, that "the Scriptures furnish no data for a chronological computation prior to the life of Abraham; and that the
Mosaic records do not fix and were not intended to fix the precise date either of the Flood or of the
creation of the world."

A sufficient illustration of the freedom with which the links in the genealogies are dealt with in the Biblical usage is afforded by the two genealogies of our Lord which are given in the first chapter of the Gospel of Matthew. . . .

The question of the antiquity of man is accordingly a purely scientific one, in which the theologian as such has no concern. As an interested spectator, however, he looks on as the various schools of scientific speculation debate the question among themselves; and he can scarcely fail to take away as the result of his observation two well-grounded convictions. The first is that science has as yet in its hands no solid data for a definite estimate of the time during which the human race has existed on earth. The second is that the tremendous drafts on time which were accustomed to be made by the geologists about the middle of the last century and which continue to be made by one school of speculative biology today have been definitively set aside, and it is becoming very generally understood that man cannot have existed on the earth more than some ten thousand to twenty thousand years. . . .

If the controversy upon the antiquity of man is thus rapidly losing all but a historical interest, that which once so violently raged upon the unity of the race may be said already to have reached this stage. The question of the unity of the human race differs from the question of its antiquity in that it is of indubitable theological importance. It is not merely that the Bible certainly teaches it, while, as we have sought to show, it has no teaching upon the antiquity of the race. It is also the postulate of the entire body of the Bible's teaching—of its doctrine of Sin and Redemption alike: so that the whole structure of the Bible's teaching, including all that we know as its doctrine of salvation, rests on it and implicates it. There have been times, nevertheless, when it has been vigorously assailed, from various motives, from within as well as from without the Church, and the resources of Christian reasoning have been taxed to support it. These times have now, however, definitely passed away. The prevalence of the evolutionary hypotheses has removed all motive for denying a common origin to the human race, and rendered it natural to look upon the differences which exist among the various types of man as differentiations of a common stock. The motive for denying their conclusiveness having been thus removed, the convincing evidences of the unity of the race have had opportunity to assert their force. The result is that the unity of the race in the sense of its common origin is no longer a matter of debate; and although actually some erratic writers may still speak of it as open to discussion, they are not taken seriously, and practically it is universally treated as a fixed fact that mankind in all its varieties is one, as in fundamental characteristics, so also in origin. . . .

27

Calvin's Doctrine of Creation
1915

It is a sign of how much has changed in American church history since the early part of the twentieth century that Warfield was able to contribute an article to *The Fundamentals* (1910-15) in the same period that he was writing his fullest statements on the acceptability of evolution as a theory for explaining development in nature.[1] Not for him was the antithesis which other theologically conservative Protestants, like William Jennings Bryan in his own day and many "fundamentalists" since, established between creation and evolution.

Long before he wrote on this subject in 1915 Warfield had taken a special interest in Darwin and the implications of Darwin's ideas for religion. In 1889 his review of *The Life and Letters of Charles Darwin* included this observation: "The root of his agnosticism, as of his rejection of Christianity, was his enthusiastic acceptance of his own theory of evolution, in the mechanical naturalistic sense in which he conceived it. We raise no question whether this was an inevitable result; there have been many evolutionists who have been and have remained theists and Christians."[2] Many years later, Warfield did in fact draw the conclusion that agnosticism was not the necessary result of a carefully qualified acceptance of evolution.[3]

Warfield's occasion for making this assessment was an exposition of Calvin's doctrine of creation. According to Warfield, Calvin's *Institutes* and his commentaries restricted the term *creation* to two specific events: the original act of God in bringing out of nothing (*ex nihilo*) the "original world-stuff," and the specific act of making the human soul. All else Calvin left to God's "providence" which actively, yet always through "second causes" built into the original creation, developed all of the specific forms of the natural world, including the bodies of humans. Calvin, again in Warfield's reading, thus rejected the popular Reformed idea of "Mediate Creation" whereby God was thought to specially create the individual forms of life, not *ex nihilo* but from material which by its nature was not

---

1. To *The Fundamentals* Warfield contributed one essay, "The Deity of Christ" (Chicago: Testimony Publishing, 1909) 1: 21-28. On *The Fundamentals* and Warfield's participation, see Marsden, *Fundamentalism and American Culture,* pp. 118-23.

2. Warfield, "Darwin's Arguments against Christianity and Religion," *The Homiletic Review* 17 (January 1889): 9-16; the quotation is from SSWW II: 140. See also Warfield's longer essay, "Charles Darwin's Religious Life: A Sketch in Spiritual Biography," *Presbyterian Review* 9 (October 1888): 569-601; reprinted in WBBW IX: 541-82.

3. For Warfield's part in the Christian use of Darwinism, see Moore, *Post-Darwinian Controversies,* pp. 71, 381n64.

capable of shaping itself into more advanced forms of life (*ex materia naturaliter inhabili*). Calvin felt rather that God shaped the various forms of life out of that original material by means of processes and capabilities which he had instilled into it, preserved in it, and superintended. Calvin's view of the development of forms, kinds, and species was thus supernatural to the core—because it was God who was in every sense responsible for it—but it was also "not only evolutionism but pure evolutionism"—because God worked it always through the "second causes" which He himself ordained. Warfield thus concludes that for Calvin: "the 'indigested mass,' including the 'promise and potency' of all that was yet to be, was called into being by the simple *fiat* of God. But all that has come into being since—except the souls of men alone—has arisen as a modification of this original world-stuff by means of the interaction of its intrinsic forces."

As Alexander and Charles Hodge before him, Warfield had preserved the harmony of Scripture and science. Unlike his predecessors, however, he was not blessed with the kind of successors who were as dedicated as he had been to the value of that harmony.

The following is from B. B. Warfield, "Calvin's Doctrine of Creation," *Princeton Theological Review*, 13 (April 1915); it is taken from WBBW, Vol. V: *Calvin and Calvinism*, pp. 299-306.

IT SHOULD BE observed that in this and similar discussions founded on the progressive completion of the world, Calvin does not intend to attribute what we may speak strictly of as progressive creation to God. With Calvin, while the perfecting of the world—as its subsequent government—is a process, creation, strictly conceived, tended to be thought of as an act. "In the beginning God created the heavens and the earth": after that it was not "creation" strictly so called, but "formation," gradual modelling into form, which took place. Not, of course, as if Calvin conceived creation deistically; as if he thought of God as having created the world-stuff and then left it to itself to work out its own destiny under the laws impressed on it in its creation. A "momentary Creator, who has once for all done His work," was inconceivable to him: and he therefore taught that it is only when we contemplate God in providence that we can form any true conception of Him as Creator. But he was inclined to draw a sharp distinction in kind between the primal act of creation of the heavens and the earth out of nothing, and the subsequent acts of moulding this created material into the forms it was destined to take; and to confine the term "creation," strictly conceived, to the former. Hence in perhaps the fullest statement of his doctrine of creation given us in these chapters (1.14.20),[4] he expresses himself carefully thus: "God, by the power of His Word and Spirit, created out of nothing (*creasse ex nihilo*) the heavens and the earth; thence produced (*produxisse*) every kind of animate and inanimate thing, distinguished by a wonderful gradation the innumerable variety of things, endowed each kind with its

4. Reference is to Calvin's *Institutes of the Christian Religion*.

own nature, assigned its offices, appointed its place and station to it, and, since all things are subject to corruption, provided, nevertheless, that each kind should be preserved safe to the last day." "Thus," he adds, "He marvellously adorned heaven and earth with the utmost possible abundance, variety and beauty of all things, like a great and splendid house, most richly and abundantly constructed and furnished; and then at last by forming (*formando*) man and distinguishing him with such noble beauty, and with so many and such high gifts, he exhibited in him the noblest specimen of His works." It is God who has made all things what they are, he teaches: but, in doing so, God has acted in the specific mode properly called creation only at the initial step of the process, and the result owes its right to be called a creation to that initial act by which the material of which all things consist was called into being from non-being. "Indigested mass" as it was, yet in that world-stuff was "the seed of the whole world," and out of it that world as we now see it (for "the world was not perfected at its very beginning, in the manner it is now seen") has been evoked by progressive acts of God: and it is therefore that this world, because evoked from it, has the right to be called a creation.

The distinction which Calvin here draws, it is to be observed, is not that which has been commonly made by Reformed divines under the terms, First and Second Creation, or in less exact language Immediate and Mediate Creation. This distinction posits a sequence of truly creative acts of God throughout the six days, and therefore defines creation, so as to meet the whole case, as that act "by which God produced the world and all that is in it partly *ex nihilo*, partly *ex materia naturaliter inhabili*, for the manifestation of the glory of His power, wisdom and goodness"; or more fully, as that "first external work of God, by which in the beginning of time, without suffering any change, by His own free will, He produced by His sole omnipotent command *immediate per se* things which before were not, from simple non-being to being—and that, either *ex nihilo*, or *ex materia* which had afore been made *ex nihilo*, but is *naturaliter inhabili* for receiving the form which, created out of nothing, the Creator induces into it."[5] It is precisely this sequence of truly creative acts which Calvin disallows; and he so expresses himself, indeed, as to give it a direct contradiction. Perhaps as distinct a statement of his view as any is found in his comment on Genesis 1:21, where the term "create" is employed to designate the divine production of the animals of the sea and air, which, according to verse 20, had been brought forth by the waters at the command of God. "A question arises here," remarks Calvin,"about the word 'created.' For we have before contended that the world was made of nothing because it was 'created': but now Moses says the things formed from other matter were 'created.' Those who assert that the fishes were truly and properly 'created' because the waters were in no way suitable (*idoneae*) or adapted (*aptae*) to their production, only resort to a subterfuge; for the

5. See the discussion in the introduction to this selection for the meaning of these Latin terms. Warfield identifies these two quotations as follows: "Joannes Wollebius, *Compendium Theologiae Christ.* (Oxford, 1657), p. 35" and "Amand. Polanus, 'Syntagma theologiae christianae,' (Hanover, 1525), v. 2."

fact would remain, meanwhile, that the material of which they were made existed before, which, in strict propriety, the word does not admit. I therefore do not restrict 'creation' [here] to the work of the fifth day, but rather say it[s use] refers to (hangs from, *pendet*) that shapeless and confused mass which was, as it were, the fountain of the whole world. God, then, is said to have 'created' the sea-monsters and other fishes, because the beginning of their 'creation' is not to be reckoned from the moment in which they received their form, but they are comprehended in the universal matter (*corpus, corpore*) which was made out of nothing. So that with respect to their kind, form only was then added to them; 'creation' is nevertheless a term used truly with respect to the whole and the parts."

Calvin's motive in thus repudiating the notion of "Mediate Creation" is not at all chariness on his part with respect to the supernatural. It is not the supernatural-ness of the production of the creatures which the waters and earth brought forth which he disallows; but only the applicability to their production of the term "crea-tion." On verse 24, he comments thus: "There is in this respect a miracle as great as if God had begun to create out of nothing these things which He commanded to proceed from the earth." Calvin's sole motive seems to be to preserve to the great word "create" the precise significance of to "make out of nothing," and he will not admit that it can be applied to any production in which preexistent material is employed. This might appear to involve the view that after the creation of the world-stuff recorded in Genesis 1:1, there was never anything specifically new pro-duced by the divine power. And this might be expressed by saying that, from that point on, the divine works were purely works of providence, since the very differen-tia of a providential work is that it is the product proximately of second causes. Probably this would press Calvin's contention, however, a little too far: he would scarcely say there was no immediacy in the divine action in the productions of the five days of "creation," or indeed in the working of miracles. But we must bear in mind that his view of providence was a very high one, and he was particularly insistent that God acted through means, when He did act through means, through no necessity but purely at His own volition. Second causes, in his view, are nothing more than "instruments into which God infuses as much of efficiency as He wishes," and which He employs or not at His will (1.16.2). "The power of no created thing," says Calvin, "is more wonderful or evident than that of the sun. . . . But the Lord . . . willed that light should exist . . . before the sun was created. A pious man will not make the sun, then, either the principal or the necessary cause of the things which existed before the sun was created, but only an instrument which God uses because He wishes to; since He could without any difficulty at all do without the sun and act of Himself." The facility with which Calvin sets aside the notion of "mediate creation" is then due in no sense to desire to remove the productions of the five days of "creation" out of the category of divine products, but is itself mediated by the height of his doctrine of providence.

It is important further that we should not suppose that Calvin removed the production of the human soul out of the category of immediate creation, in the strictest sense of that term. When he insists that the works of the days subsequent to the first, when "in the beginning God created the heavens and the earth," were not strictly speaking "creations," because they were not productions *ex nihilo,* he is thinking only of the lower creation, inclusive, no doubt, of the human body; all this is made out of that primal "indigested mass" which sprang into being at the initial command of God. The soul is a different matter; and not only in the first instance, but in every succeeding instance, throughout the whole course of human propaga-tion, is an immediate creation *ex nihilo.* Moses, he tells us, perfectly understood that the soul was created from nothing; and he announces with emphasis ("Insti-tutes," 1.15.5), that it is certain that the souls of men are "no less created than the angels," adding the decisive definition: "now, creation is the origination of essence *ex nihilo.*" It is thus with the lower creation alone in his mind that Calvin insists that all that can justly be called by the high name of "creation" was wrought by God on the first day, in that one act by which He created, that is called into being out of nothing, the heavens and the earth.

It should scarcely be passed without remark that Calvin's doctrine of creation is, if we have understood it aright, for all except the souls of men, an evolutionary one. The "indigested mass," including the "promise and potency" of all that was yet to be, was called into being by the simple *fiat* of God. But all that has come into being since—except the souls of men alone—has arisen as a modification of this original world-stuff by means of the interaction of its intrinsic forces. Not these forces apart from God, of course: Calvin is a high theist, that is, supernaturalist, in his ontology of the universe and in his conception of the whole movement of the universe. To him God is the *prima causa omnium* and that not merely in the sense that all things ultimately—in the world-stuff—owe their existence to God; but in the sense that all the modifications of the world-stuff have taken place under the directly upholding and governing hand of God, and find their account ultimately in His will. But they find their account proximately in "second causes"; and this is not only evolutionism but pure evolutionism. What account we give of these second causes is a matter of ontology; how we account for their existence, their persistence, their action—the relation we conceive them to stand in to God, the upholder and director as well as creator of them. Calvin's ontology of second causes was, briefly stated, a very pure and complete doctrine of *concursus,* by virtue of which he ascribed all that comes to pass to God's purpose and directive government. But that does not concern us here. What concerns us here is that he ascribed the entire series of modifications by which the primal "indigested mass," called "heaven and earth," has passed into the form of the ordered world which we see, including the origination of all forms of life, vegetable and animal alike, inclusive doubtless of the bodily form of man, to second causes as their proximate account. And this, we say, is a very pure evolu-tionary scheme. He does not discuss, of course, the factors of the evolutionary process, nor does he attempt to trace the course of the evolutionary advance, nor even expound the nature of the secondary causes by which it was wrought. It is enough for him to say that God said, "Let the waters bring forth. . . . Let the earth bring forth," and they brought forth. Of the interaction of forces by which the actual production of forms was accomplished, he had doubtless no conception: he certainly ventures no assertions in this field. How he pictured the process in his imagination (if he pictured it in his imagination) we do not know. But these are subordinate matters. Calvin doubtless had no theory whatever of evolution; but he teaches a doctrine of evolution. He has no object in so teaching except to preserve to the creative act, properly so called, its purity as an immediate production out of nothing. All that is not immediately produced out of nothing is therefore not created—but evolved. Accordingly his doctrine of evolution is entirely unfruitful. The whole process takes place in the limits of six natural days. That the doctrine should be of use as an explanation of the mode of production of the ordered world, it was requisite that these six days should be lengthened out into six periods—six ages of the growth of the world. Had that been done Calvin would have been a precursor of the modern evolutionary theorists. As it is, he only forms a point of departure for them to this extent—that he teaches, as they teach, the modification of the original world-stuff into the varied forms which constitute the ordered world, by the instrumentality of second causes—or as a modern would put it, of its intrinsic forces. This is his account of the origin of the entire lower creation. . . . [Warfield adds the following significant footnote at this point: "H. Bavinck in the first of his Stone Lectures ('The Philosophy of Revelation,' 1909, pp. 9–10) remarks: 'The idea of development is not a production of modern times. It was already familiar to Greek philosophy. More particularly Aristotle raised it to the rank of the leading principle of his entire system by his significant distinction between *potentia* and *actus*. . . . This idea of development aroused no objection whatever in Christian theology and philosophy. On the contrary, it received extension and enrichment by being linked with the principle of theism.' Calvin accordingly very naturally thought along the lines of a theistic evolutionism."]

28

R. A. Torrey

1898

The rise of Fundamentalism placed the Princeton theologians in an ambiguous situation. They certainly applauded the fundamentalists' adherence to scriptural infallibility, and they heartily approved the fundamentalistic insistence upon a supernatural faith. Yet they were squeamish about the anti-intellectual tendencies and the snap theological judgments that often characterized the movement. Warfield's review in 1898 of Reuben A. Torrey's compilation of Bible passages is an early illustration of that ambiguity.[1] It applauds Torrey for his faithfulness to traditional Christian devotion, but raises serious questions about his theological method. Especially disturbing was Torrey's claim that merely to gather texts from throughout the Bible on a given topic constituted an "inductive" approach to Scripture. The Princeton theologians, who rose or fell with their commitment to induction (see Selections 8 and 21), had greatly refined the concept over the years. Warfield's pain is evident when Torrey takes that carefully honed theological principle and turns it into an excuse for random proof-texting. Yet that pain did not prevent Warfield from approving the intentions and an occasional result of that debased form of induction.

R. A. Torrey (1856–1928), a graduate of Yale College and Divinity School and a younger colleague of D. L. Moody, was the first superintendent of the institution that came to be called Moody Bible Institute in Chicago. He conducted extensive evangelistic tours in the United States and abroad, and he also served as dean of the Bible Institute of Los Angeles from 1912 to 1924.[2]

The following is Warfield's review of Torrey's *What the Bible Teaches* (Chicago: Fleming H. Revell, 1898), in *Presbyterian and Reformed Review* 39 (July 1899): 562–64.

IT WOULD BE a very precious book that gave us "a thorough and comprehensive study of all the Bible has to say concerning the great doctrines of

---

1. A later illustration was J. Gresham Machen's relationship with the evangelist Billy Sunday, whom Machen wanted to see preach in Princeton, in spite of some reservations about popular revivalism in general; Stonehouse, *J. Gresham Machen*, pp. 222–28.

2. On Torrey, see Sandeen, *Roots of Fundamentalism, passim;* Marsden, *Fundamentalism and American Culture, passim.*

which it treats." Needless to say, Mr. Torrey's useful volume hardly fulfills to the letter this great promise of the title-page—which forms therefore something of a stumbling block at the threshold of his serviceable but somewhat desultory collection of Bible-readings on doctrinal topics. At the opening of his Preface, he explains more circumspectly that "it is not supposed for a moment that this book exhausts all the Bible has to say on the topics treated, much less that it takes up and exhausts every topic dealt with in the Bible." Of course, it does not. There are many of the great doctrines of the Bible which are not treated at all here—such as all those that cluster around the fact of the election of grace and all those that belong under the locus of the Church and the means of grace. And the treatment accorded to the doctrines selected for study moves far too much on the surface to have plumbed the depths of any one of them.

But though the Preface sets the title-page right on this point, it raises a difficulty of its own in the emphatic claim it puts in for the method of the work as being in an especial sense "inductive." The chief gain that has been made by doctrinal study of late years is its acquisition of a more inductive method. That is the significance of the birth of the new discipline of "Biblical Theology." Whereas there has been a tendency hitherto to formulate doctrine on the basis of a general impression derived from a cursory survey of the Scriptural material or on the basis of the specific study of a few outstanding texts isolated from their contexts, and then to seek support for it in more or less detached passages; it is becoming more usual now to rise from the thorough understanding of the teaching of complete sections of Scripture to larger and larger groups until an insight into the doctrinal whole is attained—in the unity of its historical development and the harmony of its varied expression. Mr. Torrey's method is altogether alien to this truly inductive process. He begins with isolated passages, collected under a purely formal *schema* already present explicitly or implicitly in his mind: and this is not made induction merely by arranging the texts first and the propositions which they support second, on the printed page. We have not the remotest intention of suggesting that Mr. Torrey is not striving to give the pure teaching of the Bible in these propositions; neither do we doubt that he succeeds in giving the pure teaching of the Bible in the large majority of them. We are merely animadverting on the claim put in that the method pursued in this volume has some distinguishing right to the name of "inductive." That it certainly has not.

The fact is that Mr. Torrey's method is undistinguishable from the ordinary method of the exercise known as "Bible-readings."[3] What he has given us is just a series of sublimated "Bible-readings" on doctrinal topics. Any appreciative estimate of the book must proceed on the clear recognition of this fact. If we are to regard it as a contribution to dogmatics, we must needs look upon it as moving over the

---

3. "Bible-readings" were services devoted exclusively to the linked reading of passages from Scripture. On these gatherings, see Timothy P. Weber, "The Two-Edged Sword: The Fundamentalist Use of the Bible," in *The Bible in America*, p. 110, where Torrey's *What the Bible Teaches* also is mentioned.

surface of its subject—as incomplete, insufficient and occasionally erroneous. If, on the other hand, we may accept it for what it is—a series of thoughtful Bible-readings on selected doctrinal subjects, including especially the topics of the Father, the Son, the Holy Spirit—we may gladly recognize it as an admirable example of an admirable method of teaching, from which we may all learn much. Of course the limitations of its method characterize it: and of course the limitations inherent in the author's equipment and doctrinal views condition it. Even in his Bible-readings, naturally, Mr. Torrey still teaches his Arminianizing theory of redemption, and his Keswick doctrine of the Baptism of the Spirit, as well as his burning, evangelical blood-theology.[4] As is also, perhaps, natural in Bible-readings, his exposition runs much on the surface of things and is rather external and at points even shallow. We read occasionally thoroughly misleading things: as, for example, when we are told that all of God's gifts are at the disposal of all who wish them, for there is no respect of persons with Him (p. 379), or that "numbers belong primarily to the physical world," so that the category of number can be only with difficulty applied to spiritual being (p. 20).

In such deep things as the Trinity, the Person of Christ, the idea of Eternity, Predestination and Freedom—Mr. Torrey's plumbet does not reach the bottom. But though he does not know how to discriminate between the extraordinary and ordinary gifts of the Holy Spirit and so leads his readers into very muddy water indeed, as to spiritual gifts and guidance, he does know the fundamental thing about the Holy Spirit—that He is a Person—and how to present this truth in a form so striking, so true and so enheartening (p. 225), that we should like to see his three paragraphs on it bound as a frontlet between the eyes of every Christian teacher. And though he does not know all the secrets of the divine dealing with man, as they are revealed in the Word, he does know that most fundamental secret of all—that the Holy God hates sin and punishes it because it is sin—and how to set forth God's holy hatred of sin in language as moving to the conscience as it is faithful to the Word of God (p. 39). And the best thing about the book is that it is this element of evangelical religion, laying hold of the very core of the Gospel, that constitutes its main contents. As we read, we see there are many things that Mr. Torrey has yet to learn concerning the great doctrines that the Bible teaches, but we see also gladly that there are many things taught by the Bible that he has learned and knows how to teach the Christian world, and we gladly put ourselves in these at his feet.

---

4. The Keswick Convention was founded in 1875 during Moody's successful evangelistic tour of England by the vicar of Keswick. Annual gatherings followed where the emphasis rested on prayer, the indwelling presence of the Holy Spirit, and "practical holiness." Keswick gatherings sprang up rapidly in the United States and elsewhere. Warfield was nervous about Keswick, because, as he saw it, the movement stressed a subjective concept of the Holy Spirit over the objective resources of Scripture.

29

Herman Bavinck

1903

Warfield read the works of his contemporary Calvinists, the Dutch theologians Abraham Kuyper (1837–1920) and Herman Bavinck (1854–1921), with mingled delight and exasperation. When he provided an introduction in 1898 to the English translation of Kuyper's *Encyclopedia of Sacred Theology,* Warfield praised "the depth of his insight, the breadth of his outlook, the thoroughness of his method, the comprehensiveness of his survey, the intensity of his conviction, the eloquence of his language, the directness of his style, the pith and wealth of his illustrations, the force, completeness, winningness of his presentation."[1] And he had similar words of praise for Bavinck and the other Dutch theologians under Kuyper's influence.

When, however, Warfield examined the Kuyperian approach to apologetics, he found it seriously lacking. George Marsden does not exaggerate when he concludes that Warfield was "utterly mystified by this approach."[2] The selection below, from 1903, explains in some detail why Warfield took exception to the Dutchmen. In the same year, for another work, he wrote, "It is easy, of course, to say that a Christian man must take his standpoint not *above* the Scriptures, but *in* the Scriptures. He very certainly must. But surely he must first *have* Scripture authenticated to him as such, before he can take his standpoint in them."[3] With these words Warfield restated a basic Princeton position that stretched back to Alexander's inaugural (Selection 4). Only Charles Hodge among the major Princeton theologians had ever assumed that humans did not possess the abilities in themselves to judge such issues correctly (Selection 6 and its introduction). And he expressed such opinions only some of the time. For the most part, the Princeton Theology rested on its belief that the world of facts was open alike to all people who could be convinced of God's existence and the truth of Scripture by the proper reasoning of a redeemed thinker. The weight of nearly a century's tradition lay behind Warfield's expression, in the excerpt below, that "faith, in all its forms, is a conviction of truth, founded as such, of course, on

1. Warfield, "Introductory Note," in Abraham Kuyper, *Encyclopedia of Sacred Theology* (1898), reprinted as *Principles of Sacred Theology* (Grand Rapids: Baker, 1980), p. xii.
2. Marsden, *Fundamentalism and American Culture,* p. 115, with an excellent general discussion, pp. 115–16.
3. Warfield, "Introduction" to Francis R. Beattie's *Apologetics: or the Rational Vindication of Christianity* (Richmond, Va.: Presbyterian Committee of Publication, 1903); from SSWW II: 98.

evidence. . . . Christianity . . . has been placed in the world to *reason* its way to the dominion of the world."

By contrast, Abraham Kuyper was impressed much more by the difference in approach to systematic thinking between those who were Christians and those who were not. In his *Encyclopedia* Kuyper used the term "palingenesis," which Warfield also employs below, to designate the position growing out of Christian faith or the New Birth.[4] From the standpoint of "palingenesis," the world—especially the world that is important to theologians—is marked by "the four phenomena: (1) of personal regeneration; and (2) of its corresponding inspiration; (3) of the final restoration of all things; and (4) of its corresponding manifestation of God's power in miracles."[5] Yet these "phenomena" are precisely what the nonbeliever assumes cannot be true. Kuyper admitted that "this antithesis" affected natural science only a little, but he thought that its effect on the doing of theology was immense. Thus, for him, apologetics was not the ground of faith as it came into existence but a necessary extension of faith as it encountered the world. This difference of opinion concerning apologetics continues to exercise Reformed theologians to this day.[6]

The selection which follows includes the major portion of B. B. Warfield's review of Herman Bavinck's *De Zekerheid des Geloofs [The Certainty of Faith],* in *Princeton Theological Review,* 1 (January 1903): 138–43; as taken from SSWW, II: 117–22.

I T IS A STANDING matter of surprise to us that the school which Dr. Bavinck so brilliantly represents should be tempted to make so little of Apologetics. When we read, for instance, the really beautiful exposition which Dr. Kuyper has given us in his *Encyclopedia of Theology* of the relation of sin and regeneration to science, we cannot understand why he does not magnify instead of minifying the value of Apologetics. Perhaps the explanation is to be found in a tendency to make the contrast between the "two kinds of science"—that of nature and that of palingenesis—too absolute. There are "two kinds of men"—men under the power of sin and men under the power of the palingenesis;[7] and the product of their intellection will naturally give us "two kinds of science": but the difference between the two is after all not properly described as a difference in *kind—gradus non mutant speciem.* For a critical estimate of Dr. Kuyper's view on this matter we

4. "Palingenesis" itself means "renewal by or as if by rebirth" and has been used also as a synonym for Christian baptism.

5. Kuyper, *Encyclopedia/Principles of Sacred Theology,* p. 225. The section, pp. 219–227, "The Influence of Palingenesis upon our View of Theology and its Relation to the Other Sciences," is most helpful. For a general contemporary discussion, see Herman Bavinck, "Recent Dogmatic Theology in the Netherlands," *Presbyterian and Reformed Review,* 3 (April 1892), 209–228, especially pp. 223–228.

6. See, for example, the discussion in Geehan, ed., *Jerusalem and Athens,* pp. 154–171, 275–305, 420–427.

7. On "palingenesis," see note 4 above.

should obviously take our start from an exact conception of the effects of sin on man. Sin clearly has not destroyed or altered in its essential nature any one of man's faculties, although (since it has affected *homo totus et omnis*) it has affected the operation of them all. The depraved man neither reasons, nor feels, nor wills as he ought. The products of his action as a scientific thinker cannot possibly escape this influence, though they are affected in different degrees and through different channels, as Dr. Kuyper lucidly points out, in the several "sciences," in accordance with the nature of their object. Nevertheless there is a question here rather of perfection than of kind of performance: it is "science" that is produced by the sinful object even though imperfect science—falling away from the ideal, here, there, and elsewhere, on account of all sorts of deflecting influences, entering it at all points of the process. The science of sinful man is thus a substantive part of the abstract science produced by the ideal subject, the general human consciousness, though a less valuable part than it would be without sin.

Regeneration, now, is not in the first instance the removal of sin; the regenerated man remains a sinner. It is only after his sanctification is completed that the contrast between him and the sinner can be thought to become absolute, and not till then could in any case the contrast between the intellection of the one and of the other become absolute. Meanwhile the regenerated man remains a sinner: no new faculties have been inserted into him by regeneration; and the old faculties common to man in all his states have been only measurably restored to their proper functioning. He is in no position therefore to produce a science different in *kind* from that produced by sinful man: the science of palingenesis is only a part of the science of sinful humanity, though no doubt its best part: and only along with it can it enter as a constituent part into that ideal science which the composite human subject is producing in its ceaseless effort to embrace in mental grasp the ideal object, that is to say, all that is. Indeed, even if palingenesis had completed its work it may be doubted whether the contrast between the science produced by the two classes of men could be absolute. Even sinful men and sinless men are alike fundamentally men; and being both men, they know fundamentally alike. There is ideally but one science, the subject of which is the human spirit, and the object, all that is. Meanwhile, as things are, the human spirit attains to this science only in part and by slow accretions and through many partial and erroneous constructions. Men work side by side at the common task, and the common edifice takes gradually fuller and truer outlines. As Dr. Kuyper finely says himself, in the conflict of perceptions and opinions those of the strongest energy and clearest thought finally prevail. Why is not the palingenesis to be conceived simply as preparing those stronger and clearer spirits, whose thought shall finally prevail? It is not a different kind of science that they are producing: it is not even the same kind but as part of a different edifice of truth. It is only the better scientific outlook, and the better scientific product, striving in conflict with the product of fellow workers to build itself into one edifice of truth, which rises slowly because of sin but surely because of palingenesis.

Only in God's mind, of course, does science lie perfect—the perfect comprehension of all that is, in its organic completeness. In the mind of perfected humanity, the perfected ectypal science shall lie. In the mind of sinful humanity struggling here below, there can lie only a broken reflection of the object, a reflection which is rather a deflection. The great task of science lies in completing the edifice and correcting this deflection. Sinful man cannot accomplish it. But he makes the effort and attains his measure of success, a success that varies inversely with the rank of the sciences. The intrusion of regeneration prepares man to build better, and ever more truly as the effects of regeneration increase intensively and extensively, until the end comes when the regenerated universe becomes the well-comprehended object of the science of the regenerated race. Now it would seem a grave mistake to separate the men of the palingenesis from the race, a part of which they are, and which is itself the object of the palingenesis. And no mistake could be greater than to lead them to decline to bring their principles into conflict with those of the unregenerate in the prosecution of the common task of man. They will meet with dull opposition, with active scorn, with decisive rejection at the hands of the world: but thereby they shall win their victory. Just as the better science ever in the end secures its recognition, so palingenetic science, which is the better science, will certainly win its way to ultimate recognition. And it is in this fact that the vindication of Apologetics lies. Here too the "man of stronger and purer thought"—even though that he has it is of God alone—"will prevail in the end." The task of the Christian is surely to continue hopefully to urge "his stronger and purer thought" in all its details on the attention of men. It is not true that he cannot soundly prove his position. It is not true that the arguments he urges are not sufficient to validate the Christian religion. It is not even true that the minds of sinful men are inaccessible to his "evidences": though, in the sense of the proverb, "convinced against their will they remain of the same opinion still." On the contrary, men (all of whose minds are after all of the same essential structure with his own, though less illuminated than his) will not be able to resist or gainsay his determinations. He must use and press the advantage that God has given him. He must insist and insist again that his and not the opposing results shall be built into the slowly rising fabric of truth. Thus will he serve, if not obviously his own generation, yet truly all the generations of men.

We are not, we repeat, absurdly arguing that Apologetics will of itself make a man a Christian. But neither can it be said that the proclaimed gospel itself can do that. Only the Spirit of life can communicate life to a dead soul. But we are arguing that Apologetics has its part to play in the Christianizing of the world: and that this part is not a small part: nor is it merely a subsidiary or a defensive part—as if its one end were to protect an isolated body of Christians from annoyance from the great surrounding world. It has a primary part to play and a conquering part. The individual, to be sure, does not need to become a trained apologist first, and only after and as a result of that a Christian. The individual is prone vastly to overestimate himself: it ordinarily does not require the whole "body of evidences" to convince him. But surely he does require that kind and amount of evidence which is requisite to convince him before he can really be convinced: and faith, in all its forms, is a conviction of truth, founded as such, of course, on evidence. And this kind and amount of the evidences constitutes "Apologetics" for him and performs the functions of Apologetics for him. When we speak of Apologetics as a science, however, we have our eye not on the individual but on the thinking world. In the face of the world, with its opposing points of view and its tremendous energy of thought and incredible fertility in attack and defense, Christianity must think through and organize its, not defense merely, but assault. It has been placed in the world to *reason* its way to the dominion of the world. And it is by reasoning its way that it has come to its kingship.[8] By reasoning it will gather to itself all its own. And by reasoning it will put its enemies under its feet.

Let it not be imagined that with all this we have done away with the "certainty of faith" as distinguished from "certainty of knowledge." We have only opened the way to a proper appreciation of the difference between the two. This difference is obviously the difference between faith and knowledge. And the difference between faith and knowledge is not that knowledge rests on evidence and faith does not, or that knowledge rests on sufficient evidence and faith does not, or that knowledge rests on grounds objectively or universally valid and faith does not. The difference is only that they rest on different kinds of evidence—knowledge on "sight" and faith on "testimony." The whole question of a "certainty of faith" turns, therefore, simply on the question whether testimony is adapted to produce conviction in the human mind, and is capable of producing a conviction which is clear and firm—a *firma certaque persuasio*. If we judge that it is, we shall have no choice but to range alongside of the various forms of "certainty of knowledge," whether resting on sense-perception, immediate intuition, or rational demonstration, a "certainty of faith" also, resting on convincing testimony. This "certainty of faith" has nothing in it particularly mysterious; it is no more "incommunicable" than the "certainty of knowledge" and no more "subjective." Testimony that is "objectively" valid for the establishment of any fact should be "subjectively" valid to establish it in the forum of any mind; and only such testimony should be valid to any mind whatever. But a conviction grounded on testimony is obviously of a different variety from a conviction grounded on "sight" and will have characteristics of its own. Chief among these is that in it the element of "trust," which is of course present in all forms of conviction (for knowledge itself rests on trust), is peculiarly prominent. In this fact only, so far as we can see, lies whatever relative justification it is possible to give to the notion that the certainty of faith is of a "lower" order than the certainty of knowledge, and bears a "more subjective" character. It does not appear, however, that either of these epithets is properly applied to it. There seems to be no reason why—if testimony is adapted to produce conviction at all—the conviction produced by testimony may not be as strong and as "objectively valid" as that produced by "sight" itself; that is, why it should not rise into "certainty." For "the certainty of faith" is obviously no more the product of faith than "the certainty of

8. Warfield repeats almost these same words in "Introduction" to Beattie's *Apologetics*, ssww, II: 99.

knowledge" is the product of knowledge. Strictly speaking, it is just that faith itself raised to its eminent degree. No doubt, if by "certainty," "assurance," we mean the emotional accompaniments of the conviction—the rest, confidence, comfort, happiness, we find in it—it would be the product of faith; but so would the "certainty of knowledge" under such an understanding be the product of knowledge. In itself, however, it is just the conviction itself, and its validity depends only on the validity of the testimony on which it is grounded. If that testimony is really adequate to the establishment of the fact, the conviction founded on that testimony is as valid as any knowledge founded on "sight" can be. . . .

30

William Newton Clarke
1910

Into the twentieth century Warfield maintained the Princeton conviction that the
Bible was the sole reliable guide to the history of God's activity in Christ and,
thus, to the entire Christian faith. In this defense Warfield carried high the banner
of Alexander and the Hodges. The excerpt below offers an example of how
Warfield reacted to those who wished to maintain something of the old Jesus but
with new methods of biblical criticism.

William Newton Clarke (1841–1912), whose book Warfield attacks, was a
Baptist minister and theologian who had moved in his life from believing (with the
Princetonians) that the Bible was God's unique propositional revelation to a more
modern opinion that Scripture represented a refined record of religious encounter with God. His book, *Sixty Years with the Bible: A Record of Experience,*
charted that evolving perception of Scripture. Clarke was known in American
theological circles especially for *An Outline of Christian Theology* (1898) which
was the first full-scale American treatment of theology from a consistently
modern position.[1]

The following is the conclusion of Warfield's review of William Newton Clarke,
Sixty Years with the Bible (New York: Charles Scribner's Sons, 1909), in *Princeton Theological Review* 8 (January 1910): 165–67.

O NE OF THE effects on the reader of the impression of mere drifting
which Dr. Clarke's narrative conveys, is a feeling of the insecurity of his final position. This position is one of perfect freedom over against the Bible, but at the same
time one which in some sense finds in the Bible the revelation of God in Jesus
Christ. When defining his attitude as a theologian towards the Bible (p. 210), he says:
"According to the principle that I accepted and acted upon, a system of Christian
theology has God for its center, the spirit of Jesus for its organizing principle, and
congenial truth from within the Bible and from without for its material." This is, of
course, to make very little of the Bible in our theologizing. Not all its declarations
are to be worked into our system and none of them have "the element of finality."

1. On Clarke, see William R. Hutchison, *The Modernist Impulse in American Protestantism*
(Cambridge: Harvard University Press, 1976), pp. 117–121 and *passim;* and Wacker, "The Demise of
Biblical Civilization," in *The Bible in America,* pp. 128–130.

Only such of them as are "congenial," that is, as are "congenial to the spirit of Jesus" as we conceive that spirit, are to be used by us; and these only along with any other notions which we may consider "congenial" to that spirit which we may think discernible outside the Bible. Thus the Bible is deprived of all uniqueness as a source of theology and as "authority" is set altogether aside. But, at least in Dr. Clarke's view, that "spirit of Jesus" which he makes the "organizing principle" of "Christian theology" is the gift of the Bible to us. He even declares (p. 253): "It is certain that the Bible gives us knowledge of Jesus, and that Jesus gives us knowledge of God, and that God as Jesus reveals him is the true light of life. Our sacred book is thus our guide to Jesus, to God, and to life divine." In so saying a certain uniqueness seems to be reserved to the Bible in its relation to our theologizing. We should be glad to think so; but we are constrained to add that we miss any solid grounding for even such a uniqueness. Dr. Clarke assures his readers, no doubt, that the faith that the Bible gives us the knowledge of Jesus "has been established in long human experience, and can be trusted." But he leaves them in grave uncertainty what amount of knowledge of Jesus the Bible gives us, and what kind of Jesus we may confidently derive from it. Dr. Clarke has committed himself far too deeply to the "new critical views" of the Bible to be able simply to take off of the face of Scripture as it stands the Jesus which lies open to view on it. And if he did, this Jesus by His whole attitude towards "the Scriptures" as truly as by His express declarations regarding them would compel him to retrace his steps and to accord to the Scriptures that plenary authority as a witness to fact and doctrine alike which he has discarded. But if he is not to take off from the face of Scripture the Jesus that lies openly there, what Jesus does the Bible give true "knowledge of"? The "liberal theologians" of the last generation, discarding John in favor of the Synoptists and the other Synoptists in favor of Mark, and discriminating in Mark between the tradition of which he is the bearer and the theology which he superinduced upon it, managed to find "knowledge" in the Bible of a Jesus who fairly reflected in his teaching their own liberal thought. Our twentieth-century "eschatologists," working in their own way on the Biblical text, find "knowledge" in the Bible of an "ecstatic Jesus," the fair representative of first-century Judaistic fanaticism. Which Jesus is it, or what Jesus is it, that Dr. Clarke finds that his eminently untrustworthy Bible gives him "knowledge" of—who in turn is to give us our knowledge of God that is to stand as our test of truth—in the Bible and out of it? Obviously our conception of Jesus will depend on the view we take of the Scriptures from which we derive that conception; and if we are now to turn around and make our view of the contents of Scripture depend on the conception of Jesus which we derive from our reconstructed Scriptures, we seem to be in danger of falling into a circular movement of thought which promises us no very obvious issue. It would seem that we ought to find a starting point somewhere.

The fact appears to be that simple drifting scarcely offers us a safe guide for our theology or for our view of the Bible. We may follow Dr. Clarke's driftage with a profound interest and a deep sympathy. But the mere fact that he has drifted through these stages and feels comfortable and assured at the end of them, scarcely commends them to us as stages of opinion we should like ourselves to drift through or an issue at which we should ourselves like to arrive. We have an old-fashioned prejudice for reasoned views of truth; and we are in our hearts convinced that the Jesus which the Bible gives us is the Jesus of the orthodox faith. We are not unaware of the difficulties which attend both convictions. But we never expect to attain convictions on any matters of importance which are not attended with difficulties. And we prefer to rest our convictions on their own proper evidence and to leave the difficulties to be dealt with in detail as occasion offers and opportunity serves. If we could be convinced of nothing which offered difficulties to our faith, we could scarcely believe in God, or Man, or Salvation. The hardest thing to believe about the Bible, to our thinking, is that it can be a different kind of a book from what Jesus and His Apostles declare it to be. And the most difficult task we can conceive anyone setting himself is that of holding to the Jesus of the Bible and at the same time not holding to the Bible of Jesus. It is a task we may feel sure has never been accomplished. He who no longer holds to the Bible of Jesus—the word of which cannot be broken—will be found on examination no longer to hold to the Jesus of the Bible. The new Bible he has constructed for himself gives him a new Jesus, and his whole system of truth, brought into harmony with what he considers the spirit of this new Jesus, is eccentric to the system of truth which is taught us by the real Bible which is placed in our hands by the real Jesus, to whom it bears consentient witness.

31

Jonathan Edwards
and the New England Theology
1912

When Warfield was asked early in the century to write the article on Jonathan Edwards and New England theology for *Hastings' Encyclopedia of Religion and Ethics,* he had the opportunity to review once again the main Princeton complaints against New England. The essay began, however, with fulsome praise for Jonathan Edwards. Despite his "individualisms," Warfield held him to be a powerful and consistent Calvinist. Like Charles Hodge before him (e.g., ST, II: 217), Warfield's own commitments to Common Sense prevented him from understanding Edwards completely. In particular, he did not see that Edwards's own careful use of reason was directed largely at liberating himself from the assumptions of the "age of reason" rather than aligning himself with it.[1] Still, Warfield honored Edwards as the greatest speculative thinker in the history of American Calvinism.

It was much otherwise when Warfield turned to the "Edwardeans" of later New England theology. For a century, the theologians at Princeton had roundly denounced New England's errors—where it had undermined the substitutionary theory of the atonement, underestimated the effects of Adam's fall, overvalued the natural capacities of human beings. Warfield here recapitulates these errors with a special focus on the "Pelagianizing" system of Nathaniel W. Taylor. In passing, it is intriguing to note how a change of perspective enabled Warfield to place a higher value on the work of Edwards Amasa Park than had Charles Hodge (Selection 17). From Warfield's point of view, with Calvinism of any variety at a premium in New England, Park's mediating position now had much to recommend it.

Notwithstanding his harsh judgments, Warfield's comments on the New England theologians lack the fire of Hodge's polemics. Warfield was now in a different situation, where European modernism and its American counterparts posed more serious threats to Protestant orthodoxy than the lingering errors of New England conservatives. In addition, Warfield was now living in an age where academic controversy and popular religious disputing had grown much further apart than they had been in Charles Hodge's day, when an attack on the errors of a popular revivalist (e.g., Finney) could grow into a full-blown exercise in

1. A near contemporary of Warfield who saw this in Edwards more clearly was Joseph Haroutunian, *Piety Versus Moralism: The Passing of the New England Theology* (New York: Henry Holt, 1932). It is also the central theme of Norman Fiering, *Jonathan Edwards's Moral Thought and its British Context* (Chapel Hill: University of North Carolina, 1981).

detailed theology. This period was past. Even to Warfield, who had lived through
the last chapter of the great New-England-Princeton debates, the world seems
to have become a narrower place, the demands of academic theology more
exacting, the distance between church and academy considerably broader.

This selection is from B. B. Warfield, "Edwards and the New England Theology," *Encyclopedia of Religion and Ethics*, ed. James Hastings (1912), 5: 221-27;
as it appears in WBBW, Vol. IX: *Studies in Theology*, pp. 527-36. Again, names
mentioned in the essay receive short biographical descriptions in the index.

THE PECULIARITY OF Edwards' theological work is due to the union
in it of the richest religious sentiment with the highest intellectual powers. He was
first of all a man of faith, and it is this that gives its character to his whole life and all
its products; but his strong religious feeling had at its disposal a mental force and
logical acuteness of the first order; he was at once deeply emotional, and, as Ezra
Stiles called him, a "strong reasoner." His analytical subtlety has probably never
been surpassed; but with it was combined a broad grasp of religious truth which
enabled him to see it as a whole, and to deal with its several parts without exaggeration and with a sense of their relations in the system. The system to which he gave
his sincere adhesion, and to the defense of which, against the tendencies which
were in his day threatening to undermine it, he consecrated all his powers, was
simply Calvinism. From this system as it had been expounded by its chief representatives he did not consciously depart in any of its constitutive elements. The
breadth and particularity of his acquaintance with it in its classical expounders,
and the completeness of his adoption of it in his own thought, are frequently
underestimated. There is a true sense in which he was a man of thought rather
than of learning. There were no great libraries accessible in Western Massachusetts
in the middle of the eighteenth century. His native disposition to reason out for
himself the subjects which were presented to his thought was reinforced by his
habits of study; it was his custom to develop on paper, to its furthest logical consequences, every topic of importance to which his attention was directed. He lived in
the "age of reason," and was in this respect a true child of his time. In the task
which he undertook, furthermore, an appeal to authority would have been useless;
it was uniquely to the court of reason that he could hale the adversaries of the
Calvinistic system. Accordingly it is only in his more didactic—as distinguished
from controversial—treatise on "Religious Affections," that Edwards cites with any
frequency earlier writers in support of his positions. The reader must guard himself, however, from the illusion that Edwards was not himself conscious of the
support of earlier writers beneath him. His acquaintance with the masters of the
system of thought he was defending, for example, was wide and minute. Amesius
and Wollebius had been his textbooks at college. The well-selected library at Yale,
we may be sure, had been thoroughly explored by him; at the close of his divinity
studies, he speaks of the reading of "doctrinal books or books of controversy" as if

it were part of his daily business. As would have been expected, he fed himself on the great Puritan divines, and formed not merely his thought but his life upon them. We find him in his youth, for instance, diligently using Manton's "Sermons on the 119th Psalm" as a spiritual guide; and in his rare allusions to authorities in his works, he betrays familiarity with such writers as William Perkins, John Preston, Thomas Blake, Anthony Burgess, Stephen Charnock, John Flavel, Theophilus Gale, Thomas Goodwin, John Owen, Samuel Rutherford, Thomas Shephard, Richard Sibbes, John Smith the Platonist, and Samuel Clark the Arian. Even his contemporaries he knew and estimated at their true values: Isaac Watts and Philip Doddridge as a matter of course; and also Thomas Boston, the scheme of thought of whose "View of the Covenant of Grace" he confessed he did not understand, but whose "Fourfold State of Man" he "liked exceedingly well." His Calvin he certainly knew thoroughly, though he would not swear in his words; and also his Turretin, whom he speaks of as "the great Turretine"; while van Mastricht he declares "much better" than even Turretin, "or," he adds with some fervor, "than any other book in the world, excepting the Bible, in my opinion." The close agreement of his teaching with that of the best esteemed Calvinistic divines is, therefore, both conscious and deliberate; his omission to appeal to them does not argue either ignorance or contempt; it is incident to his habitual manner and to the special task he was prosecuting. In point of fact, what he teaches is just the "standard" Calvinism in its completeness.

As an independent thinker, he is, of course, not without his individualisms, and that in conception no less than in expression. His explanation of the identity of the human race with its Head, founded as it is on a doctrine of personal identity which reduces it to an "arbitrary constitution" of God binding its successive moments together, is peculiar to himself.[2] In answering objects to the doctrine of Original Sin, he appeals at one point to Stapfer, and speaks, after him, in the language of that form of doctrine known as "mediate imputation." But this is only in order to illustrate his own view that all mankind are one as truly as and by the same kind of divine constitution that an individual life is one in its consecutive moments. Even in this immediate context he does not teach the doctrine of "mediate imputation," insisting rather that, Adam and his posterity being in the strictest sense one, in them no less than in him "the guilt arising from the first existing of a depraved disposition" cannot at all be distinguished from "the guilt of Adam's first sin": and elsewhere throughout the treatise he speaks in the terms of the common Calvinistic doctrine. His most marked individualism, however, lay in the region of philosophy rather than of theology. In an essay on "The Nature of True Virtue," he develops, in opposition to the view that all virtue may be reduced ultimately to self-love, an

---

2. Edwards developed these views in his work, *Original Sin* (1758). Warfield goes on to discuss "mediate imputation," which is the idea that Adam passed on his corrupt nature through natural generation, so that all children of Adam are born as corrupt and therefore are considered guilty before God. This view, advocated by Jonathan Edwards, Jr., was opposed to the traditional Calvinistic (and Princeton) view that all humanity stood with Adam in condemnation before God, and that this forensic status was the crucial element in original sin.

eccentric theory of virtue as consisting in love to being in general. But of this again we hear nothing elsewhere in his works, though it became germinal for the New England theology of the next age. Such individualisms in any case are in no way characteristic of his teaching. He strove after no show of originality. An independent thinker he certainly claimed to be, and "utterly disclaimed a dependence," say, "on Calvin," in the sense of "believing the doctrines he held because Calvin believed and taught them." This very disclaimer is, however, a proclamation of agreement with Calvin, though not as if he "believed everything just as Calvin taught"; he is only solicitous that he should be understood to be not a blind follower of Calvin, but a convinced defender of Calvinism. His one concern was, accordingly, not to improve on the Calvinism of the great expounders of the system, but to place the main elements of the Calvinistic system, as commonly understood, beyond cavil. His marvelous invention was employed, therefore, only in the discovery and development of the fullest and most convincing possible array of arguments in their favor. This is true even of his great treatise on the Will. This is, in the common judgment, the greatest of all his treatises, and the common judgment here is right. But the doctrine of this treatise is precisely the doctrine of the Calvinistic schoolmen. "The novelty of the treatise," we have been well told long ago, "lies not in the position it takes and defends, but in the multitude of proofs, the fecundity and urgency of the arguments by which he maintains it." Edwards' originality thus consists less in the content of his thought than in his manner of thinking. He enters into the great tradition which had come down to him, and "infuses it with his personality and makes it live," and "the vitality of his thought gives to its product the value of a unique creation." The effect of Edwards' labors was quite in the line of his purpose, and not disproportionate to his greatness. The movement against Calvinism which was overspreading the land was in a great measure checked, and the elimination of Calvinism as a determining factor in the thought of New England, which seemed to be imminent as he wrote, was postponed for more than a hundred years. . . .

It was Edwards' misfortune that he gave his name to a party; and to a party which, never in perfect agreement with him in its doctrinal ideas, finished by becoming the earnest advocate of (as it has been sharply expressed) "a set of opinions which he gained his chief celebrity in demolishing." The affiliation of this party with Edwards was very direct. "Bellamy . . . and Hopkins," says G. P. Fisher, tracing the descent, "were pupils of Edwards; from Hopkins, West derived his theology; Smalley studied with Bellamy, and Emmons with Smalley."[3] But the inheritance of the party from Edwards showed itself much more strongly on the practical than on the doctrinal side. Its members were the heirs of his revivalist zeal and of his awakening preaching; they also imitated his attempt to purify the Church by discipline and strict guarding of the Lord's Table—in a word, to "restore the Church to its Puritan ideal of a congregation of saints." Pressing to extremes in

3. Warfield's note: "'A Discourse Commemorative of the History of the Church of Christ in Yale College during the First Century of its Existence,' New Haven, 1858, p. 36."

both matters, as followers will, the "Edwardeans" or "New Divinity" men became a ferment in the churches of New England, and, creating discussion and disturbances everywhere, gradually won their way to dominance. Meanwhile their doctrinal teaching was continually suffering change. As Fisher puts it, "in the process of defending the established faith, they were led to recast it in new forms and to change its aspect." Only, it was not merely the form and aspect of their inherited faith, but its substance, that they were steadily transforming. Accordingly, Fisher proceeds to explain that what on this side constituted their common character was not so much a common doctrine as a common method: "the fact that their views were the result of independent reflection and were maintained on philosophical grounds." Here, too, they were followers of Edwards; but in their exaggeration of his rational method, without his solid grounding in the history of thought, they lost continuity with the past and became the creators of a "New England theology" which it is only right frankly to describe as provincial.

It is a far cry from Jonathan Edwards the Calvinist, defending with all the force of his unsurpassed reasoning powers the doctrine of a determined will, and commending a theory of virtue which identified it with general benevolence, to Nathaniel W. Taylor the Pelagianizer, building his system upon the doctrine of the power to the contrary as its foundation stone, and reducing all virtue ultimately to self-love. Taylor's teaching, in point of fact, was in many respects the exact antipodes of Edwards', and very fairly reproduced the congeries of tendencies which the latter considered it his life-work to withstand. Yet Taylor looked upon himself as an "Edwardean," though in him the outcome of the long development received its first appropriate designation—the "New Haven Divinity." Its several successive phases were bound together by the no doubt external circumstance that they were taught in general by men who had received their training at New Haven.

The growth of the New Divinity to that dominance in the theological thought of New England from which it derives its claim to be called "the New England Theology" was gradual, though somewhat rapid. Samuel Hopkins tells us that at the beginning—in 1756—there were not more than four or five "who espoused the sentiments which since have been called 'Edwardean,' and 'New Divinity'; and since, after some improvement was made upon them, 'Hopkintonian,' or 'Hopkinsian' sentiments." The younger Edwards still spoke of them in 1777 as a small party. In 1787, Ezra Stiles, chafing under their growing influence and marking the increasing divergence of views among themselves, fancied he saw their end approaching. In this he was mistaken: the New Divinity, in the person of Timothy Dwight, succeeded him as President of Yale College, and through a long series of years was infused into generation after generation of students. The "confusions" Stiles observed were, however, real; or, rather, the progressive giving way of the so-called Edwardeans to those tendencies of thought to which they were originally set in opposition. The younger Edwards drew up a careful account of what he deemed the (ten) "Improvements in Theology made by President Edwards and those who have followed his course of thought." Three of the most cardinal of these he does not pretend were introduced by Edwards, attributing them simply to those whom he calls Edwards' "followers."[4] These are the substitution of the Governmental (Grotian) for the Satisfaction doctrine of the Atonement, in the accomplishment of which he himself, with partial forerunners in Bellamy and West, as the chief agent; the discarding of the doctrine of the imputation of sin in favor of the view that men are condemned for their own personal sin only—a contention which was made in an extreme form by Nathaniel Emmons, who confined all moral quality to acts of volition, and afterwards became a leading element in Nathaniel W. Taylor's system; and the perversion of Edwards' distinction between "natural" and "moral" inability so as to ground on the "natural" ability of the unregenerate, after the fashion introduced by Samuel Hopkins—a theory of the capacities and duties of men without the Spirit, which afterwards, in the hands of Nathaniel W. Taylor, became the core of a new Pelagianizing system.

The external victory of the New Divinity in New England was marked doubtless by the election of Timothy Dwight to the Presidency of Yale College (1795); and certainly it could have found no one better fitted to commend it to moderate men; probably no written system of theology has ever enjoyed wider acceptance than Dwight's "Sermons." But after Dwight came Taylor, and in the teaching of the latter the downward movement of the New Divinity ran out into a system which turned, as on its hinge, upon the Pelagianizing doctrines of the native sinlessness of the race, the plenary ability of the sinner to renovate his own soul, and the self-love or the desire for happiness as the spring of all voluntary action. From this extreme some reaction was inevitable, and the history of the so-called "New England Theology" closes with the moderate reaction of the teaching of Edwards A. Park. Park was of that line of theological descent which came through Hopkins, Emmons, and Woods; but he sought to incorporate into his system all that seemed to him to be the results of New England thinking for the century which preceded him, not excepting the extreme positions of Taylor himself. Reverting so far from Taylor as to return to perhaps a somewhat more deterministic doctrine of the will, he was able to rise above Taylor in his doctrines of election and regeneration, and to give to the general type of thought which he represented a lease of life for another generation. But, with the death of Park in 1900, the history of "New England Theology" seems to come to an end.

4. These are the errors which so exercised the Princetonians, especially Charles Hodge in his long polemical career.

Archibald Alexander's Philosophical Sources for His Lecture, "Nature and Evidence of Truth," October 1812

AT THE CONCLUSION of his 1812 manuscript on epistemology Alexander listed at least some of the reading that helped shape the lecture. The hand and ink at this point in the manuscript (housed in the Speer Library of Princeton Theological Seminary) seem to be the same as those of the actual lecture itself, so with some confidence it may be said that Alexander had perused at least these works before embarking on his career at the seminary. The following is a transcription of Alexander's "bibliography" to which I have added numbers in the left margin to facilitate the brief comments below. (I have not reproduced Alexander's irregular underscoring.)

On the subjects treated in this lecture consult:

1. Locke on the Understanding
2. Beattie on Truth
3. Reid on the Mind
4. ——— on the Intellectual and active powers of man
5. Buffier's First Truths
6. Oswald on Common Sense
7. Berkeley on Human Knowledge
8. Encyclop. Brit. Sit. Metaphysics
9. Velthusius De Initiis Primo
10. Philosophiae juxta fundamenta
11. Clarissimi Cartesii
12. Duncan's Logic
13. Stewart's Philosophy of the mind
14. Watt's Improvement of the mind
15. ——— Logic
16. Descartes' Meditations

Alexander's reading divides itself naturally into four categories. In the first are the seminal works of early modern philosophy, René Descartes (1596-1650), *Meditations on First Philosophy* of 1641 (16), and John Locke (1632-1704), *An Essay concerning Human Understanding* of 1690 (1). Although Alexander frowned upon Descartes' attempt to *prove* his own existence, he nonetheless followed Cartesian paths in building epistemology upon sense data and native reasoning rather than on received traditions or divine revelation. Alexander was more indebted to Locke whose theories of perception and reasoning are foundational in this lecture. To those two works could be added Bishop George Berkeley (1685-1753), *Treatise concerning the Principles of Human Knowledge* of 1710 (7). Berkeley's extension of Locke's ideas into a thorough-going idealism was one of the spectres which Alexander sought to exorcise.

By far the larger share of Alexander's reading, however, was made up of works from the Scottish school of Common Sense. Of the 17 works listed in this "bibliography" (Alexander included two works under #4), at least 8 and probably 9 fit into this category. Most important philosophically were the titles by Thomas Reid (1710-1796), *Inquiry into the Human Mind on the Principles of Common Sense* of 1764 (3), *Essays on the Intellectual Powers of Man* of 1785, and *Essays on the Active Powers of Man* of 1788 (both 4). Reid's most important successor, Dugald Stewart (1753-1828), contributed *Elements of the Philosophy of the Human Mind* of 1792 (13) to Alexander's reading. Alexander also drew on the popularizations of Common Sense Philosophy by James Beattie, *Essay on the Nature and Immutability of Truth in Opposition to Sophistry and Scepticism* of 1770 (2), and James Oswald, *An Appeal to Common Sense in Behalf of Religion*, published in two parts in 1766 and 1772 (6). The work of the French Jesuit Claude Buffier (1661-1737), *Traité des vérités premières* of 1717 (5), had anticipated some of Reid's arguments by making much of "common sense" in rebuffing various forms of scepticism. *The Elements of Logic* (12) by William Duncan, published in a Philadelphia edition in 1792, also came out of Reid's circle. The same may be said of the article on Metaphysics (8) from the *Encyclopedia Brittanica*, which was published in Scotland and which reflected the special influence of Dugald Stewart during the period when Alexander would have been reading it (its second edition appeared 1777-1784, third 1788-1794, and fourth 1801-1810). The modern study by S. A. Grave, *The Scottish Philosophy of Common Sense* (London: Oxford University Press, 1960; Westport, Conn.: Greenwood Press, 1973), is essential reading for the nonspecialist who desires to understand the intellectual world of which Alexander was so much a part.

A third category of Alexander's reading consists of less influential, miscellaneous works, including textbooks by the English hymn writer and nonconformist theologian, Isaac Watts (1674-1748), on *Logic*, 1725 (15), and *The Improvement of the Mind*, 1741 (14), which discussed study habits; what was apparently a compendium on *The Introductory Principles of Philosophy* (10); a work concerning Descartes (11); and an older theological work by the Calvinist theologian Lambert van Velthuysen (1622-1685), *On First Principles* (9).

The last category has no books. But it is clear from the content of Alexander's lecture that he had read David Hume with care (e.g., on the uncertainty of proof for cause and effect in *A Treatise of Human Nature*, 1739 and 1740, and on the improbability of miracles in *Enquiry Concerning Human Understanding*, 1748). The absence of Hume's works from this list, and of his name from the lecture, is especially striking inasmuch as Alexander devoted almost the entire exercise to a refutation, along lines suggested by Reid and his followers, of Hume's epistemological and religious scepticism.

Selective Bibliography

This bibliography is divided into the following sections:

1. Manuscripts
2. Bibliographies and Indexes
3. Major Books of the Major Princeton Theologians
   Archibald Alexander
   Charles Hodge
   Archibald Alexander Hodge
   Benjamin Breckinridge Warfield
4. Secondary Works
   Princeton Seminary and General Studies on the Princeton Theology
   Archibald Alexander
   Charles Hodge
   Archibald Alexander Hodge
   Benjamin Breckinridge Warfield
   Other Princeton Figures
   Theological, Intellectual, Cultural, Denominational Background
5. A Check List of Dissertations and Theses on the Princeton Theologians

It should be stressed that no section of this bibliography is exhaustive, although care has been exerted to assemble as complete a listing of secondary works as possible. The list of the Princetonians' own books in Section 3 should be supplemented by the specialized bibliographies of Section 2 which provide a much fuller picture of the range of the Princetonians' works, including the vast numbers of their contributions to periodicals.

1. Manuscripts

It should come as no surprise that archival resources for studying the Princeton theologians are concentrated in Princeton. The Manuscript Division of the Firestone Library of Princeton University houses papers of Charles Hodge and his family, as well as of several other early leaders of Princeton Seminary, like Samuel Miller and Ashbel Green, who had ties to Princeton College. The Speer Library of Princeton Seminary contains some manuscripts from all of the Princeton theologians. These include Warfield's own collection of his widely scattered contributions to periodicals, as well as some of his letters which came to the seminary through the good offices of John E. Meeter. The Speer Library also houses Warfield's extensive personal library. The papers of J. Gresham Machen are at Westminster Theological Seminary, Philadelphia. Additional concentrations of papers by, and concerning, the Princeton theologians are located at the Presbyterian Historical Society in Philadelphia and the Historical Foundation of the Presbyterian and Reformed Churches, Montreat, North Carolina. Smaller collections are to be found at the Library of Union Seminary in New York City (letters from A. A. Hodge to Charles Briggs), the Library of Rutgers University, New

Brunswick, New Jersey (some papers of Charles Hodge), and other depositories cited in *The National Union Catalogue of Manuscripts*. It should also be noted that the fulsome nineteenth-century biographies of Archibald Alexander (by J. W. Alexander), Charles Hodge (by A. A. Hodge), Joseph Addison Alexander (by H. C. Alexander), and the *Forty Years Familiar Letters of James W. Alexander* (ed. by John Hall) present lengthy extracts from the Princetonians' private papers.

2. Bibliographies and Indexes

It should be noted that many of the works listed in Section 4 contain extensive bibliographical material on the Princetonians as well.

Armstrong, William P. "Index of *The Presbyterian and Reformed Review* XI (1900)–XIII (1902) and *The Princeton Theological Review* I (1903)–XXVII (1929)." *Princeton Theological Review*, 27 (July 1929), 487–587.

Biblical Repertory and Princeton Review. Index Volume from 1825 to 1868. Philadelphia: Peter Walker, 1870–1871.

Burr, Nelson R. "The Princeton Theology," pp. 999–1003 in *A Critical Bibliography of Religion in America*, Vol. IV, Parts 3, 4, and 5 of *Religion in American Life*, eds. James Ward Smith and A. Leland Jamison. Princeton: Princeton University Press, 1961.

Dulles, Joseph H. "Index to Volumes I–X, 1890–1899." *Presbyterian and Reformed Review*, 10 (October 1899), 727–798.

Gapp, Kenneth S. "The *Princeton Review* Series and the Contribution of Princeton Theological Seminary to Presbyterian Quarterly Magazines." Typescript, Speer Library, Princeton Theological Seminary, 1960.

Gunn, Roland. "Bibliography of Archibald Alexander." Typescript, prepared for Roger R. Nicole, Gordon-Conwell Theological Seminary.

———. "Bibliography of Archibald Alexander Hodge." Typescript, prepared for Roger R. Nicole, Gordon-Conwell Theological Seminary.

Kennedy, Earl William. "Authors of Articles in the *Biblical Repertory and Princeton Review*." Typescript, Speer Library, Princeton Theological Seminary, 1963.

———. "Writings about Charles Hodge and His Works. Principally as Found in Periodicals Contained in the Speer Library of Princeton Theological Seminary for the Years 1830–1880." Typescript, Speer Library, Princeton Theological Seminary, 1963.

Meeter, John E., and Nicole, Roger. *A Bibliography of Benjamin Breckinridge Warfield 1851–1921.* Nutley, N.J.: Presbyterian and Reformed, 1974.

3. Major Books of the Major Princeton Theologians

This partial list of published books also contains information on where these various volumes are still in print (as of 1981–1982 catalogues). For each author, books are listed in chronological order by date of first publication. Many of these works went through several editions in their authors' own lifetimes.

Archibald Alexander

A Brief Outline of the Evidence of the Christian Religion. Princeton: D. A. Borrenstein, 1825.
The Canon of the Old and New Testaments Ascertained; or The Bible Complete without the Apocrypha and Unwritten Traditions. New York: D. A. Borrenstein for G. & C. Carvill, 1826.

Evidences of the Authenticity, Inspiration, and Canonical Authority of the Holy Scriptures. Philadelphia: Presbyterian Board of Publication, 1826. In print, Arno and New York Times, New York.

A Selection of Hymns, Adapted to the Devotions of the Closet, the Family and the Social Circle. New York: Leavitt, 1831.

Counsels of the Aged to the Young. Philadelphia: Key and Biddle, 1833.

History of the Patriarchs. Philadelphia: American Sunday School Union, 1833.

History of the Israelites, from the Death of Joseph to the Death of Moses. Philadelphia: H. Perkins, 1834.

Thoughts on Religious Experience. Philadelphia: Presbyterian Board of Publication, 1841. In print, Banner of Truth, London.

Biographical Sketches of the Founder and Principal Alumni of the Log College. Princeton: J. T. Robenson, 1845. In print, Banner of Truth, London.

A Brief Compend of Bible Truth. Philadelphia: Presbyterian Board of Publication, 1846.

A History of Colonization on the Western Coast of Africa. Philadelphia: W. S. Martien, 1846. In print, Arno and New York Times, New York; Greenwood, Westport, Conn.

Theological Essays. New York and London, 1846.

Practical Sermons: To be Read in Families and Social Meetings. Philadelphia: Presbyterian Board of Publication, 1850.

Outlines of Moral Science. New York: Charles Scribner, 1852.

A History of the Israelitish Nation, from their Origin to their Dispersion at the Destruction of Jerusalem by the Romans. Philadelphia: W. S. Martien, 1853.

Practical Truths. New York: American Tract Society, 1857.

Charles Hodge

A Commentary on the Epistle to the Romans. Philadelphia: Grigg & Elliot, 1835. In print, Eerdmans, Grand Rapids; Banner of Truth, London.

The Constitutional History of the Presbyterian Church in the United States of America. Philadelphia: Presbyterian Board of Education, 1840.

The Way of Life. Philadelphia: American Sunday School Union, 1841. In print, Baker, Grand Rapids; Banner of Truth, London.

A Commentary on the Epistle to the Ephesians. New York: R. Carter & Bros., 1856. In print, Baker, Grand Rapids.

Essays and Reviews: Selected from the Princeton Review. New York: Robert Carter & Bros., 1857.

An Exposition of the First Epistle to the Corinthians. New York: R. Carter, 1857. In print, Eerdmans, Grand Rapids; Baker, Grand Rapids; Banner of Truth, London.

An Exposition of the Second Epistle to the Corinthians. New York: R. Carter, 1857. In print, Baker, Grand Rapids; Banner of Truth, London.

Systematic Theology. New York: Charles Scribner's Sons, 1872–1873. In print, Eerdmans, Grand Rapids; J. Clarke, Cambridge, Eng.

What is Darwinism? New York: Scribners, Armstrong, and Company, 1874.

Conference Papers. New York: Charles Scribner's Sons, 1879. In print, as *Princeton Sermons*, Banner of Truth, London.

A. A. Hodge

Outlines of Theology. New York: Robert Carter & Bros., 1860. Rev. and enlarged ed., 1878. In print, Zondervan, Grand Rapids.

The Atonement. Philadelphia: Presbyterian Board of Publication, 1867.

A Commentary on the Confession of Faith. Philadelphia: Presbyterian Board of Publication, 1869. In print, Banner of Truth, London.

The Life of Charles Hodge. New York: Charles Scribner's Sons, 1880. In print, Arno and New York Times, New York.

Inspiration, with B. B. Warfield. Philadelphia: Presbyterian Board of Publication, 1881. In print, Baker, Grand Rapids, with notes, introduction, and bibliographies by Roger R. Nicole.

Popular Lectures on Theological Themes. Philadelphia: Presbyterian Board of Publication, 1887. In print, as *Evangelical Theology,* Banner of Truth, London.

B. B. Warfield

An Introduction to the Textual Criticism of the New Testament. London: Hodder and Stoughton, 1886.

The Power of God Unto Salvation. Philadelphia: Presbyterian Board of Publication, 1903.

The Lord of Glory. New York: American Tract Society, 1907.

The Saviour of the World. New York: Hodder and Stoughton, 1914.

The Plan of Salvation. Philadelphia: Presbyterian Board of Publication, 1915. In print, Eerdmans, Grand Rapids.

Faith and Life. "Conferences" in the Oratory of Princeton Seminary. New York: Longmans, Green, 1916. In print, Banner of Truth, London.

Counterfeit Miracles. New York: Scribner, 1918. In print, Banner of Truth, London.

Revelation and Inspiration, Works: Vol. I. New York: Oxford University Press, 1927. In print, Baker, Grand Rapids.

Biblical Doctrines, Works: Vol. II. New York: Oxford University Press, 1929. In print, Baker, Grand Rapids.

Christology and Criticism, Works: Vol. III. New York: Oxford University Press, 1931. In print, Baker, Grand Rapids.

Studies in Tertullian and Augustine, Works: Vol. IV. New York: Oxford University Press, 1930. In print, Baker, Grand Rapids; Greenwood, Westport, Conn.

Calvin and Calvinism, Works: Vol. V. New York: Oxford University Press, 1931. In print, Baker, Grand Rapids.

The Westminster Assembly and Its Work, Works: Vol. VI. New York: Oxford University Press, 1931. In print, Baker, Grand Rapids.

Perfectionism Part One, Works: Vol. VII. New York: Oxford University Press, 1931. In print, Baker, Grand Rapids.

Perfectionism Part Two, Works: Vol. VIII. New York: Oxford University Press, 1931. In print, Baker, Grand Rapids.

Studies in Theology, Works: Vol. IX. New York: Oxford University Press, 1932. In print, Baker, Grand Rapids.

Critical Reviews, Works: Vol X. New York: Oxford University Press, 1932. In print, Baker, Grand Rapids.

The Inspiration and Authority of the Bible [selected mostly from *Works, Vol I*]. Philadelphia: Presbyterian and Reformed, 1948. In print, Baker, Grand Rapids; Presbyterian and Reformed, Phillipsburg, N.J.

The Person and Work of Christ [selected mostly from *Works, Vol III*]. Philadelphia: Presbyterian and Reformed, 1950. In print, Baker, Grand Rapids; Presbyterian and Reformed, Phillipsburg, N.J.

Biblical and Theological Studies [selected mostly from *Works, Vol II*]. Philadelphia: Presbyterian and Reformed, 1952. In print, Baker, Grand Rapids; Presbyterian and Reformed, Phillipsburg, N.J.

Calvin and Augustine [selected from *Works, Vols. IV and V*]. Philadelphia: Presbyterian and Reformed, 1956. In print, Baker, Grand Rapids; Presbyterian and Reformed, Phillipsburg, N.J.

Perfectionism [selected from *Works, Vols. VII and VIII*]. Philadelphia: Presbyterian and Reformed, 1958. In print, Baker, Grand Rapids; Presbyterian and Reformed, Phillipsburg, N.J.

Selected Shorter Writings of Benjamin B. Warfield, Vols. I and II, ed. John E. Meeter. Nutley, N.J.: Presbyterian and Reformed, 1970 and 1973. In print, Presbyterian and Reformed, Phillipsburg, N.J.

4. Secondary Works

Princeton Seminary and General Studies on the Princeton Theology

Balmer, Randall H. "The Princetonians and Scripture: A Reconsideration." *Westminster Theological Journal,* 44 (1982), 352–365.

———. "The Princetonians, Scripture, and Recent Scholarship." *Journal of Presbyterian History,* 60 (Fall 1982), 267–270.

Biographical Catalogue of the Princeton Theological Seminary, 1815–1932, compiled by Edward Howell Roberts. Princeton: Trustees of the Theological Seminary of the Presbyterian Church, 1933.

The Centennial Celebration of the Theological Seminary of the Presbyterian Church in the United States of America at Princeton, New Jersey. Princeton: Princeton Theological Seminary, 1912.

Hart, John W. "Princeton Theological Seminary: The Reorganization of 1929." *Journal of Presbyterian History,* 58 (Summer 1980), 124–140.

Hodge, Charles. "Retrospect of the History of the Princeton Review." *Biblical Repertory and Princeton Review. Index Volume,* no. 1 (January 1870), 1–39.

Hoffecker, W. Andrew. "The Devotional Life of Archibald Alexander, Charles Hodge, and Benjamin B. Warfield." *Westminster Theological Journal,* 42 (Fall 1979), 111–129.

———. *Piety and the Princeton Theologians: Archibald Alexander, Charles Hodge, and Benjamin Warfield.* Phillipsburg, N.J., and Grand Rapids: Presbyterian and Reformed, and Baker, 1981.

Illick, Joseph E., III. "The Reception of Darwinism at the Theological Seminary and the College at Princeton, New Jersey." *Journal of the Presbyterian Historical Society,* 38 (September 1960), 152–165; (December 1960), 234–243.

Lindsay, Thomas M. "The Doctrine of Scripture: The Reformers and the Princeton School." Pp. 278–293, *The Expositor,* Fifth Series, Vol. I, ed. W. Robertson Nicoll. London: Hodder and Stoughton, 1895.

Noll, Mark A. "The Founding of Princeton Seminary." *Westminster Theological Journal*, 42 (Fall 1979), 72–110.

Sandeen, Ernest R. "The Princeton Theology: One Source of Biblical Literalism in American Protestantism." *Church History*, 31 (September 1962), 307–321.

Vander Stelt, John C. *Philosophy and Scripture: A Study in Old Princeton and Westminster Theology*. Marlton, N.J.: Mack, 1978.

Woodbridge, John D., and Balmer, Randy. "The Princetonians' Viewpoint of Biblical Authority: An Evaluation of Ernest Sandeen," in *Scripture and Truth*, eds. Woodbridge and D. A. Carson (Grand Rapids: Zondervan, 1983).

Archibald Alexander

Alexander, James Waddel. *The Life of Archibald Alexander*. New York: Charles Scribner, 1854.

"Archibald Alexander." *Biblical Repertory and Princeton Review. Index Volume*, no. 1 (January 1870), 42–67.

De Witt, John. "Archibald Alexander's Preparation for his Professorship." *Princeton Theological Review*, 3 (October 1905), 573–594.

Hodge, Charles. "Memoir of Archibald Alexander." *Biblical Repertory and Princeton Review*, 27 (January 1855), 133–159.

Jackson, Gordon E. "Archibald Alexander's *Thoughts on Religious Experience*, a Critical Revisiting." *Journal of Presbyterian History*, 51 (Summer 1973), 141–154.

Loetscher, Lefferts A. *Facing the Enlightenment and Pietism: Archibald Alexander and the Founding of Princeton Theological Seminary* (Westport, Conn.: Greenwood, 1983).

Mackay, John A. "Archibald Alexander (1772–1851): Founding Father," in *Sons of the Prophets*, ed. Hugh T. Kerr. Princeton: Princeton University Press, 1963.

McKim, Donald K. "Archibald Alexander and the Doctrine of Scripture." *Journal of Presbyterian History*, 54 (Fall 1976), 355–375.

Nelson, John Oliver. "Archibald Alexander, Winsome Conservative." *Journal of the Presbyterian Historical Society*, 35 (March 1957), 15–33.

Okholm, Dennis. "Biblical Inspiration and Infallibility in the Writings of Archibald Alexander." *Trinity Journal* [Trinity Evangelical Divinity School], 5 (Spring 1976), 79–89.

Charles Hodge

Barker, William S. "The Social Views of Charles Hodge (1797–1878): A Study in 19th-Century Calvinism and Conservatism." *Presbyterion: Covenant Seminary Review*, 1 (Spring 1975), 1–22.

Cashdollar, Charles D. "The Pursuit of Piety: Charles Hodge's Diary, 1819–1820." *Journal of Presbyterian History*, 55 (Fall 1977), 267–274.

"Charles Hodge." *Biblical Repertory and Princeton Review. Index Volume*, no. 2 (1870), 200–211.

Danhof, Ralph J. *Charles Hodge as Dogmatician*. Goes, The Netherlands: Oosterbaan and le Cointre, 1929.

Discourses Commemorative of the Life and Work of Charles Hodge. Philadelphia: Henry B. Ashmead, 1879.

Hodge, Archibald Alexander. *The Life of Charles Hodge*. New York: Charles Scribner's Sons, 1880.

Hogeland, Ronald W. "Charles Hodge, The Association of Gentlemen and Ornamental Womanhood: A Study of Male Conventional Wisdom, 1825–1855." *Journal of Presbyterian History*, 53 (Fall 1975), 239–255.

Holifield, E. Brooks. "Mercersburg, Princeton, and the South: The Sacramental Controversy in the Nineteenth Century." *Journal of Presbyterian History,* 54 (Summer 1976), 238–257.

Nelson, John Oliver. "Charles Hodge (1797–1878): Nestor of Orthodoxy," in *The Lives of Eighteen from Princeton,* ed. Willard Thorp. Princeton: Princeton University Press, 1946.

Olbricht, Thomas H. "Charles Hodge as an American New Testament Interpreter." *Journal of Presbyterian History,* 57 (Summer 1979), 117–133.

Patton, Francis Landey. "Charles Hodge." *The Presbyterian Review,* 2 (January 1881), 349–377.

Proceedings Connected with the Semi-Centennial Commemorative of the Professorship of Rev. Charles Hodge, D.D., LL.D., April 24, 1872. New York: Anson D. F. Randolph, 1872.

Shriver, George H. "Passages in Friendship: John W. Nevin to Charles Hodge, 1872." *Journal of Presbyterian History,* 58 (Summer 1980), 116–122.

Stein, Stephen J. "Stuart and Hodge on Romans 5:12–21: An Exegetical Controversy About Original Sin." *Journal of Presbyterian History,* 47 (December 1969), 340–358.

Wells, David F. "The Stout and Persistent 'Theology' of Charles Hodge." *Christianity Today,* August 30, 1974, pp. 10–15.

A. A. Hodge

Patton, Francis Landey. *A Discourse in Memory of Archibald Alexander Hodge.* Philadelphia: Times Printing House, 1887.

Paxton, William M. *Address Delivered at the Funeral of Archibald Alexander Hodge.* New York: Anson D. F. Randolph, 1886.

Salmond, C. A. *Princetoniana. Charles & A. A. Hodge: with Class and Table Talk of Hodge the Younger.* Edinburgh: Oliphant, Anderson & Ferrier, 1888.

B. B. Warfield

Allis, O. T. "Personal Impressions of Dr. Warfield." *Banner of Truth,* 89 (Fall 1971), 10–14.

Craig, Samuel G. "Benjamin B. Warfield," pp. xi–xlviii in *Biblical and Theological Studies.* Philadelphia: Presbyterian and Reformed, 1952.

Fuller, Daniel P. "Benjamin B. Warfield's View of Faith and History." *Journal of the Evangelical Theological Society,* 11 (Spring 1968), 75–83.

Gerstner, John H. "Warfield's Case for Biblical Inerrancy," in *God's Inerrant Word,* ed. John Warwick Montgomery. Minneapolis: Bethany Fellowship, 1974.

Grier, W. J. "Benjamin Breckinridge Warfield." *Banner of Truth,* 89 (Fall 1971), 3–9.

Krabbendam, Hendrick. "B. B. Warfield vs. G. C. Berkouwer on Scripture," in *Inerrancy: The Extent of Biblical Authority,* ed. Norman L. Geisler. Grand Rapids: Zondervan, 1980.

Murray, Iain, et al., ed. "Warfield Commemorative Issue, 1921–1971." *Banner of Truth,* 89 (Fall 1971).

Nicole, Roger. "The Inspiration of Scripture: B. B. Warfield and Dr. Dewey M. Beegle." *The Gordon Review,* 8 (Winter 1964–65), 93–109.

Parsons, Mike. "Warfield and Scripture." *The Churchman* (London), 91 (July 1977), 198–220.

Patton, Francis L. "Benjamin Breckinridge Warfield—A Memorial Address." *Princeton Theological Review,* 19 (July 1921), 369–391.

Peter, J. F. "Warfield on the Scriptures." *Reformed Theological Review,* 16 (October 19, 1957), 76–84.

Rogers, Jack B. "Van Til and Warfield on Scripture in the Westminster Confession," in *Jerusalem and Athens,* ed. E. R. Geehan. Nutley, N.J.: Presbyterian and Reformed, 1971.

Swanton, Robert. "Warfield and Progressive Orthodoxy." *Reformed Theological Review,* 23 (October 1964), 74–87.

Torrance, T. F. Review of Warfield's *Inspiration and Authority of the Bible. Scottish Journal of Theology,* 7 (March 1954), 104–108.

Van Til, Cornelius. "Introduction," pp. 3–68 in *The Inspiration and Authority of the Bible.* Philadelphia: Presbyterian and Reformed, 1948.

Wallis, Wilbur B. "Benjamin B. Warfield: Didactic and Polemical Theologian." *Presbyterion: Covenant Seminary Review,* 3 (April 1977), 73–94.

Westblade, Donald. "Benjamin B. Warfield on Inspiration and Inerrancy." *Studia Biblica et Theologica,* 10 (April 1980), 27–43.

Other Princeton Figures

James Waddel Alexander

Forty Years Familiar Letters of James W. Alexander, ed. John Hall. New York: Charles Scribner, 1860.

"James Waddel Alexander." *Biblical Repertory and Princeton Review. Index Volume,* no. 1 (January 1870), 67–82.

Joseph Addison Alexander

Alexander, Henry Carrington. *The Life of Joseph Addison Alexander.* New York: Charles Scribner's, 1870.

"Joseph Addison Alexander." *Biblical Repertory and Princeton Review. Index Volume,* no. 1 (January 1870), 82–91.

Moorhead, James H. "Joseph Addison Alexander: Common Sense, Romanticism and Biblical Criticism at Princeton." *Journal of Presbyterian History,* 53 (Spring 1975), 51–65.

Lyman Atwater

"Lyman Atwater." *Biblical Repertory and Princeton Review. Index Volume,* no. 1 (January 1870), 94–96.

Starr, Harris Elwood. "Lyman Hotchkiss Atwater," in *Dictionary of American Biography,* I: 416–417. New York: Charles Scribner's Sons, 1928.

A. B. Dod

"Albert Baldwin Dod." *Biblical Repertory and Princeton Review. Index Volume,* no. 1 (January 1870), 151–155.

Ashbel Green

Green, Ashbel. *The Life of Ashbel Green, V.D.M.,* ed. Joseph H. Jones. New York: Robert Carter & Bros., 1849.

William Henry Green

Davis, John D. "William Henry Green." *Presbyterian and Reformed Review,* 43 (July 1900), 377–396.

J. Gresham Machen

Marsden, George. "J. Gresham Machen, History, and Truth." *Westminster Theological Journal,* 42 (Fall 1979), 157–175.

Russell, C. Allyn. "J. Gresham Machen: Scholarly Fundamentalist," in *Voices of American Fundamentalism.* Philadelphia: Westminster, 1976.

Stonehouse, Ned B. *J. Gresham Machen: A Biographical Memoir.* Grand Rapids: Eerdmans, 1954.

Samuel Miller

Miller, Samuel, Jr. *The Life of Samuel Miller.* Philadelphia: Claxton, Remsen & Haffelfinger, 1869.

Theological, Intellectual, Cultural, Denominational Background

The following are works which place the Princeton theologians in their historical and theological contexts. Many of them contain extensive material on the Princeton Theology and the relationship of that theology to wider spheres of Christian and American life.

Ahlstrom, Sydney E. *A Religious History of the American People.* New Haven: Yale University Press, 1972.

———. "Theology in America: A Historical Survey," in *The Shaping of American Religion,* eds. James Ward Smith and A. Leland Jamison. Princeton: Princeton University Press, 1961.

———. *Theology in America: The Major Protestant Voices from Puritanism to Neo-Orthodoxy.* Indianapolis: Bobbs-Merrill, 1967.

———. "The Scottish Philosophy and American Theology." *Church History,* 24 (1955), 257–272.

Armstrong, Maurice W., et al., eds. *The Presbyterian Experience: Sources of American Presbyterian History.* Philadelphia: Westminster, 1956.

Baird, Robert. *Religion in the United States of America.* New York: Arno and New York Times, 1969 [1844].

Barker, William S. "Inerrancy and the Role of the Bible's Authority: A Review Article." *Presbyterion: Covenant Seminary Review,* 6 (Fall 1980), 96–107.

Beardslee, John W., III, ed. and trans. *Reformed Dogmatics: Seventeenth-Century Theology through the Writings of Wollebius, Voetius, and Turretin.* New York: Oxford University Press, 1965 [reprint, Grand Rapids: Baker, 1977].

Berkhof, Louis. *Introduction to Systematic Theology.* Grand Rapids: Eerdmans, 1932 [reprint, Grand Rapids: Baker, 1979].

Bowden, Henry Warner. *Church History in the Age of Science: Historiographical Patterns in the United States 1876–1918.* Chapel Hill: University of North Carolina Press, 1971.

Bozeman, Theodore Dwight. *Protestants in an Age of Science: The Baconian Ideal and Antebellum American Religious Thought.* Chapel Hill: University of North Carolina Press, 1977.

Brown, Ira V. "The Higher Criticism Comes to America, 1880–1900." *Journal of the Presbyterian Historical Society,* 38 (December 1960), 193–212.

Brown, Jerry Wayne. *The Rise of Biblical Criticism in America, 1800–1870: The New England Scholars.* Middletown, Conn.: Wesleyan University Press, 1969.

Cecil, Anthony C. *The Theological Development of Edwards Amasa Park, Last of the Consistent Calvinists.* Missoula, Mont.: Scholars Press, 1974.

Collins, Varnum Lansing. *President Witherspoon.* New York: Arno and New York Times, 1968 [1925].

Conforti, Joseph A. *Samuel Hopkins and the New Divinity Movement.* Washington and Grand Rapids: Eerdmans for the Christian University Press, 1981.

Cross, Barbara M. *Horace Bushnell: Minister to a Changing America.* Chicago: University of Chicago Press, 1958.

Dillenberger, John. *Protestant Thought and Natural Science: A Historical Study.* Nashville: Abingdon, 1960.

Dollar, George W. *A History of Fundamentalism in America.* Greenville, S.C.: Bob Jones University Press, 1973.

Finney, Charles G. *Memoirs of Rev. Charles G. Finney, Written by Himself.* New York: AMS Press, 1973 [1876].

Foster, Frank H. *A Genetic History of the New England Theology.* Chicago: University of Chicago Press, 1907.

Geehan, E. R., ed. *Jerusalem and Athens: Critical Discussions on the Philosophy and Apologetics of Cornelius Van Til.* Nutley, N.J.: Presbyterian and Reformed, 1971.

General Catalogue of Princeton University 1746–1906. Princeton: By the University, 1908.

Grave, S. A. *The Scottish Philosophy of Common Sense.* Oxford: Clarendon Press, 1960.

Haroutunian, Joseph. *Piety Versus Moralism: The Passing of the New England Theology.* New York: Henry Holt, 1932.

Hatch, Nathan O., and Noll, Mark A., eds. *The Bible in America: Essays in Cultural History.* New York: Oxford University Press, 1982.

Hoeveler, J. David, Jr. *James McCosh and the Scottish Intellectual Tradition.* Princeton: Princeton University Press, 1981.

Hofstadter, Richard. "The Revolution in Higher Education," in *Paths of American Thought,* eds. A. M. Schlesinger, Jr., and Morton White. Boston: Houghton Mifflin, 1963.

Holifield, E. Brooks. *The Gentlemen Theologians: American Theology in Southern Culture, 1795–1860.* Durham, N.C.: Duke University Press, 1978.

Hood, Fred J. *Reformed America: The Middle and Southern States, 1783–1837.* University, Alabama: University of Alabama Press, 1980.

Hovenkamp, Herbert. *Science and Religion in America, 1800–1860.* Philadelphia: University of Pennsylvania Press, 1978.

Howe, Daniel Walker. *The Unitarian Conscience: Harvard Moral Philosophy, 1805–1861.* Cambridge: Harvard University Press, 1970.

———, ed. *Victorian America.* Philadelphia: University of Pennsylvania Press, 1976.

Hudson, Winthrop S. *Religion in America.* Third ed., New York: Charles Scribner's Sons, 1981.

Hutchison, George P. *The History Behind the Reformed Presbyterian Church, Evangelical Synod.* Cherry Hill, N.J.: Mack, 1974.

———. *The Problem of Original Sin in American Presbyterian Theology.* Nutley, N.J.: Presbyterian and Reformed, 1972.

Hutchinson, William R. *The Modernist Impulse in American Protestantism.* Cambridge: Harvard University Press, 1976.

Kelsey, David H. *The Uses of Scripture in Recent Theology.* Philadelphia: Fortress, 1975.

Kuyper, Abraham. *Principles of Sacred Theology,* trans. J. Hendrik De Vries, intro. B. B. Warfield. Grand Rapids: Baker, 1980 [1898].

Loetscher, Lefferts. *The Broadening Church: A Study of Theological Issues in the Presbyterian Church Since 1869.* Philadelphia: University of Pennsylvania Press, 1957.

Marsden, George M. "The Collapse of American Evangelical Academia," in *Faith and Rationality,* ed. Nicholas Wolterstorff (Notre Dame, Ind.: Notre Dame, 1983).

———. *The Evangelical Mind and the New School Presbyterian Experience.* New Haven: Yale University Press, 1970.

———. *Fundamentalism and American Culture: The Shaping of Twentieth-Century American Evangelicalism.* New York: Oxford University Press, 1980.

———. "On Being Reformed: Our Present Tasks in the American Setting." *Reformed Journal,* September 1981, pp. 14–17.

May, Henry F. *The Enlightenment in America.* New York: Oxford University Press, 1976.

Meyer, D. H. *The Instructed Conscience: The Shaping of the American National Ethic.* Philadelphia: University of Pennsylvania Press, 1972.

Miller, Perry. *The Life of the Mind in America from the Revolution to the Civil War.* New York: Harcourt, Brace and World, 1965.

Moore, James R. *The Post-Darwinian Controversies: A Study of the Protestant Struggle to Come to Terms with Darwin in Great Britain and America, 1870–1900.* Cambridge: Cambridge University Press, 1979.

Nichols, James Hastings, ed. *The Mercersburg Theology.* New York: Oxford University Press, 1966.

———. *Romanticism in American Theology: Nevin and Schaff at Mercersburg.* Chicago: University of Chicago Press, 1961.

Noll, Mark A. "Christian Thinking and the Rise of the American University." *Christian Scholar's Review,* 9 (1979), 3–16.

———. "Who Sets the Stage for Understanding Scripture? Philosophies of Science Often Provide the Logic for our Hermeneutics." *Christianity Today,* May 23, 1980, pp. 14–18.

Numbers, Ronald L. *Creation by Natural Law: Laplace's Nebular Hypothesis in American Thought.* Seattle: University of Washington Press, 1977.

Oleson, Alexandra, and Brown, Sanborn C., eds. *The Pursuit of Knowledge in the Early American Republic: American Scientific and Learned Societies from Colonial Times to the Civil War.* Baltimore: Johns Hopkins University Press, 1976.

———, and Voss, John, eds. *The Organization of Knowledge in Modern America, 1860–1920.* Baltimore: Johns Hopkins University Press, 1979.

Princetonians: A Biographical Dictionary, eds. James McLachlan and Richard A. Harrison. Princeton: Princeton University Press, 1976, 1981, 1982.

Rennie, Ian. "Mixed Metaphors, Misunderstood Models, and Puzzling Paradigms: A Contemporary Effort to Correct Some Current Misunderstandings Regarding the Authority and Interpretation of the Bible. An Historical Response." Typescript, Institute for Christian Studies, Toronto, 1981.

Reynolds, David S. *Faith in Fiction: The Emergence of Religious Literature in America.* Cambridge: Harvard University Press, 1981.

Rogers, Jack Bartlett. *Scripture in the Westminster Confession: A Problem of Historical Interpretation for American Presbyterianism.* Grand Rapids: Eerdmans, 1967.

———, and McKim, Donald K. *The Authority and Interpretation of the Bible: An Historical Approach.* San Francisco: Harper & Row, 1979.

Sandeen, Ernest R. *The Roots of Fundamentalism: British and American Millenarianism 1800–1930.* Chicago: University of Chicago Press, 1970.

Saum, Lewis O. *The Popular Mood of Pre-Civil War America.* Westport, Conn.: Greenwood Press, 1980.

Sloan, Douglas. *The Scottish Enlightenment and the American College Ideal.* New York: Teacher's College Press, 1961.

Smith, Elwyn. *The Presbyterian Ministry in American Culture.* Philadelphia: Westminster, 1962.

Smith, Gary S. "The Spirit of Capitalism Revisited: Calvinists in the Industrial Revolution." *Journal of Presbyterian History,* 59 (Winter 1981), 481–497.

Smith, Hilrie Shelton. *Changing Conceptions of Original Sin: A Study in American Theology Since 1750.* New York: Scribner's, 1953.

——, ed. *Horace Bushnell.* New York: Oxford University Press, 1965.

Smith, Timothy L. *Revivalism and Social Reform in Mid-Nineteenth-Century America.* Nashville: Abingdon, 1957.

Turretin, Francis. *The Doctrine of Scripture,* ed. and trans. John W. Beardslee III. Grand Rapids: Baker, 1981.

Van Til, Cornelius. *The Defense of the Faith.* 2d ed. Philadelphia: Presbyterian and Reformed, 1955.

Veysey, Laurence R. *The Emergence of the American University.* Chicago: University of Chicago Press, 1965.

Wells, David F. "The Atonement in American Theology, 1820–1840." Typescript, ca. 1978.

——. "Nathaniel William Taylor: Theologian of Revival." Typescript, July 1978.

Welter, Rush. *The Mind of America 1820–1860.* New York: Columbia University Press, 1975.

Wertenbaker, Thomas Jefferson. *Princeton 1746–1896.* Princeton: Princeton University Press, 1946.

Willis, E. David. "The Material Assumptions of Integrative Theology: The Conditions of Experiential Church Dogmatics." *The Princeton Seminary Bulletin,* n.s. 2 (1979), 232–250.

Woodbridge, John D. "Biblical Authority: Towards an Evaluation of the Rogers and McKim Proposal." *Trinity Journal,* n.s. 1 (Fall 1980), 165–236; expanded as *Biblical Authority: A Critique of the Rogers/McKim Proposal* (Grand Rapids: Zondervan, 1982).

Wright, Conrad. *The Beginnings of Unitarianism in America.* Boston: Starr King, 1955.

5. A Check List of Dissertations and Theses on the Princeton Theologians

Princeton Seminary, Princeton Theology Generally

Balmer, Randall H. "The Old Princeton Doctrine of Inspiration in the Context of Nineteenth-Century Theology: A Reappraisal." M.A., Trinity Evangelical Divinity School, 1981.

Clyde, Walter Raymond, Jr. "The Development of American Presbyterian Theology 1705–1823." Ph.D., Hartford Theological Seminary Foundation, 1939.

Haines, George Lamar. "The Princeton Theological Seminary, 1925–1960." Ph.D., New York University, 1966.

Hoffecker, Andrew W., Jr. "The Relation Between the Objective and Subjective Aspects in Christian Religious Experience: A Study in the Systematic and Devotional Writings of Archibald Alexander, Charles Hodge, and Benjamin B. Warfield." Ph.D., Brown University, 1970.

Johnson, Deryl Freeman. "The Attitudes of the Princeton Theologians Toward Darwinism and Evolution from 1859 to 1929." Ph.D., University of Iowa, 1969.

Livingstone, William D. "The Princeton Apologetic as Exemplified by the Work of Benjamin B. Warfield and J. Gresham Machen: A Study in American Theology 1880-1930." Ph.D., Yale University, 1948.

Nelson, John Oliver. "The Rise of the Princeton Theology: A Genetic History of American Presbyterianism Until 1850." Ph.D., Yale University, 1935.

St. Amant, Penrose. "The Rise and Early Development of the Princeton School of Theology." Ph.D., University of Edinburgh, 1952.

Scovel, Raleigh Don. "Orthodoxy in Princeton: A Social and Intellectual History of Princeton Theological Seminary, 1812-1860." Ph.D., University of California, Berkeley, 1970.

Charles Hodge

Berg, Kenneth P. "Charles Hodge, Controversialist." Ph.D., University of Iowa, 1952.

Deifell, John Jay. "The Ecclesiology of Charles Hodge." Th.D., New College of the University of Edinburgh, 1969.

Kennedy, Earl William. "An Historical Analysis of Charles Hodge's Doctrines of Sin and Particular Grace." Ph.D., Princeton Theological Seminary, 1968.

Lazenby, Henry F. "Revelation History in the Theologies of Karl Barth and Charles Hodge." Ph.D., University of Aberdeen, 1982.

McAllister, James L., Jr. "The Nature of Religious Knowledge in the Theology of Charles Hodge." Ph.D., Duke University, 1957.

Murchie, David Neil. "Morality and Social Ethics in the Thought of Charles Hodge." Ph.D., Drew University, 1980.

Richards, Walter Wiley. "A Study of the Influence of Princeton Theology upon the Theology of James Petigru Boyce and His Followers with Special Reference to the Work of Charles Hodge." Th.D., New Orleans Baptist Theological Seminary, 1964.

B. B. Warfield

Behannon, Woodrow. "Benjamin B. Warfield's Concept of Religious Authority." Th.D., Southwestern Baptist Theological Seminary, 1964.

Counts, William Martin. "A Study of Benjamin B. Warfield's View of the Doctrine of Inspiration." Th.M., Dallas Theological Seminary, 1959.

Cousar, R. W. "Benjamin Warfield: His Christology and Soteriology." Th.D., University of Edinburgh, 1954.

Hoefel, Robert J. "The Doctrine of Inspiration in the Writings of James Orr and B. B. Warfield: A Study in Contrasting Approaches to Scripture." Ph.D., Fuller Theological Seminary, 1983.

Kraus, Clyde Norman. "The Principle of Authority in the Theology of B. B. Warfield, William Adams Brown, and Gerald Birney Smith." Ph.D., Duke University, 1962.

Markarian, John Jacob. "The Calvinistic Concept of the Biblical Revelation in the Theology of B. B. Warfield." Ph.D., Drew University, 1963.

Trites, Allison A. "B. B. Warfield's View of the Authority of Scripture." Th.M., Princeton Theological Seminary, 1962.

J. Gresham Machen

McNutt, Charles William. "The Fundamentalism of J. Gresham Machen." Th.D., Union Theological Seminary, Richmond, Va., 1952.

Masselink, William. "Professor J. Gresham Machen: His Life and Defence of the Bible." Th.D., Free University of Amsterdam, 1938.

Roark, Dallas Morgan. "J. Gresham Machen and His Desire to Maintain a Doctrinally True Presbyterian Church." Ph.D., University of Iowa, 1963.

Related Subjects

Lane, Belden C. "Democracy and the Ruling Eldership: Samuel Miller's Response to Tension Between Clerical and Lay Authority in Early Nineteenth-Century America." Th.D., Princeton Theological Seminary, 1976.

Pope, Earl A. "New England Calvinism and the Disruption of the Presbyterian Church." Ph.D., Brown University, 1962.

Smith, Gary S. "Calvinism and Culture in America, 1870–1915." Ph.D., Johns Hopkins University, 1981.

Index of Subjects

Andover Seminary, 18, 51
apologetics, 26–27, 77–79, 107, 242, 251, 256; compared to Bavinck and Kuyper, 32, 41–42, 65n8, 302–7

Bible. *See* Scripture
Biblical Repertory and Princeton Review, 14, 22–24, 38, 153–54

Calvinism, 27–30, 38–40, 44–45; vs. Bushnell, 176–84; and Edwards, 312–14; vs. Finney, 165–75; and New England Theology, 314–16; vs. Park, 185–207; and Torrey, 300–1
concursus, as theological principle, 278–79, 297–98
Council of Trent, 84, 231

Deism, 55, 57, 121
Design, Argument from, 93–104

Encyclopedia, theological, 212, 251
enthusiasm, 53–54, 80–81, 242
eschatology, 89
evolution, 145–52, 233–37, 289–90, 293–98

Fundamentalism, 38, 293, 299–301

geology, 142–44, 215–17
German mind, 115, 157, 163–64

Holy Spirit, 26–27, 170, 178–79, 260, 301; and the illumination of Scripture, 85–86; and the inspiration of Scripture, 139, 224–25, 232, 276, 285–88
humanity, antiquity of, 288–92; special creation of, 296–97; unity of, 100–4, 292

inerrancy of Scripture, 41–42, 137, 145, 222; in church history, 273–74; of original autographs, 268–74. *See also* Scripture

inspiration of Scripture, 77–79, 135–41, 213–15, 218–32, 280–88; biblical passages in support of, 281–84; in church history, 281; plenary, 226; verbal, 226–28. *See also* Scripture

Jesus Christ, 52, 90–91, 111, 113, 136–37, 158–59, 190–91; and Scripture, 282–84, 308–10

Mediate Creation, 293–95
Mercersburg Theology, 155–64
miracles, 78, 107

Negroes, 104
New England Theology, 182–84, 311–16; and Edwards Amasa Park, 184–207
New Haven Divinity, 315–16

Oxford Movement, 159, 162

Pelagianism, 158, 315–16
Presbyterian and Reformed Review, 23–24
Presbyterian church, 23–24, 176; debate over Scripture, 220, 268–69
Presbyterian Quarterly and Princeton Review, 23–24
Presbyterian Review, 15, 23–24, 219
Princeton College, 20–22
Princeton Theological Review, 23–24
Princeton Theological Seminary, 18–20, 55–58
Princeton Theology: development, 38–40; flourishing and passing, 36–38; modern controversy, 11, 41–45, 220; 19th-century culture, 34–37, 46; publications, 22–24; Reformed Confessionalism, 27–30; religious experience, 33–34; Scottish Common Sense Philosophy, 30–33; Scripture, 25–27; society and politics, 47; theologians, 13–18. *See also* individual themes and topics
prophecy, 78–79
Protestantism, 157–64

Index of Names

The following abbreviations are used in the index, PTS = Princeton Theological Seminary; BRPR = *Biblical Repertory and Princeton Review.* Consult the Table of Contents for polemical targets of the Princeton theologians. Grateful acknowledgment is made to John Stackhouse and Mrs. Anne Edgin for assistance in the preparation of the indexes.

337